My Narrowboat Life fron
By Daniel Mar

CH00730609

www.danielmarkbrown.com

To EFB

A Brief Boaty Introduction from the Author!

What sort of person would try to live on a tiny, thirty foot long narrowboat, built in 1987, with very few comforts? Well, somebody like me!

More accurately, a twenty-five year old version of me, a version of myself who was not sure about what I wanted to do with my life and even less familiar with anything at all to do with boats. This is the very simple introduction to my life as it was when I found myself signing the papers to take ownership of Narrowboat Tilly.

I could never have imagined in mid 2012, that the following four years would see my life with Tilly go through incredible highs, a few low points together with a countless number of miles pedalled down muddy towpaths and roads on winter cycling commutes!

Luckily, as a keen diary keeper, I managed to record a lot of the mini-adventures and perfect rural moments in writing. Along with these diaries, my thousands of photos and video clips act as a visual diary of my time onboard, allowing me to look back at a specific time and place exactly as it was during my canal experience.

Using these resources, along with the endless inspiration of my rural mooring sites, I released several short kindle books about my life afloat as it happened. Here for the first time, all six books that make up "The Narrowboat Lad" series, are compiled together in one handy volume!

I hope that you will enjoy reading through these books, whilst seeing a glimpse into the most important time of my life. As I edited this collection and re-read these short books, barely a month after selling Tilly and moving into my own place on dry land, I found that the stories and moments highlighted in this book took on a new significance. The events you will read about, no matter how trivial, such as simple brief encounters with wildlife, people, or even just extreme weather conditions, they were all important enough to me at the time to make me record and share them with anybody who would listen!

The words you are about to read, were written by what I now realise was a lad in his twenties, having the absolute time of his life! It may have been a simple existence in a lot of respects, a very basic and sometimes uncomfortable period, but my time with Narrowboat Tilly was truly time well spent. The impact of experiencing such a different lifestyle, so early in my life, is too big to truly contemplate so soon after the end of my boat life.

Attempting to live simply, spending as much time as I could in quiet rural places, often with nobody else in sight, being so close to nature so much of the time, all these things barely scratch the surface of the experiences that have shaped my world view, values and ideas of what is truly important in life. Somehow ending up with millions of views on YouTube represents the extreme opposite of what I had in mind when I moved onto Tilly for a quiet obscure life, yet that too has been an eye opening experience.

Boat life has fundamentally changed me, definitely made me a better person, and given me the sort of memories I could have never imagined.

So, here is how it all happened... from beginning to end.

The Narrowboat Lad

The Narrowboat Lad
By Daniel Mark Brown

www.danielmarkbrown.com

To all my friends and family who have given me
the support I needed to make my dreams a reality.

Introduction: The Dream Realised

Writing an introduction to this book has been an unexpectedly difficult task. At first it seemed like something that could be done with a simple, "Welcome my dear readers" type of comment, or one of those generic introductions that don't really introduce anything about the book, who it is by, or what it is about. As I sat and thought about the seemingly simple task, I realised that what I was trying to do was introduce my entire life, everything that I have ever wanted, everything that I have in the world and how I have found myself being asked by complete strangers if I am *the narrowboat lad.*

Suddenly it was not so simple, so instead of the introduction described above, please enjoy the following short story...

A lonely figure walks down a dark towpath on an October night, it is barely half-past-eight yet it has been dark for hours, a sure sign that the winter is already trying to force autumn to hurry along so that Jack Frost can have his dominion over the scene. The night is bitingly cold and the figure is wrapped up in layers of clothing, wearing a thick pair of gloves, a good hat, and of course a scarf, and as he rounds a long corner he looks upon a heartwarming sight.

A small narrowboat sits moored to the bank, a light is on inside, and even through the closed curtains throws a yellow tinted glow onto the grass verge that runs between the canal and path. The smell of burning wood meets the figure's nostrils as he gets closer, and a little smoke with the occasional orange glowing ember can be seen leaving the chimney, before disappearing into the dark night air.

The figure walks up the path to draw level with the boat, and hops across the muddy grass, before stepping up onto the stern, outside the rear door. He takes one last look around him, no other boats in sight, has a final glance up into the starry sky, as astronomy is one of his passions. He then pulls out a bunch of keys far too heavy to be floated by the large cork keyring, turns one in the keyhole and opens the door. He is immediately hit with a wall of heat, a huge relief from the chilly night outside.

OK, so if you didn't guess that was not a story at all, the figure is me, and that is literally what has just happened before I sat down to start this introduction for this book, about my first steps into becoming a full time live-aboard. Welcome to the story of how I came to live on a small narrowboat called Tilly.

Dry Land

One of the criticisms that I have often seen in reviews on books based on narrowboating is that too few words are devoted to actual boating and time on the water, and as I am now approaching my first year aboard there is a lot to talk about, however, allow me briefly to start with a little background from a now seemingly distant past shrouded in the mists of time...

For many years I had lived in my parents' home while working in a supermarket, that is the mundane sentence that starts this short chapter on pre-boat life. I had never known what I wanted to do with my life, and ultimately spent my childhood and early twenties doing nothing but playing video games. When I first got a job in a supermarket the only real impact it had was that I could afford a lot more games and consoles, but then almost in one moment something changed, and I realised that I had got everything wrong for all this time.

What it was that made me suddenly start walking around all the local countryside and ultimately ending up never being sat in front of the telly with a controller in my hand, is up for debate, but the change was profound and I started walking hundreds of miles a month, every month. No real goal, just getting out and enjoying the countryside, listening to endless podcasts and audiobooks as I went, taking a book to read, or even a pen and pad to sit down and write a short story or two.

My entire attitude to life changed, and after a while when I realised that I was spending far less money as my new passion of getting out walking was near enough free, just taking something to eat and drink and that was the only cost of the trip. I decided to drop from full time hours at work to just sixteen, and I suddenly had all the time in the world to get out and do stuff.

As bad luck would have it after a few months of this I found myself with a hernia, not painful or particularly damaging to everyday activities, but definitely not something I would have chosen to have happen. Following the operation I had two months off work, for the majority of the time I was stuck in the house becoming increasingly frustrated at missing the good weather to be out wandering the hills in.

Despite having no real problems in the world, I could not stop my mind from turning to a generally downbeat and dark place. I was heading into my mid twenties, still had no plan or idea of what I wanted to do in life, I was still living in the family home with no chance of owning my own home, and even being unlikely to find a place to rent without having to bundle in at least one friend. I would have to go back to full time hours, and end so quickly my second chance at youth, and having free time to spend outdoors in the middle of nowhere, doing nothing with my life at all.

In a lovely gesture of getting me out of the house two friends and I went to the local stretch of canal and hired a canoe. Sat there, letting them do the paddling and hard work, still claiming that I was not to do anything too physical, I took in the sights and sounds of a perfect summers day on the canal. As we passed a few moored boats, one of them had a "for sale" sign in the window. It was at that point that in a passing comment one of us joked that I could live on a boat... Maybe I took the joke a little too seriously!

So it was that a random trip on a canoe and the most innocent of comments changed the course of my life forever! At the time none of us could have imagined that within three years I would be sailing my own little boat down that very stretch of canal.

Within the next few days the idea popped back into my head, and just out of curiosity I started to look at boats for sale on the internet. As I was still relatively housebound, this grew into an increasing obsession and I started to learn about the various aspects of what it meant to live on a boat. At this point it was still not even a dream or even a half formed idea that I might actually do it, but as time went on I started to see a clear choice of two lifestyles before me.

After two months the doctors signed me off to get back to work, which duly gave me that inherent confidence boost to start getting back out there into the world again. This time though, whenever I was in the midst of society's hustle and bustle I was seeing everything through a new prism, a view that had an alternative on its peripheral. Was I going to struggle to pay an extortionate rent, utility bills and goodness knows what else for the rest of my life, or was I going to do the unthinkable and not live in a house at all?

Everywhere I turned I saw people struggling their lives away locked in a battle over the practical issue of money, working every hour they could to sustain a standard of life that was no more than acceptable, and yet never having time to enjoy it. I saw people who worked their entire lives to retire with something in the bank, only to have a blow dealt to them by fate that would stop them from ever reaping the rewards of a life spent working, worse still, I saw how close I was to entering this forty year cycle. Living on a boat was starting to seem like a necessity. I started to put money aside and I started to do some real research.

At the time I was looking into buying a forty-five foot boat in the region of £25,000, it would take me years to buy outright but I was determined not to have any debt hanging over me, as it seemed it would go against the whole idea of getting a boat in the first place. Once I had the boat, by my maths, I would easily be able to pay for the running costs as well as standard living costs on only sixteen hours a week at minimum wage. This would protect my way of life, I would still have all the time in the world to go out walking and do all the things I loved to do outdoors, and with a boat I would be able to start my trips from a different place each, week and would already be out in the countryside from the moment I stepped off the stern.

Once this idea had taken hold I started to go through life with a certain sense of relief, and the more time that passed, the more I felt that I was getting closer to a goal and a purpose, for the first time in my life I had something that I wanted to do, something that I could work towards.

The Hunt

After a year had passed I had saved up more than I had expected, and some of the smaller boats I had been viewing online became affordable, temptation started to creep into my mind in the form of a thirty foot boat, it was not what I had intended, but soon enough I was in my friends' car travelling out to see a twenty-eight foot boat that didn't even have an inboard engine.

I stepped onboard Jess at Norbury Wharf and felt overcome, she was a small vessel, that could not be disputed, but two things hit me instantly. First, she was not the boat that I would want to live on. Secondly, I could easily live on board a boat that small. As I walked up and down the short distance between the bedroom, bathroom, kitchen and living room, I saw that everything I needed was all there. Heating, sleeping, eating, washing, living. Thirty foot would be enough!

The next few months passed in a blur and a panic as I realised the terrifying truth, that I could see a boat and be living on it within a week, a few days even. I was gripped by fear at leaving home, I was utterly unnerved at the prospect of living on and even just travelling solo on a boat, I was clueless about real life with cut apron strings, but more than anything I was excited that it could be happening at the drop of a hat.

I viewed boats locally and far afield, some I loved, some I didn't, and I had a few moments of crisis when I thought it was all a terrible idea and I had been wasting my time. As the end of summer approached I became increasingly desperate and convinced that I had to do the deed, and had to do it soon. The intangible influence of increasing impatience was with me the day that I first saw Tilly.

Moored at Great Haywood, Tilly was a thirty foot Springer Narrowboat built in the mid Eighties: being a Springer she was unusual due to her square back end (rather than the rounded stern of a traditional narrowboat) and very large deck space outside. This meant that there was even less space inside. Stepping down the few steps from the large outdoor area, the boat is entered with the shower room and toilet to your left, before the space opened out to a small living room containing a sofa-bed and a set of cupboards. The all important fireplace complete with wood burner sat central in the boat's length, and on the right hand side. After this lay the kitchen with sink, oven and fridge, and at the very front was a small seating area that also turned into a bed, before the front doors that opened up onto a small front deck.

She was decorated with dark wood and magnolia panelling, and despite needing some work doing was seemingly in good condition. I knew within the first minute onboard that this was my boat. With an asking price of £12,000 she was within budget, and the following day I made an offer of £10,000 before settling at £11,000. I had bought a boat! All the doubts and fears I had ever had about the idea became an intense dread that I fell into during the brief moments that I was not over the moon and grinning like a fool.

The First Day

After several phone calls and a few days, arrangements were made to make Dan and Tilly official. A date and time was set for the obligatory signing of papers and handing over of keys, and with incredibly large butterflies in my otherwise empty stomach, I set out in my Nan and Grandad's car packed full of the basic necessities of life, to head to Great Haywood and become a boater.

Never in my life had I had such nerves and fear run through me, as we got nearer and nearer to our destination I felt like I was going to faint, and I felt my voice taking on its usual quiet stuttering tone that only made the feeling more intense. We arrived at the marina at the same time as the previous owners. In a daze I was shown around the boat and taught about all kinds of switches and taps that I was too nervous to really recall only an hour later. Then back to the boat sales office we went, papers were signed and keys were handed over. At twelve forty-four on Tuesday 24th of July 2012 I became a boat owner. Happiness surged through me as I sat once again in my grandparents' car while we made our way back down the short distance to Tilly.

The first job was to take bedding, food and basic living supplies on board, the second and far more important job however, was to sit down and eat the rolls and crisps that my Nan had made for us. The first meal onboard, a good start to boat life.

After an hour or so my Nan and Grandad left to make the long trip back home, I was to stay onboard and be picked up by my friends the following day, giving me a chance to start to tidy and clean Tilly up ready for the big trip home, to be started in less than two weeks time. I had planned a route from Great Haywood to Ellesmere that stood at ninety-six miles long with sixty locks to navigate. I had set aside two weeks holiday for this to be undertaken, a decision that turned out to be very fortunate.

At that point though the idea of moving Tilly anywhere was the least of my worries, and on a perfect summer's day I opened all the windows and doors and set about cleaning every surface I could put a cloth over. After a couple of hours of cleaning with an unnatural enthusiasm and a grin that probably struck passers by as a little strange for basic chores, I decided that my arms had had enough, and for the first time ever, locked the door and set off on a walk down the Towpath. I was living the dream at last.

As I walked down the busy stretch of canal with its residential moorings and live-aboard boaters, passing traffic travelling carefully down the canal at painstakingly low speed, it started to really sink in that this is what I was now a part of. The cheerful greetings and random conversations with strangers only served to increase the overwhelming feelings, joy and a sense of relief that I had finally gone through with it, were the main sensations gripping me, that on more than one occasion that day led me to have a few teary moments in the privacy of my new home.

Looking back on that first day it seems somehow appropriate that I instantly started to walk the surrounding area, without even realising it I was doing what I had hoped having a boat would help me to do, get out in the countryside in a far wider area than I could have realistically walked to from my previous home. The sun shone and I covered a good few miles in three separate walks up and down the towpath and around the beautiful village of Great Haywood itself, I am glad to say that this spirit of exploring the calm quiet countryside has become a cornerstone to living onboard.

The First Night

It had been a long day, filled with emotions, cleaning and a good deal of walking, so around eleven o'clock I started to feel the hand of sleep on my shoulder, I rolled out my sleeping bag onto the sofa-bed and pressed play on my iPod to listen to another chapter or two of The Lord of the Rings, one of my favourite audiobooks. I lay there in the darkened boat, not a sound to be heard apart from the occasional trickle of water. The front three windows did not have curtains at this point so it was anything but private, this did however give me an incredible view from my bed up through the windows into the sky.

Astronomy has for many years been one of my passions, and I was hoping that living on a boat would allow me to moor up miles away from the nearest town and enjoy some relatively light pollution free stargazing. I wasn't however quite prepared for this to happen within the first twelve hours of boat ownership.

As I lay there unable to get to sleep, nerves and excitement still keeping my mind occupied, I decided that I needed to go outside and look at the sky properly, the time was around midnight when I paused my iPod to enjoy the scene in silence. When I stepped up onto the stern I was greeted by an incredible dark sky, the summer constellations were out in full force above me, in that moment of utter peace looking up to a night sky filled with familiar stars I think that the days events finally sunk in. For about a quarter of an hour I stood looking, walking up and down the sides to angle my view around an overhanging tree, then all at once I felt like I was ready to sleep. I went back inside, wrapped myself up in my sleeping bag, and fell asleep in my own home for the first time.

Tap tap tap. Rattle, tap tap. That was the sound I woke up to, barely past six in the morning I awoke in a daze with no idea what was making such a strange noise on the canal side of the boat. I lay still listening intently, I couldn't figure out the source of the noise at all but I knew one thing, I didn't like it. I got up and stuck my head through the back door looking down the side of the boat, relief, two ducks were pecking away at the algae growing on the hull. A rude awakening after my first night onboard, but just about the best alarm clock I could ever have asked for.

I knew that there was no chance of getting back to sleep as the joy of being on a boat took over again so I resumed The Lord of the Rings audiobook for a while as I got dressed, washed and ready for another day. My enduring memory of that morning is the sound of whistling kettles and the smell of bacon that permeated the area from the surrounding boats as eight o'clock rolled around to nine.

It was another hot day, this time with a complete cloud covering, giving it a very humid and close feel which only added to my sense of dread at the prospect of moving Tilly up to the nearby marina. It was a short distance and took only ten minutes to walk, but the long unbroken line of residential boats on the canal made it a daunting prospect. I was waiting for my friends to arrive before making the trip, more people on board more people to blame if things went wrong, or at least that was my plan. The wait did nothing to settle my fear of moving, and in the early afternoon when they were on board it was time to face the music.

I turned the key in the ignition to the "heat" marker for a few beeps, then right over to "start", the engine burst into life and I let the key rest in "run", another moment of life to remember! We untied the ropes and pushed her out to set off, the three of us novice sailors feeling on top of the world… until the immediate issue of not knowing whether the engine was in neutral or not! There was a small red button on the gearstick that we had assumed needed to be pressed in, but as I revved the engine higher and higher we were going nowhere other than sideways towards a very expensive looking boat. I pulled the gearstick back to the upright position, the red button popped out and I pushed the stick forward, with a rush of disturbed water behind us we slowly moved forwards, and after twenty minutes of painstaking travel found ourselves at the marina.

At this time I was still unaware of exactly what you could and couldn't do when it came to mooring up on the canal and so I had decided to play it safe and leave Tilly in a marina for five nights until the following Tuesday when my two weeks holiday from work began. A marina employee was kind enough to come onboard and guide us to our mooring spot, or maybe he took one look at me and thought *"this is not somebody I want steering a boat around here"*.

Safely nestled in the back of the marina I said my silent goodbye to Tilly and headed back to the mundane everyday life that I had known for so long, never have I known five days to last so long as those days leading up to the big trip home.

A Long Way to Travel at 4mph

I found myself once again in my Nan and Grandad's car travelling the long way out to Great Haywood Marina, this time with my friend Helena as a passenger along with every possible thing that we may need on a two week boating trip that would see Tilly travel ninety-six miles and through sixty locks to finally arrive at Ellesmere, the first place on the map that I considered close enough to my old home, to declare as my new home.

The plan was simple. Helena would be my shipmate for as much time as possible, returning home and being dropped off by her husband every few days, while I stayed on board and tried to edge closer at any moment I found myself alone.

I was terrified, I was scared of locks, I was scared of other boats, I was scared of clear open stretches of water. The presence of anybody else on board was vital to my own self confidence, and therefore the success of the trip itself. With this sense of fear of everything, the importance of what was happening in my life was inflated ever more out of proportion, leading to more worry, and to me obsessively documenting everything both in video and in writing in my newly started boat diary. With this little black book of memories I have rebuilt the tale of two weeks in summer.

It was the last day of July, a Tuesday, that Helena and I were dropped off at the boat and left there to start the slow dawdle back home. We had a quick salad roll each and then carefully steered Tilly around the marina to fill up with diesel at the reception. £45 for forty-five litres after taking the domestic non taxed amount into consideration. Little did I know that that last forty-five litres I put in to fill up the one-hundred and fifty litre capacity would be the only diesel I would have to put in for a year. The same helpful chap who had steered Tilly into her mooring, was there on hand and gave me a few quick tips on the engine and which parts did what, then with a cheerful "farewell and good luck", we were off!

The first day's travel had the instant stress of travelling down some very busy stretches of canal, often with boats moored up on either side. To say that I took things slow would be an understatement, even by narrowboat standards. I felt like we were constantly drifting towards every boat that we met, and the long stretches of boats moored bow to stern took on the image of a very expensive crash barrier to hit.

It was only a mile until we found the first lock, this was it, the moment of truth. Luckily there was a lock keeper on hand and from his presence alone our fears were reduced. I wasn't prepared at all for the way the water would push Tilly around, as Helena and the lock keeper raised and lowered the paddles to fill the lock then open the gate to see Tilly emerge unscathed through the first lock of the sixty separating us from home. It was a beautiful moment, the sun was shining and we were finally doing the deed. We made what I thought was excellent progress that first day, four more locks fell to our new found skills, and ten miles of water were put behind us.

We moored up, for the first time using mooring pins, I hammered them down into the ground for all I was worth and tied Tilly so tightly that it was difficult to unmoor the next morning. The evening was perfect, a clear sky for the sun to set in, while we sat around just up from the last lock of the day, the sound of the running water seeping through the gate mixed with a distant motorway. Two things that even at the time we noted were a world apart, in ten minutes the cars were travelling further than our eight hour day had produced, but there was only one way I wanted to travel.

While obsessively checking the mooring pins, I was surprised to see a black cat casually strolling along the towpath, Helena also clocked it and we smiled and said the usual things like "Aaaawww" and "Psss psss psss" to try to attract it towards us. When it jumped up onto the boat moored ahead of us we looked at each other in surprise and our reaction to seeing it then enter into the boat through a cat flap on the back door can only be described as hysterical.

After seeing about a dozen dogs we could not believe that there was a cat living on a boat, it somehow seemed to be the most amazing and cute thing we could have imagined. So ended the first day.

We woke early the following morning eager to start the trip and at almost bang on eight o'clock we started the engine and set about travelling through the nearby locks at Penkridge. During the first few hours of travel we were able to observe how fast other boats were travelling, and I came to the conclusion that I had been travelling at less than half the speed that everybody else was powering along at and not wanting to become known as Dan the Slowest Boater in the West, I floored it, or at least moved the throttle a little closer to a ninety-five degree angle.

This made for a day of great progress, once again smiled upon by a scorching sun, we managed a full twelve hours of travel and progressed twenty-three miles closer to home and put another nine locks behind us.

With great progress being made boat life seemed to be going perfectly, we were treated to several perfect nature scenes, passing only a few foot away from a perched kingfisher and then seeing him take flight and skim along the canal only inches from the waters surface. We saw more herons than I had ever seen in my life up to that point, and when it comes to ducklings, well I don't think it would be an exaggeration to say we saw at least one-hundred maybe even as many as two-hundred!

So it was that that days travel went perfectly through the ideal countryside surrounding the majority of the canal from Penkridge, becoming increasingly industrial as we touched the very edge of Wolverhampton and then returned to perfect countryside as we approached Gnosall. Perfect except for one brief moment. As we travelled down a barren stretch of canal a few miles up the Shropshire Union, the ignition panel started to beep and the oil light came on. This caused me to go into an instant panic, not known for my calm approach towards unexpected problems, I was thrown into a wild struggle to get the boat all of the five foot across the canal to the towpath. I wildly waved the tiller from side to side and shouted for Helena to get ready to jump off and pull us in, while I thrust us into reverse briefly making the engine work harder as I revved far too high in the chaos.

Needless to say, looking back, all I had to do was move over to the side and stop, which is what happened, in the heat of the moment though it seemed like the worst thing that had ever happened. We pulled over and stopped for tea to give the engine a chance to cool down. I looked through a manual and found that I understood little enough of it to make further reading useless at that point, so I told myself that it was just overheating from being run for nearly ten hours straight. After tea we moved a few more miles to moor at Gnosall, and I promised myself we would take it easier the next day to avoid stressing the engine further.

On the morning of day three of the trip I was still kidding myself that I was going to try to take it easy rather than get home as fast as I could. Then as soon as we had pushed off from the side and started travelling, I had instantly fallen into the trap of thinking "We will just go fast for this first part" then adding "We will keep the speed up until the next bridge" and so on.

We very quickly found ourselves at Norbury Wharf, the marina that we had visited to view the first ever boat I had considered buying. It was, as it always seems to be, a hive of activity. I carried out the unspeakable task of emptying the toilet and bought a few new fenders to protect Tilly from my still rookie driving. Then it was time to start the real part of the day's trip, we were hoping to make it to Market Drayton as it would be an easy place for Helena to be picked up from and taken home in the evening.

The stretch of canal seemed simple and an easier days travel than we had yet done, there was a small warning about a narrow stretch but that was not really a consideration, a narrow canal for a narrowboat, seemed like a fine idea to us right until the moment we entered the narrows.

A narrow stretch of canal can be very narrow indeed with barely enough room to squeeze one boat at a time through, this can be a tough driving challenge for a novice or even an experienced boater. The narrows that we met that day are still my least favourite stretch of canal. On one side there was a towpath in various states of repair, on the other was what I can only really describe as a cliff face, stretching a few dozen feet upwards it worked with the trees hanging from the opposite bank to create a very dark, close, claustrophobic atmosphere. The rock face was very uninviting above the water and even less inviting below the waterline, to my horror we occasionally strayed across and hit some of the frequent underwater obstructions that the stone made, and once again my "heat of the moment" calm was put under immense pressure. Luckily we had followed what turned out to be a far more experienced boater into the area who helped wave us on or hold us back when we met oncoming traffic. At length though we emerged and found a calm, quiet place to eat dinner before heading on towards the five locks leading into Market Drayton.

The Tyrley Locks are barely a mile away from the town centre of Market Drayton and yet as the weather turned in an instant to pouring rain that mile seemed to stretch out indefinitely. We were caught in the middle of the "after dinner rush" as boat after boat headed downwards towards the town. This had the advantage of the community spirit of everybody chipping in together to get as many of us through the locks as fast as we could, but also had the drawback of being stuck in the middle of heavy traffic waiting over half an hour to get to each lock, until finally emerging on the final mile straight to moor up at Market Drayton.

So with only a short stretch of uninterrupted canal left to travel for the day there was surely nothing that could go wrong... Beep beep beep flash flash flash went the oil light! This time I managed to keep calm and tried to keep us moving towards somewhere we could moor up, a cement and hardcore towpath meant that the stretch of canal we were overheating along was no good to stop on. A minute or two passed...

"What is that smell?" ... "Is that smoke?" ... "It is!"

I stopped the engine immediately and luckily we were drifting towards the side, I jumped off and pulled us over, still nowhere to moor up. Helena took the ropes to hold us in to the bank, while I hopped onboard and lifted up one of the boards of the deck. A mist of blue smoke greeted me, a sickly chemical smell rising into the air with it. I looked at the engine, it looked fine and I had no idea what I was looking for anyway. We debated on what to do and agreed we needed to move a little further, so we could at least moor up and let her rest properly.

With the deck boards up we started the engine and moved very slowly into Market Drayton and just as we found an overnight mooring spot, the lights came on, the smoke returned. We moored up and I set about despairing of everything and over dramatically rueing every decision I had ever made. Just a normal night in then!

I reread the engine manual, and after the engine had cooled for a few hours fiddled around with water caps and managed to add another litre of water into the cooling system, a fact that gave me great relief and when Helena was picked up we all sat around saying that the lack of water in the system must have definitely been the problem. That evening plans were made for me to meet my family a few miles up the canal at the Adderley Locks in two days time, leaving me with a simple easy three mile stretch of plain canal to travel the next day. I was still nervous about my first ever trip on my own, but knowing it was only a few miles up the canal took some of the pressure off.

That evening I enjoyed the time on my own, calming down from the previous few days excitement and planning a calm day of cleaning before the short trip to the locks. Taking a takeaway pizza back to eat on the deck while the last light of the sun faded into darkness, was probably the most content I had ever been in my life.

I had a lazy morning not getting out of bed until half past eight, a huge rest compared to the previous days. I did a spot of cleaning and then thought I would walk up the canal to my destination in order to reassure myself that I could handle my first solo trip later on in the day. It was a three mile trip, so the walk added up to six miles, the sort of walk I had done many times before and on the flat towpath it was easy going. I liked what I saw, simple wide canal, only a few bridges and nothing out of the ordinary.

As I walked back down the final straight towards Tilly it struck me as odd that I could see most of her side when the angle of the canal seemed to suggest I should only see her bow. She seemed to twist a little revealing even more of her side… NO!

I started running and have never run so fast as I did that day, she had broken free of her moorings and was floating around blocking the entire canal. Arriving at her side I saw that the front was still tied, but the back mooring pin had been pulled out of the boggy towpath, I jumped onto her and ran to the stern, starting the engine up in a panic and fetching her back over to the side. I had arrived back just in time as a boat emerged through a nearby bridge. I hammered the pin back in and retied. Another criss averted, another heart stopping moment to act as a lesson.

Seeing the danger of staying moored in the spot I was in, I was spurred on to get the boat trip over and done with so I could relax again. So in the early afternoon I set off, keeping my speed low, after about five minutes of travelling the beeping and flashing started, I kept calm, I was on my own, but I could deal with this, I started to move towards the towpath, but within seconds of the warning light coming on something terrible happened.

PUFF! A loud hiss and sound of high pressure gas escaping all at once was accompanied by the sight of a cloud of steam streaming through all the gaps on the deck around me. I smashed my hand at the engine "off" button and drifted bow first into the bank. I jumped off and hammered the pins into the ground with mightier smashes of the mallet than I had ever mustered. I lifted up the deck boards and saw a red pipe no longer attached to wherever it had come from. My moments of panic up to this point had been little other than small blips, now on my own miles away from anybody, I knew I had a real problem and had to be a grown up about it.

I paced up and down the boat frantically not knowing what to do before grabbing everything I owned into a backpack and walking down the towpath away from Tilly. I was not entirely sure what my plan was. I would call into the boat yard I had passed barely two minutes ago and ask for help, why I had my bag, and as one of the chaps at Orwell's boat yard said, *"all my worldly possessions"* I am not sure, but it was reassuring to have what amounted to a camera, change of clothes and some maps with me.

A sheepish, shy Dan walked into the boat yard to be greeted by three people who looked like they knew their boats. A relief. I recounted my tale and looking down the canal seeing just how close I was to them, an engineer whose name I unfortunately never found out, walked back down to Tilly with me. He looked at the engine and tilted his head this way and that, occasionally making a sound as if to say *"what is going on down here?"*

At length he reattached the pipe and we ran the engine, he pointed to a tank I had previously ignored known as the header tank. It was positioned above the deck by the ignition, and while running the engine in neutral we poured litres of water down it for it to seemingly disappear. While the engine was running, he noted that there was a loose nut on the engine fixtures that kept the engine from breaking loose and offered to tighten it up at the yard if we spun the boat round. I was keen to have anything done to help the engine at this point, so we just about managed to find room to turn Tilly on the canal and back to the boat yard we went. In the back of my mind I was starting to think *"How much will this set me back?"*

The job at the yard was simple enough but we once again found the header tank empty. After asking where I was travelling to, I was told to keep topping up with water and that I should at least be able to get back home and then get it fixed properly then. I dared to ask "So what do I owe you then?" The engineer looked at the others and took in a breath through his teeth as if ready to sting me with a bill before smiling and saying "Go on then bugger off!"

I needed no second telling and promptly said my thanks, I can't recall ever being so grateful to a stranger for anything in my life, then set about the short three mile trip... again. I had filled up some water bottles from the tap and kept them on the deck ready to top up the header tank that fed down into the rest of the engine and cooling system. Every few minutes I was able to pour in another litre and a half bottle. I had no idea if this was meant to be happening or not, but it made for an interesting time juggling the tiller and topping up water for three miles.

Soon enough though I was relieved to see my destination, a forty-eight hour mooring spot just down from the five Adderly Locks. I pulled up and hopped off pulling Tilly in closer to the side only to hear a horrible scraping sound at the stern, *"What now?"* I asked myself worn out from the day's drama. I looked into the water to see a line of slabs sticking out of the bank wall two foot or so below the surface, the bow was high enough to pull into the side but unfortunately Tilly's backend was just too low to be able to pull her in properly.

I jumped back on and moved a little further only to find this row of slabs blocking me on my repeated attempts. Feeling ever more disheartened and wanting to just curl up and put a blanket over me, I once again had to show the rare quality of being grown up enough to deal with a very minor problem. I turned around and ended up travelling a mile back on myself to moor up by a small wooded area. That night I was asleep as soon as my head hit the pillow. Boat life was not what I had hoped for at all.

Fast forward twenty-four hours and I was back in high spirits, in love with boat life, excited and impatient to get Tilly to Ellesmere so I could really start making her my home. I had awoken to a bright morning and set about turning Tilly back around and travelling back up to the locks to meet my Mum, Nan and Grandad. They had been a little delayed so I had moored Tilly back up where I had spent the night and sat out on the deck reading up on Roman history. Sat out there on the stern in the middle of nowhere I was reminded just what it was that I had wanted from boat life, and that inherent peace and tranquility was the epitome of my desires. When they arrived I made my way up to the first lock to meet them, my mum had still yet to see Tilly in real life so jumped on board straight away and set to work nosing around in true motherly fashion! She seemed happy enough with her findings so that was good enough for me!

The five locks at Adderley were dispatched with surprising ease considering that I was the only one of us to have ever been through a lock, and I was stuck on board trying to steer Tilly through unscathed while constantly pouring water into the header tank. With a team of four though our progress through the locks was much smoother and faster than when Helena and I were struggling away running up and down from gate to gate. The fantastic weather was also a bonus, and coupled with our progress, made for some pretty high spirits, high enough that we decided to continue on from the Adderley five to tackle Audlem.

Audlem was a place on the map that had been a constant worry for me. The village of Audlem is situated almost equidistant along the canal between Market Drayton and Nantwich, adding to its traditional postcard charm is an attractive stretch of canal and canal side buildings, including the obligatory pub that is required in these places. It is an ideal place to moor up, and if you so wished, you could get some very nice photographs in the area. So what was my worry then? Well the problem for me as a novice boater planning my ninety-six mile trip home came in the form of the fifteen locks spread over one mile of canal as you pass Audlem.

Luckily our high spirits gave us the "can do" attitude that is required to carry a group of amateurs into a very long hard day. After completing the Adderley five then the first two of the Audlem set, we moored up and sat down for some dinner, butties, rolls and crisps. Classic. It was around this time that I was relieved and overjoyed to hear word from Helena, she would be dropped off at Audlem so we could attempt to get to Ellesmere in the next few days. High spirits rose higher and we embarked on another ten locks.

The hours of that August Saturday rolled away in a stream of opening and shutting lock gates, lifting and lowering paddles, pouring water into the engine, holding Tilly by the bank as other boats rose towards us, and the occasional mishap to break the cycle. The first and only attempt at lock working from my Nan ended when she lifted the catch to let the paddle down without holding onto the windlass first. The paddle of the lock gate sped downwards spinning the windlass on the shaft at high speed before it flew off and into the lock, never to be seen again. It was a comical moment to look back on, but one that left my Nan a little shaken up at the time. The danger of a flying windlass may sound like a joke, but the potential damage a windlass to the face could do is not something to take lightly.

So with my Nan becoming my shipmate in order to, as she said *"get out of harms way"* for the rest of the day, it was with tired arms that my Mum and Grandad got back onboard after we had moored up right in Audlem. Now past five in the evening another round of butties was enjoyed by all before they headed back down the canal to the car, leaving me to await Helena's return to Tilly.

As my family were leaving there were some very loud rumbles of thunder, the sky darkened and the heat became stifling, it helped to create a strangely quiet atmosphere as boats moored up for the night around me. Helena arrived in the increasingly muggy dusk and we decided to move a little way around the corner and pass through the final three locks. Before heading through them however I thought we had better refill the water tank. Tilly was now noticeably slanting backwards as the water supply in the front had been diminished by ten hours of pouring it into the engine. When I lifted the water tank panel to see the water level as it filled, I was amazed to see that I had poured what must have been nearly one hundred litres into an endlessly thirsty engine. With no idea where the water was going I tried to put the sheer weight of that volume of water out of my mind while the tank slowly refilled.

The very moment that I had reeled up the hose pipe and started the engine the Heavens opened. Some of the loudest raspy thunder cracked the sky overhead, while a torrent of water fell from the sky. Three locks later we were soaked through and desperate to moor up. I used the mooring hooks to attach us to the metal canal siding for the first time and we headed indoors, then within ten minutes the sun was back out and we enjoyed a beautiful sunset over perfect countryside. Typical!

Sunday morning broke with a perfect blue sky interrupted only by a bright warming sun and a few wisps of cloud. Audlem had been done, we were a few miles away from joining the Llangollen Canal and being closer to home than ever, things were not just looking up, they were looking almost completed. Only thirty-two miles remained, the main bulk of the locks were behind us, it was looking possible that the following morning may see us wake up early and be leisurely cruising down into Ellesmere for dinner.

We had a few miles simple travel into Nantwich and in the interest of allowing the engine a rest, moored up and headed into the town for a walk around and a top up of supplies, which broadly meant walking back to the boat with a bag full of chocolate and pop.

After a pasty for dinner we set off again, travelling a very slow two miles to find the four locks that greeted us at the start of the Llangollen Canal where it branched off from the Shropshire Union that continued up to Chester and Ellesmere Port. The locks were already in use by a descending boat, which was lucky for us as it meant the water was on our level once the gates were opened.

Helena walked up and prepared to start working the locks while I took my usual role of being the one to batter Tilly against every lock surface I could, while keeping an eye on the header tank water level. I was left holding Tilly to the side while the descending boat exited the locks, I read with some worry the warning sign on the lock wall telling boaters to lift their fenders. It was advice I was keen to take, but with the wind pushing Tilly away from me and then the flow of water as the lock was emptied and the boat moved through into the canal, I was unable to jump on board to lift all of the thin rubber fenders that hung over each side, eight in total.

I thought that I would get into the lock and then quickly lift the remaining fenders before we let any water in, with the lock clear and gates open I moved Tilly calmly into the thin lock opening. This was it, I was finally entering the home stretch of canal that would lead to my destination... But after the first ten foot of Tilly had entered the lock disaster struck. The thin rubber fenders I had not yet been able to lift towards the front of the boat had wedged us solidly in place, even though they were only an inch thick they made us too wide to pass. Feeling us stop rather abruptly, I had no idea what the problem was and assumed that the flow of water had just pushed against us, so I revved the engine to try to force us in against it, no luck.

I then tried to reverse and found that that direction was also a no go. It was at this point that I realised what had happened. I ran down the side of the boat and saw the fenders wedged in position. I grabbed them and pulled and pulled with all my might, my legs and back pressing against the damp slimy lock walls covering me in a horrible muck that added to the chaos of the moment. They would not move. I ran back to the stern and slammed into full reverse once again, losing my composure utterly, as I found myself dealing with a situation that I did not realise was surprisingly common. The engine revved and the water was churned up all around me as the propeller forced it under the boat. Still no luck, not one inch moved. I was meant to be taking it easy on the engine and to my horror as I revved and revved somewhere seemingly from below deck, a long beep sound could be heard. I knew I was standing over the batteries and this new sound instantly saw me put the engine into neutral and listen for a few moments. Now not wanting to push the engine, I ran back to the stuck fenders and heaved and heaved until one of them finally came up, the tiny bit of room freed up saw Tilly instantly wobble in the disturbed water and I knew we were safe. I quickly ran around and scooped up the remaining fenders throwing them in a rush onto the roof, in turn spraying mud and slime from the lock walls all over the boat.

We moved completely into the lock and everything returned to normal, except my heart rate which still needed a moment of calm later on to find itself relaxing. That is the scene of my less than triumphant entry onto my home canal. The remaining three locks passed without incident and after a mile or so of travel we decided to moor up for another engine rest period. The day was increasingly hot as the sun enjoyed an uninterrupted dominance of the sky, and on lifting the deck boards to investigate what the beep from the engine may have been, we were greeted by a wall of heat, another thing to worry about for the day.

While we were sat moored up somewhere in the middle of the Shropshire countryside sheltering from the sun, one of the key elements of the trip revealed itself. It wasn't the endless engine trouble, it wasn't the fact that every tiny problem seemed to be massive and was blown well out of proportion by our lack of experience or knowledge of almost all aspects of boating, it was the heavy downpours that would interrupt otherwise perfect summers days. Huge claps of thunder could be heard in the distance and far away rain showers could be seen across miles of open fields. We took this as our cue to try to move a little bit further along the canal before we got another soaking.

Wrenbury became our destination and as we moved the few miles and four locks towards the small village with the famous lift bridge, everything seemed back on track. The stress of the day disappeared and spirits rose even higher when Helena started to pour a bit more water into the header tank and found that within seconds the water overflowed onto the deck. It was a moment of great celebration as it seemed that after hundreds of litres, wherever all the water had been heading to, had finally been filled. What a relief to be free of the burden of constantly trying to fill that tank. We were a little worried that there seemed to be some dark smoke coming from the exhaust, but put that down to us not really paying attention to the exhaust fumes before. So in high spirits we continued on our way.

It took only minutes for us to realise our error, the header tank started to steam and then boiling hot water started to spray and splutter from the header tank out onto the deck. Looking back to the exhaust it was clear that the dark smoke was not meant to be there. We pulled over to the side, mooring up just as a downpour consumed us. Sheltering inside trying not to think about anything whatsoever, I distracted myself looking at how I could try to store some of my possessions. Built into the front end of Tilly was a seating and bed area that had generous storage underneath the seat cushions, I lifted the lid to find some very damp wood. It was wet to the touch and below the waterline. That was it, the last straw. I started to lament once again everything that I had ever done and a teary eyed Dan sat and sulked inside, while Helena set about washing the outside of the boat after the rain had passed. What was boat life going to be?

The seventh day of the trip started very early, we were determined to start in the cool early morning to give the engine as much of a chance as possible, and so it was that before seven we were sat rising up the first lock of the day. No boats to rush us, and no glaring sun to exacerbate the overheating issue. This was the first day of my new approach to narrowboating which was based on the simple idea: *"Move the boat as far as you can and be happy about it"*. It was a simple change in mindset that put me and boats back on speaking terms and after a very long day of travelling with frequent stops to let the engine cool we were amazed, overjoyed and in disbelief that we had managed to travel ten miles, rise up through thirteen locks, and moor up at Whitchurch.

It was the perfect day, taking it slowly had been a breath of fresh air. Just enjoying the trip as a trip rather than an urgent quest to get to Ellesmere had opened up my eyes to just how amazing it was to be on a boat miles from anywhere with nothing but fields, trees, farms and perfect countryside scenery around us. When we realised that we were approaching Whitchurch and were soon going to get to the

Grindley Brook stair case locks, the last locks on the trip it was as if another weight was lifted from our shoulders. I was now confident that I could travel the final stretch on my own, a spot of luck as Helena was due to be picked up and leave the boat for the last time later that evening.

The highlight of the day was passing through the famous Wrenbury Lift Bridge. It lifts a small section of the main access road to the small village and as such is a rather fancy bridge as far as the canal goes. I stayed by Tilly holding her to the side while Helena took the magic BW key that opens services and facilities along the canal, down to the bridge control panel.

Watching from a distance I saw Helena figuring out the process. First of all the barrier had to be put across the road to make sure no cars drove straight into the canal, then inserting the key into the electric control panel and holding down the button things really took off. Lights and a siren started to sound as the road slowly lifted to allow me and Tilly to pass under, before slowly descending back into place. The barrier was hastily moved out of the road, and Helena just managed to jump back on board as my steering had left us floating at all kinds of angles over the canal.

So with a great day of progress, countryside and canal behind us, Helena left the boat for the final time of the trip. I had a peaceful nights sleep and awaited my Dad's first visit to the boat the following morning. As a bonus I got to watch a heron only a few feet away while I was doing the dishes, boat life was back on track!

My Dad and Helen (who was also carrying the soon to be born Ezara) arrived early in the morning. It had been a damp grey start to the day that brightened up considerably on their arrival as if to give me the best possible chance of wowing them with a short narrowboat trip. They seemed suitably impressed and happy with my humble floating home, and we sat around while I talked at length about the trials and tribulations of the eighty three miles I had previously travelled.

Unsurprisingly talk soon turned to starting her up and having a little trip of our own. My Dad drove his car a few miles down the canal and walked back up to us so that Helen did not have to carry herself and the baby back up the towpath. We travelled three miles down the canal, which I was very pleased about, as it meant that we passed through three lift bridges out of four that lay in the few miles heading away from Whitchurch.

A lift bridge was not quite as terrifying as a lock to a novice like me as it didn't have the element of danger that locks inherently contain, they are however a real pain in the backside for a solo boater having to moor up, wind up the bridge, go back on board and steer through, before re-mooring and going back to wind the bridge down. Having a helper on board meant that even at the very slow pace we were travelling to nurse the poorly engine, we made good steady progress and on passing the third bridge, it was time for our paths to part.

I took this as an opportunity to moor up and give the engine a rest. Taking it slow had become in one single day the only way I would travel for at least the next year. No rushing, no worries, no overheating? I set off an hour or so later, looking at my series of canal maps had made me impatient to attempt to make it all the way to Ellesmere, it was around midday and I had only nine miles until mission accomplished.

The final obstacle for me to overcome was the nearby fourth lift bridge. I approached it with a clear canal ahead and behind, which was a relief meaning there was no pressure or any reason to rush. I moored up, ran over the bridge with my windlass to crank the bridge up, found the mechanism stiff but soon enough the bridge was raised, and as I stepped away from the crank realised a rookie mistake. I was now trapped on the opposite side of the canal from Tilly. Instinctively I had moored on the towpath side of the canal instead of right up by the lift bridge and on the opposite bank. I looked at the gap where the bridge had once sat and considered taking a running jump. I could jump it easily I reckoned.

SPLASH! It turned out to be just beyond my ability to clear the gap, I managed to sprawl my arms and body forwards enough to land on the opposite bank from the waist up, however from my shins down I was utterly canal bound. Slightly shaken and very glad that there was nobody else around to witness this moment, I steered Tilly through the narrow opening that the bridge usually sat in, and moored up on the same side as the lift bridge operating mechanism. I slowly let the bridge back down and then realised that it was then irrelevant on which side I had moored Tilly, as with the bridge in place both sides were equally accessible. Another lesson learned and another moment to give the engine a rest.

I was now starting to get excited and once again let my impatience get the better of me and started moving closer to the goal, as the various bridges and landmarks rolled past I was ecstatic. The stretch of canal between Tilly's bow and Ellesmere was slowly shrinking, and as I kept checking the map at each numbered bridge I was counting down the miles. The sun was beaming, I was almost home and the canal was passing through some incredible local countryside. Then in the way that I had become accustomed to, and at a painfully close three miles away from the destination, disaster struck, the light flashed and the tone beeped. With more composure than previous emergency stops, I pulled over to the side and found nowhere quite suitable to moor up. I walked the boat for a few metres before deciding to just hold her in to the side for ten minutes before starting her up again and trying to make it a few hundred metres further around a corner to moor up in a designated place on the map.

I made the two minute long trip and moored up, examining the map and seeing just how close I was, I knew that I would not be able to just leave it, and my impatience won its third victory of the day. It speaks volumes about my change in attitude that the overheating had not just led me to sulk and say everything was rubbish before going to bed at four in the afternoon. *"Slowly but surely"* was, and remains, my boating motto and it is a fantastic way to travel. Setting off again after barely half an hour of rest for the engine, I thought I was guaranteed to make it. Once again however the heat warnings started within minutes and I realised that I had to admit defeat, mooring up and checking the map I found myself only two miles from Ellesmere. That was close enough for me to call home!

Keen to investigate the last few miles and even more keen to get to a chippy after nearly two weeks of chip based abstinence, I put *all my worldly possessions* into my backpack and enjoyed the short walk into the town. The canal passed by Blakemere and I was amazed to recognise the sights from a trip that my friend Jono and I had been on that saw us spend over six hours walking all over Ellesmere and its surroundings looking for geocaches. The shore of Blakemere and the canal are barely ten metres apart, creating one of the most idyllic mooring sites I have ever seen where you can have what amounts to a massive lake as the view through your windows, offering a stark contrast to the usual countryside and fields.

Walking past this point was a key moment in the trip and in fact my life up to that point. I realised that in only minutes I would be on the other side of the short Ellesmere Tunnel, and therefore where I considered the final destination. I had still only walked about ten minutes from the boat, I really was this close to home. I stopped and looked over the mere and in one moment all the emotions of the last week or so rushed through me, the stress, the fear, the joy, the excitement and now the relief and realisation that I was back. I stood there alone at the edge of Blakemere, the sun setting and the sky turning from blue to purple and pink, and I cried for reasons too numerous to list and too vague to really know myself. I felt amazing and as I regained my composure I pulled out my video camera to record a short clip for my video diary of the trip back home, but as I tried to talk I was overcome again. I walked into Ellesmere, managed to find myself some chips and sat down in the town centre eating them on a bench. I was back!

That night I had probably the best nights sleep of my life and waking in the morning I was keen to travel the last two miles and get myself through the tunnel and moored up at a place I had scouted out the night before. In the early morning and with the canal kept in the shade by overhanging trees, it was a little chilly as I passed Blakemere and entered the tunnel. At eighty metres long Ellesmere Tunnel is not the longest of tunnels, but certainly not a feature to dismiss, certainly not as it was mine and Tilly's first tunnel. About twenty metres in I strayed to close to the side and various parts of Tilly started to scrape along the wall, chipping paint and throwing bits of brick onto the deck. I hated to do it, but going through the tunnel, the final obstacle on the trip, I had to jump off and pull her along for about forty metres, using the fender to stop her from scraping along the wall. Just before exiting the tunnel I jumped back on board and emerged feeling like a hero completing a long adventure, within ten minutes I had moored up and was walking back into the town. I was home. We were home, my new home was home!

I caught a bus from Ellesmere back to what I could now call "My Old Home" or "My Mum's House" in Oswestry in order to get some supplies and also some plastic and polystyrene tiles to start work on the bathroom. Once I was stocked up I had a lift back with my Grandad stopping en route to pick up Helena who would sleep on board, and so for the first time also be able to enjoy Tilly without the stress of having a ten hour day of travelling when we woke up! To say we were relaxed would be an understatement. On the evening of Wednesday 8th August 2012 we were living the dream. Mission Accomplished. Now I could start making Tilly into a real home, my home.

Making Home

It was a Thursday morning when Helena and I woke up with the realisation that this would be the first day that she would step off Tilly without having seen the engine so much as switched on. Being a Thursday left me another three nights onboard before I would be waking up to bike into town and return to work, just enough time to start getting Tilly more homely and shuffle my best friends on and off the boat, having had a taste of the canal (not literally.)

I had spent the previous evening testing out my "fake tiles" in the bathroom, which on Tilly contained a portable toilet, shower, sink and boiler. The plan was to tile two walls, paint the remaining two and place some shelves, while also covering up the below sink area with a shower curtain, creating some hidden storage space. The tiles looked fantastic and as I spent the next day or so slowly adding more to the walls, the grubby old bathroom became a much nicer environment. I was very keen to get the bathroom sorted before I had to return to work as I felt it was the least presentable area of the boat, and also I was not keen on the worn out looking cream and slight rusty tint the existing decor had taken on.

Helena left early on, and I set about more tiling while I awaited the arrival of one of my best friends, Jono. On his arrival we spent a good hour or so climbing over the boat while I excitedly talked about everything that had happened, and pointed at things on the boat, and tried to sound like I knew what any of it really was! After settling down and enjoying a dinner of noodles, bread and Pepsi, we unmoored and made our way down the busy stretch of canal surrounding Ellesmere basin, we stopped and filled with water, while I emptied the rubbish and toilet. Jono took the tiller for the first time, both of us shirtless and warmed by an unobstructed high noon sun, we were the ultimate holiday makers as we moored up once more around a mile from our starting point. Life was good and two happy boaters had a few great hours onboard before Jono headed back home, and I set about tiling once more. This set the precedent for many great days and nights with friends on Tilly.

The tiling went better than expected to the point that I ended up using my last tiles that very day. In my impatience I decided to hop on the next bus back to Oswestry to buy as many as I could carry, and then in the still glorious weather jump on my bike and ride back to Tilly. The significance of having my bike onboard should not be underestimated, as for the previous few years I had been riding my bike at least two-thousand miles a year. Cycling had taken over from walking as my main hobby, and I had built up a great deal of stamina when it came to biking. Knowing that pedal power was going to be my main way of commuting from Tilly to work, to friends, to *my old house,* to almost anywhere I needed to be in a hurry, I had really focussed my efforts in the months leading up to purchasing a boat, and the eight mile ride to Ellesmere was no problem, maybe even easy compared to some of the more extreme riding I had done in the previous months.

When I arrived back onboard I locked up my bike on the stern and contemplated the freedom I had now gained by its presence. It felt great, boat, boots and bike all together at last! My three favourite things, all I needed was to get my small telescope onboard and life would be complete. More pressingly though I had a bathroom wall to make complete, and the tiling resumed in earnest. Hours later as the sun was lowering at last, I looked around a fully tiled bathroom with a rather fetching shower curtain now covering the under sink space too I had a small amount of painting to finish the job, but the real work was done.

Feeling pleased with a fantastic day of tiling, boating, biking and Jono-ing I stretched my legs with a late evening walk into Ellesmere, walking past the mere itself, before finding myself instinctively drawn to the local takeaway. Needless to say I returned to Tilly clutching a large Margarita pizza, large chips and bottle of Pepsi. I sat down and tucked in while listening to a little more of the BBC radio version of The Lord of The Rings. Perfect!

The following day I decided was finally going to be a day of real rest. The first day since that now distant memory of Great Haywood Marina that Tilly would not move. I spent the day measuring and contemplating decoration, walking around fields and the canal, and making the most of being able to live in such a location. The joys of boat life were really starting to sink in, I could not believe I was actually doing it. I was vaguely aware that this was a time to enjoy as one of the key points in my life, and that however hard the trip home had seemed to be at some points, and no matter how deeply I had despaired only a week earlier with an overheating engine and endless miles to travel, I had finally got to a place that I could settle down, literally in terms of the boat but also personally.

The trip home had seen me forced to face up to problems, problems that with my novice mind seemed to be the worst problems I could have in the situation. Looking back I can smile at how out of proportion my reactions were, but at the time while on my own and miles away from anyone, I had never had to really get myself out of difficult situations before. Living a sheltered life in the family home, where work was only a ten minute walk away, and the worst things that happened involved getting lost on a walk ten miles from home or arriving a few minutes late from work in the evening. I had been in some ways lucky to live with an unknown ignorance of any real difficulty, which had only served to make my boating problems that much worse in my mind. I knew I had been lucky to have a good childhood, even though I spent an unreasonable amount of it indoors playing computer games which grew into an outright obsession. As I grew, but did not really mature, it took until I was in my early twenties before the outdoors bug bit me and I left that electronic world behind me. Sat on a little boat at Ellesmere I still had no real problems and was thankful for that, I had however, been shown how immature I was as a person with how extreme my reactions had been, and how not having a *real* adult around at all times I had hated and dreaded having to face things myself. It was a realisation that had not just been thought about and a conclusion reached, but demonstrated time and again with my moody attitude that would last only a few minutes until whichever minor problem of the moment had been dealt with.

I sat and tried to write about this realisation at the time, but the words would not come to me. Maybe I was still figuring it out, now though, I can see that my outlook on the world and way of dealing with things has been on an ever increasing level of sense and reason since those few weeks in the summer of 2012. I am still far from perfect and prone to panic, but at least now I know I am being ridiculous!

The following day another best friend made his first trip to Tilly. It was another great sunny day and the fact it was a Saturday gave the day an even more cheery feeling as many friendly boaters came and went while me and Mike or Manning as I only ever refer to him as, spent a fantastic five hours onboard, once again with me excitedly giving him the grand tour of the tiny thirty foot boat. We enjoyed two small trips, and I ended up moored back past the marina again, and decided to leave Tilly there over the rest of the weekend. I was due back in work the following day and the good towpath surface was a bonus for biking into Ellesmere, before the ride up the infamous Brow hill, not exactly the sort of contours I particularly wanted to see first thing in the morning.

After a long day of climbing over the boat and looking at the engine, as well as quizzing Manning on his perspective on interior design and decoration I should follow for Tilly's small interior, it was time for him to catch the last bus, and for me to have one last holiday moment, and get chippy chips for my tea. Then as the evening drew into night I fell asleep knowing that the holiday was over, and that I was about to start truly living on a boat.

At five minutes to seven on the morning of Sunday August the eleventh while the silence around the Ellesmere basin was broken only by early morning birdsong, another sound suddenly burst into life. My alarm clock! It was time to return to work and for the first time commute by bike from another town. I woke up with a start and in a panic that I was going to be late, rushed around to make the boat respectable to anybody who might pass by on another boat and look in through the windows. I rushed to get dressed, hopped on my bike and started the eight mile ride into town, obsessed that I was going to be late despite setting out two hours before I was due to start. I pedalled as fast as I could the entire way. I arrived at *my mums house* only 50 minutes later, absolutely worn out and ready to get back into bed, but at least I consoled myself that I was over an hour early.

I had some cereal for breakfast and wasted an hour on the internet. So the routine was set for all future work days, another element of boat life, the commute, was settled in my mind. Now I was living my simple everyday life, if that happened to include sixteen miles of bike riding and an eight hour shift, then I was just going to have to get used to it.

Returning home to Tilly turned out to be easier than expected. Jono had come out for our traditional favourite, French bread pizza for tea, with the hope of watching some of the meteor shower later in the evening. I caught a lift back with him and the pizza was delicious, the weather on the other hand did not turn out so well, clouding over leaving us very lucky to have seen one shooting star by pure luck. The evening was another pleasant demonstration of how just by being on a boat in the middle of the countryside, everything just seemed inexplicably better, After Jono left I fell straight to sleep, once again I would be heading to work the following day, luckily working a late shift meant I could catch the bus. I set a late alarm clock but as had become a common theme of boat life already, was woken up by passing traffic almost uniformly at eight in the morning, sometimes a little earlier by very keen boaters.

Over the next few weeks I really did settle into the basic principles of boat life. I became less stressed about constantly moving every couple of days as I figured out the mooring rules, and it hit me that I really could moor up in some of the most amazing pieces of countryside for up to two weeks before moving along. I enjoyed the incredible peace and dark nighttime skies of some of the familiar stretches of canal that I had walked dozens of times in the past. St Martins became a favourite place of mine, offering an incredible view both during the day and night, with flat fields surrounding parts of the canal in almost three-hundred-and-sixty degrees. A few hundred metres around the corner from one of my favourite pubs, The Poachers Pocket, became another favourite offering a five minute bike ride to Helena's house, and a thirty minute ride into Oswestry for work.

It was this new understanding of the mooring rules and the opportunities for a perfect view from every window, that really helped me fall for boat life. I had been concerned about the potential difficulty of getting to work and back on my bike if I could move only to places marked for mooring, some of which would leave me a long ride down the towpath alone, before getting to a road to really start progress on my commute. Other mooring problems that had concerned me included the potential to have to move Tilly on work days if I had been on a forty-eight hour mooring. As it dawned on me that I really could moor anywhere apart from one very small stretch that specifically said "Private. No Mooring", I was amazed at how much pressure this took off me. Other boaters told me that nobody was checking and it didn't really matter, but I was keen to stick to the rules to get a feeling of living properly by them and with boating now limited to short distances, I was no longer living in dread of having to start the engine up. With family and friends onboard I enjoyed many regular short trips that saw me progress up and down the canal in many happy hours and nervous moments of letting others take the tiller.

My new confidence in leaving Tilly in one spot for more than a day or two allowed me to spend a great deal of time painting and decorating Tilly's ever modernising interior. Given that Tilly is split into only two rooms, the bathroom and then everything else, it may not be a surprise to learn that the bathroom was my first completed part of the boat. White walls and fake tiles gave it a new clean look and feel, a new portable toilet, shower head and shelves turned it into a room that I was far more comfortable with, both in terms of having it as a place of daily use, and also for the use of guests who I now hoped would not think my facilities quite so primitive.

When it came to the main living space I decided to stick with the safe option of magnolia for the walls with the thin border strips of wood painted a light blue. The floor I decided to leave until after winter, my reasoning being that if I did it before the bad weather of autumn and winter arrived, then I would instantly lose the fresh feeling of a brand new clean carpet. I now know not to bother planning around the weather anymore.

The painting took longer than expected but was still completed within three weeks, once again the ever present helping hands of Helena were put to good use with a paintbrush, and over the end of August and start of September we steadily covered the previous very dark wood interior with magnolia and light blue. Some of the days that I spent painting and listening to audiobooks on my own, while the sun shone and holiday boats whizzed past rocking me and my otherwise steady brush strokes all over the place, were the best times I have had onboard. There was an all pervading sense of progress, of making a home and of growing up, and being out in the wide world... at the same places that I had been walking for years anyway!

After the tiling success in the bathroom I decided to add some warmer coloured tiles to the main room too. This began an expensive obsession, as after one wall was tiled I was so impressed with the final look, that I went on to tile more than double the intended area. Once complete though I was satisfied that Tilly was now truly my home.

There were still jobs to be done, the fire was still too leaky to use, the engine had to be seen to, and in a few months the carpet could be replaced. For me though, the most important fact was that I could now pull out a sofa-bed and go to sleep in a place that felt like home. There were a few cold nights starting to sprinkle themselves in with the dwindling summer, and my attention was finally required on the fireplace. Jono and myself made several ill fated attempts at lighting a fire, invariably ending in the fire going out within minutes, but not until it had seen that the boat was filled with smoke through the joins in the rings on top of the fire, intended to allow you to add fuel and heat pans and kettles.

As the weather got colder I added another blanket to my bed, and still kept putting off actually getting something done with the fire, as I tried to sort out things back at the old house, as well as figure out what I needed and where I would store them on the boat. There was plenty to get on with and during the daytime the cold nights without a fire were easy to ignore, then between the hours of twelve midnight and eight in the morning I would bitterly regret not getting it sorted, only to start the cycle of putting it off all over again as soon as I was up and dressed for the day.

I could have made the fire issue far less of an issue by running the engine which was also connected to a radiator on the inside, as after twenty minutes of engine running the radiator would be quite warm and only got hotter from there. However, with the engine still drinking water, leaving it to run in neutral and warm the boat up was simply not an option, I could have run the engine and stayed outside on the deck filling the header tank every ten minutes, but that would have ironically made heating the boat very cold work.

Finally, after I had settled on the things I needed to have onboard and the things I definitely did not want onboard anymore, I had to sort something out for the engine and fire. Looking back, it could have been a desire to avoid any potentially costly work or repairs that had helped me focus on the *free* jobs I had to do on Tilly. Mentioning the engine at work one day, it became apparent that of all the incredible luck somebody that I had been working with for four years had previously worked at a marina, and still did BSS boat safety surveys. We arranged a day that he could come out and take a look just to see if there was an obvious problem, and then maybe put me in touch with someone who could fix it at a good price.

The day before our meeting I moved Tilly down to a local pub for easy walking access, and in an amazing twist of fate the header tank did not take any water at all. I revved and revved to try to make it drink but to no luck. After a short trip, and happy that the day before getting the engine looked at, the problem seemed to be fixed, I left the engine on while I moored up and made myself some tea. After an hour or so all the water remained where it had started. I was hugely relieved and confused but it seemed that somehow after weeks of pouring hundreds of litres of water into it, the engine had finally been satiated. That was the start of a beautiful time onboard with much more enjoyable travel and short boat trips, without the worry of the header tank hanging over me.

My friend came round the following evening and we lifted the boards to reveal the engine. He agreed with previous comments that it was probably the head gasket and asked if there was anything else I wanted him to look at. Taking the opportunity, I asked about the leaking fire on the chance that he may know a bit about them. That was the second moment that led to an amazing period of time onboard. He took one look at it and said words to the effect of "It is full of ash and needs emptying" and, "If you open this ash tray then it will let a draught through and take the smoke out." Later on after he had left I couldn't help my curiosity and emptied the ash from the fireplace and then set some paper and dry grass on fire. It burned perfectly, no smoke leaked, I placed about eight pieces of coal in, they started to burn, it got very very warm.

It was a revelation, all I had had to do was open the ash tray door at the base of the fire by a few millimetres and the smoke was carried straight up the chimney and out of the boat. I had never used a real coal fire or wood burner before, so had assumed that I would need to at least cover the bottom of the fire with fuel, then just to make sure it burned I had added a few more pieces of coal. Big mistake! Within twenty minutes the fire was burning so hot that I had opened the windows, this was not enough and soon I had the doors open too. This helped, but even with a strong through draught I had to strip down to just shorts and slippers. I had learned a valuable lesson. Don't overfill the fire.

Living The Dream

Suddenly finding myself with the basic abilities of both keeping myself warm twenty-four-seven and being able to move Tilly without storing ten litres of water in bottles right by the header tank, I was on top of the world again, and life on a narrowboat had never seemed like such a good idea. Making my short trips up the canal back to Ellesmere and then back to Trevor (the place not person!), I really did reach a new level of boat satisfaction which ultimately led to a couple of weeks in which I didn't do much at all. I felt that I could finally rest after two months or so of stressful boat trips, work, painting, trying to get the basic elements of a home on a boat, I finally felt carefree enough to become lazy. The majority of the work was done and it seemed that I had not stopped since buying Tilly at the end of July, by the end of September I was worn out, but I was at least worn out with a smile on my face.

It was a strange time to look back on as although I did nothing for a while, it was the first time that I was truly just living a normal day to day life surrounding the boat. When I had had all the work to do I may have been on the boat all day everyday, but I was there doing work rather than enjoying the simplicity and silence that I had bought a boat to achieve. As soon as the jobs were done I started to live on the boat rather than work there.

Soon enough however I was bored of doing nothing and resumed my obsession with youtube and began an incredible amount of filming onboard, random life updates, boating tutorials, scenery. I was pointing the camera everywhere. As a result my YouTube channel steadily grew in popularity which spurred me on even more, once I had reached a psychological milestone of getting one-thousand views a day and having more minutes watched than there were in each day, I managed to bring my habit under control. With this new base of endless comments and questions flooding in on all my videos, I was no longer ever short of anything to do.

I would record and edit videos all week onboard, and then when I rode my bike into town for work would leave my laptop at *my old house* plugged in and bombarding YouTube with upload after upload. This has pretty much become my standard routine, and to this day I am grateful that I have the stroke of luck that my parents house is right next to my workplace. It has saved me a lot of trouble that some boat dwelling folks do not have the easy solution that I do, being able to leave my work uniform ready to put on, as well as a safe place to leave my bike and any other possessions I may have with me.

I spend time at friends' houses and frequently visit home over the working weekend and sometimes during the week. Some people may think I am cheating at boat life, but I never intended to buy a narrowboat to just sit inside it all day doing nothing. Having Tilly as a mobile base in the middle of the countryside has proven to be an even greater an experience than I could have imagined. My commute to work is the perfect example of why I love boat life. I hop on my bike by seven in the morning and it is very rare that more than five days pass without my commuting route changing, sometimes longer, sometimes shorter, entering town from many different roads but almost universally involving a ride through some of the postcard countryside of Shropshire. Making the trip back out after work has proven to be the perfect way to leave the events of the day behind me. In the bitter cold or pouring rain it is certainly not ideal, but getting back to Tilly, throwing some logs onto the fire and hanging my dripping clothes above it to dry off, is one of the most profoundly satisfying ways I have spent my evenings.

Over the past year having a home that is constantly on the move has allowed me to really get out into countryside that I would never have had the opportunity to, in my previous everyday life. I used to walk from Oswestry to places on the canal as the destination, now I start at the canal and am already surrounded by nature before I even step out of the door. This has resulted in an incredible amount of exploring both on foot and by bike. Being able to ride around deserted lanes at any time of day or moored up by the sign for a footpath and then within ten paces finding myself in a field of crops is incredible. I have been walking and biking for many years now but the experience of the moving front door has opened up walks I never imagined, and seen me lost in places I could never guide you back to as a result.

In good weather this is perfect, Tilly is my home with an infinite garden but just like my commute the weather can also turn it into a not so infinite wonderland. Tilly is a thirty foot boat, but due to her very large outdoor cruiser stern, there is only fifteen foot of actual living space indoors. This makes a rainy day a day of very little movement, and over the course of my first autumn onboard we had more than a few rainy days. Spending a day in front of a roaring fire reading and writing may sound like an ideal way to weather out a storm, but there is a point at which it will become tedious.

When the poor weather took hold and we were treated to day after day of downpours I became frustrated at not being able to get out, just as I had done when living in a house but amplified by several factors. I had made the decision not to have a television onboard, this was based on the fact I rarely watched TV and so didn't see the value of paying for a license and using up battery power to run it. I also had no internet access at all and with my mobile phone costing me a grand total of £7.50 it did not come with any distracting features of its own. It was not until the bad weather that I missed having internet access, and when the long nights started to draw in as well, I knew my days without an internet connected phone were numbered.

So with a shiny new iPhone I found myself back in touch with the world, adding some more social elements to what was sometimes a very secluded lifestyle. With internet access came the return of one of my favourite things, podcasts, for many years I have spent countless hours a week listening to all sorts of podcasts as well as producing many hours of my own. This time around though I was just a listener, adding all kinds of background noise to my time onboard, the boredom that had started creeping in vanished, and when I rediscovered audiobooks other than The Lord of the Rings, I was over the moon to be able to have forty hour long recordings to act as a constant source of entertainment for weeks on end. My already strong love of reading and writing were now finally not my only sources of distraction for the rainy days and dark nights.

As winter drew closer I found myself in genuine boat life routines, collecting and cutting wood, adding antifreeze to the engine and running the water from any pipes over night in fear they may burst if things started freezing up, then trying to find the balance between a fire that will burn until the morning, and a fire that will make you sweat so much that you can't get to sleep. Waking up to open the curtains and find ice frosting up the windows and blotting out a view of frost covered fields was fantastic, and stoking up the fire in the mornings I don't think I have ever been so cosy or had such a feeling of warmth and protection from a cold outside world. The start of winter was fantastic and when I moved to Chirk Bank for my winter mooring I couldn't have been happier.

Winter moorings are scattered around the canal network and throughout the spring and summer are usually forty-eight hour mooring points like any other, however, from the months of November through to March you can pay a varying cost per foot of your boat to stay at these places longterm. Chirk Bank is located around six miles from Oswestry and the nearest place I could find to stay long term for cold winter commutes, it also happened to be the very stretch of canal that I had considered my true home canal. I had walked it at least a hundred times at a guess, and it had been the start and end point on so many long distance walks I had done that I was very happy to live there. I knew a few of the local residents and it was fantastic to be a part of a small community again rather than just a passing traveller.

I started my winter mooring in December and stayed through until the end of February. The previous few months had been a fantastic introduction to boating but mooring up knowing that I had no pressure to move for the next few months, was a strange feeling. I was sad to not have the sheer joy of meandering slowly down a canal on a boat for no other reason than the joy of boating. However, at the same time the increasingly hostile weather was making the trips down the deserted canals to mooring spots that might see me having to walk over a mile of muddy towpath just to find the nearest bus stop to head out and find supplies, was a less than inviting prospect. From Chirk Bank there was no towpath, just a few feet of grass and then a gravel area in front of the nearby houses, and the nearest bus stop was less than two minutes away. The thirty minute bike ride into Oswestry was equally welcome as an easier commute than some of my previous mooring places, without too many hills separating me and my workplace.

December passed in a blur, having a fixed point as my home gave me a sense of permanence which allowed me to further settle into life onboard. I was in the literal sense living at one of the places that I most regularly walked to prior to having Tilly. Starting out at Chirk Bank now opened up bike rides right down the canal to the busy tourist town of Llangollen, and walks for miles around the local small hills, all the time knowing that if I wanted to return home I needed only to find the canal then follow the perfectly flat path back to my doorstep.

My weekly life now included walks and bike rides through some of my favourite places and countryside and occasional bus trips out to Wrexham. I even started to walk the eight miles into Wrexham, do my shopping and then get the bus back, good exercise and with a purpose. Similarly my bike rides into work were fantastic, no muddy tracks or towpath, just straight to the road and riding in the right direction.

The mornings did become bitterly cold. One Sunday morning had been forecast as particularly cold so I had set my alarm a little earlier for half six to give me plenty of time to walk in for work if it was too cold to bike all of the way. Waking up I found the thickest frost of the year so far, covering everything, almost appearing to be a slight snow covering with its thickness. My bike lock was frozen solid and took a bit of a kicking to unlock, but soon enough I had set out on the road. I managed to ride for ten minutes until my hands, even though in thick gloves, were so cold that I had tears in my eyes and had to stop, the sheer pain of my freezing fingers being chilled by the artificial windchill created by riding a bike. The rest of the ride was painful, I couldn't get my hands warmed up and had a stream of tears from my eyes the entire way. Frequent stops, and riding one handed alternating which hand I used on the handlebars, was the only way I proceeded. The trip took twice as long as normal at fifty minutes, another lesson learned. Luckily I had been given some battery powered heated gloves. They were well used.

After the initial shock of my winter commute and taking on a few tips to stop my hands freezing, I really enjoyed the rides, the frost covered fields and hedgerows that glistened in the bike lights, the absolute silence and darkness of the roads, and the sense of being one of the few people up early in the mornings. Having my own deserted town to ride around for a few minutes of fun before going to the house to change into my work clothes and put in eight hours before getting on the bike and riding back, once again in the darkness of winter. It all felt good. I had over the previous few months slowly seen the sun move through different phases of rising and setting while I was riding in and out of work, but with my early winter starts and a very early evening sunset, it provided a certain sense of silence and calm to start and end the day with, a silent ride through the darkness.

My biggest daily feature however was keeping the fire going, but not making the place too hot to be comfortable. I had struggled from day one to find the balance in fuelling the fire, and when the cold weather closed in on the canals it was more testing than ever. The number of nights that despite freezing temperatures outside I lay sweating in bed covered by the lightest blanket I had, (just in case anybody could see through a crack in the curtain), is uncounted. Waking up in the morning however, to find a smouldering fire keeping the temperature at a cosy level, while opening the curtains to reveal a frost covered world outside, was the perfect start to the day, and some of those moments go down as the best moments onboard. Sitting with slippered feet up in front of the fire, eating a bowl of cereal, and starting on the audiobooks first thing in the morning while seeing the very occasional walker pass by all wrapped up in winter clothes, is exactly as ideal as it sounds, one of the very few things in life that lives up to expectations.

The fire needed fuel however, and so every week to ten days I would head out into the local area and in some cases towpath side wooded areas, to collect dried old broken branches from the ground. Travelling with two saws and an axe in my bag to start sawing and slicing up amidst the trees was another stereotypical boatman activity and one that I thoroughly enjoyed, and was surprisingly popular with my friends and family as something to go out and do for an hour or so if they were visiting. The chunks of wood were then stored under a huge tarp I had fixed to Tilly's roof with bungee hooks. I would keep a cycle of topping this up and having some by the fireplace to be dried out and ready to burn at a moments notice, sometimes though I could be seen out in my pyjamas in the small hours of the morning desperately trying to pick some dry pieces of wood from the roof.

During this time of short winter days and damp drizzly conditions the canal and towpath emptied of people. I had a fellow boater moored up nearby as well as the row of houses, but in my position moored slightly further on than the space opposite these, I never really saw many people coming and going. I was not quite prepared for how empty the canals became. After the last half term school holiday in October that saw a small rise in boats around the area the amount of boats that I would see in a week dropped to single figures. From the summertime and seeing hundreds of boats, I started going for days on end with no sightings of another boat moving on the canal. Later in my winter mooring time, when I would move Tilly a mile or so just for a change of scenery for a night before returning to my usual place, I discovered that I was the only boat sometimes in four miles of canal. A very odd change of pace and one that made what had previously been very rural mooring spots, even more isolated and peaceful. The boat trips that I made along the deserted canals were some of the most pleasant I have done, and I look forward to having what one boater described as "Your own private canal" again. With no traffic I could take things as slow as I wanted, there was no worry about meeting boats at awkward points in the canal and if I needed to stop for any reason, there were simply no other boats to take up any moorings.

As Christmas approached I decorated Tilly with as many battery operated strips of fairy lights as I could find room for, with those outside and in, the fire crackling away, while candles lit the interior with a dancing orange tinted light, there has never been a time of my life that felt more *"like Christmas"*, as we would have said at school. It was very important to me that I woke up on board on Christmas morning despite the offers of stopping in town to save the bike ride in. As my first Christmas onboard I couldn't wake up anywhere but on the canal.

Waking at a luxurious half-past-eight I set about the modern day tradition of texting everybody to wish them a good day, and then diving into the presents that I had on board. My delight at finding a remote control boat in one of them can not be overestimated, I instantly gave it a spin. Standing on the stern on Christmas morning sailing a tiny boat up and down the side of Tilly, saying various greetings to the local residents, or as I now called them, my neighbours, I knew it had been a good decision to stay onboard. Later I biked to a friends house for a while before riding into town for a fantastic family dinner and all the usual cracker pulling, overeating and festive cheer that can be expected.

This was the jewel in the crown of my new life, a shining example of how I always imagined life should be. I was ecstatic and had high hopes for the next few months and what they would bring, as I planned to stay in my winter place for three months more after having such a great experience so far.

Luckily we never have bad winters… Oh!

December passed quickly and without incident and heading into the new year I got bitten by the "lets change around Tilly's layout" bug. Myself and friends would spend hours debating how to change things and what could go where and how it would best be laid out to use the space available. It was like living through the initial weeks of getting Tilly back home again but only on a bigger scale, having lived onboard for a while at this point I knew exactly what I did and didn't want or need, and on the fifteenth of January myself and Jono ripped out the front seating and bedding area to create more storage space, and deal with the damp in the corner. I am still not really sure what my plan was ever going to be to replace this area, and to this day the bow end of the interior looks a lot tidier but has only ever been used to store coal, wood, bedding and a telescope.

Once this first dramatic event had taken place there was no stopping me. I pulled up all the carpet and floor tiles, removed a cupboard entirely, and sawed a few feet off the worktop by the sink to make the living area bigger. I controversially got rid of the fridge (in favour of keeping things cool by floating them in the main water tank) and had eyed up some new furniture, flooring and carpet.

In an amazing bit of productivity Jono and myself managed to lay carpet tiles through the living area, stopping at the kitchen in only a few hours. It was a small space, but the quality of the workmanship is probably still the most professional thing in the entire boat. Never have two people been so pleased with themselves, at least not since we had cleaned the oven one bizarre afternoon. It may seem an odd recollection for me to bring up here, but it was very very clean afterwards, never before have I used a screwdriver and a duster together! My Grandad had also come up to help take away some of the huge amount of scrap wood that we had created while demolishing the front bed set up as well as half of the sofa bed, leaving myself one half to sleep on while the work was ongoing. This was my only piece of furniture left at that point.

The surge of home improvement was however stopped in its tracks on day three when I awoke to find snow on the ground. It was an amazing moment and I had been looking forward to being able to be all warm and cosy inside, while a snowy canal scene surrounded me. However Chirk Bank became inaccessible for a day and the delivery of my chairs by my Grandad was delayed until the next convenient time. This was no big deal, I thought I would head into town on the bus and get some flooring for the kitchen. No bus service. I was stuck!

Realising that I was there for the day with nothing to do, I looked around and enjoyed just how amazing the snowy scene before me was. A little smoke made its slow ascent from Tilly's chimney and a few chimneys of the local houses, the local geese that usually appeared so white now looked yellow and dirty in comparison to the snowy ground that they waddled over. The snow made everything bright and crisp and as it melted in a circle away from Tilly's chimney, my perfect winter scene was realised. A happiness descended on me that helped to take the edge off my re-entry of the boat, looking around inside I saw that it had been vital for me to go into town to get any progress done on the interior. Instead I was stranded on a boat that had half a sofa bed as its furniture, no chairs, no cupboard to store food in, (I was still in need of shelves to fill the place once occupied by the fridge), nothing but bare floorboards for half of the floor, and about two square metres of exposed insulation and just plain boat hull where the bed had been removed from the bow. It was going to be a long day. My phone beeped as a text arrived, "did I want to go sledging?" That day turned instantly from boring to brilliant, I quickly put my boots back on and trudged up the snowy road.

The following morning brought even more snow, but this time at least there had been time for the roads to be gritted. Keen to make up for lost time I headed into town, bought some "wood effect" flooring strips for the kitchen and rounded up my Grandad for a quick run out to the boat, complete with tub chair and stool. Things were finally taking shape. Laying the floor was easy and the strips of laminated style vinyl flooring made an incredible improvement to the front end of the boat. Looking clean and bright the space seemed bigger and more open, equally the black tub chair that sat in the corner while the sofa bed half was pressed flat against the wall made the small fifteen foot long interior seem huge compared to only a few days previous, when the sofa bed itself had taken up most of the room.

It had been less than a week and Tilly had changed fundamentally inside. I was amazed, there was still work to be done but now I had a proper little living room that took less than two minutes to become a bedroom and a much cleaner brighter place to live in. The old brown carpet was now a very short length red carpet, the dark kitchen floor was now light wood, and the (awful) dark brown leather seating and bed at the bow was entirely gone. The finishing touches were small jobs, adding shelves to my new cupboard, a few more tiles for the walls, and a few newly revealed areas to paint.

Almost as rapidly as the progress inside the snow melted outside, and we all thought very little of it. Some years we didn't get any, and it had been a great novelty to have two days of good snow covering. I was glad to have taken the opportunity to go sledging and to have been able to be onboard Tilly when it fell. As January passed, Tilly was completed inside and life returned to the new routine of boat life. I got through more coal than I had done previously, and at one point found myself wheeling forty-five kilograms of the stuff two miles on a hand cart. Life was definitely back to normal!

I remained in my winter mooring at Chirk Bank until the end of February, at which point I had started to get the urge to travel again. I was very keen to cross over the famous Pontcysyllte aqueduct. A world heritage site, the aqueduct is a popular tourist attraction and a main feature of many holiday boat trips, going there during March however, is a different prospect. The canals are still almost empty in the area at this time, and so I thought it would make a pleasant trip and holiday before starting the proper bulk of the year's travel.

February had passed without much of note happening, the theft of my bike was certainly not a great way to draw my time at Chirk Bank to a close, but the significance of such events can only spoil things as much as you let them. We had more snow coverings over the middle of the month and were once again thrilled by the novelty of a few days consistent snow. It still failed to become a big, feature but I continued to burn coal like it was going out of fashion and frequently overfilled the fire and sweated away like a very hot fool on a boat.

The arrival of March saw a very unexpected break in the cold and rain with an exceptionally hot couple of days. Shorts and T-shirts were worn, and Tilly was mopped from the tip of the bow to the back of the stern outside, but after looking very smart, it took only three days for the rain to return and bring all the leaves and muck from the trees down with it! I persuaded Helena to join me on a four day holiday to the Pontcysyllte aqueduct and Trevor Basin and the sun shone on us almost constantly.

The day of the aqueduct crossing was a beautiful chilly but bright day, blue skies but you could still see your breath. The layout of the canal allowed us to go across the aqueduct then immediately turn around and cross over it again, heading back to where we started from, two crossing with barely two minutes between them. More than the various architectural features, the aqueduct is famous for one thing. There is no railing on the water side, and standing on a crossing boat puts literally nothing between you and a one-hundred-and-twenty foot drop. It is exceptionally narrow, just wide enough for a boat to cross, and to the one side a very thin path that makes walking across and meeting someone coming the other way a hair raising, possibly very wet experience. The path has tall iron railings to the outside, but these are not to be found on the water side at any point along the slow trip across.

Taking turns on the tiller, Helena and I peered over the edge of Tilly down at the playing fields below, the irrational feeling that we were suddenly going to jump or fall over the edge for no reason really took hold. A fantastic experience, a wide river flows underneath towards one end, and the hills stretch off away to Llangollen giving the crossing an incredible backdrop, scenic, terrifying, and all from the back doorstep. I took the opportunity to go inside and look out through the windows. To look out from your kitchen window and not even be able to see the side of the aqueduct is an odd experience. From inside it was almost as if I was standing in a plane or helicopter slowly flying across the valley. Reaching the Trevor basin I jumped off onto the bank and turned her around by hand, before jumping, literally, back on board and doing it all again!

With another item on the *"Things you have to do on a narrowboat"* list crossed off, we moved down a mile or so to a mooring spot at the far end of the village of Chirk. This would be a good place to spend a week or so and left me with a commute of around nine miles, but a relatively flat route including roughly two miles of canal. Riding a bike that far down a very dark secluded and empty canal at eleven at night can be a haunting experience, the creek of the trees, the sound of unseen running water dribbling into the canal, and the rustle of animals fleeing your path. By the time I was back on board after work it seemed as if everything prior to the last few miles of riding had been in another lifetime.

Being moored up right out of society has always had a great positive effect on my productivity, especially if I don't have a strong internet connection on my phone. Writing, recording videos or just simply getting on with odd jobs, rural mooring with no distraction other than an audiobook playing in the background has been a bonus in many ways I could not have predicted. However, it does pose the problem of being a very long bike ride if I need anything urgently or have something to do in town. This led me to jump at the chance of spending the night in *my mum's house* when I found out that I would be the sole occupant, and able to continue the month's long process of sorting through my old belongings for things to sell. That was a Thursday night. Waking on Friday morning I could not believe what I saw through the window.

At least six inches of snow covered everything in sight, cars were stuck at the bottom of the shallowest of hills, walkers were finding it hard going as they sank up to their shins, and the postman was having the workday to end all workdays. I had only one thought, I had to get to Tilly and get the snow off the roof. Snow continued to fall unbroken all day long until my Grandad and myself were able to dig the car off the driveway, and very slowly make the trip to my out of the way mooring place. My fear for what we would find must have shown in my voice despite my best brave face to cover it, as my Grandad walked down the towpath with me "Just to see what it was like". She was still afloat but there was a total covering of at least six inches, in some places eight, where the snow had been blown into smooth curves rising up the inside of the stern.

I immediately set about knocking as much snow off as I could while my Grandad made his slow way back home. This was the heaviest snow I had ever seen. The TV had been a constant stream of the chaos across the country as things ground to a halt, power cuts, roads blocked and accidents spread over huge parts of the nation, leading to an all consuming sense of embattlement with nature. After brushing the snow from half of the roof I went inside for a rest, the weight of the snow still on the right hand side was tipping the boat steeply to that side and I had to go straight back out and get the rest off. It took a while but the safety and relief I felt knowing that she was now back to her normal weight in the water was immense. I spent the remainder of the day enjoying the walk up and down the towpath experiencing snow drifts well in excess of a foot, and exchanging comments with the rare walker I met and the even rarer boater.

With winter scenes through the window the likes of which I had never seen in my life, I warmed myself with a roaring fire and placed a saucepan of tomato soup on top of it. I was living the dream!

Around four in the morning I awoke with a start, there was shouting outside in the distance. Stepping up onto the stern I was shocked to find another four inches or so of snow had fallen and recovered the whole of Tilly. The voices seemed to be coming from a road bridge a few hundred metres ahead. I listened but in the sleepy state I was in couldn't figure out what was going on and assumed that it must have been kids or something. I did not consider that it was so early in the morning that almost nobody should be out in the heavy snow. When I awoke at eight I was greeted by a very unexpected sight.

A minimum of six inches of snow once again covered Tilly. I stepped up onto the snow covered deck and looked around. To the rear there were two snow covered boats that had arrived late in the evening the previous night, and as I turned to the front, I saw a sight that shocked and scared me. An enormous tree had fallen across the canal. Intrigued at the sheer size of it and the possibility of the canal being genuinely blocked by a fallen tree I darted inside, put some proper clothes on, and walked the short distance to the obstruction. It was carnage. Somebody had already been down the towpath and cut the branches so that at the very least you could walk past, but the canal was completely blocked. There were three separate trees that all merged into one tangled mess across the entire width of the canal and beyond. There was no way I would be travelling anytime soon, so my plans for the day were instantly cancelled as I received word that the second night of heavy snow had been widespread throughout the area, and as I could see for myself, it was still falling.

As I walked back to Tilly a thought suddenly struck me. The trees were now occupying an area of the canal that when I had gone to bed the previous night was filled with a holiday boat. The shouting and voices I had heard in the small hours of the morning suddenly made sense. I felt guilty at dismissing it as mischief at the time as having such a huge tree fall on your boat in the middle of the night must have been a terrifying ordeal. I thought I would walk down the canal a little later in the day to see if the boat was anywhere to be found, and if they were ok or needed anything. Luckily I found the boat had made it to the safety of a nearby marina. A relief for everybody I imagine.

I relit the fire and boiled the kettle, a mid morning cup-a-soup was called for, it was Saturday, and I needed to be in work at nine the following morning. It was an impossible bike ride in the conditions of snow and ice, none of my family could get as far as the end of their driveways, and public transport was out of the question for the foreseeable future. One option remained, walk it. This was not an option I particularly wanted to take as the nine mile trip meant that I had no choice but to leave Tilly that afternoon and spend the night at *the old house* when I was desperate to stay on board and hold the fort with snow clearing duties should the snowfall continue. Work was however, not a thing to miss and I made the decision to set out at midday.

I ran all the water out of the pipes, topped up the fire with coal to allow it to heat the boat for as long as possible after I left, and wrapped towels around anything I was worried about being frosted or iced up on my return. Leaving at midday on Saturday my working hours would leave me stranded on dry land and away from Tilly until first thing Tuesday morning. I bade farewell and with a backpack full of food and water started the slow walk into Oswestry. I was going to call in at my friends four miles away at Weston Rhyn for a break before the final five miles, to the still empty house.

The snow was roughly a foot deep down the stretch of towpath adjacent to Tilly, and it did not indicate that the next two miles of towpath I had to walk before joining the road would be an easy walk. Within five minutes of walking I had discovered that the gently winding path the canal took along with the varying tree cover and terrain, had allowed the snow to build up in some places to being thigh deep. I found myself wading through snow at many points, the easy parts of the trek still saw a shin high build up of the stuff. Passing Chirk marina I had seen a few smaller trees fallen across the canal but not blocking it, and considered how lucky it was that more of the larger trees had not fallen. This sentiment was soon to be proven as utterly incorrect.

The canal passed through a brief stretch of open countryside before heading into a thickly wooded area with trees lining either side of the canal for nearly a mile. Along this stretch the snow on the ground was reduced to around eight inches, but the trees had taken the brunt of the snow's pitiless falling. In less than two miles of canal I counted fourteen serious obstructions, each one alone was enough to make the canal impassable and in some places I had difficulty just continuing on the towpath. The scene was in so many ways perfect, snow on the canal, no sign of humanity, and an eerie sense of calm broken only by the creaking and snapping of trees with the occasional full on branch snap, fetching wood and snow tumbling down to the ground.

As I got closer to Chirk Tunnel I was already worn out, wet feet and bitter cold on my face, yet sweating heavily from all the layers I was wearing, coupled with the very physical nature of the snow walking. Traversing another obstruction caused by a group of trees falling from the steep bank that edged the towpath, I saw another thing that struck fear for Tilly into my heart. My friends boat was moored just ahead of Chirk Tunnel and a tree had come down right across the canal. I could not tell if it had hit his bow or not. It was a close shave. Arriving alongside I was amazed and relieved to find it had fallen merely one foot in front of the very tip of the boat. Tilly was not under any huge trees, but even a small one would be more than unwelcome to find onboard in a few days time.

The remaining walk was one of very slow progress and discomfort as my wet feet in my shin high boots were rubbed by the damp fabric, but despite the fear, pain and general lack of progress for far too much effort... I loved it! It remains one of my favourite walks to date, I was able to see amazing scenes from not only my doors and windows but also up close. The kind of footage that is shown on the news to the viewers' responses of "Oh how lovely" and so on. That day I was able to live it. It was a shame to have to leave

Tilly, but I was not going to miss two days of work while I had access to an empty house right on the doorstep going to waste. The walk was brought to an abrupt end when my friends decided to dig their car out of the driveway when a local farmer saved the day by ploughing the local roads. After being stuck in their house for a few days they needed food supplies, and I was more than happy to accept a lift!

The nights I spent away from Tilly were plagued by my own mind thinking up scenarios and asking ""What if? My fears would not have been soothed had I have known that less than two miles away a boat had sunk under the weight of snow at the Trevor Basin. When I learned this fact I was never more glad to have been out there scraping snow off the roof at every opportunity. When I was finally able to get back to her on Tuesday I was relieved to find that everything was in order, if a little frozen inside and out. Some of the trees had been cleared by the winning formula of a boat and chainsaws, but it would not be until a few days later that I would finally be able to move along.

Once the canal was clear I wasted no time in getting closer to town to avoid any more repeats of the fiasco of the previous weekend that had seen me stuck in a house, when I felt like I needed to be on the boat more than ever. I travelled to St Martins, stopping slightly earlier than anticipated when my hand simply became too cold and my arm too sore to continue working the tiller. As I tied the ropes and then stepped inside I was reminded of just how amazing it was to be able to move my entire home, so that even while I had been freezing and sore barely two minutes previously, I was already warming up in front of a still smouldering fire, and with a radiator also piping hot from the days engine usage. Moving Tilly through what even in normal conditions was an area of fields, hills and countryside, had been even more of a spectacle with a covering of thick snow kept in place for well over a week by the consistently cold temperatures.

Just before the snow finally disappeared and let spring start to make progress across the country, I was treated to an amazing moment of natural beauty, the kind that only happens in story books. I was having my tea sat as usual listening to a podcast, when I saw a large white bird fly very low over the boat and across to the far side of the canal. I sprung up from my seat and looked through the window to see a barn owl perched on a fence post about thirty foot away. I was in awe. I was stood looking through the window of a boat surrounded by snow on all sides, at a bird I had never seen at such close range before. The brown and white feathers and wide face were amazing enough, but when it took to the air and circled the area occasionally diving down to the ground and attempting to dig into the snow for some poor being it had discovered, I thought it could have easily been a scene from a book written many years ago. The show lasted for half an hour until the bird moved just out of sight, my pasta had gone cold but it was an incredible experience, a truly beautiful moment of boat life to end my first winter. The perfect way to send myself into my first full summer season afloat.

The Narrowboat Lad

Out of the highs and lows of my first year on board Tilly there have been many moments that have seemed to be the turning point of when I truly became a live-aboard boater, when a pipe blew off the engine, when I passed my first kingfisher, collected the first armfuls of wood for the fire, the first time that I added sixteen miles of biking to my working day. The list of first narrowboat experiences is seemingly endless and not one moment can truly be chosen as the turning point between land and canal. Every new thing that I have come across in the past year, both the good and the increasingly rare bad, have been moments that I have silently said to myself "This is it, you are doing it properly now!" That was until recently when introducing myself to new people I have been met with responses like: "Oh yeah, Dan, you're the narrowboat lad right?" With a smile like the Cheshire Cat I confirm my identity!

I have been that narrowboat lad since day one to the people around me. My obsession with finding a dramatic moment that I can say was the start of my real life afloat was simply based on my love of the romantic image of boat life. I wanted a moment of watching a smokey chimney or a long hard day on the tiller, to sit back and say "this is it", which I have done far too many times at every opportunity. The truth is however that my boating life started in the mundane moment when the previous owner handed over the keys while we sat in his car looking across the canal at my new home. When those keys entered my hand my life changed forever.

People have often asked me if I am always going to live on a boat, my reply is always an unquestionable "yes." The next question is often "why?" The response is impossible to truly sum up in words, spoken or written. I could talk at length about the peace and quiet of the countryside around me, the amazing sights of nature I have seen as a part of everyday life, or the freedom of being able to move home everyday if I wished. I can sum up how cheap a small boat like Tilly is to run and how my quality of life has been improved by having a very minimal base cost of living, how being able to work part time with no debts and (touch wood), no significant costs in the foreseeable future allows an inherently less stressed state of mind to arise. The outdoor lifestyle I have built around living on a boat, with bike rides, walks and wood collection a standard part of day to day life can be talked of and told, but none of it really sums up why I hope to stay afloat forever more.

The lifestyle, the waking up to see a heron looking in at me from across the water, the short cold trips on the deserted winter canal, lighting a fire in the middle of the night after it has burned out, it all feels right. Living on a boat somehow suits me, the luxury of a big spacious house, the on call pizzas of the town or city, the consistent strong internet connection of modern urban life are all fine, great in fact, but there is something missing, something that even years before I had thought of living on a boat, I was looking for on my twenty mile walks or during my freezing cold midnight astronomy sessions on the outskirts of town. Something that I have found in the middle of nowhere on a tiny boat in the rain. Is it peace? Is it a closer connection to nature? A sense of being where I am meant to be, in the trees and fields? Maybe all of these things are one, maybe none of them are the reason, but at night when all I can hear is the occasional drip of water and rustling of trees outside, I know that I am right where I should be. Going nowhere slowly.

Dan's Narrowboat Life

Dan's Narrowboat Life

By Daniel Mark Brown

www.thenarrowboatlad.com

For everybody who has ever believed in me, encouraged or
helped me… or at least sat and listened to me talk endlessly about
boats!

Setting the Scene

When I signed the papers to buy my narrowboat home in mid 2012, I never could have imagined the events that would make up my life afloat. I had many doubts and fears, but also a huge amount of excitement at the prospect of a quiet life in the countryside. I was filled with ideas of tranquil moorings and sunny summer boat trips… Little did I expect that my life onboard would also see me scrambling around in the dark at three in the morning, walking the boat down the canal to get away from a barrage of bird droppings from the trees above! This unpredictable, mixed bag of often surreal and amusing day to day experiences is what I love about living on a boat. Being able to unmoor and move along. Changing your scenery, your neighbours, commute, local town, and more, leads to a lifestyle that can at some points be almost all tranquility, but, never the same.

As I write this introduction I am lucky enough to be well into my third year afloat. During that time I have seen the best of what narrowboat life can offer, but also some of the more troublesome aspects of life on the move. For example it is great to wake up and find snow on the ground, until you actually have to go to work in it or get supplies to the boat. These negative moments have been very rare in my experience afloat though. My main issues have all arisen from being a total boating novice at age twenty-five, yet finding myself living on a boat! However, as I approach my twenty-eighth birthday, I now find myself wishing that I had had a boat for a lot longer and have no plans of leaving the water anytime soon.

This book is intended to bring more of my experience of the canal than ever to life. Beyond the anecdotes and "quick guide" style writing and videos that I have been producing for the last few years. I hope that the new approach of this book will help show what my life is like in a wider context, inviting you onboard to join me for an entire year of my life. (The year in question is 2014). Being a keen keeper of diaries and obsessively filming and photographing things for the internet, I have not only got my memories, but also a vast library of recorded reference material.

Using all of this I have tried to create a written documentary of my life. Starting with the wet weather of winter we will see an amazingly warm spring turn to summer. Autumn will set in and bring peace back to the canals as the holiday traffic melts away until we arrive back at winter, with extremely quiet canals that are at some points literally closed to traffic, both floating and by foot.

I am hoping to show the variation and also similarities in my own life as the seasons, neighbours and locations change throughout the year. There will of course be plenty of anecdotes and my bad decision making, that throw in a far more random and unpredictable series of events than they could/should otherwise be.

There are a couple of things I would like to mention briefly about the content of this book. I have tried to keep it focussed on my personal boating experience of the year. There are many different tangents that I could go off on, writing about all the "off Tilly" adventures, but I felt that this would add unnecessary and irrelevant tales and fluff to the book. I have seen criticisms of narrowboat books for just that, a non boating aspect, and have always tried to avoid it, I have however thrown in a few side stories just to add a little context to my life.

I have also tried to keep away from too much minute detail, a very close look at a year of narrowboat life could become a very slow, long-winded and boring account. Things such as when I went shopping, what I bought, every detail on emptying toilets at service points etc, would not make for pleasant reading! I have tried to stay general, attempting to say what my experience of the year was, rather than exactly how it unfolded day to day.

I was lucky to have a very good year afloat. There was only one real problem during the period and it was hardly a problem at all, narrowboat life is not all sunshine and smiles, but during my year of recording and writing the following words there just happened to be an awful lot of both! There have been hard times that I have written about in the past and I am sure there will be hard times ahead, that is the nature of life itself, I have just been lucky to avoid them so often.

Finally, during the following text I have referred many times to "a friend" or "friends". This is out of general respect for their privacy. I would never wish to draw attention to those who did not want it or give away too much from somebody else's life. I just thought I would mention this to not appear rude or ignorant when sometimes failing to name individual people. I am lucky to know many people on and around the canal and I greatly appreciate all of their help, and the advice born from their greater experience of canal life.

Without further ado, we must get onboard and head off for a year afloat. The high points, the very few lows. A year of travelling, peaceful mooring, busy holidays and pottering around in the countryside awaits. Or to sum up this entire introduction in a single sentence: "I'm Dan Brown and this is my narrowboat life!"

A Very Quiet, Wet Start to the Hottest Year on Record

Writing the opening to this book has been a great challenge. A challenge that I have met in every piece of writing I have ever done on life afloat. Trying to introduce not only myself, but also Tilly the narrowboat, the scenic Llangollen Canal and my entire way of life in a few paragraphs. At one point I was tempted to simply write a list of bullet points and give up writing forever! Hopefully the following pages will do the job and if I am very lucky, they may even prove to be interesting or entertaining. Writing about my year afloat has been a fun process and taught me more than I expected.

The way that the year is split into sections of similar activity or inactivity is something I have not properly grasped the impact of on my life before. The winter months spent in one or two locations melt into one long period of calm, quiet time of an almost hibernation like peace. The spring and summer months bring a lot of movement and changing scenery and with it a lot of cycling to get to and from work, or even just to the shops for a pasty. Soon autumn slowly fetches the canal to a gentle restful peace for the winter again. Having your surroundings go through such changes and being so close to nature certainly has an effect on your outlook, mood and activity.

If you had walked down the towpath in the vicinity of Chirk Aqueduct during January then you would have almost certainly bumped into my humble thirty foot long home, Tilly. Thirty foot does not sound very big for a narrowboat. It isn't! As you continued to walk on past Tilly and saw the large open stern area at the back of her dark green body you might have thought "That is a nice little day boat". Meanwhile the chimney might have been smoking and you may have heard me talking to a camera inside or even heard me reading whatever book I was writing at the time out loud to myself on an empty boat.

The point I am labouring to tell you is that Tilly is small. Not only small, but also as old as me, being on the water since 1987. This has the side effect of her also being relatively basic. Luckily I am generally a back to basics kind of person and the idea of simplicity was something that appealed to me about life afloat. The basic layout of Tilly is fifteen foot indoor space with a ten foot stern to sit and eat on in the summer, and a five foot open bow area to the front that is often filled with coal and wood for the winter.

Indoors, you would step down through a door next to my bathroom, complete with shower, sink, boiler and toilet. Beyond this is my living room/bedroom. It is hardly grand, cupboards for storage sit opposite a sofa bed. The kitchen area follows with a sink, cupboards and cooker. The remaining few feet are taken up with a desk to the right and more storage to the left. A wall with two small stable doors and windows marks the end of the interior. Amidst all of this next to the cooker but opposite the bed is the heart of the boat during winter. The fireplace. It contains a small cylindrical wood burning fire with a chimney leading up to the ceiling. It is an odd creation with no door or window but a series of rings on the top that can be lifted to add fuel or sit a pan on top for cooking. The origin is unknown but the important thing is that it keeps the boat warm when the weather needs it to. Sometimes it keeps the boat a little too warm. The idea of a narrowboat being so hot that windows and doors need opening in mid winter is one that I never would have believed in prior to actually having to do it!

That is a brief introduction to Tilly. Tiny and basic but the place that I call home. Or do I? When asked, I may say that I live on a boat but the reason that I live afloat is so I am able to live in all sorts of amazing rural places. The Shropshire and Welsh border area in general is my real home. A region that is very green and filled to the brim with the sort of farmland and countryside that would suit an oil painting. I have enjoyed walking and cycling in the perfect scenery for a very long time, and one of the main factors that culminated with my desire to live on a boat, was to put all of that on my doorstep. Another way to consider it, is that I am really just moving a floating base with all my "stuff" in it around the countryside.

The amount of walking and cycling that I have done in the past around the canal and places like the aqueduct at Chirk certainly measure in the triple digits. By living afloat these locations became the starting points to set out on bike rides or the daily backdrop to a simple trip for a snack from a local village shop. Which brings us back to where we started on our imaginary walk down the towpath and past Tilly.

For the first three months of the year I stayed mostly around a small village by the name of Chirk Bank, right on the edge of the English side of the Welsh Border. In only a matter of minutes it is possible to walk from the village, over the old stone arched aqueduct and find yourself in Wales and at the small town of Chirk. It is a hilly area that leads into an ever more undulating landscape as Wales and the Berwyn mountains open up to you.

Tilly usually sits on the canal just around the corner from a canal-side pub and out of direct line of sight of any fixed buildings. Opposite lies a flat boggy field that can also include a pond if it rains enough! The towpath is, during winter, a mixture of mud and stones and the course of the canal itself is made up of a long series of sweeping curves. The towpath is edged with a small wasteland of bushes, before the back of a (luckily quiet) industrial estate ends the greenery. This is almost all hidden by bushes these days, but once was a good shortcut through to a nearby garden centre and restaurant. Once upon a time a local friend of mine caught me and a girl suspiciously emerging from the bushes... I don't think I ever did get a chance to explain that we were simply trying to look at a wide range of home and garden furnishings!

The stretch of canal just described is very much like the miles of canal that continue both ahead of and behind my/Tilly's winter home. If anything, it remains almost completely rural with the occasional main road crossing overhead or unexpected industrial site breaking up the greenery. There is no shortage of idyllic mooring places on the Llangollen Canal. Even at the height of summer it is easily possible to find a place to moor for the vast majority of the canal. Sometimes you can be seemingly cut off from all of society during the long light evenings as the holiday traffic rests for the night. Other times a gang of holiday making pirates, complete with costumes, may be your neighbours for the night.

The Llangollen Canal is truly a beautiful stretch of water, at roughly forty-four miles in length it runs on a winding course through Shropshire. From Nantwich it dances over the border into Wales and back several times before finally heading miles into the Welsh countryside to reach its final destination of Llangollen. A small town, well known for its steam trains and bridge over an incredible river of white water and fast flows. There is an additional branch of rural and, if possible, even more beautiful canal known as the "Monty" or more officially as The Montgomery Canal. This is a further seven miles of bliss, especially as it sees very little traffic compared to the Llangollen's popularity as a holiday destination.

Llangollen plays a big part in my winter life as a hub for walking, and often a destination for cycling. My home at Chirk Bank is roughly nine miles of canal from the town. A bike trip to the local bakery for a pasty, will normally take around three hours to complete. The trip could be done in far less time but I like to add in some incredible hills and hard work to make it more of an event. Not a bad way to spend a day and keep fit, as long as the weather is on your side.

But we are getting ahead of ourselves, who am I who finds myself adrift in the green lands of Shropshire and Wales? For those who are lucky enough to have never seen any of my hundreds of videos online, I am Dan Brown. At the time of writing this I have been living onboard Tilly for over two and a half years and loved (almost) every moment.

Tilly has allowed me to enjoy the countryside and outdoor pursuits that have been my love for a decade. Running such a tiny home, and with only me in it, has allowed me to survive comfortably on part time work hours in a supermarket. My friends and family, as well as workplace, are luckily spread along the canal or at the very least, a reasonable commute from it. At best I can go and bother some friends after only a short walk from the boat. My commute to work can take anywhere from fifteen minutes to approaching two hours which we will see more of later in this book.

Starting this book with Tilly moored in the Chirk Bank area seems somehow suitable, as not only do my best friends live just minutes away from the canal, but it is also the area that as a child we would visit on Sunday afternoon trips out. As I grew older and started walking as a hobby it also became one of my most frequently visited destinations. Maybe it was seeing the boats moored up or crossing the aqueduct that planted the seed of my future lifestyle quietly in the back of my mind. Now though, during winter the area is my home.

But why am I talking about spending months in one place rather than getting out and exploring the canal that I have just sung the praises of? Well that comes down to something I am a big fan of. The Canal and River Trust's "Winter Mooring Scheme". As I do not have a full time mooring spot I am classed as a continuous cruiser on narrowboat Tilly. Being a continuous cruiser means that I have to stick to certain rules, the rule that has the largest impact on my life states that I can't stay in one, loosely defined, "place" for more than fourteen days. This is not a great hardship, boating down the canal is what I do and love! There is however a five month period that acts as an exception to this rule, "The Winter Mooring Period" which as the name implies takes place over the winter months, from November to March. To take advantage of this you have to pay a fee depending on the length of your boat. Luckily my small boat also means a smaller fee, for the full five month period of 2014 into 2015 it cost £212.80 to have Tilly moored at the canal side long term.

There are rules attached to this as well, such as not mooring within a certain distance of a marina and not overstaying in specifically marked areas. For me though these are not issues I really have to deal with, and I am able to stay for the winter in some beautiful areas. On a practical level though it is vital. During the cold and often icy months I am able to stay within a reasonable commute of work, friends and family and have good access to public transport to local towns for supplies.

This of course can be a lifeline if a particularly bad winter demands a constantly burning fire or makes cycling very risky on icy roads. That is how I ended up finding my quiet place, just out of sight of anybody but also within a few minutes walk of civilisation.

During 2014 I spent most of January through to March in this area, making a few brief trips to fill up the water tank from a tap at the side of the canal just over a mile away. It is always enjoyable to start the year with no concern about moving the boat. No worries about leaving her moored up in an unknown area, and relatively short, easy twenty-five minute cycling commutes into work during the dark an cold mornings. Having friendly neighbours who know if anything is amiss and will keep an eye on Tilly is also reassuring while I am away, the list of positives goes on.

The fact that this is also a scenic and rural area with a number of very quiet spots I could move to if I wanted total peace, is definitely a bonus. However I still don't think I could ever settle down anywhere all year long just yet. A sense of restlessness often leads me to even more activity than usual after a couple of months in one place. In 2014 this saw me purchase a kayak during January. It turned out to be one of my very rare good decisions.

January was a wet month, and a windy month. Initially the kayak did not get the use I had hoped for, but when the weather allowed, my friends and I made full use of it. Being a light weight inflatable kayak meant that it could easily be moved and carried, more importantly it was easy to throw over the side of the boat and step into without ever touching dry land. This led me to keep making short trips in it at random times of boredom throughout the day until finally I got a bad back!

While I was cursing the moderately bad weather for spoiling our fun, there was seriously bad weather causing massive scale flooding down south. An image of a canal lock so completely surrounded by flood water that it appeared to be merely a few posts sticking out of a lake rather than a few foot of water in a narrow channel, has stayed with me as clear as the day I saw it. It made me appreciate what truly bad weather could be, and very thankful that it almost never visits the Shropshire area. It did however act as a demonstration of how mild the winter had been, rain rather than snow, and it was mud not ice that you would be likely to slip on.

This impacted life in many different ways. The warmer days meant less fuel on the fire and of course less money spent on coal. There were also very few "chilly boat moments" of waking up in the small hours to discover the fire had gone out and that there was ice forming on the windows... Which unfortunately has been know to happen in my earlier days on Tilly... Putting a balaclava on while you wait for the fire to get warm at four in the morning is not the way I would choose to start my day!

The lack of ice also allowed me to get on my bike without fear of injury. Especially as my work hours usually mean that in the winter not only do I set out in the dark but also return after sunset. The joy of not having to sit on a bike seat covered in frost is also something that I could never communicate. So it was that my first period of short twenty-five minute cycling commutes to my mother's house, fortuitously located mere minutes away from the supermarket that I work in, were done more often in sweaty rain rather than bitter cold. A difficult choice to make if given the option of one or the other, but a guaranteed lack of ice is always preferable.

An average week in January was very similar to an average week from any of the first three months of the year. That could even be broadened out to include the final two months of the previous year too. Two days spent doing my job, one day spent tinkering and giving the boat a "proper" clean, and at least one good walk or bike ride. If the weather allowed it then I would hop out into the kayak multiple times in one day at the height of my obsession. The first quarter of the year passed peacefully and doesn't really lend itself well to the way that I wanted this book to be written. Rather than a narrative of events and descriptions of travelling down the canal every so often, winter at Chirk Bank was a very calm time. Enjoying the dry days as they came, I would still often be caught out in rain and storms that left me sat in front of the fire while my clothes hung over it to dry.

An unfortunate side note to the initial kayaking love occurred on one of my first solo trips. In my usual way I was hoping to make a quick video while I was out, I fixed my camera to a miniature tripod and placed it at the front of the kayak which was floating around on the still water. For some reason I did not think to myself that it would be a bad idea to leave this tripod freestanding and then get into the kayak. Needless to say, adding myself to the situation rocked the kayak somewhat and after tapping the side of Tilly the tripod fell over. It was almost one of those overly dramatic, slow-motion moments. The tripod rocked, fell onto its side and the curved surface of the kayak allowed it to slide elegantly into the water, never to be seen again. It was the first of two lost cameras for the year, the canal may be a little camera shy it seems.

When not working or doing something useful, which I should really rephrase as "most of the time", I would be with friends, pottering around onboard or walking and biking different routes. Evenings spent up at my nearby friends house would often see me walking or cycling down slippy wet towpaths in the middle of the night then quickly lighting the fire. On rare occasions I would arrive back onboard not only dry but also to find the fire was still burning and Tilly was already a warm haven to escape the cold night air.

By the end of January however, I did finally need to take Tilly down to a nearby water point at St Martins to fill up the tank. St Martins is another small village, it has a supermarket that is unusually large for such a location and the usual collection of old churches and winding country lanes. The canal does not run through the village itself but is situated about a twenty minute walk downhill. It is separated only by a few fields width at the nearest point. Walking up the winding public footpaths, through fields, between cows and crossing small bridges over trickling streams is one of my favourite walks into any town or village anywhere on the canal. The farmland is the sort of rolling small hills and streams that would be used in adverts to bring back ideas of what it was like in "the olden days".

The area directly around the canal though is incredibly flat, the non village side is completely flat for a good distance which offers a huge visibility and great views of the low hills on the horizon. It is a favourite spot of many people lucky enough to frequently pass through the area by boat. It is a good sign of the area's beauty that many people who I have spoken to online, who are not from the area, often remember it more than any other place from their trips excluding the local aqueducts.

Filling Tilly with water is an easy task. Simply moor up by the canal side taps, attach your hosepipe, make sure the other end is definitely going into your water tank and let the water flow. The act itself may be easy but the trip that I had down to the tap itself was unfortunately very windy.

The distance from Chirk Bank to the St Martins water point is barely two and a half miles, or just over an hours travel at my speeds. The canal, as described earlier, runs through perfect countryside. For a lot of the distance the canal and towpath are lined with a thin layer of trees which, when lit up by a low winter sun gain a lovely hint of yellow, adding to the perfect nature of the area. The day that I travelled down was just such a day, quite cold too, which added a perfect blue sky to complete the winter scene. The wind kept me on my toes with regards to steering but luckily the canal was still near enough empty due to the time of year. When I finally did moor up for the day I had a smile on my face at a safe uneventful and calm trip overall. It wasn't until getting back inside that I realised I had lost a hat, a glove and a mat overboard in the wind... Another example of why you should never let your guard down while boating!

I decided to hang around for a while in this area of flat surroundings, peace and cows. Not only because of how nice an environment it is, or even because of the fantastic commute up into the village. The rural location coupled with the low horizons all mix together to create a great place for astronomy. A telescope is one of the very few items that I have as a luxury onboard Tilly. The canal at this point running so far away from any major light sources lends itself to some fantastic dark sky conditions. I have been extremely lucky to see shooting stars, peer at planets and star clusters in some wonderful areas, St Martins is again one of the my favourite places around, the ease of access over winter makes it irresistible.

Unfortunately though, it was a very rare thing during a warm, wet, winter to get any good clear skies. I did manage one good night of stargazing before slowly moving in very short trips back up towards my original mooring for the year. Often, during this early part of the year, I did find myself seeing some incredible sunsets. The low horizons of St Martins and early bedtime of the sun, both increasing the chance of a spectacular end to the day. The often cloudy sky, was, on one occasion at the end of 2013, lit up with such a vibrant pink and purple colouring that I have used a photo of it to open my videos ever since. Being able to walk up and down a very straight mile of canal, while looking to the low hills on the horizon with a sunset slowly vanishing and a fading, being a tiny figure below the other worldly sky above, was a pleasure. Being able to then get inside a warm boat and be tucked up safely out of the evening chill is what boat life can add as the icing on the cake.

On the few nights that the night sky was clear, the temperature also dropped accordingly. Again the advantage of having a floating haven nearby came into its own. A sky filled with stars but very little light pollution is the perfect mix. Walking a few foot away from the stern door, planting a telescope down on the towpath and then looking up at tens-of-thousands of stars invisible to the naked eye is humbling to say the least. The smell of smoke in the air and the occasional flicker of a burning ember rising from the chimney, serve to show just how close to home I remain at these moments, regardless of how remote the images in the telescope maybe.

I have always been given a sense of just how tiny the world is during these experiences. With one eye pressed to the eyepiece, it is possible to scan the sky and see hundreds of thousands of stars in a few moments. The occasional galaxy that comes into view, such as Andromeda, could contain a trillion stars, while only taking up a small part of your view of a tiny part of the sky. All of these things can be seen from a few feet from Tilly, containing everything that I own. A tiny home, that, even if I used it to travel the entire length of the canal network I would barely have seen a fraction of a single country on our planet drifting through space. Humility is hardly the word. If the weather turns nasty, the choice of picking up the telescope, jumping onboard and being in bed within two minutes seems almost an impossibly mundane way to end an evening of stargazing.

I sometimes find myself facing unexpected weather conditions slightly further away from Tilly's salvation. At the end of January one such moment occurred at the most inopportune moment, when I had kayaked two miles downstream. The original plan had been to go out walking, but when the weather had forecast huge rainfall and thunder the plans had been cancelled. On waking up to a blue sky, a stiff breeze but ultimately dry day greeting me through the window I was a little miffed. Not wishing to waste one of the few dry days of the year so far, I thought it was only right to get in the kayak and see where I ended up. The wind was not too strong and was mostly at my back, every now and then it did catch me off guard, the lightweight inflatable kayak being easily knocked off course, but also almost equally as easily realigned.

I was enjoying a pleasant morning at a leisurely pace until the world grew a little darker and the sky a lot more grey. Paddling a kayak is a peaceful experience, just the natural sounds around you with the odd splash of your paddles. Imagine how disturbing it was to all of a sudden find an awful lot more splashing going on around me, as not only rain but also hail started to fall.

As could be imagined, on my trip back upstream to Tilly the pace was not quite so relaxed. The wind that had been at my back was now working against me, and when I reached the open and exposed stretch of countryside immediately surrounding Tilly, it blew harder than ever.

The flat fields and low horizon served only to allow me to watch the huge rain clouds approach at alarming speed. I paddled, it rained, it poured, and I was sure I had heard thunder. I was lucky enough to get back before the worst of it hit. Still I found myself out on the stern in the rain, trying to stop the kayak blowing away downstream, to the delight of the lucky person who may have found it and gone for an unexpected canal based trip by paddle power. After strapping it down and hoping for the best, I sat out the storm inside. The odd feeling of being a child again came over me coupled with a very specific, yet indescribable, hollow sensation in my chest every time lightening flashed across the sky. I had definitely heard thunder on my way back. It was a good job that I wasn't attempting to kayak by kite power!

As February rolled in, the weather became one of the biggest features of daily life. I wrote in my diary at several points during the first two weeks of the month that it was unpredictable in the extreme. At one point I noted that I had never seen the towpath muddier, but then the following day talk about how the sun had been beaming all day before being followed by a huge downpour. For any overseas readers of this book who may have heard of the British stereotype that says we are all obsessed with the weather, I am afraid that this book will do little to dispel that myth! Due to the large amount of time I spend out in the elements, the weather is probably more of an obsession for me than most. I just thought I would put this little note in now to prepare you for the coming pages of weather references.

More unpredictable than anything else was the morning of Monday February 10th. I had planned on having a nice early morning, waking up and then boating back towards the starting point of this book. I wanted to do this nice and early in the morning as I was working during the afternoon, so wanted to leave myself plenty of time to cycle into town and get ready.

When I awoke I found it to be freezing cold outside, ice and frost everywhere... Joined by snow! It was only a light covering but there was snow still falling. Of all the days to have one of the only two days of snowfall of the year, it was only right that fate should deliver it on my first planned early morning trip.

I wrapped up warm until I became something akin to a walking sleeping bag. Prizing apart the frozen mooring ropes I was gleeful at the idea of boating upstream with snow in the air. Leaving the ever whitening flat farmland of St Martins I was treated to familiar scenery in an unfamiliar winter coating. The mud of the towpath, frozen then covered by a white layer undisturbed by boots. Every field, hedgerow and house looking like something from a Christmas card.

The images that have stayed with me more than any others though are the canal specific items. Namely the humpback bridges and boats that I passed. When I reached a stretch of canal that was lined with trees on either side I felt like I had fallen through the wardrobe into Narnia. Spindly, naked branches topped with snow, white fields behind, acting as a perfect background. With each passing moment the snow seemed to get thicker and the ground whiter, the roof of Tilly slightly higher with snow.

As I passed through each bridge I was chilled to the bone by the wind being funnelled through. The snow seemed to line any irregularity or protruding feature in the brickwork of the bridges, highlighting these points and making the scene look immensely rustic. As I passed by the few boats that were moored, I really was looking at a true canal stereotype, a smokey chimney poking through a snow covered boat roof, melting a small area with its heat. Had I not been so cold I might have had a tear form in my eye from the over romantic nature of what I was seeing.

In the end I travelled only a mile or so upstream to a canal side, pub, restaurant and hotel called The Lion Quays. Located so close to St Martins and even closer to my original mooring place (with its own nearby pub, "The Poachers") it is still surrounded by the countryside that offers so much. It is slightly unfortunate to have one of the few main roads of the area cross over the canal just by the pub. This is not the worst thing ever and shouldn't be too devastating to the resting boater, but it does tend to add a drone of passing cars into the background. Something that many parts of the canal are often almost entirely free from. On a personal note I enjoy this site as it offers a slightly longer commute than other local places but one that is an awful lot less hilly. A very gentle ride of around seven miles is more than welcome when finishing work and cycling out to Tilly in the middle of the night.

After mooring up I had the slight problem of getting into town. Buses were likely to be a suddenly withdrawn luxury, I might wait at a bus stop only to find them cancelled. An issue that I had run into on a previous winter's unexpected snowy day. As has happened many times, I was again saved by having friends close to the canal. The Jaspers just up the road informed me that they would be going into town and that if I could get to their house I would be welcome to have a lift with them. Not wanting to leave my bike onboard I made one of the slowest most careful journeys I have ever ridden down the towpath. I was putting the first marks in the fresh snow with my tyres and didn't want them to abruptly end with a swerve into the extremely cold water. I am pleased to say that I arrived at my destination about as dry as I was when I had set out, but far more chilly and with a nose as bright and red as Rudolph himself. Arriving in town with plenty of time spare before work, I had managed to squeeze in another great boaty memory within a few hours of waking up. Just the way I like a work day to begin.

As great as half a day of snow had been, the biggest national weather event during this time however was "The Big Storm" of 2014. The south of England had been battered by storms and under huge quantities of flood water for a long time at this point. The misery being added to with the arrival of one of the UK's worst storms on record. High winds and huge rainfall hitting most of the country.

February the 12th was the day of impact for the worst of the weather. Shropshire and the local canals were not flooded like the south was enduring, the Welsh border region very rarely has to take the full brunt of any severe weather, on this occasion we were very lucky to escape the worst. What we did have though was about as destructive a night of high winds and rain as I have ever seen.

I heard a couple of loud cracks during the late afternoon and early evening, it took me only an hour or so to discover one of them had been the sound of an enormous tree falling across the nearby lane. I have never seen a tree so large knocked down and battered on the ground. Even as it lay sideways, its trunk was higher than my head. I could find no way to walk around or even climb over it, so large, tangled and broken were its branches. Other trees were victims all around. It took me a few days to find them one by one, but the canal was blocked by a couple of fallen trees less than a mile away. Another tree only a few hundred feet away had been snapped at an odd place about halfway up its entire height.

It was another moment of life that sums up how small and feeble we as humans are when compared to the forces of nature. Waking up the following morning to find that it was a calm day was a stark contrast to the previous day's events. I was grateful for the calm as I had been stupid enough to find myself onboard with a bike crippled by a puncture with no spare inner tube or repair kit. The outcome of this lack of forethought was that I had to push my bike seven miles into town! It was slow progress, but did give me the opportunity to see just how many trees, signs and roof tiles had been tossed around like paper planes in the wind. Had I have known how much damage was being done I don't think I would have slept a wink on Tilly. The fear of not only stray trees coming our way, but also any airborne menace would not have created the usual relaxing environment onboard.

Valentine's Day also sticks out for me to mention as it again sums up, albeit in a depressing manner, my general, unplanned walking and pottering around the canal and countryside. On the February day of love I was not living up to the occasion. I note in my diary, that in the evening, rather than wining and dining, I was making the short walk from Tilly, up onto a country lane that rarely sees any traffic and then down to a local garage to pick up some junk food. While checking my facts I discovered that I was so impressed by the size of a king size Lion Bar that I even took a picture of the said purchase. Two chocolate bars and a bottle of pop, a grim reminder of a Valentine's Day spent with a destructive love of mine, food.

March soon came around and found me making an uneventful short trip to moor back at Tilly's original location. Being the final month of winter mooring, I told myself that I would get some of the little jobs done onboard, painting, sanding, tightening screws and fittings, cleaning out various corners of the exterior. I may have told myself that is what I was going to be doing, but in reality I really just enjoyed the last of my time in the area. A slight calming of the weather helped me get out kayaking, walking and biking even more than the previous two months.

One of the things I spent a big chunk of my time on over the end of February and early March was a short documentary entitled "The Narrowboat Lad". YouTube has long been a big hobby of mine. Creating short videos about my life afloat was, and remains, something that I thoroughly enjoy doing. But my boat videos are only the most recent form my hobby has taken, even before YouTube had past its first birthday I had been posting videos about any old thing, mainly games related, back when I never left my mum's house unless a new release was out in Woolworths games section.

Towards the end of 2013 and over the first two months of 2014 an amazing thing had happened. Nearly one-hundred-thousand people were tuning in to my videos each month. I was flabbergasted to say the least! It had been incredible when the previous year ten thousand people had been tuning in, but the latest figures seemed ridiculous. On the strength of that new viewership I thought that I had better try and make videos worthy of being watched. The Narrowboat Lad was my first attempt at a "proper" video. It took, what seemed like forever, to put together. Ten months on I look back at it and pick out so many flaws that I can barely watch it. Amazingly though, during that time it has been viewed nearly thirty-thousand times. The sort of figure that I would have never dared to imagine while putting it together.

I mention this now as it is a good illustration of what I do with all the free time I am lucky enough to have. When I am not doing something outdoors and away from the boat I am often found in three states. The first is sat at my desk writing or rewriting something like the lines you are reading right now. The second is sprawled out listening to podcasts or audiobooks. The third is wildly waving my hands around, as I half talk and half shout at a camera over excitedly about what fun and games I have been up to recently.

I have been humbled to have thousands of people join me for life afloat via YouTube. This year saw the moment that I finally started to receive so many messages and comments that I could no longer respond to them all. But I am no less grateful for every message that I get. Every moment that anybody decides to spend looking at me talking gibberish, while waving at the scenery surrounding Tilly on that particular day, is a moment I could barely be any more humbled by.

During my quiet an unproductive March onboard I had no idea that for the rest of the year YouTube would become a huge defining factor of life afloat. The best part of one and a half million people would glance at my videos during 2014, which, by the time the busy summer period arrived, would mean that more boats than ever would go past Tilly with a shouted "Hello" or other gesture of recognition. I do not wish to dwell on the topic, but thought that as so many people reading this will have found the book by watching my videos I had better give you all a nod and a great big thank you!

Let's Get Moving!

During the last week of March, I hopped onto my bike and for the final time of the winter mooring period, rode down the familiar country lanes from Chirk Bank to Oswestry. There I left my bike at my mother's house, met a friend, and then stocked up on supplies for Tilly, ready to resume continuous cruising for the spring and summer. Laden with goods, we caught the bus back out to Tilly. Arriving, I put the shopping away before we unmoored to make the short trip down to the St Martins water point. After filling up, on an entirely calm uneventful day, I attempted (and completely failed) to reverse Tilly up stream for a night or two. Rather than engine power, it was far easier for the two of us to simply walk Tilly back upstream a little, narrowboats unfortunately have no rudder based steering when in reverse. If you start to drift off course while in reverse, the only remedy is to start going forwards, unless you have bow thrusters which Tilly is not blessed with.

As I had left my bike in town in order to fetch out supplies on the bus, we decided to walk home together. We walked down the towpath, passing the two locks that marked the only change in canal level for around twenty miles, where the Grindley Brook Flight at Whitchurch promises plenty of physical work for the passing boater.

It was a mild afternoon that we found ourselves walking home on. The straightness of the canal seemed to make the mile long towpath walk seem a lot further. Again the cloudy sky sat over flat fields and farmland in every direction. Arriving at a very nice pub "Mad Jack's", we joined a country lane that took us to a main road into the tiny village of Whittington. known locally for the picturesque ruins of its castle. Whittington is a place that I have biked and walked to on many occasions. The castle has proven to be so alluring to me that I find it almost impossible to pass on foot without a quick walk up and around its stony skeleton.

Despite my terrible reputation for directions, I managed to convince my friend to take a shortcut over the fields to the back of Oswestry, rather than walk alongside the main road to town. He was less than impressed when my first attempt at finding the shortcut took us down a dead end residential road, leaving us looking like two suspicious characters to say the least. When I did get my act together though, we found ourselves doing what we both loved. Hopping over fences and gates as we veered from field to field attempting to at least stay roughly on track with the designated right of way. With the sun sinking ever lower in the sky, we finally found Tarmac under our boots once more and were soon going our separate ways. Reunited with my bike I stayed at my mother's house for a good fill of food and to rest my legs before pedalling off and away into the darkness.

The following day I was up early to start my decent of the two locks, finally exiting the small stretch of water that had been my winter home. The sky was filled with an unusual haze, tinted with the colour of a freshly risen sun. It was in this gently lit, orange tinted world, that I slowly descended the first lock. A process that I had done many times and slowly felt more comfortable with, yet never relaxed while doing. Just as the lock was fully drained a towpath jogger came by and said hello. He introduced himself as a fellow boater who was moored up just down the canal by Mad Jack's.

We chatted away while each of us opened a gate to let Tilly free. He was generous enough with his time to stay behind and close the gates for me, which was a big help as it meant I did not have to move Tilly out of the lock, moor up, then walk up and close the gates before going back to Tilly to continue. Thanking him, I told him that I would see him around as we would probably be neighbours when I moored up by Mad Jack's myself later on that morning. The second lock passed again without incident, but also without a second pair of hands. The only major event on the trip was the fact that the promising but murky sky had transformed from slightly golden in colour to simple, standard, grey. I later learned that this odd haze was the remnant of a sandstorm that had carried a small part of the Sahara Desert across Europe and over to the UK. Another demonstration of how small the world truly is.

All in all I was happy that my cruising had begun with a calm trip and a friendly new face. The friendly, travelling, wood carving craftsman, proved to be a person I would unexpectedly, but happily, bump into throughout the year, sometimes not even close to a canal, but in Oswestry on a supply run.

I moored up about thirty seconds bike ride away from the front of the pub, with a thin row of trees edging the towpath and the sight of a work colleague's boat on the offside. I should mention that this boat was out of the water. For the last few years it has sat on the bank while its renovation is completed. A fantastic hobby and the location of a great many conversations between the owner and myself. Having known each other for almost eight years, it was a surprise to both of us to one day bump into each other on the canal, both on our own boats.

This mooring location is again a favourite of mine due to its easy access to friends and family, a relatively flat commute to Oswestry and once again it's wonderful rural location. Despite my love of that particular area of the canal, the two week cruising rule would mean that by the end of April I would be over nine miles away, and as close to Oswestry as the canal runs.

April brought in some warmer weather, it certainly threw in some awful rain storms too, but overall it was a fantastic month for being outdoors. Not only do I know this from memory, but also while reading through my diary entries from April I found that I repeatedly mention the incredible weather. Two lines make the point as clear as possible, *"Have had some really great walks and rides from Frankton... Can't stress that enough!"* and *"Loads of really great weather and proper nice times... Especially long trips with the bike over fields from Frankton..."* The first thing to take away is that I use the term *"really great"* far too much, but more importantly I was loving the unexpectedly good weather and getting some excellent use out of it.

It was just as well that the weather was rising to the occasion as there was a lot of cycling to do. In an unusually early bid for calm, not only did my mum go on holiday for a week, but the following week my grandparents also took a trip up to their caravan on the Welsh coast. This left me in the position of what has recently been declared by my grandfather as "Head Gardener". A tongue in cheek overstatement of my actual basic duty of keeping the plants watered and also feeding any animals that may look up to me and meow or bark.

So not only was I able to enjoy some great, prematurely summery, boating but I was also blessed with kayak trips that did not involve hailstones or thunder. The addition of the empty houses, and filling the cat's stomach gave me plenty of reasons to get out on my bike. The benefit of having friends and family within easy biking distance of the canal certainly shines through when the opportunity of hijacking somebody's bath presents itself.

Tilly has a shower onboard that gets regular use during normal life afloat, but the luxury of a bath is not one that I can always turn down. There are not many narrowboats that have baths due to the huge amount of water that they take to fill compared to how much water you can store onboard. The space limitations of a boat also play their part but, as me and my friends have often mused, a bath is like lifting the lid on your water tank and diving in with a bar of soap. Not an activity that I have tried or recommend.

Cycling between Tilly and town was an almost daily commute at one point. These times are ideal for meeting up with friends, buying supplies or even using the house as a base for launching walks further into Shropshire. I have often found that in times when I have the option of staying at a house for a few days, I soon find myself itching to get back to the canal. Even a place as rural as Oswestry, with countryside available within twenty minutes of the town centre, is just not the same as opening the curtains and already being "in the middle of nowhere".

There was little more that I could have asked for during this first month of cruising. I took things nice and slowly, steadily moving down the canal over the course of about five to ten short trips. My preferred way of traveling is normally to spend a few days in one place then move along for another few days and try to work these trips around weather conditions and visiting friends or family. The perfect mixture of good weather, good company and good boating can create memories that will last a lifetime.

Spending the last few years out walking, biking and boating around the canal, I have been able to discover some excellent little places to moor. Often slightly away from the main mooring areas, but still frequently just within sight of a boat or two. Security alone is a good reason for this, but the time I do spend hidden away is often a time when I find myself at total peace. Being able to find these places and scout them out ahead of actually boating to them, is all part of the fun and adds an extra reason to go out on some very long walks to the shops. If I walk down the canal late one evening and find that a good place is completely empty of boats, while Tilly is currently nestled in a row, I may be tempted to move along the following morning, especially if I have a lot of filming that I want to get done. There is an overwhelming shyness that builds up within me if I find myself standing on the stern talking to a camera while other people are quietly going about their lives.

April was still a quiet month, a small surge of traffic was brought in due to the continued good weather but in all honestly it was quite nice to see a few boats around and speak to people who were in all stages of their lives. The retired boaters cruising the canals for fun, the holiday makers quizzing me on the best places to moor by pubs, and plenty of walkers on the towpath.

Slowly switching scenery brought with it a changing set of dog walkers and local people as I moved into, and out of, "their territory." It is from local people that I have learned the most about the canal. The history and forgotten features long covered by moss and grass have steadily started to come back to life through fragmented conversation and discussion with people who, in some cases, saw the canal in what seems to almost be a different landscape altogether.

However, with a canal as rural as the Llangollen, there are a great number of miles which have very few villages or even houses nearby. Certainly few enough houses that leaves the title "regular walker" a vacant position at some of my more remote mooring places. During April I started to drift into a couple of these as I moved away from Mad Jack's towards the very small Village of Lower Frankton a couple of miles cruise away. Lower Frankton is more a group of scattered houses loosely grouped together around a junction in the canal, rather than a traditional idea of what a village should look like.

At these points despite still being around a thirty minute bike ride from town, I am certain that I could go for days without seeing more than a handful of walkers. Peace and quiet like this needs to be enjoyed to its fullest before the summer holiday rush begins. Enjoy it I did!

Through spring I tried and failed to master the art of the sketch. Many half finished drawings are hidden away in a sketchbook onboard Tilly, a reminder of what promised to be a year defining new hobby during the first half of the year. Being blessed to have so much free time, or at least time I get to spend doing things I enjoy, such as writing this book, I have often found myself putting off one job after another. Being able to continually say that I will do it next week or, at worst, next month has not helped me get anything done at all. When faced with the enjoyable prospect of filming and editing a quick video, or instead painting the fiddly finishings inside Tilly, the camera would be rolling in an instant. As the weather gets increasingly warmer and dryer throughout the year, the addition of increased outdoor pursuits acts as the final nail in the coffin of getting things done. With the fantastic weather of early spring, my attempts at completing jobs soon fell away to writing, filming, walking and biking... and of course actually going to the job that allowed me to do all these things!

On the day of my birthday my family came out to join me as we descended through the Frankton Locks and onto the Montgomery Canal. We moored up in one of the most remote places on the entire seven mile stretch of the Montgomery. Most of the canal bank on these seven miles is unsuitable for mooring, due to the shallowness of the canal, long stretches of reed covered bank, or the structure of the bank itself. This means that if you find the designated mooring areas full, then you may have a very long trip on your hands.

The canal itself is extremely rural, going beyond the Llangollen's level of countryside, at some points seeming to entirely leave the outside world altogether. Between the junction at Frankton and its end around the small village of Maesbury, the canal cuts through an extremely flat area of farmland. There is only one real village of note that it runs through around halfway down at Queen's Head.

To add to the serenity there is a rule of letting no more than twelve boats a day descend or ascend through the locks, I have been amazed to find that even this low limit has only been met once on a day that Tilly was making the passage. The lack of travellers seems to stem from the canal's lack of any exciting features (such as the Llangollen's epic tall aqueducts and tunnels), dead end after just seven miles, lack of moorings and narrow nature. All things that I can understand but also exactly what makes it a canal that I love. Another rule peculiar to the Montgomery keeps the canal quiet. You are only allowed to stay on the entire canal for fourteen nights. This is intended to keep the few moorings vacant, but of course does not always guarantee that you will end up where you want to be.

This was the case on my birthday, after finding the first and only real mooring place on the top end of the canal full we had to abandon ship about a mile further on, and moor up to some temporary mooring mushrooms. They are intended only to let boats pass single file over a very small aqueduct, barely even noticeable. Due to the canal being so quiet it is extremely unlikely that two boats would ever meet here, so they are generally used as a mooring point. An extremely isolated place that I would be visiting again unexpectedly later in the year.

After leaving the boat for a while to go off for some more birthday fun, I returned later to continue my trip downstream. Considering that the "Monty" length of canal is only seven miles in total, there is a gap of three and a half miles between the mooring point by the top locks and the next official place downstream. So it was that a peaceful and uneventful trip ended with me and Tilly nestled between two locks, not an ideal or recommended place to be, but a place that I finally decided was enough for one day. A visit from a few friends rounded out the day and led me to a sleepy, lazy evening onboard.

The rest of April passed calmly with plenty of time spent enjoying the surroundings. The flat fields for miles were a welcome change to the hilly terrain of most of Llangollen's surroundings. The lack of any hills is especially welcome when it comes to commuting into town. Maesbury, my mooring location at the bottom of the Monty, is the nearest place that the canal runs by Oswestry. At less than three miles, with hardly any change in elevation, I find that I get on my bike and ride around more than ever. Easy cycling around the many empty lanes. Biking into Oswestry in the evenings and doing a few laps around the silent town, then heading back to the boat without ever taking my feet off the pedals, sometimes just biking up the towpath to see who is about. Just being out and about, a good start to what looked like it would be a great summer of cruising.

Boating and Bird Poo

The end of spring and early summer brought every great bit of boating and weather I could have hoped for. By May 7th Tilly was back on the Llangollen and being rocked around by more boats than she had seen all year. The trip back up the Montgomery had been a one day trip from bottom to top, having two friends onboard. All of us on a boat and with a bike each, led to another set of great memories being made. After all, who doesn't love a day that ends with three figures carrying bikes on their backs across fields of crops?

I feel as if I spent most of the month moored around what I describe as the Ellesmere area, but in actual fact I covered at least a dozen miles. The village small town of Ellesmere sits almost on top of the canal. A large supermarket is literally built on an old wharf, very handy for shopping. The name is taken from the large lake of Ellesmere, a feature that is truly beautiful. The mere sits in the "old part of town", a very attractive area to say the least. A walk from the canal over a steep bank leads you through winding lanes with names such as "Love Lane" that take you past old ivy covered houses and the towering church of St Mary.

Walking down between these features and seeing the mere open up in front of you, is just one of many moments from my life of drifting from place to place, that seems like it could be happening two-hundred years in the past. The fact that Ellesmere is such a picturesque place would be enough to make it a regular stop on my travels, the fact that it also happens to be one of the few places with any shops for miles around, guarantees it.

During early May, Tilly was moored at a placed called Tetchill. Again, the settlement is a collection of a few dozen houses and very little else. There is a long string of boats moored at the edge of a field, or as it is also known, "marina" that I have jealously eyed up, hoping to get a spot at on many occasions. For Tilly though, the mooring was a little downstream and opposite an open field raised slightly to roughly boat height on the far side. It was a very strange horizon to have, the sky meeting the earth literally twenty-five feet away. The only odd addition to the sky line for any moored boats would be the wind turbine which serves as a marking for the village for miles around.

The reedy overgrown far bank, then skyline almost immediately above make a nice view through the window. The weather was throwing in the occasional bad day but spring had proven itself to be full of good weather and even better times. My evenings in Tetchill were spent in peace as I worked away on a book and continued my obsessive filming and editing of everything I did. I would give myself a break to walk around and actually move my body every so often. A walk down the canal to a bridge that would lead to a farmer's track, which in turn would lead to Tetchill itself. A quick lap of the square shaped road layout would lead me back to the track and down to the canal once more. If I was feeling very energetic then I would break into a run, before immediately regretting the choice and reaching for my inhaler.

The cycling commutes to work were not huge, just a little further than any others at that point in the year. The unfortunate part being that the first mile, right from stepping off the stern, was up to the top of a local hill known as "The Brow". It is great to cycle down as the last thing you do before getting home from work, but as the first thing you do on the way to work it is not quite so much fun.

This hill was also rude enough to plant itself between me and almost all of my local friends houses too. As I spent many days out and about with friends and family around this time, I had to be sure to pack a "normal" set of clothes to change into out of my designated "biking" set of clothes. The warm weather was not too desirable when it came to such energetic activities, but it was ideal for drying out my hand washed clothes on my washing line made out of a pair of bungee hooks hung on the side of Tilly. So it balanced itself out.

It was from this location that I enjoyed a few trips out on the bike, with friends, and to friends houses. Returning on one day I found myself deciding to prolong the ride with a quick detour down unexplored roads. Imagine my joy when I reached the top of the hill, then started to travel downhill on a road I had not been on before, only to discover that it had no turnings in the direction I wanted to travel. Before I knew it I was at the foot of the opposite side of the hill and had to ride back up to the top again to take my familiar one mile road down to Tilly. It was another road that I placed on the "avoid" list.

Later in the evening I was disturbed by a scratching on the side of the hull. I peered into the darkness and found myself almost face to face with a swan. A truly beautiful creature it was too. I went outside and sat on the stern for a few minutes, the swan coming closer to take a look at me. It was a moment of tranquility. Swans are not too common around the area I tend to boat in, Ellesmere seems to be the only place you are likely to see them. This wanderer had made its way down to Tilly and decided to effectively do the equivalent of knocking on my door at ten to ten in the evening. I often feel that these are special moments, nature is literally making itself known to me, even if unintentionally. Even the most hard hearted, angry or fearful person must surely find something calming and soothing in an unexpected call from a swan.

Over the next few weeks Tilly slowly moved down to Ellesmere and then through the small tunnel to the best mooring place for miles around. Blakemere, the huge tree lined lake is, for a good few hundred metres, hugged by the canal. This literally means it is only a few steps away from your boat. There are many points where it is possible to moor your boat aligned with a break in the trees, when you open the curtains in the morning it is a breath taking sight.

One of my great pleasures is standing in the kitchen, either washing up or at the cooker, depending on which way Tilly is facing. Doing such a simple task is nothing on its own, but when you are staring across a huge expanse of water, especially as the sky turns into the many colours of sunset, it takes on a status of more of an event than a chore.

Walks to the shops, commutes and just general walks for walking's sake were begun or drawn to a close at Blakemere. About as picturesque a backdrop as you could ask for. A picnic table a few seconds walk away was the perfect place to sit and have a snack or write in my diary, enjoying the total three-hundred-and-sixty degree experience of nature. One of my only neighbours during this time was once again a swan, possibly the same one from Tetchill. Getting off the boat and walking over to the bank of the incredibly clear watered mere was often enough to attract the swan's attention from right across the water.

Seeing a swan slowly approach you over a period of minutes is a mesmerising, hypnotic experience. The swan would get closer at a very slow speed, which was made even slower by the zigzagging route that it would take. The changes in direction were so subtle that I missed them for the first two years of mooring in the area but once I noticed them it was impossible not to see them. Waiting to see at what point it would twist its course slightly then turn back and repeat, a few minutes of total mind emptying zen-like peace.

May had very nearly passed without incident when, on the twenty-ninth, I finally decided it was time to take a trip from the scenic banks of Blakemere and have a look further down the canal. It seemed to be a calm evening, so I unmoored Tilly and waved farewell to the scenery.

After a couple of long bends I found myself approaching a series of moored boats just as another boat was heading up from the opposite direction. Technically it was my right of way, but I am always a lot happier to pull over if in doubt, rather than go ahead and risk an incident. Luckily the other boat started to pull in before the moored boats, so I continued. As with many places on the canal it may appear as if there is plenty of room for boats to pass, but I knew just how shallow the far side was, this was the side that I would have had to go on if the other boat had charged ahead towards me.

As I moved slowly past the moored boats I was a little concerned to see the other boat move back out and start coming up the narrower stretch of free canal. "Oh dear", was the thought in my head. I was beyond the point of no return so had to try and get far enough over to avoid a head on collision, but also not end up like many of the holiday boats that I have seen, beached and struggling to free themselves from the shallow water. The first sign that things were not going well was when the camera and tripod that I was filming the trip on, were knocked over and dragged along the roof by low hanging branches. Then just as the two bows of our boats were passing the worst feeling in the world occurred. The whole of Tilly sharply lifted up on the right hand side. She had hit something in the shallow water. I could not say if it was the muddy bottom of the canal, a rock or a tree root, all I know is that it was one of those moments of heart pounding panic.

The boat passed in an unrecognised instant as my entire focus was now on Tilly rocking from side to side, something that should almost never happen on a narrowboat and certainly never from a violent impact below the waterline. Luckily she did not get stuck, it seemed that the pull of the water, disturbed by the other moving boat, helped to immediately pull the bow sideways off the object.

Even though the whole incident was over in about thirty seconds I was (probably excessively) shaken. One of those horrible feelings of dread consumed me from the pit of my stomach and I just wanted to moor up as soon as I could. Anything that happens above the waterline I have always felt that I can deal with, but something below the waterline, that I cannot see or fix really does leave me with a terrible feeling of dread. The fear of what might be going on out of sight was enough to cut my trip short, bringing it to an instant end after I had passed the remaining moored boats. When I checked the camera, that had been filming the entire time, even while on its back after being knocked over, I discovered that my intended relaxed trip down the canal had ended after only eight minutes. I moored up and was happy to just potter around onboard and give the outside a quick mopping down to end the night in a much calmer way… or so I thought.

The evening passed into night-time quietly enough. I was still right on the bank of beautiful Blakemere. There were a few overnight fishermen camped out silently nearby, there was not a sound from the neighbouring boats behind Tilly either, bliss. As I snuggled up in bed an odd thing started to happen, at irregular intervals it sounded as if something was thumping the boat. Every twenty minutes or so, I would hear another thud. I went up onto the stern and couldn't see any signs of debris on the roof or hear any wildlife scuttling away. I couldn't even be sure where on the boat the sound was coming from. I got back in bed and tried to settle.

As I lay there, the mystery noise kept breaking the silence. One thump and then nothing for another few minutes, then again. Thump! Silence… Thump! As I waited for sleep to take me, I found the sound slowly taking over my mind, listening and concentrating, waiting for the next one to try and figure out where or what it was. An idle mind waiting to go to sleep cannot help but be driven to distraction by an unsolved mystery like this, but eventually I did fall asleep.

Later, with the sound of another impact on the boat I was awoken, the sound was still quiet but loud enough to stir me from goodness knows what dreams. I could not say for certain what the time was, other than it was definitely after two in the morning. I got up and had a look around through the back door. It was pitch black and silent outside. With my torch I suddenly discovered to my horror what the noise had been... What I can only describe as some giant bird droppings had been collecting on the stern and rear part of the roof. Not only that, but they had also been falling from a great height. The result was that my freshly mopped boat was looking rather unpleasant. Worse than that, when I went back inside to go to sleep my mind was now completely awake and distracted about the fact that every time I heard the sound, the mess was getting a little bit worse.

I lay in this state of half dazed, irrational fear of bird poo for probably the best part of an hour. At which point I couldn't take it anymore. I looked at the time, it was just after three in the morning. I decided to just deal with it. So it was, that at something past three in the morning I crept out of the boat silently in order to not disturb the nearby fishermen and boats.

Stood on the towpath next to Tilly, I looked at the metal chains I had used to moor up to the corrugated metal piling canal siding. A very noisy metal on metal setup. I had to untie the ropes and then as slowly and gently as I could lift the chains out without them touching the side of the narrow gap they went through on the bank. Once they were out, I held onto Tilly and walked her at a snails pace for a mere fifteen foot, just enough to take her out of the target zone of the bird who must have been having a chuckle at the scenario unfolding below. The entire trip of half a boat length took me twenty-five minutes to complete. A trip that was not even a trip! I managed to get back into bed for four o'clock.

I am glad to report that I did not hear a sound for the rest of the night. The moral of the story, sometimes when nature calls, it literally does come knocking, but in a vastly more unpleasant way than a graceful swan tapping the side of your boat! I delayed my alarm in the morning to try and catch up with some sleep... Unfortunately the boat that went past at five to seven in the morning had other plans for me! Oh well, almost three hours of sleep was better than none.

Brilliant Boating and Bad Decisions

As June moved in to replace May as the month of the moment, the weather just about stayed bright, there were a few ups and downs and the odd inadvertent soaking to the skin. After the incident with the bird, I had moved down the canal, away from Ellesmere and any airborne threats. I found myself moored by an extremely small village by the name of Bettisfield.

There is roughly thirteen miles of canal between Ellesmere and the next place of any size, Whitchurch. That thirteen miles is extremely empty and quiet, featuring a lot of flat land and open fields. There is a huge flat swampy expanse of ground around the halfway mark that has the rather wordy title of "Fenn's, Whixall and Bettisfield Mosses National Nature Reserve". Bettisfield sits just at the edge of this area, there are no shops and only a few roads. It is roughly a mile from the nearest main road, and the next two biggest places around are equally shopless and miniature in size.

If supplies are needed then the canal towpath is the quickest route for a walker or cyclist to find civilisation, over eight miles to the nearest shop in Whitchurch, or just over five miles back to Ellesmere. It is at this point that my commute into Oswestry takes on a bit more of a daunting prospect. Apart from a longer distance of about fourteen miles, the route is also a little more hilly. Definitely not the hardest thing anybody has ever had to do, but something that needs to be considered when setting alarms and viewing weather forecasts. The influence of a strong headwind or pouring rain not only on the travel time, but also the happiness of the cyclist is immense.

To offset this issue I had booked my holidays from work to occur largely when I was likely to be out in these far away lands. Coupled with the summer holidays of friends and family I had tried to make sure that at the very least, if I had no choice but to stop in town overnight when working, I could do it in as useful a way possible. Resuming my summer job of watering plants and feeding cats, sometimes a dog too, I enjoy the chance to spread out in a house with more than two small rooms. Having a bath is like leaving the earthly realm for a moment!

However, as June progressed I would make a series of poor decisions and turn my simple cruising plans upside down. Before we leave the topic of holidays I would like to briefly mention a quick trip that my friends and I made up to my nan and granddad's caravan on the Welsh coast. On June 3rd we travelled up to the coast by a village called Llwyn Gwril, a perfect Welsh village, complete with annual village fete and a beach a short walk away. This was a highly anticipated trip as it would be the first time that I was able to take the kayak on the sea.

After arriving we unpacked and had something to eat, then at the first possible moment I was out inflating the kayak. We walked down to the beach and found that the stiff breeze in the air had made the sea less than calm. Typical that the weather would not be on our side the one moment that it was vital. I wrestled with the kayak in the shallow water for a while but eventually made it in. Channelling all the spirit of my childhood holidays, spent in the area with an inflatable dinghy, I was both over the moon and terrified. Being sat upright in what was little more than an air bed with a hole in the middle, floating on a choppy sea was a little different to the beautiful sunny days on a perfectly flat canal.

The experience was fantastic but it really did make me appreciate just how calm and still the canal water is. One thing that you definitely do not get on the canal is a seal following you at what it decides is a safe distance, popping its head above water suspiciously at random intervals. As with all good things the time passed at an alarming pace and our quick one night stay was soon over.

As if to sum up how relaxed boat life can be, when I was dropped off at Tilly the following day, I couldn't decide exactly what I wanted to do. I had been thinking of moving down the canal a bit further and as I dragged the kayak down the towpath, I finally made the decision to go for it. I arrived back onboard took a moment to unpack and then started unmooring.

It was an overcast evening that saw me make a very short two mile trip, no rush, no panic, just a trip down a very sparsely populated canal in an even less inhabited countryside. I moored at Balmer Heath, a locality so rural that its nearest four villages do not boast even so much as a corner shop between them. The area blends into one large region of countryside with the previously mentioned Whixall and nature reserve. What the region lacks in corner shops and amenities it makes up for with a much higher percentage of "very nice" houses than a lot of the local region.

Walking and cycling around the area was a welcome change of scenery. Although the countryside may have looked almost the same as the rest of the Shropshire/Wales border, it has always been a great pleasure of mine to head down unknown roads and paths. Occasionally in areas like this it is possible to follow a country road and slowly see the surface deteriorate into a muddy track, this is usually followed by the realisation that you have actually been travelling down somebody's driveway. This happened on more than one occasion while I was in this area, the worse thing was that it happened on the same road! I was out cycling and found myself being shaken around by a road that turned into some kind of 4x4 test track and ultimately a dead end. Then a few days later when some friends and I had been out in their car we tried to take a shortcut and ended up at the same place. I decided not to share the news that I had been here before, my reputation with directions being less than favourable already.

When out in places that nobody knows me, and my friends and family are miles away I sometimes feel that I should be seeing more of them, or for that matter just more of anybody. I am not prone to loneliness and between getting outdoors, listening to audiobooks, filming and writing I do not ever really stop and sit on my own doing nothing at all, which probably helps an awful lot.

The solitude of the more remote places I have moored has on some occasions seemingly allowed me to utterly step out of "real life". Spending a few days in an area that lets me be on my own, seeing only the passing walkers on the towpath and boats, having little or no internet access helps me get things done. It was during June that I released my last narrowboat book, so for the weeks prior to launch I spent a great deal of time rewriting sections, proofreading and rewriting again. Something that I love doing, but loved even more when sat on a boat in the middle of a sun drenched canal with birds, boats and the occasional dog walker or rambler as the only passers by.

So it seemed that June was going to pass in a peaceful countryside location, with a destination of Whitchurch to be crawled towards, slowly but surely. Everything was falling into place with my holidays from work and family leaving their houses and pets to look after. I was looking forward to a month of relaxing and cycling all over the place. The intention was to move in a few short trips down to Whitchurch, taking my time to enjoy some of my less frequented mooring places along the way. The month ended with Tilly moored up twenty-five miles in the opposite direction of my intended destination!

On June 11th I had arranged to meet my father by the canal. We drove the short distance to Whitchurch and had "chippy chips" for tea, sat overlooking a few meadowy fields bordered by a residential area. Again, my photos of this day are evidence of how incredibly sunny and warm it was. We walked a few miles up and down the canal and took a look at the Grindley Brook locks, he had never seen a set of three locks in one single staircase before and I must admit that the structure is pretty impressive. The surroundings seem to make it seem less intimidating than if it were placed in a more isolated spot. It is sided by a proper Tarmac path and even a cafe, a destination hugely popular with tourists during the day time, but as we were there in the evening it was almost entirely empty.

After a few miles put beneath our boots we headed back up to the canal bridge near Tilly. Before he left, we had a long conversation sat on the bridge like the days of old. It was a deep conversation about many things, life, the past, the future and more importantly, the present. As I walked down to Tilly and heard the distant beep of a car horn signalling his final departure, I felt my mind move back to my immediate plans. All day long I had been mulling over making a big change of plan. Turning Tilly around and going all the way back up beyond my winter mooring area, just over the border back into Wales and staying in Chirk Marina for a month or two.

This decision was based on a few factors, firstly as the canal was starting to get busy I would not have minded getting out of the main flow of boats during the peak holiday months. I had lost a drinking glass every so often due to them being tipped over while in a cupboard by a passing boat, when I later opened the cupboard door out they would roll, never to be used again. All part of boat life and not the greatest of hardships I know.

The second reason was that I had been putting off redecorating the interior of Tilly all year long. Half out of always finding something better to do, half out of not wanting to be stuck in a tiny environment, painting then sleeping in the paint fumes, I thought that if I headed to the marina I could paint onboard in the day, then bike to a friend or family member's house to sleep before returning the following day until the job was done. My asthma has never got on well with paint fumes, and my eyes certainly did not appreciate the original decoration of Tilly a couple of years back when I had first bought her.

The third reason, and the reason that will make you immediately dismiss the first two reasons as even counting in the decision at all, was that staying in Chirk Marina would have been ideal for meeting and spending time with my, recently met, girlfriend. A rarity in my life, we were getting on great, but I was getting ever more distant in a literal geographic sense!

So it was that in the mid evening, with a sun still beaming in the sky I turned Tilly and set off to get as far as I could before night crept in. It was a boat trip that I will remember for a very long time, there were very few boats moving as everybody had settled for the night which made progress very slow. More boats moored means slower travel as you pass and considering how slowly I have always taken things anyway, it meant dropping into neutral every now and then.

As the sun crept lower, the trees were lit with an increasingly orange light, the shadows they cast became huge stretched caricatures of their structure. The only people I saw, were either fishing or milling around doing odd jobs on their boats. As I approached Ellesmere the sun sank further. Reaching the short tunnel I did my common practice and jumped off Tilly using a rope to pull her through. Tilly's stern has an unusual guard rail around it which tends to catch on the sides of tunnels very easily as it sticks upwards rather than leaning in slightly. I was travelling upstream so it was a fair amount of effort to pull her through, against the force of tightly channelled water. If it was downstream then I would have had to do almost nothing at all, the general flow would have pushed her slowly through. No such luck on that particular evening.

Emerging on the other side, I made sure to put my headlight on and use the lights off my bike to make it clear that I was moving. It was still light and visibility was good but I like to play it safe. Due to Ellesmere's popularity as a mooring place and the increased traffic, there were boats lined up literally as far as my eyes could see. This made the trip through the area extremely slow, I did not meet another boat so did not have to worry about trying to pass alongside moored boats. Once clear of the main moorings I was very keen to moor up for the night. The sun had crept down in the sky and the first hint of darkness was creeping in. The extra slow passing through Ellesmere had used up the last of my desire for boating that day, when you see a family including very young children walk past and away from you on the towpath, you know that you are going nowhere slowly!

I was keen to make some good progress the following morning and set an alarm for soon after six o'clock, I knew that I would not meet any moored boats for a long time so would not be disturbing anybody. The alarm went off and I opened my eyes to find an early morning so sunny that it could have easily been mistaken for the middle of the day, I was made up! By the time I had woken up properly, put the boat in order and actually got moving, I was glad of the early alarm.

Heading off upstream through what were again silent canals, it was not until around a very slow mile and a half away that I actually met another boat, even then it was still moored up. Passing the Frankton Locks I loved seeing people onboard their boats getting ready to start their day. It would have been a very busy day judging by all the activity. I reached the huge line of boats moored along the canal at Maestermyn Marina, and was again very grateful to just about miss any oncoming traffic while moving alongside some very expensive looking boats.

At length I found myself with the New Marton Locks in sight ahead of me. A return to St Martins many months before I had intended to! I moored just down from the lower lock, deciding that enough was enough for one day.

This is a good moment to take stock of what I had just done. Despite planning my entire year and holidays from work around a simple cruising plan for Tilly, I had turned around and gone almost back to the starting point. I was moored at one of the places I had a very easy commute into work, rather than the intended opposite. My nan and grandad had gone on holiday so I also had the use of a free house, and of course gardening duties, meaning that I could have stayed there in total peace over my work days had I have been moored miles away. On top of that, my work holidays were also now going to be clustered around a time that I was closest to home. I did doubt the quality of the decision at this point, but not as much as I would do in the coming days.

After a few days of rest and constant biking in and out of town, a friend and I took Tilly up through the locks and all the way to Chirk Marina. It was an amazing day, sun and blue skies but with plenty of big fluffy clouds much like a child's painting. In no particular rush we made the most of the experience of crossing Chirk aqueduct. In good weather it acts not only as a passage for boats, but also as a giant historical viewing platform. The viaduct that stands slightly taller to its side is equally magnificent with its huge stone arches acting as an iconic frame for the hilly valley and green view behind it. Amazing views from the aqueduct were soon plunged into total darkness as we entered Chirk Tunnel.

Tackling the tunnel with two people was a lot easier than dragging Tilly through Ellesmere tunnel on my own, my friend stayed onboard at the tiller while I held on to a rope and walked, if she strayed to the side I pulled her back... Much easier than sheer brute force, something that I definitely lack!

We moored just by the marina entrance, where I was left on my own to start further doubting my decision to move all the way back and beyond the year's starting point. I had enough doubt that I delayed my trip to go and book my mooring place for a few days.

At length I decided that I was going to stop in the Marina for at least one month, probably two. I walked around and booked my spot, then had a look at the slot in the rows of boats and felt a little sad that I was going to be spending the summer months there rather than out on the canal. The fact that it had been pouring down frequently during the last few days and even on that very morning, didn't seem to warn me of the change in weather conditions that was happening.

Later on in the evening I thought I would move from the canal and take my place alongside a much bigger boat, safely tucked away at the far end of the still waters of the marina. I was a little further up from the entrance, so I untied Tilly's ropes and started to walk her backwards. As I did, the heavens opened and it hammered down with rain. It poured so much that I had to take shelter under the trees lining the towpath, still holding Tilly by the ropes. What a sorry sight this drenched narrowboat lad must have been. Right by the entrance there also sits a section of forty-eight hour moorings, handily with accompanying mooring rings. When the rain continued seemingly indefinitely, I just gave up. I stepped back out into the full deluge and walked Tilly to the two day mooring and quickly tied up to the rings. Needless to add that no sooner was I inside, sulking and drying off, than it cleared up for a few minutes, then poured down again!

I am not entirely sure why but this experience seemed to make up my mind that it had been a terrible mistake to come back. I had enjoyed my stay at the marina previously, but much preferred to be out in the ever changing countryside locations that the canal had to offer. The following day I had to walk back around to the marina office and with my tail between my legs, cancel my mooring. They were fine with my very quick change of heart, but I felt no less of a total wally!

Back to Square One

During the end of June I hovered around on the outskirts of the marina, not quite sure what my plan was. I recall around this time that for some reason I was being given an awful lot of sandwiches to take home to the boat with me by my mother, either when I finished work over the weekends, or had just been in town visiting. An odd detail to remember but unwrapping some sandwiches with salad spilling out of the sides was certainly a pleasant addition to being sat on the stern of a narrowboat, as the sunny evenings drifted into a chill tainted twilight.

As I had not been in the area for a very long time I decided to stay for a while. Although the marina is named after Chirk it is positioned a little awkwardly to walk from the marina to the village. The problem is really caused by the railway that runs alongside the canal, not right next to it, but a field or so away, it follows the long sweeping curve of the water and cuts the land in half for walkers. There are bridges to get over the line at both, Chirk Tunnel itself and at the shorter Whitehouse Tunnel, neither of which actually stand very near the village and shops, although Chirk Tunnel can claim to be on the very edge of the village. If the railway line was not there then the area would be nothing but the usual rural scenery criss-crossed with public footpaths, I am sure. However, by having to first walk to the bridges, then to Chirk, it makes a round trip to get supplies roughly an hour long depending on your mood.

This did not really bother me, it was more the fact that there were no real options for the walk, no branching footpaths, no fields or styles, just plain old towpath and Tarmac. But it was always good to stretch my legs when the weather looked like it could be stable for more than three minutes! Regular walks to buy milk, salad and an onion bhaji or two, were a good demonstration of what I love about life out on the canal. A simple task such as going to the shops involved lots of walking, plenty of narrowboats both moored and moving, and the occasional conversation with somebody that could have been a local dog walker or equally, could have been on a boating holiday from halfway around the world. Summer on the canal, very busy, potentially soaking, but filled with all kinds of people, most of which are friendly to a shy stuttering Shropshire lad.

Mooring opposite a marina makes me feel slightly uncomfortable, almost a feeling of doing something naughty, although that is probably just me and my overly sensitive, nervous manner. I felt a slight relief and release to be on the move again on July 1st. I woke early to beat the regular early morning holiday traffic and at barely a moment past eight o'clock I was on my way. Luckily the unpredictable weather had decided to shine upon me and Tilly with a beautiful morning.

I passed the few other boats moored by the marina as people were still stirring, lots of dressing gowns and toast to be seen. The trip was just a short two mile meander downstream, really I just wanted to get the tunnel and aqueduct done and out of the way before the canal truly came to life. It is a common sight to see a string of boats floating around as the traffic backs up waiting to enter the tunnel at Chirk. Just as I have in the past waited for hours to get down through the two New Marton locks, I wished to avoid spending too much time milling around waiting my turn at the tunnel.

The trip went as smoothly as I could have hoped, looking at my photos from the day I can see that while I was on the aqueduct there was not a person to be seen, boater or walker. The trip took almost an hour, an average speed of below two miles per hour, just the way that I like it. The aqueduct crossing was really the only moment where Tilly was out in the sun directly. The section of canal before the tunnel being covered by huge trees to either side, and the final destination of Chirk Bank being obscured by a mixture of trees and cottages... And of course the bank that it is situated on.

The image of the aqueduct, and adjacent viaduct with a lonely boat travelling on its solitary watery road would make for an excellent poem I am sure. The experience of being on that boat certainly made for an excellent morning. With the sun directly beaming against the stonework from a clear sheet of blue sky, the image really pops! As mentioned previously, the aqueduct is a great place to view the world from, or at least the idyllic portion of the world in line of sight, between the great stone arches. This momentary experience is the kind of event that I could fill a book with, disjointed, singular moments of beauty, tranquility, nature or a mixture of the three. To be fair that may actually be a description of this book! Moments like that are what make boat life so appealing and alluring to an over romantic dreamer like myself. They also provide the endless scenery and video footage that make up a huge part of my videos online. My stock line being "Nobody wants to look at my ugly mug so lets take a look at some scenery"!

Taking Stock

At this point in the book I would like to take a break from the travelogue and speak to you a little more directly about this particular year afloat. Especially the summer months. As I mentioned in the introduction I wanted to keep this book focussed on the boating element of my life. I feel I should point out that apart from the general walking, kayaking and biking I was doing in the immediate surroundings of Tilly, the summer did bring many trips with friends and family to various locations. Nothing hugely exciting, but all things that break up the continued canal scenery with something a little different. The weather for the summer failed to live up to the promise of spring and became incredibly unpredictable, swinging from extreme opposites of sunshine to showers, sometimes multiple times a day.

I do not wish to bore you with every trip I took, such as staying at a friend's parent's house in the local countryside and spending an evening shooting an air rifle at a can of coke and a bottle of Mountain Dew. Neither do I wish to keep repeating the story of walking down the towpath with a bag of rubbish to throw in a skip at a boat service point or stopping to fill up with water when I pass through the locks at New Marton. Emptying the two toilet tanks that I have onboard whenever passing Maesbury or Ellesmere for example may not make for pleasant reading, but equally you may not be reading this book to hear that I felt extremely dizzy and disorientated from riding the Smiler at Alton Towers theme park! (As a side note I would like to say that The Smiler is the best ride I have ever been on... admittedly I have been on very few!) I have noticed that this approach may make me seem like a very solitary figure at times. That may be true to a certain extent, but without saying every few paragraphs "and then me an a friend biked in some big circles", it is difficult to really communicate the passing often unplanned trips that go along with the boating element of my life.

I have decided to just focus on a few key moments for the summer so as to avoid repeating myself as we travel back down the same stretch of canal that the beginning of this book took part on.

Seeing the full growth of the greenery in summer certainly changes the canal, most noticeably on many of the long curves and bends, that have ever reduced visibility due to the overgrown nature of the offside of the canal.

Barely three weeks after leaving Chirk Marina, Tilly would again be moored at Maesbury on the Montgomery, avoiding the summer traffic of the main Llangollen for a couple of weeks. Those three weeks alone saw several amusing incidents and many more days of perfect and not so perfect weather.

One of the scariest moments of the year came in early July when I decided to finally take the kayak through Chirk Tunnel. I had kayaked over the aqueduct on many occasions during the winter and been right up to the mouth of the tunnel, never daring to go through it. I thought I would make a video of the event and began by filming a few safety thoughts first. I spoke a great deal about making sure that if you enter a tunnel you are as visible as possible and well lit for boats to see you. I demonstrated how I had my LED head light as well as two big seventy-two LED lights attached to the kayak, just to make absolutely certain that I was visible.

I made the short journey up to the tunnel, paddling over the aqueduct, I had deliberately chosen a mid afternoon time that I thought would be one of the few quiet points of the day. There were plenty of tourist out on the towpath and plenty of photos were taken as I glided past on the kayak. The temptation for people to get a picture of a kayaker on the aqueduct seemed to be very strong, but the strength of politeness and shyness also seemed a force to be reckoned with. The result was that as I passed by I heard a few camera noises from phones that were held casually as if not taking a photo at all!

Reaching the tunnel I milled around for a moment trying to ensure that I got the shot I wanted with my camera, then, deep breath, I started paddling like never before. The force of the water wasn't too much of an issue but the odd effect of being in a four-hundred-and-twenty metre long tunnel was something I had not thought about. After a certain amount of paddling it felt as if there was no progress being made. A slight feeling of claustrophobia kept my arms going though, and at length a marker on the tunnel wall showed me that I was at the halfway point. I paused for a moment simply enjoying and taking in the surreal surroundings. Sat at a height that was basically *in* the water with over two-hundred metres of tunnel either side of me in almost total darkness, just my lights and what was literally the light at the end of the tunnel to guide my way.

I paddled out into the light and found myself grinning from ear to ear, I had finally done the one bit of kayaking I had been scared of and it was great! Even better than that, I was about to turn around and do it again. I hovered around the canal, well away from the tunnel entrance, for a while as a boat was coming upstream. It seemed to be a very long time in passing through, partly due to my excitement, and partly due to the fact that it does take a long time to power upstream through the darkness.

Once the tunnel was clear I floating back into the abyss. Paddling down, I now found it slightly less pleasant as the place was filled with boat fumes, but going with the flow of water was easy going, to make up for the fog. As I got to roughly a third of the way in, I saw a boat pass the entrance on the far side, it moved out of sight to the temporary mooring mushrooms and I breathed a sigh of relief. A figure walked up and peered into the tunnel, a good sign too... But moments later the boat came back into view.

As the tunnel entrance ahead became filled with the silhouette of a boat I started to shout. "Hello! Hello!?" then a louder "HELLO, I'm on a kayak!" This is probably the only time of real panic that I had during the entire year, a real deep down panic at potential and immediate danger. The boat moved further and I paddled like a man possessed, shouting "There is someone here!" In a moment of perfect timing, it seems that a walker had entered the tunnel and started to move up towards me, unlike the boaters who were understandably unable to hear me over the noise of an engine in a small stone walled tunnel, he heard me and, I believe, raised the alarm.

The boat stopped coming towards me, the stern was only a few feet into the tunnel when I arrived. Personally I would have walked Tilly back out from that distance. Instead they opted for the more interesting decision (for me anyway) of pulling the boat to the side and allowing me just enough room to squeeze past. As I used my hands to move between their boat and the wall, we exchanged a few cordial remarks and I breathed a sigh of relief as I emerged into the sunlight.

I was quizzed about what had happened as I slowly floated over the aqueduct lined with tourists, and was pleased to get back to Tilly just around the corner. Another few moments of narrowboat life that were unpredictable, interesting and more than anything, terrifying. The story acts as the perfect and ironic way to show how you can never be too careful and shouldn't take anything as a given fact. Only minutes earlier I had been recording a piece to camera about how many lights I had on myself and the kayak to be safe, then halfway through the actual trip it had all been proven as useless. If the boat had continued to approach, then I would have had to scramble out of the kayak and through the railings onto the towpath. I am not sure how well that would have gone, in a panic and the dark, I hope never to find out!

In early July a couple of friends and I went for a mini adventure. A single night of camping and a lot of walking in Yorkshire. I could write at great length on the short period as it involved so many moments of fun, scenery and the ridiculous comedy that the three of us combined seem to create and enjoy.

What little I will write though is that being picked up from right beside Tilly on a drizzly morning was a great start to the trip. We drove the distance to the foot of the first hill in a fully laden car and within hours were putting our boots on grass and gravel. I had started the day with a little attempt at painting in a notebook onboard Tilly. Leaving that to dry, it would turn out to be us who would be wet by the time we returned the following day.

The weather had been glorious all week, but as mentioned even just walking twenty foot to the car from Tilly it was raining. Our first day of walking was done in cloud, a little mist but relative dry. The hilly, uneven terrain of Yorkshire was a stunning change of scenery, even if it was a little grey looking.

After the three of us had piled into a tent overnight, we set about a full day of walking. Heading up the the remaining two of the three famous peaks of Yorkshire (Whernside, Ingleborough and Pen-y-ghent, for anybody interested) and a couple of other associated hilltops. The beautiful summer weather had well and truly deserted us. Up and up we walked, then down again slightly wetter than we set out. On the final ascent of the day we started to get a little wetter, then on the peak, with a visibility of a dozen metres at best, we really got wet.

So wet that we broke away from the beaten track and cut almost diagonally back to the car. I could describe just how soaked we were for a few paragraphs but nothing sums it up better than one simple moment. On the drive back we decided to stop at a motorway service station for some food. On parking we realised that only one of us had enough dry clothing to actually go inside, one friend and myself were in various states of undress with clothing hanging or spread out on the few patches of free space. A good trip all round!

On being dropped off at Tilly, the first task was to get the fire lit, by eight-thirty the chimney was smoking and a very wet Tilly was warming up with trousers and coats over the fireplace. I stood on the stern under a grey sky, every surface was covered in water. Thirty-five hours previously I had been leaving a similar scene, I had returned after a fantastic trip as if no time had passed. The painting was dry but both Tilly and I were soaked, one out of three ain't bad.

Not Quite a Disaster

The theme of vanishing off for an adventure before coming home to a calm boat in the evening is one that defines my vision of an ideal life. Being blessed to live it for even a brief moment is something I can never take for granted, the frequent downpours of rain that punctured the sunshine over the following months only served to make the good times seem even better.

I enjoyed the summer boating, taking the obvious choice to start Tilly up and untie the ropes on the better days rather than those more suited to the ducks. However when I found myself moored at Maesbury, the shortest commute to work, it really showed how bad my decision to come all the way back upstream had been. The time that Tilly spent closest to Oswestry was also time sandwiched right between when I had stacked up a large portion of my holidays from work. Instead of being at the furthest point away for the year as I had expected and planned for, I was literally at the closest possible point. Similar to how my family members had taken holidays when I ended up by the locks.

With this in mind I decided that it would be a good idea to try and boat out to that furthest point as soon as I could. Almost in an attempt to pretend the return journey had never happened. With my allotted time on the Montgomery Canal running out I decided that I would spread the trip over a few days of gentle travel but soon be at Whitchurch… the title of this chapter "Not Quite a Disaster" is probably a bit of a giveaway that things didn't go to plan.

On a very warm evening I made a five mile trip, almost the length of the Monty itself to the very small aqueduct mentioned earlier in this book. I travelled very slowly and took the locks at a sensible pace, travelling alone and with no exact destination or time in mind, I just enjoyed being on the move.

At one point I found myself interrupting some kind of kayak based game of basket ball. No honestly! At a turning point, near a water sports club storage shed, I was amazed to discover the spectacle. There were even nets suspended over the canal on wires. Once I was spotted approaching, not only did the players scatter, but the nets themselves were hauled out of the way. Fascinating, I have never been a pitch invader before but it seems that that is exactly what I became for a few brief moments!

As the evening drew on I decided to play it safe and moor Tilly to the temporary mushrooms by the tiny aqueduct that sits amidst some incredible flat farmland. Giant trees line patches of the canal, old field boundaries and sometimes just seem to have grown at their own will, randomly dotted in the countryside. There is nothing really to see, and that is what makes it so beautiful.

After mooring up, I just happened to check the water level in the cooling system. My heart sank, it was, as far as I could tell, empty. The old problem that had plagued me when I first bought Tilly was back! For over a year she had been running fine. Now, moored up, I discovered that no matter how much water I would pour in, it would all soon vanish from the header tank, visible just above the deck.

Once upon a time this endless pouring away of water was worrying to distraction for me as a novice boater. On that night I seemed to just accept it and deal with it. Surrounded by peace and rustling animals, the ever common screech of buzzards flying overhead, these were consolation enough for any problems or costs that I might be about to face. A good night's sleep soon followed, and the next day I moved up through the locks and onto the Llangollen. I asked every possible person what they thought the problem may be, but unfortunately no answers seemed to satisfy any of us. I later learned that no answer could explain it when I was giving out completely incorrect information... Another classic moment of my lack of technical knowledge being shown off in full.

The intention had been to go straight to Ellesmere but instead I moored at Tetchill, not wanting to risk it. A calm day of filming and editing followed, the first in a series of boat life documentaries I was putting together. The effort involved was huge but enjoyable, made all the more difficult by the fact that I had lost another camera to the canals muddy murk while attempting to film a video on how to use a lift-bridge while down at Maesbury. It was getting an expensive hobby!

Somehow the year had passed at an alarming pace. I found myself limping to Ellesmere well into August. During a working weekend I found myself looking online for engine advice and decided to try a sealant that simply needed to be poured in with the water. My sort of simple solution, in both senses of the word.

When I tried this I was gutted to discover it had little or no effect at all. I had a backup plan though… Get actual help from an engineer! Before I walked around to Blackwater Marina, located right by the services and general basin at Ellesmere, I had one last job to do. That was to stock up on water for the engine. I had a few spare bottles that I needed to fill, not wanting to move the boat, I did the strangest kayak trip of my life. I paddled for only a few minutes, drifted up to the boating services and right behind the proper full-size narrowboats, hopped out of the kayak and dragged it up onto the side. I then proceeded to fill a series of two litre bottles before throwing them into the front of the kayak, pushing it back into the canal and then paddling off again. I am not entirely sure how it appeared to any onlookers, but just like the feeling of being moored opposite a marina, I had a feeling of hi-jinx and naughtiness as I vanished around the corner.

What followed was a slightly embarrassing marina visit. I walked around and explained the problem. Walking back to Tilly with a friendly engineer I had a feeling of dread at what the problem may be revealed as, and more terrifyingly how much the resolution would cost. From the day that I bought Tilly I had believed and told people her engine was raw water cooled. I could even point to the pipes that went from the engine out into the canal. Within about five minutes of seeing the boat, the engineer had discovered that this was not the case at all.

It was revealed that on the underside of Tilly's big backend there was a pipe that ran from the inside pipe, around the swim, just above the propeller and back into the engine on the other side. The information I had been given when I bought her was incorrect and I had literally spent two years telling it to people! When I had had this leaking water problem in the past, it had seemed to be a real mystery with the only explanation being a blown head gasket. That itself didn't satisfy many people.

So from two years of guessing, one man had spent a few minutes and discovered that it was nothing more than a small hole in a pipe that nobody else knew had existed! We checked his diagnosis by having a short trip into the marina. As there was little that could be done about it without her coming out of the water I was given a lot of full large water bottles and an apologetic bill for a minimum amount of about £7.99. I left the marina and moored up on a long, very straight length of canal nearby, among many boats. I was over the moon. The problem was not fixed but it was at least now identified and better yet, identified as non disastrous and hopefully a low cost fix when Tilly next leaves the water for hull painting.

With this renewed sense of calm I decided to stay in Ellesmere for a week, a couple of friends wanted to come and visit so it was an easy place to meet them. The relief and short rest was also a time that I finally made some progress on painting the interior, a job I had been putting off all year long. August, the true summer month delivered probably the worst weather all year. If it was not raining then wind would often take its place. Windy conditions being less than ideal for both boating and biking.

With my plans for a quick trip to Whitchurch shattered and some progress on the painting underway, I started to long for a marina for a month again. It had crossed my mind a number of times and I had called in at Maestermyn on my way past just to inquire, but they were full, the two other online marinas at Maesbury and Tetchill were easy to check merely by walking past. I couldn't believe it when I got to Tetchill and saw that at just the point I might have moored there, the single vacant spot was filled. The marina at Ellesmere was also full so I decided to go ahead with my now much slower trip to Whitchurch.

There and Back Again (and a few random thoughts before the end of the year!)

So it was that at long last after a huge amount of unplanned backtracking, total disarray and confusion over whether I was or wasn't going to end up in a marina and an awful lot of cycling, I was finally on the way to Whitchurch. Had I have stayed with my original plan, then more than likely I would have not been able to resist a quick trip further down to Wrenbury. A tiny village at least as rural as most of the other locations named in this book, but with the addition of an electric lift-bridge. A novelty that I have wanted to visit ever since passing through there when I first brought Tilly home.

Whitchurch, a place that at one point seemed to be on the other side of the world rather than a few miles away, is a fantastic town. It is only small but has all the features that you would expect. Big old churches, an unrecognisable Roman construction, and of course the canal running up to its very edge. Almost more impressive than these in this modern day is the amount of independent shops, including a bakery, my favourite of all buildings! The layout of the town is ideal to make it seem even more quaint. The high street is a street on an unusually steep hill, lined with buildings of various age and style, when you walk to the top you find yourself opposite the impressive sandstone church of St Alkmunds. For the fast food junky in a hurry there is even a McDonald's with drive-thru on the outskirts... Something for everyone! But to be serious, Whitchurch is equally equipped with some brilliant traditional pubs, traditional both in the way they look and what is contained within.

Being a decently sized town it also features a couple of supermarkets and chain stores for good measure. Trains and buses can be caught to other nearby bigger towns, but unfortunately not directly to Oswestry. Equally the canal is well endowed with facilities just by the Grindley Brook locks. Again, toilets, rubbish and water, the trilogy of narrowboat service essentials, are all side by side on the towpath.

To say that August had begun with Tilly moored at Maesbury, then the slight hiccup with the engine had slowed progress to a standstill for a certain period, I was happy to draw the month to a close with Tilly tied up seventeen miles down the canal at Whixall. Unfortunately, due to the fact all of my timing and holidays were now out of sync, there were a few weekends that I had to stop at either my mother's house or a friend's house between work nights. The commute from Whixall was around sixteen miles to Oswestry. With the now frequently grey skies and stiff breezes, that distance seemed like a lifetime.

As I approached Whitchurch itself the commute ultimately found itself at a massive twenty-two miles. That is the sort of distance that I may enjoy biking as part of a fun day of riding for pleasure, but as a start to a work day and end to a work day, I hope you can forgive me for deciding to pass on the opportunity of a forty-four mile round trip with a quick shift at work in between!

This was a strange time. The weeks spent so far away from almost everybody I knew, my closest friends and family at least, were oddly calm. September seemed to pass in a blur of increasingly shorter walks up to Whitchurch for supplies and a pasty and a cake from the previously mentioned local independent bakery. The strangest part was how much I felt utterly relaxed while on Tilly. It may have been some of the big bike rides into town that were taking it out of me or maybe just the slightly cooling temperatures, but I seemed to spend a lot more time onboard rather than hopping over fences and crossing fields in the surrounding area. What it was exactly, I couldn't put my finger on, but my memories of the time somehow make me feel like it was quiet, something I am not used to.

As time passed and I moved in my usual short but frequent trips from mooring to mooring, I discovered many hidden gems. In an unfamiliar area that I had not moored in ever before, I could scarcely wait to tie the ropes before walking off to follow a footpath or two into the fields surrounding the canal. It was business as usual, audiobooks playing, podcasts being downloaded, videos filmed and this book in its middle stage of planning and writing. But it was with a different view, a different set of people as regular towpath walkers, and in some cases seemingly nobody at all.

One of my favourite tricks during the spring and summer is to get in my kayak with a bowl, and paddle over to the far side of the canal that in various places has a bounty of blackberries like nothing I have ever seen. When I still lived at my mother's house I would always be out walking and often have a nibble on some of the few patches of wild growing berries that I found. Sometimes if I discovered a big patch I would return to the spot prepared with a bag for the horde.

What I have found with the canal is that not only are there huge stretches of blackberries to be found, they are also almost impossible to get to. The casual walker would be unable to cross the canal water, and from the berries rear they would be protected by their jagged, tangled brambly barbed bodies. The kayak is the best tool for collecting them.

There was however one mooring place that this inaccessibility of natural fruit was turned on its head. It has frequently popped into my mind ever since and I can't wait to return to it sometime. A few miles outside of Whitchurch there was a newly constructed wooden siding to protect the bank on the towpath side. It was unsuitable for mooring, but immediately before and after it were sections marked as forty-eight hour locations. As I passed I decided that it would be a good place to stop, and in the blazing sun I noticed the selection of newly placed picnic tables, what better place to sit down with a diary to do some writing?

When I walked up to the tables I noticed that all over the ground lay a familiar fruit. Damsons! A countryside favourite of mine that I don't find very often. I am not sure how many times I must have walked past them on my marching up and down to Whitchurch, but as soon as I had moored by the spot, I somehow had time to see them. I immediately looked up and realised I was surrounded by damson trees. Needless to say that I consumed more damsons during those two days than probably the previous five years of my life combined. I think that the same could likely be said for the other boats that moored up in the area. Talking to fellow passing boaters, while you are both collecting fruit from a tree, is an experience that I don't think I would have ever expected to have in my life.

This small anecdote may again serve to paint the idyllic scene of boat life and it certainly was a high point. To balance it out things were not so perfect when, due to my poor planning earlier in the year, I ended up having to get two buses on an indirect and ultimately three hour long route to Oswestry. This took place on the day before work, then arriving at my mother's house, hopping on a spare bike to ride out of town five miles to sleep at a friend's house over my working days. A lesson well learned, stick to the plan!

A less old fashioned anecdote from this period and general area comes in the form of the quest for a decent phone signal. On September 9th Apple held a conference to unveil the new iPhone and the Apple Watch, two highly anticipated gadgets as you can imagine. Tilly was moored within the long stretch of canal approaching Whitchurch that doesn't have very good regular phone service, not to mention 3G for internet use. I was very much interested in seeing what all the hype was about, particularly the watch, a device that I feel I want but would never use.

It was again a lovely sunny evening and as the conference got underway at around six, I set out with my phone and iPad on the quest for a connection. I strolled down the towpath and walked off up the lanes that frequently cut across the canal via lift bridges. Nowhere I went seemed to have an answer. At length I started a slow walk back to Tilly eyeing up some steep sided towpath that led to what I hoped were fields free of livestock.

Deciding to give it one last go, I scrambled up a loose soil and tree covered bank and delicately stepped over the low barbed wire fence, just low enough to avoid a nasty accident. The field that I emerged into was being allowed to meadow up, rows of trees seemed to be planted in such a way that they specifically looked picturesque. Importantly for me at the time, my phone started to beep with the endless stream of notifications that had been backing up while out of range.

I sat down amidst the long grass, dried and dying, I was careful of the thistles and sitting under the curious gaze of the unknown animals that scuttled around in the undergrowth. I was underwhelmed by what I saw unfold at the conference, the old tech nerd in my character surfacing for a brief moment. I was distracted by my surroundings, a sun creeping closer to the ground, ever more intensely pink in colour. A haze descending over the world around me, how could a watch with a screen compete with that?

As things wrapped up I allowed myself a moment to just enjoy the surroundings. No more peering at a screen and seeing the world reflected in it, just looking directly at the world. What was this life I was building for myself? Something as mundane as an Apple conference had just taken place in a rural Shropshire field with an audience of one. How times had changed. In years gone by an Apple conference was to be witnessed sitting at my giant computer perched on a desk in my room. Now it had become an event witnessed with quite possibly no other human being within half a mile in every direction. A change that I can imagine would drive some people to madness, but seemed ok at the time.

An internet connection was once a thing that I took for granted, an essential item that must be maintained. But onboard Tilly in her travels to nowhere and back, an internet connection was often a luxury to be cherished and used for keeping in contact with people and very little else. Days could pass where it was easier to go kayaking than it was to get online. A forced calming down and step back from the world.

Within the next month Tilly would find herself being chugged up to Whitchurch, passing through lift bridges in a hilariously unskilled manner. Then turned around and chugged all the way back, again unskilfully through the lift bridges, in preparation for winter to start again.

The lift bridges on the outskirts of Whitchurch, plus one further away at Whixall, provide a feature I don't very often use on the canals. It was one of these very bridges, that when first passing through just after purchasing Tilly, I found myself getting stuck on the opposite side of the canal from my boat, and failing to quite jump the full width of the canal.

This time no such drama unfolded, but I felt that due to the fact they are one of the few features on the canal where other people can be backed up waiting for you, namely the vehicles trapped either side of the canal while you have the bridge hoisted up in the air, that I put myself under a certain pressure that made me rush things. Rushing and boating do not mix, in many cases it is impossible, and even if it is, then it is likely going to lead to lapses of concentration.

Floating up to a bridge blocking the canal and mooring the nose of your boat is simple enough. So too is the act of using the same tool you use on locks, a windlass, to crank the bridge up. I found that if at this stage a couple of vehicles rolled up then I would immediately feel like I had to get it done, which is never a good idea. Moving Tilly beneath the bridge by hand seemed to take twice as long as usual. Pulling her to a stop the other side and tying up became a timed challenge, instead of a simple task similar to what had taken place at three in the morning earlier in the year. Sloppily tied knots would let her gain a little too much slack, and bang about at such an angle she would touch both banks of the canal. On one occasion I was relieved to see another boat approach, so as I handed over the reigns of the lift bridge and moved Tilly out of their way, I was then gutted to discover I had left my windlass on the ground on the far side of the canal. I pulled Tilly over and quickly caught up with them, in what seemed like a moment of childhood where you may have kicked a ball into a neighbour's garden, I had to ask for my windlass back.

The many and myriad moments like these that are sprinkled into my regular boat experience can never be underestimated. From passing conversations with boaters of all kinds, to spending an hour helping a boating friend fetch his boat down through a series of locks on the Monty. Shouting "All Clear" while walking through a tunnel to allow a boat to enter without having to stop, there are many tiny ways in which the community, not only of people on boats, but also people just enjoying the canal in general, help each other out. There are also many big ways the community is connected, but that is for another book. (I would also like to add at this point that after the kayak tunnel incident I can only wish anybody who takes my advice the best of luck!)

The last two months, before winter mooring began again in November are tricky ones to write about. This chapter is already seeming to jump around from topic to topic, as I do not wish to repeat my earlier writing on just how much I loved being out in the slightly more distant area of Whitchurch. Nor do I wish to talk of how great it is to arrive back at somewhere like Blakemere for one single night then leave it in Tilly's wake for the year, probably not to return for seven months at best.

As summer vanishes and so to does a large amount of the holiday traffic, things can often seem like they are entering a very long decline. The cooling weather, (we were lucky enough to be treated to another mild autumn and winter) the nights drawing in and the trees slowly yellowing all create a sense of peace and almost sadness.

This is not to say that the canal is a drab place to be, anything but. When the autumn colours really kick in it is one of the nicest times of year to be out. Waking up on a chilly morning with a clear sky and bright sun beaming golden light onto already golden leaves is a pleasure beyond words. It is just that unfortunately sometimes this does bring with it long periods of rain, or in the worst case scenario, a mixture of ice, wind and snow. Nothing can be more disruptive to a cyclist's trip to work than hidden ice patches on the road, as I discovered long before I ever dreamed of a boat. (Long story short: I once fell off my bike with a laptop in my backpack, unsurprisingly it is a not a story with a happy ending!)

The people who you meet on the canal are often different to the main bulk of the summer holiday traffic. Livaboard boaters rather than holiday makers. People with a huge amount of experience and wisdom to disclose. The sort of people who make me feel as if I have never stepped foot on a boat in my life. It is this time of year that I really like walking on the towpath, seeing really well used and lived in boats moored up is not only heartwarming and stereotypical in some cases, but also potentially inspiring to see how other people use the space on their boats.

A string of moored boats with smoking chimneys on a frosty morning is a nice view to wake up to, especially when you you step outside and realise that your boat too is one of the scenic string of smoke enshrouded dwellings. How to truly describe these times on the canal escapes me, a lot of this book has been based on anecdotes and descriptive writing, a small glimpse at the events and places of a year afloat. It seems that for my own limited ability, these are the best ways to communicate my love of the canal and life afloat. As we enter the final stages of the year and also this book I hope you will forgive me if I continue to throw in anecdotes to try and exemplify my unique version of an entire lifestyle lived in many different ways by thousands of different people. The last few years of my life have been my own attempt at living on a boat in a way that suits me. This book definitely seems to have lived up to its title of "*Dan's* Narrowboat Life" not only focussing on my tiny experience of life afloat, but also written in the style that I seem to be living, a casual passing from moment to moment with a vague plan that I keep getting distracted from!

From the pre-winter mooring months there are a couple of moments that have stayed with me. For example the day that when moored at Blakemere I was out walking and received a message on Facebook containing a photograph of a painting of Tilly that had been done by a kind stranger from the internet. A moment that made me beam from ear to ear. As I walked back along the towpath I saw a boat that seemed vaguely familiar, out of the corner of my eye I spotted movement onboard. I turned to find that it was, again an internet based recognition. A couple who had stumbled upon my YouTube videos and had been in contact with me for a while, I hopped on their boat and we moved the short distance around to Tilly and moored up. What a coincidence I thought, a painting and then this! As we moored up their large boat between Tilly and another boat, a lady got off the boat ahead of us and walked down to me.

"Dan?" The question that I have been amazed to have been asked many times in recent years. A brief conversation about my online antics and some more talk about how strange it is that people recognise me from YouTube followed. Then the usual handshakes and photographs were taken, with me almost certainly doing a ridiculous, awkward thumbs up gesture! All in all an amusing afternoon!

As a perfect evening set in with a view of Blakemere from Tilly, I stood on the stern talking to the chap off the boat I had enjoyed the short ride on earlier in the day. Moored stern to stern we stayed on our two vessels as darkness really took hold of the scene. Talking in hushed tones (a great rarity for me!) it was another perfect end to the day. My blue LED lights threw out their soothing light inside Tilly, and we chatted until the familiar figures of my two friends emerged from the darkness of the towpath.

The following morning I set off to pass through Ellesmere once more and stop at the services for water and a more grizzly business. Just before I left I was handed a bag by the previous day's boat ride giving, literal "stern" talking, friend. When I later looked at the contents I found a handmade heart trinket and a note. Even as I write this sentence now, the heart hangs in front of me on the wall, with the oil painting of Tilly above.

Possibly the simplest, most everyday, moment that I enjoyed an unnatural amount as winter mooring drew nearer was mopping the roof while on the other side of Ellesmere. It took place after an evening that had been long and lazy. With not another boat in sight, I had felt that I could stand around on the stern watching the sunset and tinkering, while an audio book of the History of Britain played loudly in my breast pocket. At length I decided that I would not mop the roof until the morning. So I went inside and did a bit more tinkering and time wasting. I made my bed up and prepared to have an early night.

Something told me that I couldn't rest until the roof was mopped though, I have no idea what it was, or why it was so urgent, but I started to mop the roof in the dark. I had my audiobook playing from my top pocket and routinely stopped to look at the clear sky full of stars above. It was senseless yet perfect. I could not tell exactly what had and hadn't been mopped, nor could I gauge whether or not I was just spreading more mess around rather than removing it, or just how badly the windows were going to be streaked by the dirty water dripping down them from above. Yet it was brilliant. Every now and then a satellite passing overhead would catch my eye and I would stop to track its progress, testing my knowledge of which stars and constellations it was passing.

The biggest obstacle was the chimney, not only was it pouring out smoke that made my clothes stink the following day, but it also kept dropping ash onto the wet roof. I moved my coiled rope to the worst area and hoped for the best. Seeing the dirty mop water turn to steam around the base of the chimney, then quickly fade as a gentle mist was so pleasing that I had to deliberately splash water on it a few times to repeat the tiny spectacle. The simple pleasures of being able to stand on your own roof!

The drawing in of the post summer evenings created many of these moments, simple activities normally done by daylight being pushed back into darkness. Commutes down the towpath under a starry sky in both the morning and the evening are a joy to be a part of. A walk over farmland by moonlight while making an evening trip to the shops, a simple stroll to stretch my legs after an evening of fireside book editing. As November approached all these experiences became regular, or if not regular, at the very least, accepted parts of life.

What did happen when November finally arrived and winter mooring began again? Not much! The last leg of my trip back to the exact position that this book began with me describing, was the best trip I had made for a while. A chilly morning but with a bright sun behind me. The trees were well on their way to autumnal perfection. Before I set out on Tilly I had cycled down the towpath to check that the mooring place was clear. It was.

The weather was perfect, the canal was void of both boats and people, the countryside was the same as it always was, perfect. As Tilly emerged around the last corner and my destination was in sight, I felt a relief that did not signify any previous worry, but rather the sensation of simply being home.

Between November 1st and the end of the year I would only move a few hundred feet around the corner to moor up slightly closer to the pub and adjacent carpark, making it easier to get some coal onboard. The familiar commute to work was welcome, and the familiar faces of the towpath as friendly as when I left them. The calm canal was cut to total stillness for almost all of November and December due to the closure of the canal at multiple places including the draining of Chirk Tunnel itself. I finally did the very last bits of painting... But later was dismayed to find that my Christmas decorations pulled huge chunks of the paintwork off when they were removed. The simple job of painting seemed impossible to finish, having somehow stretched itself out for the best part of a year.

A lot of time was spent creating this book throughout November, I had been working on a few titles off and on for a while and finally focussed on "Dan's Narrowboat Life". Some days I would spend hours writing, only to then rewrite it all the following day, slow progress but an enjoyable experience that I can't seem to stop myself from taking part in.

November at its heart was truly the ultimate in quiet months, literally in terms of the canal. Even onboard it was a time of sitting down in silence or painting with the sound of Roman history ringing in my ears from podcasts and audiobooks. November was a grey but great month, no extreme weather, no drama, no worries. Very little to write about in this book! The most exciting event was decorating Tilly for Christmas, even the majority of this was done during December. Six-hundred lights went up, along with the usual tinsel and cards, on a thirty foot boat that is an awful lot of clutter to add on the inside, and a fair amount of lights to add outside. It is however fantastic to just enjoy a festive boat as a base for some peace and calm when the chaos of Christmas descends in other areas of life.

That is fundamentally what Tilly represents. A refuge, a place to call home, somewhere to relax, somewhere to keep my things in order, to then go out and do other things. She is my floating headquarters to launch exploratory operations from. The heart of my life and yet not the limit of my life.

The real story of the month was biking home during the dark nights, getting the fire lit, then sitting down as the boat warmed up while binge listening to *The History of Rome* podcast.

The Rise of the Potato Man

December brings us to the final part of this book. I am glad to say that, like most of the year before it, it is a pleasant end. The weather was the commonly experienced mixed and unpredictable series of elements. Windy days broke up periods of chilly bright days. Pouring rain would make itself a moderate nuisance with ice only occurring on a couple of occasions.

Tilly remained moored just down from the pub, and the canal continued to be almost entirely silent except for the sounds of me splashing paddles into the water as I kayaked up and down a short mile long stretch every now and then. As far as great adventures and epic drama goes, there was very little to be had while I sat at my desk, still writing, occasionally adding wood to the fire.

At the beginning of the month I reached a terrible dilemma. My second portable toilet tank was approaching its full capacity. In normal circumstances a quick trip by boat could solve this issue, but with a canal cut up by winter maintenance, draining and lock gate replacement, things were not so straight forward.

The short trip around the corner on Black Friday was not only ideal for getting closer to the road and car park for the sake of getting supplies onboard... it also proved vital to get waste off-board. On a very cold, early December morning, I placed a toilet tank inside a black bin bag, hoping to disguise my cargo and placed it onto a sack truck. With a backdrop of a beautiful blue sky, green fields with highlights of white frost in the shade, and a canal bridge lit up by the sun, I dragged a full toilet down the (fortunately empty) towpath to meet my grandfather in his car. Luckily when travelling by car, rather than boat, your destination can be reached a lot quicker. Within twenty minutes or so of the pick up point, we could reach any number of marinas and canal side facilities to do the deed of emptying one toilet into another almost comically giant toilet. At this point I will close the door on the small room that holds the chemical toilet emptying facility and attempt to forget the experience! As amusing or unpleasant as it may sound, it is in all seriousness not the worst thing to have to do. When I consider that it marks the most unpleasant points of life afloat, the infrequent nature of the job is another small price to pay for what narrowboat life has to offer a lover of the outdoors.

If we turned back the clock a little, and revisited the end of November, an unexpected thing happened. While the boating side of life was extremely quiet, I was amazed to find a new point of interest on my Tuesday commute. In the centre of Weston Rhyn, a trailer based kitchen had turned up and was selling baked potatoes. Better known locally as *jacket* potatoes. One of my top three favourite food items.

Throughout December, Tuesday night became potato night! With me leaving the boat, walking up the hill to the village and then buying myself and my friend a jacket potato each. Of all the fillings available I had to keep it traditional and have cheese and beans. Delicious! In the strange way that these things tend to take on an unknown significance, I would find myself looking forward all week long for the next potato night. I would make sure that I left my bike at my friend's so that it would be a simple walk up to make the purchase. Then after eating at their house, and maybe staying for general chat and company, I would get on my bike and ride straight downhill back to Tilly. Arriving within minutes, in the pitch black of the often cloudy, damp nights Tilly's exterior Christmas lights were like a shining beacon, promising to be a cosy refuge from the elements. If everything went to plan I would open the door to find a wall of heat hit me and the fire still smouldering away.

Rarely have I been so content with life than on these nights. I would often make my bed up before I left, so that if it was a late night at my friend's I could arrive, lock the bike, add some fuel to the fire and crawl into bed. There was something very Christmassy about the whole experience. Leaving a boat covered in lights and returning to it gleaming in the dark. Wrapping up warm, lighting my way with a torch down the towpath. Standing chatting, as the smell of the food filled the air while it was prepared only feet away. Eating homely food with friends before setting out back into the darkness. It all went together perfectly with the time of year. Even now, while editing this book, "potato night" is an activity/meal that I am thoroughly enjoying. The weeks that I have missed this treat have just not been the same!

To say that the canal had been quiet during the November to December period would be an understatement. As the canal was closed for maintenance in all directions, it was at some times literally impossible for boats to reach Tilly. Bizarrely, after not seeing a single boat on the move for nearly two months it was a genuine surprise when on the morning of Saturday December 20th, I heard the tell tale hiss of a propeller cutting through water. I looked up to see a small fibreglass cruiser heading downstream and almost did a double take! A boat? Moving on the canal? I had almost forgotten that that was a possibility.

It was in this peaceful way that December slipped away, uneventful, yet still near enough perfect. The Christmas period saw me busier than usual as I had agreed to join in the suddenly abundant overtime at work in the run up to the big day. Being in a shop full of people for eight hours and then coming home to a festively lit boat on a silent canal only served to make the two seem even more extreme. The hectic reality of "real life" and the stereotypical peace of a narrowboat bobbing about in a mild breeze.

When Christmas Day finally arrived I awoke on Tilly and discovered sunlight streaming in. Always a good sign. I got dressed and grabbed my backpack, which I had packed the night before, ready for a quick exit. Standing on the stern was a moment of utter happiness and calm. Being mid morning on Christmas Day there were barely any cars travelling on the road in the distance, leaving the scene quieter than ever. An entirely unbroken blue sky housed the sun that streaked through the spindly trees next to the towpath. The well lit fields were as green as the sky was blue. The air had a chill to it that told of how cold the night had been, the mud of the towpath told the same story as it was in many places frozen solid. Twinkling frost covered a few patches of Tilly, and the entire roof of a nearby boat.

I walked up the hill to my friend's house where I had left my bike the previous night. We enjoyed the usual fun and games of Christmas, and then I was off cycling into Oswestry for a great family Christmas at my mother's house. Classic. I cycled back out in the mid evening and was quite successful in having an early night, ready for the early bike ride and shift at work on Boxing Day.

When I was about two miles into my Boxing Day commute I was very cold. The dry weather had been a blessing on Christmas Day, had it have rained then the roads would likely have been far too icy to cycle on. When I arrived in town I was the coldest that I had been for a very long time, the weather forecast did not offer much hope for the return trip either.

I went to work and did a short four hour shift before returning to my mother's empty home in the wind driven, bitter rain. As I gathered up my things the rain turned to sleet, which within ten minutes then turned to snow, lots of it. I decided to wait for a while and see how things turned out, unfortunately the only change was that a total covering of snow stuck to the ground and continued to build. In a perfect twist of fate my ever present friends from Weston Rhyn, happened to be in town. Collecting me, they were kind enough to drop me off barely a minutes walk away from Tilly, what a sight she was!

The snow had not yet given her a total white covering but it was quickly heading that way. The Christmas lights on the outside, the background of snowy trees and fields and the chimney that was smoking as soon as I could possibly light the fire, all made a scene worthy of a Christmas Card. I think I could have cried that this scene was where I could cosy up and call home. In addition to this perfect scene to return home to, an extremely kind friend from the internet had been passing by and left me some presents onboard too, an act that really was the definition of generosity.

Lighting a candle and sitting in front of the fire, warmth came back to me and Tilly in unison. Never has the sound of crackling wood been so welcome.

Another Year Gone, Being Grateful For Everything

As with the passing of the year, we now also find ourselves at the end of this short account of my time on Tilly during 2014. I wanted to end this book on a personal note and talk about a few of my regrets and also directly to everybody who has followed me on this journey, through either this book or online. I hope that you have enjoyed this very brief look at how my days are spent and how the various elements of my life afloat progress or stay the same throughout the year. All in all it was the sort of year that I would be happy to repeat, minus some of my bumbling errors of judgement, mainly the decision to go to Chirk Marina and then not stay there.

I also feel that I let myself down with how long it took to paint Tilly's interior which then contributed to why I didn't even think about touching up the cracked and flakey parts of the exterior paintwork. Small jobs like those are what the saying "a stitch in time saves nine" are all about.

One of my biggest regrets for the year with regards to life in general, was the lack of serious long distance walking, camping and adventuring in general. Despite an obsession with the outdoors and spending a huge amount of time outside, I feel that the second half of the year saw me retreat into the calm peace of the immediate countryside more than ever. Certainly not a bad thing, but while the good weather was available I should have been out with a tent on my back, halfway up a hill… Although that sounds like it might be a bit hard going!

The real point of this book however was to hopefully give an overview of the different things that narrowboat life can offer to the rural wanderer. The Llangollen Canal is a very well situated stretch of water for scenery and countryside footpaths, something that I am truly grateful for. I have on many occasions talked about how lucky I feel to have stumbled into this boaty lifestyle. If for any reason I had to give up boating right now, I would consider it to have been a great blessing to have spent even just a few years on the water.

Watching the seasons and surroundings change and pass by from the same windows, spotting wildlife from the doorstep, meeting friendly faces, or sometimes not seeing a person all day. There are so many things that I am grateful for, that I dare not list them all at the risk of boring you to sleep, even if you have made it this far into the book. To have done this and been able to enjoy it while in my twenties, is a true blessing, I hope to continue trying to carve out my irregular, poorly planned life for as long as I can. A year like the one you have just joined me for does very little to persuade me to change course.

I am also grateful to have been able to share my time afloat with so many people around the world. It has been an odd experience to suddenly find people viewing my videos more in twelve months, than in the previous four years combined. To be able to speak to strangers who somehow know me is a jarring experience, to have people bring gifts or letters to my door on a random summer afternoon is even more unexpected, but admittedly very pleasant.

I don't think that I can ever do anything to deserve such things, but I am incredibly thankful to every single person out there who has helped influence my life. From simply viewing a video, or meeting me after travelling halfway across the world then handing me a thoughtful gift of a poetry book, every gesture is an act of kindness that I could never live up to, or ask of anybody. So thank you all for everything.

I wanted to end this book with this short simple chapter of thanks and gratitude as I feel that it is the sort of thing that when said aloud sounds awkward or forced. I find that it is far easier to write something down and communicate my feelings or thoughts on something without room for misinterpretation. So thank you all for everything.

These final lines of this book, the ones you are reading right now, are being written just before midnight in early January 2015. I am sat at my desk onboard an incredibly warm boat, despite the freezing temperatures outside. Fairy lights line the interior, and directly in front of me, at head height, is the oil painting of Tilly and heart mentioned earlier. Constant reminders not only of how lucky I have been in life but also of just how many great people there are out there in the wider world. My bed is set up and ready for sleeping in, but I feel like it is going to be a while before the fire has cooled enough to feel comfortable. I will continue editing and rewriting parts of this book for half an hour or so. Then crawl into bed on this tiny boat, sat on a calm canal, barely a sound to disturb me apart from the low roar of the fire. Drifting off to sleep in this environment I could be anywhere, but I am not, I am home.

I will leave you with this scene of boat life tranquility and calm night time relaxation. Thank you very much for reading... and until the next time, Farewell!

Three Years Afloat

Three Years Afloat

By Daniel Mark Brown

www.asortofinterestinglife.com

To everyone who has ever given me one second of their time
to talk about boats!

Hello There Folks…

Writing the introduction to this book about my narrowboat life, three years after it began, seems surreal. It feels as if no time at all has passed since I had never so much as stepped foot on a boat, yet alone owned, and then passed through various phases of obsessively worrying about it, then relaxing and enjoying my floating base! Somehow three years have happened in the blink of an eye, at the very least, I am happy to say it has been a blink of an eye that has resulted in some of the best times of my life.

When I bought Tilly, my tiny thirty foot narrowboat at age twenty-five, I really didn't know what my plan was. I had abandoned plans to vanish off down the canal adventuring, which was my original idea, for a very long time, while I saved up for a boat. In the run up to buying a narrowboat the logic seemed perfect, "buy a boat, then go boating". When the moment of purchase got closer, I had to face up to the realities of buying a boat with only one day of narrowboat experience. To put it bluntly, I didn't have a clue what I was doing. I had read about locks and lift bridges, about mooring rules, boat licenses and even toilets. But I had not had any actual experience.

It is one thing to know the theory of working a lock, but quite another to slowly steer your boat between the soaking wet, ominous walls for the first time. Scraping from one side to the other, and feeling that the walls towered above you with a deliberate menace, trying to put you off balance to make a mistake in front of an experienced lock keeper.

On the other side of things, it was also fantastic in my pre-boat days to talk endlessly with friends, fantasising about where we could moor, or go on short trips for a night or two. To have those first experiences of waking up, then opening the curtains to a canal and fields on one side, then look through the opposite window to see even more fields on the other, was magical. Throw in the cameo appearances of all kinds of animals and wildlife, and the rural canal scenes could often fit themselves in, unobtrusively, among a book of fairy tales. Old ruined and crumbling buildings, huge buzzards flying overhead, giving their screeching cry that only a bird of prey can muster, a horizon made of blue sky and green grass, all these features have blended together many times, to create a sense of gentle adventure into a time almost forgotten. In the interest of balance, I should also point out that at other times during the last three years, weeks of rain, bad weather and dark winter nights have made life less than easy, and certainly not as enjoyable as the happy summer boating stereotype. But, variety is the spice of life!

The aim of this introduction was to illustrate just how varied my own narrowboat experience has been during the last three years, and highlight that, despite my occasional terrible steering and lack of knot tying skill, I have learned a lot from my time afloat. The following book is a collection of thoughts and experiences that I have tied together into a series of themed chapters. That is the official sounding description of this book at least, what this book really is at it's heart, is me doing what I love to do… Talk about boating!

Before going any further I would like to start with a diary entry from the early period of my boat life. A snapshot of a day that featured so many of the stereotypical images of narrowboat life, that it almost seems impossible to me that it happened during the last few years.

A Diary Entry

Thursday 17th October 2013

Today I awoke to find a very chilly but bright boat, opening the curtains to reveal a bright blue sky reflected on the huge watery expanse of Blakemere. A large lake barely twenty foot away from Tilly, moored up at the side of a comparatively murky brown looking canal. The huge trees on the far banks of Blakemere still held the yellow tint of the rising sun.

After getting dressed and having a quick wash, I decided that I would use this dry but cold break in the weather to cut all of the wood that I had been storing onboard, so that it could be dried next to, and then used in the wood burner. I was lucky enough to have enough wood to last a good few weeks dropped off by my friends Ollie and Helena. This donation had been collected from his parents' new house, as his mum continues her tireless work creating the ultimate cottage garden.

The already short pieces just needed an extra cut here and there to make them fit into the fireplace, my stove being an unusual cylinder shape, seemingly built by an individual for the purpose of fitting an awkwardly shaped boat hearth, before I bought Tilly. Along with the new delivery of wood, I had a huge collection that I had kept on the roof looking like a group of makeshift barge poles. Grabbing the short bow-saw, I realised that it was entirely rusty, blunt and uncared for. After trying to cut the first piece of wood, I decided to lock the door and take the twenty minute walk down the towpath into Ellesmere.

Soon enough I returned with a brand new saw, twice the length and with a spare blade, some mooring chains and a bag full of junk food. In the short time that I had been away, the weather had completely changed and grey clouds now filled the sky, while rain showers blew over every few minutes. I had been planning to move a few miles down the canal in the evening, but after the previous few days of rain, decided to move right there and then.

Without so much as going inside, I put my bag on the roof, untied the ropes and bid farewell to the scenic shores of Blakemere. The trip took only about an hour and passed pleasantly. The rain poured then eased repeatedly as I made my way through the nearly empty Ellesmere basin and down to the incredibly rural Tetchill. Barely two miles travelled in an hour. Fields as far as the eye could see and only two other boats on the move, peace and relaxation at its best.

I decided to cut the trip slightly short by mooring at Tetchill when the rain reached such a level that it was tempting me to try and speed up, something that I never do, and that doesn't mix well with narrowboats. In the usual way, within about five minutes of tying the last rope and getting inside to shelter, the sun was back out and a very warm afternoon ushered itself in. I needed no more prompting and was straight back outside trying out the new saw, suddenly it was a much easier job to get the stash of wood down to size. The sudden burst of activity, and the new ease at which I got it done, made the whole thing quite enjoyable as I sawed, axed and snapped away listening to audiobooks... for three hours. This created an amount of fire ready wood that would easily be able to keep me warm for at least three weeks to come, plenty of time to top up the supply.

With a satisfied feeling I put the saw and axe away, but looked at Tilly and saw a boat covered in sawdust, bark and grime in general, and set myself the next task of getting her cleaned up. All the fresh cut wood was placed in boxes under the front cover that would keep them dry, yet also make them accessible from inside through a set of stable doors. Then with nothing more than a mop and a canal full of water, Tilly was transformed into something resembling a gleaming model of how a narrowboat should look, plus a few bits of rust and chipped paintwork.

The temperature started to dive, as did the sun in the sky, at around five o'clock which as far as I was concerned was a great excuse to end the jobs of the day. I went inside and made a quick snack of porridge before taking a short three mile walk down the canal and into the village of Tetchill itself. Not only was this a perfect little walk around a quaint country village with a sunset sky, but it was also a practical exercise in trying to keep some movement in my back, three short walks a day has been my goal, and also cure to a reoccurring bad back, or at least that is my excuse for my obsession with walking all the time. It works, and my back rarely aches now, so keep those boots at the ready I say!

Returning to Tilly I put some of the recently cut wood to good use as I lit the fire, and took the opportunity to heat up a pan of tomato soup over it with a very liberal sprinkling of mixed herbs for good measure. This was the first wood burner heated food of the season. Another sign of the winter I am a little more prepared for.

It's not the size, but what you do with it that counts.

The size of Tilly is something that has caused a lot of discussion over the years, as I try to explain the layout to people who have not seen her, or try and convince the sceptics that you can really get everything you need in such a small space.

To have a thirty foot boat that has a ten foot stern, is not necessarily the greatest of choices for a livaboard boat, especially when the bow has a further five foot outdoors. It is not the end of the world though, in fact the large stern is quite handy during the good weather, as it means that even with a bike or two locked on the deck, there is still room for sitting out and eating with friends, along with travelling when loaded up with people or bikes. The spacious stern does look huge when seen from inside the fifteen foot interior, and on some occasions, with maps out, or lots of stuff in general strewn around inside, I have eyed the outdoor area with a certain feeling of lament that it is not covered over to use as a bedroom!

The interior does hold everything it needs to though, or to word it more accurately, everything that *I* need it to. Bathroom, boiler and shower, sofa bed and storage cupboards, a wood burner. That selection of items already covers most of the basic needs, sleeping, clothes, cleaning, heating and washing. The front section holds the kitchen. Kitchen may be a grand term to use for what is really just a cupboard for food, a sink, cooker and general storage area. Add in my small desk area at the very front so that I can write these books, and I am happy to say that is just about all the simple things in life covered.

The issue of space and storage isn't one that I have ever had to worry about too much. As a single sailor who is more than up for camping and, on occasion, has been known to sleep in a car when our camping gear was soaked to the point of uselessness, Tilly is more than enough. If I suddenly had to take onboard a partner in maritime-crime then it would almost immediately become impossible to live with any kind of relaxation or happiness. Unless of course we both worked full time jobs and took it in turns to be the person inside the boat!

One of the biggest things that I have come to realise over the years, is that if I did have a bigger boat with just me onboard then I would end up having empty space or idle cupboards. If for example I moved up to forty foot of space, then I would make sure that some of that length went into creating a separate bedroom, but in terms of what I would add to the boat internally, I really struggle to imagine.

I wouldn't be interested in owning a television, for the last decade I have barely watched any programmes regularly. With the modern internet age truly taking hold, almost anything that I might want to watch could be streamed to a phone or tablet (depending on location and signal of course.) More importantly for my personal tastes, the thousands of hours of podcasts, YouTube and radio programmes that I love to watch or listen to, are also available at a moments notice on a device that can fit into a pocket.

The general entertainment aspect of life afloat can now be stored in a tiny glass fronted, metal encased tablet. For an obsessive minimalist, this is an excellent way to declutter any space, whether in a house or on a boat. No more collections of DVD's, CD's or books. I do miss my two book cases full of books that I still have, as just about the only feature of note in my old bedroom at my mother's house. I have never been able to part with them, and still find myself taking the odd book back to Tilly with me for a reread every now and then.

The lack of books onboard Tilly is also a sign of how over the course of my time afloat, reading has become less of a focus. Instead of reading, I have become ever more enamoured with writing. Before Tilly I had written a few short books and would write numerous short stories, ultimately leading to a collection of seventy-five published short, single page stories, and one longer tale with a secret hint of my plans to buy a narrowboat hidden at the end! On buying Tilly I started writing even more, keeping a diary with recordings of all manner of events. Sometimes these entries themselves would go on for page after page, other times they may struggle to reach a few lines, but they have all helped tremendously with putting together the books that I now love to write, just like this one, all about my experiences afloat. An ongoing documentary of my life and thoughts at different stages of my floating education.

On top of this, YouTube became a bigger part of my life than I could have ever imagined. Making videos has been a hobby of mine since before YouTube began, stretching back into the depths of time when I received my first, extremely low quality digital camera, I realised that it was a fun thing to play around with... especially with a cat running riot in the house! I used YouTube for many years and nobody really cared, I would get a few thousand views in a year and consider myself lucky. When I got Tilly and started making boat life videos, things went a bit crazy. While getting the final edit of this book ready I am amazed (and a bit scared) to say that my YouTube videos are soon going to hit three million views in total. Quite a terrifying thought for a shy nerd with a camera and a boat.

To put it simply, writing and recording/editing videos have become the two things I spend the most time doing onboard Tilly. Listening to podcasts on the long, cold, winter nights or the long, lazy summer days, definitely needs an honourable mention. In fact podcasts can often be heard as the backdrop to almost any of my daily tasks and simple jobs afloat. Especially on some of the very long walks to the local towns or villages for supplies, walking through the countryside with the sounds of nature being interrupted by a definitive podcast series about Roman history, is a good way to spend an hour or two in my book!

This chapter started with the intention of being a simple discussion about what items I do and don't want onboard, but has clearly gone off topic. The above paragraphs really help to illuminate something that is vital to understand how my life has changed and been formed by boat life. Heading onto Tilly for the first time, I had a phone that cost £7.50 as my only communication with the outside world. Now I have an iPhone and an iPad with me, those two tiny devices have given me access to the world, regardless of whether I am on a boat, in a field or in a house. It may not be as traditional, romantic, idealistic or stereotypical as the idea of a rustic boater drifting along on his merry way, a tatty old book as his companion, etc etc. It is at the same time, a modern addition to a canal lifestyle, and in many ways, far more minimalist. Replacing, books, televisions, radios, and all manner of other individual items through apps, I have not got a need or desire to have a lot of items on top of the basics of life onboard.

That is the true heart of this chapter. While having a twenty bedroomed house may sound like a dream come true, what is its true impact or value when you can only sleep in one bed at a time? Especially as the whole idea of a boat to me, was to be able to live cheaply and spend as much time as possible out biking, walking and generally enjoying the countryside, before I am too old to truly make the most of it.

As long as I have a place to sleep that is warm and dry, with somewhere to cook and wash close by, then I am sorted. Although this may not be for everybody, in fact it is almost certainly the worst nightmare for some people, for me though, who once "cooked" a Pot Noodle on a gas stove in the footwell of a car, while trying to figure out just how two people could sleep in a vehicle so full of camping supplies and condensation, Tilly is just about right. At this point I should probably say that not only was the gas stove inside a car a very silly thing to do, and that I do not encourage or endorse that kind of behaviour in any way. Also I would like to add that we had just done an extremely wet weather walk up Ben Nevis and were pretty tired and worn out after literally wading through thigh high water on the way down... so please cut us a little slack for our actions!

That is almost a perfect illustration of how I would love to live my life full time. During the past three years I have had many long days of walking or biking that ultimately led me to arrive back onboard, worn out, aching and ready to immediately slump into bed in front of a smouldering fire. Tilly fulfilling her purpose as a floating base to let me do these walks or bike rides, or general activities in all kinds of different areas that a fixed dwelling wouldn't allow.

The opportunity to turn a simple shopping trip, that in the past would have been an unquestioned bus trip in and bus trip out, into a pair of five mile walks. Or depending on my destination a much longer walk down the towpath, through country lanes or along main roads, to reach a large town. Proceeding to walk around the town for forty-five minutes, picking up whatever shopping I had on my list and then getting the bus back to Tilly, seems almost comical when the walk to the town could have taken almost two hours to complete. That is the point of Tilly to me, to allow me the opportunity to live just close enough that I can take a normal shopping trip and by skipping the bus there, turn it into a good morning's walk. The low cost and basic lifestyle that I have tried to create is what gives me the time to actually do this, and do it now, while I am young-ish!

I may mention my age an unnatural amount during any prolonged talk about Tilly, boat life and what I do with my time. This is partly down to how I have caught myself "feeling old" and finding myself measurably less fit than I used to be. As my thirtieth birthday rolls around, I know I have been lucky to spend almost all of my twenties doing lots of active and fun things with many great people. But, I am also able to admit that in the years approaching my mid-twenties I was at my most fit. I have records of walks that I took as far back as 2009 (again proving my obsession with writing and diary entries!) that show when I was 22, I could walk five miles down a familiar country lane from my mother's house to my friend's in only a few minutes over an hour. This year I have continued to notice that when I do this same walk, it takes me almost an hour and a half, and that is when I genuinely think I am keeping my pace up. This sort of measurable pace drop really has underlined the importance of making the most of the opportunities that you have, when you have them. Tilly may not be the luxury yacht of a billionaire, but she has been worth her weight in gold with the opportunities she has given me for exploring country roads, fields and unmarked tracks, all at a gentle walking pace!

In a nut shell, that is Tilly's true value to me, far more than a sum of all her body work and interiors. Tilly is now more than ever, a way to prolong my love of wandering.

Cruising through the years of changes.

A popular and traditional image of a narrowboat, is one of an old, ornately painted boat in bright clear colours, green, red, blue, cream, all highly polished and void of any blemish. A jet black bow cuts through a murky canal, as the traveller slowly glides along on their unknown journey. The scene is usually taking place on an otherwise empty canal cutting through trees, fields and under bridges that all find themselves in a sun soaked ideal world. That is one stereotypical image, the other is the opposite time of year, an image that holds a snow covered boat with smoky chimney, and maybe even a little robin, hopping around looking for crumbs.

The winter scene that I have seen in photos, paintings, and on the local news is very often what you would expect and hope it to be. The summer cruising scene however is much rarer, all the elements exist, but getting the great weather is hard enough, getting the great weather and an empty canal in the summer, well, that is something that here on the Llangollen branch, is a little less likely to happen.

Cruising the waterways is part of the joy of living on a narrowboat for most people. Some like to travel as often and as far as they can, others like me prefer to travel less and enjoy more of the simple peace and scenery of the incredible rural backdrop, much of the canal runs through. Boating down an empty winter canal with the cold air chilling your fingers and face, is not the same as cruising along in a queue of traffic over the summer. As for leaves on the propeller in the autumn, well you get my point! Cruising on your own in the sun is only a fraction of boat life.

Many years ago I spent one day on a hire boat and travelled along a short stretch of canal around Ellesmere. It was a chilly but bright winter day, on a canal with no bigger challenge than passing through a short tunnel. It was an experience that let me know with confidence that I wanted to live on a boat, and could happily travel around on my own. Fast forward to the summer of 2012 when I stood on the stern of my own boat, ready to take her back nearly one hundred miles and things were very different. The half remembered trip of empty canals and plain uninterrupted cruising, proved to be a red herring, as dozens of locks along with all kinds of narrow single-file stretches, tunnels and aqueducts, stood in my way.

When the initial trip was complete, and I could settle into less extreme and more leisurely travel, I was exhausted and terrified of moving the boat on my own. The fact that it was the height of summer, so I was trying to gain my tiller confidence while having boats stack up behind me if I went too slow, didn't help. Nor did the flow of oncoming traffic, causing me to repeatedly get so far out of their way that I would scrape along the edge of the towpath, or even worse get beached on the off side in its shallow waters.

This was a Dan Brown who stands many miles of canal away from my current feelings. After three years of experience, I may still have moments of terrible steering and an ever more subdued feeling of dread at meeting a boat at the worst possible time, but I am now at least ready, willing and dare I say, eager, to get the engine fired up and get travelling.

The joy of cruising in my current lifestyle is immense. Making a short trip every few days, or maybe a longer trip after a week of enjoying the same mooring place, I am truly happy to float along at even less than the 4mph speed limit. The scenery and wildlife is almost unbroken, rural imagery. This chapter is going to be dedicated to the rural canal experience of being able to sit on a boat, amidst nature and witness the passing of the months, seasons and even traffic!

Living on a narrowboat that is very often moored (metaphorically rather than geographically) in the middle of nowhere, with fields, trees and the odd wind turbine as the only landmarks, has given me a very close feeling to nature. In fact sometimes when shadows of creatures walking past the windows, and rustlings of animals on the roof, feature in the dark hours before dawn, I feel a little too close to nature. Apart from the unexpected and uninvited guests, sometimes human as well as animal, the environment itself has made itself very prominent to me. When I lived at my mother's house in Oswestry, I was lucky enough to be able to walk to the supermarket that I work at, in less than ten minutes and visit other family members' houses in even less time. The changing of the seasons was only a temporary chilly patch on the way to work, or a quick dash home in the rain. For all my love of walking and biking I would not set out in pouring rain deliberately, regardless of how many times I ended up walking back in it. Walking out on bitter cold days or through scenic snowy fields, was no issue when done for the simple pleasure of being out there, and in the knowledge that a warm house and hopefully jacket potatoes for dinner, awaited me on return. This has changed with my life onboard.

Regularly mooring and commuting between three and twelve miles to work forces me to go out into whatever the weather has to offer. I have biked down roads so windy, that even pedalling downhill was not enough to stop the sheer force of the wind blowing me to a standstill. I have fallen off my bike on ice that was invisible to me in the predawn darkness. I've ridden through wetter conditions than I would have believed, seen clothes two layers under my waterproofs soaked through, and shoes so soaked and covered in mud that they have gone from "brand new" to "wear when I am doing odd jobs" in half an hour! In the huge snowfall of March 2013, I had to walk through knee deep snow for miles down the towpath to a friend's house, dig out their car and get a lift into town for work... The following day! You get the picture, suddenly adding miles onto my trip to work or sometimes even just to the nearest shop, or a friend's house, the weather is something that I can no longer ignore.

Beyond the practical realities of having to get out into the conditions, the fact that I now live with five windows and two doors that all look straight out into nature for most of the time, means that I am also totally engulfed by whatever the season is doing to the world outside. This is one of the beautiful things about life on the canal. It is possible to see the rise and fall of seasons, the huge growth of summer, with bushes pressing further over the canal, to the desolation of autumn's end, and the bare twigs that were previously the long, overhanging, branches months before.

This has a great side effect as it gives a nice variation of scenery, especially for the places that I moor in the spring, and then return to as winter creeps in. Being able to return to the exact same thirty foot of canal, eight months after I left it, and find that it has changed completely can seem to almost double the length of the canal network.

More fundamental to life afloat though, the weather alters the way I think about where I want to be and when I want to be there. As spring reaches its full life giving flow, the bright sunlight still interrupted by sharp bursts of rain, it is a refreshing break from the frequent long grey days of deep winter. Ushering in a period of dry, warm weather (that is the theory at least, in practice it is a case of hoping for the best), spring is a time for setting out and heading further afield. The good weather lends itself to pleasant bike rides, instead of a morning commute filled with bitterly cold rain and treacherous roads. A ten mile commute on a spring morning, with a sun just risen on the horizon, is preferable to one half the distance that begins and ends in the pitch black, and requiring you to scrape ice from your bike seat before sitting down!

As the weather warms up the focus turns to enjoying the outdoors and letting the light flood in, rather than trying to keep the heat indoors and stacking up wood whenever I get the chance. At the front of Tilly is a set of small stable doors with two windows that open outwards. During the autumn and winter these are kept not only shut, but covered up by a material cover that stretches from the front of the roof down at a forty-five degree angle to the level of the step around her outside, or the gunwale to put it in "boaty" words. This cover creates an almost completely waterproof area that I use to store boxes full of wood that I originally would collect and cut. These days however, the sheer amount of wood that I get offered by friends and family is more than enough, and having a landscape gardener in the family certainly doesn't hurt if you are looking for an endless supply of wood! The stable doors that sit at the front end of Tilly next to my desk can be opened from inside, allowing me to reach through and get more fuel for the fire without ever having to leave the boat. Very handy in the cold wet months.

Once the need for a stockpile of wood has lessened, I keep an emergency box of wood just in case. The cover is pulled down and rolled up and the small area in the front then becomes a porch that lets the sunlight in through the front door windows, and allows them to be opened to let a breeze roll through on the very hot days of summer. Having the front cover off Tilly doesn't only let the light and breeze in but also offers many perfect views straight down the canal ahead. The view forward is fantastic on a long strait, I have often seen herons standing still for long periods of time through a pair of binoculars, and also had fair warning when a boat is approaching at a speed slightly higher than it should.

As summer rolls on, the long days of sunlight have a noticeable effect on how often the lights onboard are switched on, and therefore if I am not travelling much, such as when I was in a marina, I find that the engine does not need to be used very much at all, as there is nothing draining the batteries that it charges while running. Running the engine can be almost a token gesture, just to keep the batteries topped up. If I ever finally get my long talked about solar panels on the roof, then things could really be quiet on the engine front. The long days are particularly enjoyable if I have a long walk planned, waking up early with the sun already up, having no time limit to tread paths I may not have trodden before, and returning hours later for something to eat, then a wash and then an early night with the sunset. It sounds over the top and romantic to the extreme but I have done just that numerous times. Days like that are why I live on a boat, just as much as the bright winter days with a roaring fire, that turn into "perfect for astronomy" clear skied winter nights before my jacket potatoes have cooked. In more recent times I have found myself being a bit lazier and walking up to the "potato man" from my winter mooring, it comes at a premium but convenience and a consistently cooked potato are hard to resist!.. Especially with some of my past, half charcoal, wood burner potato cooking efforts!

The summer months bring with them the holiday traffic, this has its own additions to the cruising experience. Setting out for various goals in the past, I have been able to join the procession of boats and sneak through bridges and gaps with the boat ahead, while oncoming traffic waits with a smile and a nod to the passers by. Long trips behind the uncertain, nervous holiday boaters have also proved to be half a blessing in the "well we can't rush so let's just enjoy the trip" mentality they create, but also a curse in that I have had to moor up after far less progress than I had hoped.

One such trip behind a nervous boater saw me moor up, get on my bike, go to my friends house twenty minutes away, have dinner and then return with two more crew members before we set out, only to find ourselves stuck behind the same boat again within two miles of canal! Being stuck on an even slower than usual, moving boat in the countryside, with the company of some of my best friends... What a terrible problem to have! Similarly one trip that was intended as a quick hop down through the two locks at New Marton, saw myself and a friend stuck for hours in a queue at the locks with more than enough time to make an evening meal, eat it and then wash up while we took turns to hold Tilly to the side of the canal.

The importance of dry conditions to mooring in some places cannot be overstated. For ease of access, myself and many other boaters will tie up a short distance from a country lane, or sometimes a relatively more substantial road. Much of the towpath remains a very bumpy beaten track, with even just a little rain it becomes surprisingly muddy and slippery. Not the sort of terrain you would want to walk or bike too far along before getting into your boat fetching half of the murky surface with you. In the summer though it can turn into a bone dry, dusty track and although very often extremely bumpy and in many cases suddenly disappearing into the canal itself, it is a much more attractive prospect to travel down. When at its best I start to moor in many of the stretches of canal that are a good distance away from roads and society. There are some incredible places that I know of, where very few people have ever spent a night due to the fact that it is not by anything such as a small town or village. Looking on a map of places of interest for holiday makers, or roads for busy livaboards to go about their business, there are large stretches of canal that come up blank. It is at these secluded places in the height of summer, that it is easy to do nothing all day but go on short walks, potter around doing odd jobs onboard, and listen to audiobooks for hours on end.

Speaking of odd jobs, summer is definitely the time for these and somehow on a thirty foot boat there is always something that needs doing. Painting is definitely a summer job as is anything that may involve moving things around inside. In a small space like Tilly I have found it is often easier to move large items such as chairs outside onto the stern if I am doing anything major, such as cutting lengths of wood or laying carpet. While writing this book originally, my granddad and myself were creating the small writing desk (mentioned earlier), to fit in a corner space at the front of the boat. The large piece of wood had to be cut outside, so, as we took tiny increments off at a time to ensure a snug fit, there was more time spent shuffling up and down the twenty-five foot or so walk between desk and stern, than there was cutting wood. (We got a perfect result in the end though!)

Autumn soon makes itself known as the perfect summer countryside starts to look a little bit subdued, leaves turning to darker shades before they change to the incredible display of golds, yellows and browns. At this point, I have now for two years in a row, discovered that I have been lazy and not done half of the jobs I wanted to do in the summer. Leave them for spring I then say to myself and then never think about them again.

It may just be coincidence, but since living onboard I feel that autumn has been bringing much stronger winds than I ever recall, maybe this once again just ties into the fact that I have to deal with it directly now. Travelling in the wind is not always fun, and I try to keep travel to a minimum. The front cover goes back up, and it becomes time for wood collection and cutting before the rain soaks everything through and makes wood collecting a very muddy, damp task.

I find that as summer turns to autumn nature also gets a little closer, spiders start to pop up in unexpected and startling places, leaves tumble down the steps to the stern door and blow in through the windows. The bathroom is normally the worst, as I keep the window open permanently, which led to a sink and floor almost totally covered in leaves after a perfect mixture of a bad mooring idea and a night of strong wind.

Travelling when the leaves are falling has the upside of the incredible golden brown scenery but the downside of the canal being full of them. Leaves on and in the water doesn't sound like a problem, and it doesn't really stop you from going anywhere, but it does stop you from getting there quickly. Even for a narrowboat, I have found travelling during autumn slow. The propeller soon gets a good coat of leaves that slows progress almost to a halt in some cases. A quick blast in reverse will spin them off, and a cloud of leaves can been seen in the water floating away behind you. Then as soon as you start to move forwards, the leaves gather again, slowing you down when they are there, forcing a quick moment of reverse gear to clear them; leaves are one of the few genuine elements of nature that have a noticeable impact on cruising. I never would have known this tip were it not for a fellow boat dwelling friend. Even when I was told, I didn't believe that it could actually have a noticeable impact, but the first time that I took the advice to go into reverse, I saw the leaves scatter then I moved back into forward gear and it suddenly felt like I had a rocket attached to the stern, I was a be-leaf-er!

The golden trees become naked of all growth at such a pace, that when the first truly bitter cold night and frosty morning arrives, it can seem as though winter has suddenly appeared like a boat with no light from a tunnel. Winter brings with it many incredible sunset skies early in the evening and many extremely cold nights, heating becomes the most important daily job onboard.

Making sure that the wood supply is kept well stocked and cut ready for use is vital. So is bundling bags of coal onboard whenever possible, to ensure a supply that will last beyond any trips you may take away from easily accessible supplies. Waking up to a fire still burning and throwing out heat is one of the cosiest feelings I can think of. Just as hearing the fire crackle nearby, while drifting off to sleep is the perfect end to a day. However sooner or later the ash will need clearing from the fire, which means that the fire needs to go out. The process varies from fire to fire but on Tilly there is a small cylindrical custom made fire, it has a lid on the top to add fuel, a wider removable section that a pan or kettle can sit in for heating, and an ash tray at the bottom that also acts as the air vent to control the flow of air, and thus the temperature of the fire. It is a small fire that can be used for about two days tops, before the ash cuts off any air flow and extinguishes the fire entirely. I make emptying it a daily task to ensure I never have to wake up to a cold boat and an un-lightable fire. I still do occasionally wake up to a chilly boat, but as time has gone on and I learned to accept these moments and not try and rush re-lighting the fire, I have found it not to be the worst thing to ever happen to me! It is worth pointing out that when it is cold, it can get extremely cold! Scraping the ash into a tray without sending it all over the carpet is still not something I can guarantee, but as long as it is all cold and not going to burn anything I consider it a success.

Getting the fire going again is now second nature, a fire lighter in first then a selection of split kindling sticks topped with larger logs once they are burning. The coal I keep for sustaining the fire through the night. This I manage to do quite well but still not with total success, and a cold boat on a frosty winter morning is about the coldest place I know. On work days I will wake up and have to get out and on my bike as soon as I can, which means the first thing that I need to do when I return, sometimes very late and nearing midnight, is clear out the fire and get it burning again. Riding a bike a minimum of five miles in the cold and then getting into a freezing boat that houses a series of very cold surfaces is something that could be better, but makes the roar of the fire all the more rewarding once it is burning well. Rubbing my hands over the top, or sprawling out on the sofa, with my feet over it, before wrapping up and getting some sleep is once again an example of the most simple yet truly enjoyable moments of boat life that make it just my sort of thing.

Winter, although the toughest time afloat, is definitely a strong contender for my favourite time of year. It forces you to do the classic things that people think of boat life involving, such as wood cutting and hanging wet clothes over a fireplace. The scenery when the snow falls, can be something straight from a painting, the sight of a smoking chimney poking out of a thick roof of snow is almost enough to make you feel warm, but the fact that it may well be your boat that you are about to climb onto and feel the wall of heat greet you opening the door, is bliss.

I love winter so much that it nearly gained an entire chapter of this book entitled "Tis The Season To Hassle Jaspers"! This title was due to the fact that I purchase a winter mooring license that allows you to exceed the two week maximum stay in certain areas, and remain for as long as five months from November to March. My mooring place of choice, is about a ten minute walk from the home of two of my best friends, Helena and Ollie. Helena was vital to the success of the original trip back home after purchasing Tilly, and was there alongside me as we both learned how to boat from scratch.

Unfortunately for them there is also a bus stop about fifty seconds away from their house, which is another excuse for me to bother them over the winter months. Having this nearby base on dry land, proves to be quite a useful and lucky break. If I have shopping to do, then I am able to catch a lift into Oswestry as their route to town near enough passes by the stern door. This is particularly handy for when I am buying big or heavy items such as kitchen roll, or bottled water. Biking into town is fine but after one attempt at biking back to Tilly with three two litre bottles of water in my backpack, I soon decided that the bus or a lift was the better option. As another stroke of luck it just so happens that Ollie works in the other local town, a few miles over the border into Wales. An early morning lift to Wrexham is perfect, arriving before a lot of the shops have opened, I get to experience the suspense and thrill of waiting for the shops I need to buy from to open their doors! Sometimes the excitement is nearly too much. A lift in, shopping and then the bus back, all before the place has really started to wake up.

Another benefit of the Jasper residence is the storage boost it gives me. At a time when I am filling up the dry space in the bow with fire wood, and being forced to spend more time indoors by worsening weather, it is very handy to have a nearby safe place to keep things like Christmas presents. As I start to pile up a small stockpile of gifts, in what was once their spare room but has since become the baby's room, they're then ready for wrapping then dropping off at various family members' homes. I don't store things that I normally have onboard off board, but it is certainly convenient to have an overflow, sometimes I have to leave the odd bag of wood up there too, then wheel it down on my little sack cart when the time is right.

The most important and beneficial thing in some respects however, is the steady access to the internet that I am allowed/covertly enjoy! Being an obsessive YouTuber I am constantly filming videos about narrowboat life and other things. I would originally upload these videos at my mother's house while I was at work, but as time has gone on and people have thrown hundreds of requests at me, I can spread the uploads a little more evenly through the week... Sometimes even getting a sneaky little gadget charge while I am at it, just don't tell Ollie! Even YouTube itself has changed dramatically over the past three years and with the ability to schedule videos, I am now less of a drain on Jasper resources!

The luck of having friends near to the canal in winter, takes away a lot of pressure that I may otherwise feel, were it not for them I would have been unable to get into town for work on some of the particularly harsh snowed under days of my first winter onboard. Without their lifts into the local towns, then my expenditure on public transport would be far higher and I would not be able to get back to the canal so quickly as I can, to enjoy even more time in the places I love.

The fact that they have an actual fixed home address is also worth noting, as I am constantly asked by potential livaboards how I cope without a fixed address. I am lucky to have access to my mother's house, so the few things that I do receive in the post are relatively uninterrupted. If it comes to a bigger or awkward to transport delivery, such as a new companion set of tools for the fire or parts for my bike, then I am able to use the Jasper residence as a delivery option for ease of access.

The most significant advantage however, that overshadows all previously mentioned uses, is the fact that having an address up the road from Tilly means it is possible for me to order my beloved takeaway pizzas and jacket potatoes. One of the great delights I nearly had to give up from my life on land! Again even my love of pizzas is waning, and becoming at best, an infrequent treat these days. Writing new pieces for this book and editing the old original text has thrown up a lot of personal observations and curious very gradual changes in my lifestyle. Once again having a love of writing creates interesting records and snapshots of how I was, but also underlines how I am.

In all seriousness though I am incredibly lucky to have such accommodating friends, so close by, and prepared to put up with so much Dan Brown invading their homes. As with all things in life like this, it is probably something I have nothing to really repay their kindness with, but at least a brief recognition for it here, and full public acknowledgement that my life is very often a team effort, maybe at least a way to show my appreciation. A rare kindness these days, that I am truly thankful for.

Travelling in the summer evenings with a sun still high in the sky or on winter mornings with sleet slowly building in the air, an empty canal or in traffic nearly brought to a halt, there is one common theme. Steering. Can you travel on a boat on your own?

A frequent question I get and always respond to with a hearty "yes"! The perfection of the stereotypical image described earlier may be rare but travelling on my own is something I greatly enjoy these days. I like to have friends and family onboard whenever possible to enjoy it with me, but when I do set out solo I often find myself humming the Pirates of the Caribbean tune, with a big grin when I catch myself doing it!

The key thing to remember about handling a huge steel tube weighing tons on your own is that it is floating on water. This makes it possible to pull on a rope attached to Tilly, and have the boat slowly move towards you, or press firmly on the hull with your index finger, and see it start to move away. In calm conditions I have been able to pull Tilly level to the bank, and then realise the mooring hooks are inside the boat, hop onboard, walk down the steps to get them, then jump back onto the bank finding that she had barely moved. A bigger boat would obviously be more difficult for me to manage on my own, I may go as far as to say quite hard to manage, but my humble thirty-footer is easy to steer with my squared non-elegant tiller. I have found that in "normal" circumstances she is also easy to moor up as long as I don't dilly dally too much and see her bow floating out towards the opposite side of the canal.

There are however, two situations that I have found as exceptions to this calm and easy travelling ideal. The first is when you are trying to hold her to the side by an unusually fast flow of water, sometimes at locks, where heavy rain can cause a huge flow of water down the overflow channels, that can often be seen at the side of the main lock. If you let your boat start to move with the water, then soon she will gain a steady momentum that could be hard to counteract without a running engine. Moving towards a narrow lock with a large swell of water pushing you off course can also lead to an unpleasant crunch of steel bow and stone lock wall!

The second and far more common issue I have found in my solo travel has been the wind. Blown into trees, narrowly missing moored boats and barely being able to hold her to the side. All part of the reason that I would rather travel in pouring rain than strong wind, in some cases travel has proven impossible with me unable to move away from the towpath to make it around boats moored ahead. The prime example of wind afloat, I will save for the next chapter in this book, when I faced one windy day on the Montgomery.

For a huge majority of the time solo boating is enjoyable, fun, rewarding and maybe plays a little to the inner adventurer who can travel miles down the canal but never leave his home. After a certain point of confidence in single handed movement, I have found myself considering it a sign of thoughtlessness and embarrassment if I accidentally let any of the ropes dip into the water as I moor. Think of the awful results, getting wet hands on a boat trip!

Moaning On the Monty, Living the Dream on The Monty!

The first time I sat down to write a narrowboat book, I had been on an epic one hundred mile maiden voyage. It was a life changing event that imbedded itself as part of my initial boating experience, making itself indistinguishable from the moment of both purchasing, and a few days later, moving onto Tilly. Two weeks of the most challenging circumstances I could have ever imagined during my previously sheltered life, a long, hard trip, and yet the greatest time of my life up until that point. Now, looking back at the years since my initial brutal education in boating, I am pleased to say that I have not had any tremendous difficulty to overcome and then write about here!

We have talked briefly about cruising, but now I invite you to join me onboard for my first trip onto untravelled canal during my first year afloat. This was the last time that I was ever really "scared" or properly stressed while boating, as you will see, it is a perfect example of how obsessively worried and quick to panic I was, over the smallest things. I feel embarrassed looking back at the incident now, roughly two years after it happened, although even calling it an incident is giving it too much credit, and my own worrying not enough blame!

The stretch was not a distant half forgotten ditch, it was in fact the stretch of canal that comes closer to my home town of Oswestry than any other, The Montgomery. After all kinds of experiences on the canals I had known so well for most of my life, the Monty was the last area to explore by boat. Of all the cruising that I have done since then, it seems that no other period of my cruising captures the bizarre mixture of experiences from high to low that narrowboat life can throw your way. It is about the only time since my initial big trip home that I have really seen any low points. For that alone it deserves a place in this book to ensure that I don't give you a sugar coated idea that boating is always perfect fun and amazing times afloat. I am extremely lucky to have been able to live my narrowboat dream and that it has been such great fun for so much of the time. It has turned out to be far better than I would have dared to hope, yet this still didn't stop me from having momentary panics and wildly downbeat feelings when the slightest thing went awry. So for a well rounded view of what exactly my life onboard can consist of, the places, the people and the panic, let us take a two week trip onto the Monty.

The Montgomery canal is an interesting stretch of water. Still undergoing a very long process of restoration, even the restored parts are separated by miles of dry canal. In fact the restoration is almost a battle with nature, even in the past months running up to publishing this book, the canal has been breached and closed for repairs. As long as it is open, in the stereotypically rural setting of Lower Frankton somewhere between Ellesmere and St Martins, a series of locks will drop a boat down from the Llangollen and onto the Monty.

Before you even get to the water you have a clue that this is no ordinary canal, when you have to phone up and book to go through the locks. There is a limit of twelve boats a day which ensures a very quiet canal, additionally there is a limit of only two weeks stay on the entire seven mile stretch to the small village of Maesbury. There is more too, the slow pace of canal life at the speed limit of four miles per hour is also slashed to three miles an hour, and then at some points even down to two miles an hour. The incredibly rural setting, slow speed and lack of traffic, are combined with unusually large sections of unmoorable banks which combine to create at many points a barren, end of the world feeling of remoteness.

I had passed by the locks several times while on the Llangollen, and been tempted to go down and see what it was like. For the first months of returning to the area with Tilly, I was too worried about my overheating engine that I for some reason, and to the frustration of those around me, just wouldn't get fixed. Another deterrent for me travelling down the Monty came in the form of several locks along the way, having never done a lock on my own. It was not until much later that I would dare to go down there, and even then I would be doing my first solo lock a few miles downstream at Queens Head.

The village of Maesbury holds the nearest point that any canal comes to my hometown of Oswestry. At only two-and-a-bit miles from my old house, I have over the years biked at a good pace to this point in less than ten minutes. It was this fact, and ease of access to town for both work and meeting friends and family, that finally got my nerves about the long slow canal, under control.

On an overcast summer day I waited for two of my regular shipmates, Helena and Ollie, and just after midday we went through the two lock staircase and then down the further two nearby locks, before taking my first wrong decision and not mooring up at the first mooring site, a site that also held facilities in the shape of water taps and bins. This was the only mooring place on the first 4 miles of canal, not a huge problem under normal circumstances, but at this point I was still uncertain of an engine I had not pushed since its earlier overheating. The passage through the locks is only open for two hours a day which causes minor traffic jams as everybody floats around waiting for their turn, lots of running in neutral is then followed by a three miles per hour speed limit, making the distance to the next mooring seem endless.

The first lock is a two step staircase which basically means that it is two locks stuck together, with the central gate leading directly from one lock into another, rather than having a short distance of canal in between. This is the assisted lock that if you turn up outside of the hours of twelve and two in the summer, you will find chained and padlocked up. With another person there helping you through it, the process is easy enough and works on the same principle as any other lock, which we will see a little closer shortly.

Deciding to pass the opportunity to moor in safety, we continued on to a very small lock that had a barely perceptible drop in water level. In preparation for travelling on my own later on, I decided to not allow anybody to get off Tilly, and insisted that due to the minimal change in height and therefore lessened risk and workload, I would do this as my first ever solo lock... The second mistake of the trip! In the excitement and panicked obsession over my engine, I utterly failed to do the simplest task of moving Tilly over to the side of the canal by the lock, and moor around the mushrooms. I just could not do it. For ten minutes I became increasingly enraged and disheartened at my failure to moor up. Tilly was banging bow and stern against both sides of canal, including a little underwater scraping, we were at all sorts of angles, sometimes with the bow on one side of canal and stern touching the other.

The ability to move to the side of the canal and stop, is just about the simplest and most basic task that I would have never said could ever cause much of a problem. Having done this hundreds of times perfectly, the fact that you literally have to do it at the end of each boat trip ensured that I was well practiced. The only difference in this case was the small overflow, where water runs from the higher level of canal around the outside of a lock, down to the lower stretch of canal. Considering that it was barely a trickle of water I could not even use that as an excuse! It was another example of how the simplest task can take far longer than it should... The pace of boat life slowing even more when mixed with the odd moment of awful driving!

When I finally did get her pulled over to the side I was disheartened and furious with myself. Getting her safely into the tiny lock was a relief, but also a time for me to dread the coming canal with its full size locks. I was less than a mile into the Montgomery and already considering turning around and going back up to the Llangollen the very next day. I knew there was a turning point ahead, and I also knew that there would be a very small aqueduct just after it, that I could moor up by. Making a sensible decision has never been one of my strong points but getting myself worked up over nothing, and then trying to make a balanced judgement, was beyond a simple quick 'yes' or 'no' or forwards or backwards answer. The aqueduct ahead was not the sort of structure that the word aqueduct conjures up. Having only a stream pass below it, the aqueduct looked more like a small bridge. The space on either side was not intended to be used for "proper" mooring, only as temporary space to allow oncoming boats to pass over the aqueduct. The fact that the Montgomery was such a quiet canal made it unlikely that I would ever be causing an obstruction. In the end the decision was made for me.

Moving out of the lock with a terrible mood descending on me, we slowly glided forwards, the canal being too shallow to moor on either side, and therefore a terrible prospect to run aground on. Before we reached the turning point the final moment I had dreaded happened. A strong smell of burning rose up from below the deck.

I found myself cursing everything that I had ever done to bring my life to this point. The general feeling was just like my first ever solo boat trip, when within minutes of starting, the engine had overheated to such a degree that one of the pipes had burst off its fitting into the engine. This time at least there was no such drama, and I was far closer to home than that dark day. In a panic and spurred on by a nose full of a burning plastic smell, I knew there was no chance of pulling over to the side, and that even if we reached the turning point we would not be able to travel all the way back up to safety. The aqueduct became the only option.

Throwing the ropes around the temporary mooring mushrooms, in an over the top and disproportional state of regret and exasperation at my own decision making, my friends took the opportunity to escape to less intense surroundings, leaving me to whip myself up into a bitter mood over the following hours.

In the middle of nowhere, well away from any sign of society, I lifted the boards of the stern to allow some air to flow around the engine. I had believed that it had been cured of its overheating miraculously in the previous months. On top of my failure at what had seemed to be the easiest lock ever, I now had the seemingly impossible task of travelling a very slow few miles further on a stretch of canal that had consistent, and in some cases deliberate, underwater obstructions making it unmoorable. If I made it successfully, I knew I would then have to think about making the entire trip back, in order to return through the locks to relative safety, still not finding a true mooring space. I knew I would be making this trip on my own which did not help.

Despite the fact that I had never been onboard Tilly at a closer point to my previous home of twenty-five years, my completely unreasonable mood made those few hours seem like the most isolated I had ever been. When it was time for tea, I decided to have my traditional quick snack that was ultimately nothing more than a mug of pasta. At this point an unknown transformation happened.

By the time I had finished eating, the clouds had all but vanished, and an evening of perfect blue sky and bright sunlight had formed. I went for a quick walk in both directions and was filled with my usual sense of love for the outdoors, perfect sunlit fields stretched in every direction, the odd row of trees here and there, and of course a perfectly scenic canal cut through it all. Ahead of me lay a huge strait that vanished at a far corner, small bushes growing and overhanging both banks. Lit up by the summer sun only just starting to dip in the sky, I was looking at my dream come true.

By the time that I stood back onboard I was in incredibly high spirits and am happy to say that never again have I felt so low or pessimistic in relation to any part of my life, least of all Tilly. I started to feel quite guilty at having been so stupid, ungrateful and shortsighted. I may have been temporarily stranded, but stranded in the most perfect, as well as one of the most rural, secluded and quiet stretches of canal for miles around. I was literally exactly where I had always wanted to be. Later on, I decided to take a bike ride ahead down the canal, I trundled down the empty, bumpy towpath with a huge smile on my face, the bumps made my tyres tangibly less inflated than before I had set out. I arrived at Queens Head, eyed up the next lock, and in a complete change of heart decided on the spot that I would set an alarm for six-thirty the next morning, and set out as soon as I could. An early start would hopefully help me reach more long term safety further down the canal, before any others moved, or I could cause potential trouble to anybody other than myself if my engine played up.

The following morning was a perfect summer morning. An early sunrise and clear sky led me to be boating down the silent canal wearing sunglasses, a T-shirt and a cap long before even seven o'clock rolled around. In total contrast to the previous day, this remains one of my favourite boat trips ever. This was one of the times that I was truly boating down the perfect stereotype of summer boating on a perfect empty canal. I knew that nobody else would be around at that hour, and that with the next mooring places being miles away, it was going to be as easy and calm a trip as I could hope for, definitely making up for the previous day. The few miles I moved took two hours, just as I was preparing to enter my first ever lock with no one else onboard, I was saved from the daunting task by one of the rare holiday boats on the Monty, who helped me down through the lock with cheerful conversation and great efficiency.

I moved a few hundred feet down the canal and then as I had planned, moored up before the next lock; I repaid the favour just done by helping the holiday makers through the lock and then went back onboard, grabbed my backpack and cycled into town to pick up a new filter for my telescope that had been delivered to my mum's house. Everything was back to normal and life was perfect!

After a brief "hello" to the family back in town, I jumped back on my bike and was back onboard for lunch time. I knew that based on the fact that the top locks were open from midday to two in the afternoon, that this far down the canal I would be extremely unlikely to meet any traffic. Those going upstream would have been long gone so they didn't miss the window of opportunity, and those coming down would still be hours of cruising away.

With this in mind, I moved the final few hundred feet to the next lock, and for the first time ever did the entire process on my own. It was surprisingly easy and straight forward, the only thing that I had not fully grasped was how long it would take. When there is one or more people involved, then one person can stay on the boat the entire time while the other opens gates, lifts paddles and so on. Working a lock single handed, you have to fill all roles.

Before you can get into the lock you need to open the first gate/gates, which means stopping and quickly mooring to the side, pushing the gate open, then jumping back onboard and steering in. Then hopping back off, closing the gate behind you, then going to the opposite end to open the paddles to either fill or empty the lock, depending on which way you are heading. The water flow then starts to move the boat, which you will then have to hold in place and keep away from the dreaded potential disaster of getting caught on the cill, which can and has caused sinking!

To keep the movement of Tilly as minimal as possible I personally only open the paddles about halfway, it takes twice as long to drain or fill a lock this way, but I would rather add even more time to the process and feel safer, than take risks I can avoid. As the water drains or fills and you stand there holding a boat in place by a rope, you have a few minutes of peace. On that day standing in a perfect rural scene, sun shining and nothing but the sounds of nature around me, the previous day could not have seemed a more distant reality.

To finish the process of getting through a lock single handed involves the final section of running around. Once the water is at the level you want to be at, you open the lock and lower all paddles, jump back onboard and move out of the lock, moor up once again, then go back to close the lock so that all gates are closed, before running back to your boat, unmooring and then finally moving on. Depending on the size of the locks and how quickly I want to move, this process has since taken me anywhere from fifteen to thirty minutes. Once again the slow pace of the canals has worn away any idea I ever had of going somewhere quickly.

I repeated this great success on the next lock nearby, and found myself on the final section of canal down to Maesbury. No more locks or anything of any note, just a canal surrounded by the most rural settings of any stretch of canal in the area. Again the majority of the bank has become impossible to moor on due to the large amount of reeds in the area, there are however a few clear points that really do see you mooring up with no sign of humanity in sight. Of course this was an opportunity not to be missed. Nature, silence, incredibly dark skies for astronomy, and a series of public footpaths that led to nowhere... I was in my element! I spent a couple of nights moored by the village, but many more out of sight.

A period of perfect weather happened to align itself with my stay on the Monty, and I made the most of it, sometimes spending six hours of daylight out biking and walking before heading inside for some tea. When I had eaten and washed up, I would find myself impatiently waiting for the stars to appear in the blackness above, and then head back out with a telescope.

One of my favourite moments of my time there was one such astronomy session. An incredible sky had given me a great view of many of the famous deep space objects, and a fantastic view of Saturn too. I had been enjoying an audiobook quietly, with the rustlings and calls of various unseen small animals and birds as the only other sound. I walked for less than two minutes to a nearby foot bridge that crossed the canal, it was an unusual type made of brick at either side of the canal but with a wooden platform that spanned the short distance over the water. I was stood on there and only a moment after having looked away from Saturn in the eyepiece, I saw two excellent shooting stars. These are not as uncommon as many people think, and once you start spending a lot of time out at night, you are likely to see many. The first was a quick one that shot a good distance across the sky, the second seemed much slower and was probably visible for a couple of seconds, more impressively, it had a very faint fire tail that was visible for a split second afterwards.

Standing on that bridge with, as far as I was aware, no other person for at least a mile in any direction, doing what I loved in a perfect setting moments away from my small floating home, I was at my happiest... My new girlfriend back in Oswestry didn't hurt the feeling either!

One of the surprisingly rare attractions that Maesbury has, is the canal side tea room, shop and canoe hire service located literally feet away from the canal. It was on one of those very canoes that the idea of living on a boat first entered into my life. While I was moored up about a minutes walk away, me and my friend Jono took one of the canoes for our traditionally overly energetic trips. Making the same trip that we had made a few times before, it was incredible to actually paddle up to Tilly and be able to hop onboard from the waterside of the stern, and make use of all the facilities and features of my entire home.

We paddled away for hours, having to lift the canoe and walk it around the locks before putting it back into the canal. Needless to say that I continued to let Jono do the more physical elements of the task, while I point to my sides and say "Oooh my hernia scars!" Canoe trips have always been a tiring affair, as we can't help but try and push further and further up the canal on each successive trip. On this particular occasion we equalled our record, and then discovered that we could duck down, and pull the canoe underneath a bridge into a disused narrow branch of water that opened into a large basin. A remnant of some long forgotten industry.

Paddling through reeds and overgrown trees, we suddenly started to talk in whispers, it was like a scene out of an adventure film, two travellers not sure where they were going, paddling a canoe down a deep jungle river. When it opened out into the basin it was still closed in by trees on every side, the huge area filled with weeds floating on the surface so thick that it became hard to paddle, and appeared as if the canoe was sat on a field of grass. We moved slowly towards the centre when we both stopped, thinking that the other had said something. When it became apparent that neither of us had, we gave a suspicious look around us. In that state of silent observation we were made to almost jump out of the canoe when a fish splashed against the surface of the water right next to us. A quick exclamation (that I refuse to describe as a scream), was then followed by shouts of "Paddle back! Paddle back!" It is random moments like those that we can laugh at afterwards and were great fun to be doing at the time, that are once again an example of just how much there is right on the side of the canal. Things that many people, including myself, have overlooked and simply do not know about, were all beyond my comprehension in the pre boat days of my life. Now though I am able to moor up with this sort of thing as a temporary garden, soon to be replaced by a new patch of land.

I have since been down to Maesbury three more times, every trip giving the same fantastic experience as the first, I am pleased to say minus the nerves! The weather was key to making the first trip so enjoyable, the general seclusion and beauty of the place can be enjoyed in any weather, not to mention the various random towpath encounters I had with some of the local residents and walkers. The canal towpaths are a great place to meet all kinds of characters, or at least they are when you live right next to them. Other boaters, walkers, daring bikers and keep fit enthusiasts of all ages along with dog walkers, CRT employers and volunteers and holiday makers from around the world, make up an incredible range of people to see and very often be quizzed by about Tilly.

While down at Maesbury I became familiar with a few people who I won't draw unwanted attention to here, but I will however give a mention to one uninvited guest. A dog walker stopped to chat one evening, while we talked away, his dog jumped up and onto the stern. A stocky brown barrel of a dog, who stood maybe two feet in height, he circled around in the open space on the stern before darting towards me pushing me down the back door steps and then running up and down the inside of Tilly's short length, soon followed by me! This has happened on more than one occasion, recently there has been a fluffy black cat walking around on Tilly in the small hours of the morning. The towpath is not only used by humans.

Speaking of people, I experienced one of those completely unexpected twists of fate one day at Maesbury services. Tilly was moored up while I saw to the job of emptying the toilet. Afterwards while it was quiet I was showing a friend what there was at this particular service point, the usual things, toilet emptying, pump out point, water taps but also a large normal toilet, a sort of laundry room and a huge shower. While we stood talking in the empty room outside of the various doors, we decided against entering into the shower as we were unsure as to whether we could hear running water. I pointed and talked in my usual loud way, and was bizarrely interrupted by a voice from behind the shower room door that asked "Dan? Is that you?" I confirmed that it was in a puzzled voice, glancing at my friend. The next thing I knew, the door popped open and out walked, still drying his hair, (but thankfully clothed), one of the local boat dwellers that I had not seen for a few months. After that, we had a pleasant trip up the canal, back into the middle of nowhere, followed by a bike ride up and down past all of the locks scouting out potential moorings.

The few hundred feet of canal between a series of locks is referred to as the "pound", the water level in these areas can rise and fall rapidly depending on the lock usage. Based on this, it is inadvisable to moor there for very long unless it's unavoidable, while you wait to move through another lock. I decided to take a chance and the following day I moored up between two locks trying to make myself believe that I knew better than everybody else. I didn't! I spent a day hopping out of the boat whenever somebody else started to ascend or descend through a lock that was a minutes walk away at most. With my windlass, (or as I still mainly call them lock handles), in hand, I helped many people get through a little faster and once again found this to be a great change of activity. Getting to see all kinds of boats close up and hear of what others were up to, it was another great day on the cut. A couple of people asked if I was staying where I was moored, as if to hint that moving out of the pound might be a good idea, but I stayed anyway. Things were fine, and another pleasant night passed onboard.

The following day I was unsure of whether or not to move or to stay one more night before making a bit of progress to have a final run at the long stretch back up to the top locks onto the Llangollen. I decided to stop where I was. During the afternoon I took the chance to make the most out of the weather and went on an incredibly long bike ride to my mother's house. I travelled on many country lanes that I had either never been on, or hadn't ridden down for a decade. I managed to sneak a place at the dinner table when I arrived at my mother's, and sorted out some more video uploads to YouTube. When I hopped on my bike and finally arrived back home to Tilly, I had a very odd sensation when I stepped up onto the stern. Instead of sinking slightly on the side I had put my weight on and then rocking around as I moved, she remained rock steady. I jumped off knowing instantly that I had made another schoolboy error. Grabbing the rail along her roof I stood on the towpath and pulled down, there was a tiny movement before a dead stop. She was sat on the bottom of the canal!

The edges are almost universally shallower than the centre of a canal, and just as I had been told, the water level of the pound had dropped during the day while I had been out. I could rock her upwards but not lower, she was just about floating, or at the very least, the bottom she was sat on was a layer of thick, squishy, mud. I knew instantly that I had to get out of there so I put my bike onboard and started the engine. With the lock ahead only a few seconds jog away, I ran up and opened the gates before running back, untying and then pushing Tilly out into deeper water. No major panic, but at just after nine in the evening it was not the quiet night in that I had envisioned when setting out on my bike. It was not until after I had fetched Tilly up through the lock and moored up in some deeper water, that I realised that I had not really given a second thought to going through the lock. Something that I had never done on my own until less than two weeks previously had already become something that I just got on and did, even when moving against my intentions as the light of the day faded.

The two weeks flew by with all the speed that is common when times are good. Seemingly moments after coming down through the locks, it was time to go back up into them. I had a slow trip up to the mooring spot around the corner from the bottom lock, and arrived there to spend my final night on the Montgomery. A final, perfect, summers night passed without event.

Waking up the following morning I could feel the boat rocking as wind howled through the trees outside, rain was being battered against the windows. I had chosen an awful day to go back up to the Llangollen. I was moored around sixty foot ahead of a water point; where I had planned to fill up from, before moving to the locks at twelve. When the rain stopped, I emerged from Tilly to untie and then walk her back the short distance to the taps. At this point I was given a serious lesson in the power of the wind against a boat.

The water point at the top end of the Montgomery Canal is located on a very short dead end that used to lead to another branch of water. This fifty metre or so arm is wide enough for about four boats to fit side by side, with forty-eight hour moorings on the far side from the water taps. As soon as I had untied the front of Tilly her bow started to drift out, so I had to run and hastily untie the back rope too. I grabbed the middle line and with all my might tried to heave her back into the side. I barely even slowed her progress down. Within seconds she had moved so far out into the canal, blown by a wind more forceful than any I had yet encountered onboard, I had no choice but to literally run and jump onto her side.

Not only was the wind blowing me to the far bank but also backwards, towards a rather nice (expensive) looking boat. We picked up speed and in my panic I could not get the engine started, I was so frantic that I was not allowing the air around the diesel to heat up, after the second attempt it was too late! We hit the concrete siding on the far bank with a crunch, then began scraping down towards the back of the moored boat. I jumped off, grabbed a fender and heaved with all the desperate strength that I could muster, only just managing to slow and stop our progress towards disaster. The slowing was probably as much to do with the friction of the hull scraping the concrete wall, as it was to do with my effort. I threw a mooring rope around a ring and breathed a sigh of relief. The exiting of the Monty was nearly a bigger disaster than the entry!

The wind was so strong that even with the engine started and running with all its power I could not get across to the tap side again without moving a good distance forwards at a slight angle. To finally get her on the correct side still required me to grab a rope and take a huge leap of faith off the stern and onto the bank. During the course of the morning the wind rose and died down in an irregular sequence, but I was finally able to fill up with water to my relief. The boat moored opposite then tried to make the move across, once again the simple and easy task in any other weather took three of us and the engine to complete! The conditions grew worse again with the return of the rain which led my fellow water point users to cancel their plan to go up through the locks altogether.

Bizarrely, in a demonstration of how much more upbeat my attitude had become since the last time I was approaching those locks, I could not wait to get stuck into them. I joined the procession of boats heading upwards as the third out of four boats wishing to rejoin the Llangollen. I had deliberately waited until I could see that the boat ahead had entered the lock, before I moved around the corner to wait my turn, just in case the wind made me unable to stop Tilly before running into the back of it.

Moving back up the locks was a slow, hard process, the wind and rain reached fever pitch and I was unable to look directly into it. Lock gates blew open before you could start letting water in, the wind blew you completely to the wrong side of the canal as soon as you left the shelter of the locks. Even without starting the engine, Tilly found her front fender bumping into the top lock gates before I had a chance to grab the ropes.

When I finally arrived at the last lock I was extremely grateful to have the help of the CRT assistant. Rising up for the final time, I managed to once again embarrass myself with some awful driving, even in a lock where you can't possibly move more than a few inches side to side. The flow of water started to pull Tilly forwards and I didn't quite react in time. I pulled into reverse but as the stern rose from behind the lock gate, the wind joined forces with the water and pushed the bow straight into the lock gate ahead. Bang! I have never hit a lock gate so hard before or since and it of course had to happen the one time that I was working a lock with a representative of the Canal and River Trust. With a chuckle and a comment of "Don't worry, it catches everyone out" they dismissed the matter graciously, I assume my face had tipped them off about how embarrassed and guilty I felt. Good times!

Once through, I realised again that just as a few nights before, I had gone through four locks in extremely unusual and probably inadvisable conditions, without having the moments of dread and pre lock nerves. I had just done it! I was however, very glad to have got it done and out of the way, given the cold and damp that had permeated my body whilst doing it. I was unsure that I would be able to control a boat properly on an open stretch of canal in such high wind. I instantly decided to call it a day on moving, instead mooring up at the first possible point, which was probably a maximum of one-hundred-and-fifty feet away from the top lock. The fire was quickly lit, my soaking clothes were hung over it to dry, and my feet were put up in front of the crackling fireplace. The benefit of moving your entire home with you was never more clearly demonstrated than when I sat there, eating sweets in those cosy surroundings, safe from the elements that I had been battling with outside, barely five minutes before.

Toilets. Services and a Clean Bottom.

A question that I get asked a lot about life onboard, even if it is asked in an awkward hushed tone, is what the situation relating to the toilet is. It seems that some people have an image of a terrible world where everything goes down a pipe, then out into the canal, creating an unearthly roadblock further downstream. A topic like this certainly is not a beautiful, romantic, high ideal of a simple life afloat, but it is a very important part of life wherever you are.

Narrowboats in general will have one of two types of toilet. Pump Out or Cassette. A pump out toilet can be very similar in function and look to a traditional toilet, the only difference being that all waste is collected in a high capacity tank which, as the name suggests, needs to be pumped out when full. These kind of toilets can have months of standard use between pump outs, whereas the cassette style toilet (also known as a camping toilet or portable toilet) is a lot lower capacity.

Tilly has a cassette onboard with two tanks for waste, the basic look of the contraption is of a plastic cube, a lid opening to a liftable seat, a piston pump to flush fragranced water down, and a tab on the front to pull out and let the waste fall into the tank below. The limited storage of these is why I found it vital to get a second tank, on average I have capacity for about three weeks before I need to find somewhere to empty out and start the whole lovely process again!

Emptying a toilet tank is the ultimate activity to test your stomach, ability to keep a steady hand under pressure and contemplate your own humble function as a human being. There are many places along the canal that you can empty both kinds of toilets, pump outs being a little rarer and requiring you to literally use a hand pump in many cases, making you feel it as you pump, shuffling everything down a pipe and off your boat. Cassette emptying is far more straightforward. Lift the toilet bowl section off the tank, pick the tank up, unscrew a cap and pour the contents into what roughly translates as a giant toilet. Needless to say it is an assault on all your senses to be doing this anywhere, but when in a tiny room designed for this single purpose and used by countless people over the hot sweaty summer days... Well I am sure you can start to build an image in your mind.

The desire for speed is held in check by the need for concentration and care, something that unfortunately not everybody has mastered, which again only adds to the potential horrendous drama of the event. Most of the time you turn up and everything is fine, the deed is done and you unmoor and put the experience behind you for the day. Unfortunately I had one rather unfortunate incident at Ellesmere services, that looking back on, now almost three years, later I can laugh about but still with a massive cringe.

Picture this, it is a rainy day, I had travelled up to Ellesmere in the hammering rain, soaked to the bone, freezing cold, and eyes stinging, I moored up on my own at the service point. Tilly is the only boat present, I connect a hose pipe to a water point and start to fill the front tank. At this point, making me jump, an anoraked man appears behind me unexpectedly, holding an empty toilet tank having walked around to the back entrance from a passing road. Many people will fetch toilet tanks by hand on sack trolleys to avoid the hassle of turning a boat around, coming down, doing the deed, then heading back to where they came from.

We exchanged a quick greeting, and off he walks as another boat arrives, a very nice looking boat, worth several times the monetary value of Tilly it would be fair to say. I take the opportunity to empty one of my tanks first, not to put too fine a point on it but the facility is a mess... Hold breath, do job, escape! While I am making the incredibly short trip between Tilly and toilet, the lady from the boat that shall not be named, jumps at the opportunity to get her task out of the way... On stepping out of the back of Tilly I am greeted to a shout of "That toilet is disgusting!" I shout back "I know!" Then there is quiet murmuring between the couple. At this point I realise that I am being accused of the terrible act, being an incredibly shy newbie to boating, pitted against two more "mature" characters on a very nice boat, I am not sure what to do, a denial seems to be even more proof of guilt in these type of moments. I say nothing and run for the cover of getting back in there with my second tank, trying to convince myself that they are not talking about me. When I emerge sheepishly and without the urgency that leaving the room normally has, the other boat is moving off as another approaches. Unfortunately above the engine I can hear a high pitched voice shouting to the newly arriving boat about the state of the toilet before a hand points back at me amid inaudible words... Just what I wanted, especially as I was only going to moor up about one hundred and fifty feet away from the scene.

This may seem like a small but embarrassing mistake, that caused me to momentarily take the blame for such an unpleasant gift left by an unknown person for all of us to not enjoy. Unfortunately the story doesn't end there. A couple of days later I was woken by the sound of an engine quite early in the morning. As that one faded a new engine sound closed in and to my horror, half asleep but suddenly snapped to full awareness, I heard a voice call out with an anger that lets me know the incident is still fresh in her mind, "That's the boat from the other day! Pull over!" Dutifully the boat is moved slowly over to moor at my bow, I jump up out of bed not sure what I am going to do if there is a knock on the door. There isn't, footsteps reach the kitchen window, the window that holds my license and boat number. A moment passes and then the boat starts to pull away. Filled with dread, I then spent the next few months expecting at any time to have a phone call from the Canal and River Trust, or a stern letter asking for an explanation to something that I hadn't done. The situation is not eased when over the following weeks I hear the original accuser and a friend of hers on another boat going past twice, pointing a finger and mumbling. But, as from the first moment the situation arose, shyness and the feeling that any sort of denial would only serve to make me seem even more guilty, kept me silent and as hidden as I could be, sometimes literally running inside if I thought an approaching boat was my assailant!

Luckily, writing this now I can think about how I should have just said, instantly, anything at all to stop the situation going further than a five second moment of blame laid at the wrong door. It is also something that now seems to have the makings of a children's television show, to see me lazing about doing simple jobs onboard out in the summer heat, to then see a boat approach with a similar look, causing me to run in and hide out of line of sight of the canal for a minute or two! What a fool! I couldn't say if I am more embarrassed by how I was too scared to speak up for myself or by the fact I was blamed for such a thing in the first place.

Incidents at the services are rare though, and far more often involve the unexpected shower of water when your hose pipe comes off the tap. Water points are far more common than general all round facilities. In seemingly random places, miles from anywhere, it is possible to find two or three taps in a row waiting to be used. Filling up with water is as simple as turning on a tap and pointing a hose pipe where you want the water to go.

Other services other than rubbish disposal, toilets and water, are normally covered by the many marinas scattered along the canal. If you are looking to fill up with diesel, pick up a new gas bottle, or undertake any serious work on your boat, then popping up to your nearest marina(s) is the way to go. For example, my friends and myself were able to disassemble the inside fittings of the boat and then slowly rebuild in a way that has made the space my own, yet when it came time to pull her out of the water entirely, and get her hull blacked, we did not have any of the appropriate equipment, experience or skills.

It is worth noting that although marinas are far more common, since I have been onboard Tilly on the Llangollen Canal, a fuel boat has started making trips up the canal every other week. Diesel, coal, wood and more, all being delivered right to your floating doorstep! I can vouch for the quite literal doorstep delivery, after spending nine hours onboard Fuel Boat Mountbatten on a perfect sunny day. Travelling down the canal on a seventy foot working boat loaded with supplies was a fantastic experience. Making two great new friends of the owners, as I filmed endless clips to put together into a short film, was definitely a great way to spend the day. Seeing an active working boat making deliveries also only served to intensify the "olde world feeling" that I so often enjoy out on the canal. I could write and talk endlessly about the fuel boat, but will save that for another time, lets get back on the topic of taking Tilly out of the water!

My glaring lack of dry dock ownership led me to ask around at a few of the local marinas, before deciding to take Tilly down to one of the most rural places I have ever been to, Whixall. There is a beautiful, silent, marina there that exemplifies the traditional image of a silent narrowboat scene. In the middle of a ten mile stretch of incredibly rural canal to begin with, Whixalll marina is then situated on a short branch of very narrow, overgrown canal, that leads only to itself, making it even more secluded.

Travelling down to the dry dock situated out there miles from anywhere was a pleasure, a slow trip made even slower by the inclusion of a few lift bridges along the way. It was a perfect summer day when my friend Helena and myself, woke up and made the final few miles down stream, through a huge expanse of flat marshland giving the unusual ability to view for miles around, while nudging the tiller left and right, trying to squeeze past some fancy looking boats.

The first time I took Tilly for blacking, it was an easy process... I tied Tilly up at the marina and let somebody else do it! The dry dock at Whixall is a large warehouse style building, with a small pool to fetch the boats into before pumping the water out, leaving the boat hopefully resting safely on a set of plinths. Tilly having an awkward, slightly V shaped hull, had to be propped up with a couple of railway sleepers, something that ensured that before leaving her, every possible item that could fall over, move around or otherwise rock and roll with a potentially tipping boat was solidly in place. Drawers were taped shut, chairs were wedged across the width of the boat and all my plates were wrapped in blankets!

The phone call I received two days later saying that she was out of the water, and everything was fine was one of those moments of sudden relief that reveals how stressed you have actually been about something. I slept well that night, sleeping as I was in my old bed at my mother's house, where I was sheltering as a homeless boater for a few days.

The job of blacking was done in just four days. Once out of the water a high pressure jet washer is used to blast away the grime and scrape away any paint that will come off. After a period of drying the time comes to get a paint roller on a big stick, and start layering up the thick coats of black paint that will hopefully keep the rust away for another year or two of cruising. Just as keen as I was to see Tilly out of the water, was my grandfather, so we hopped in his car and went off to see the spectacle. After a thirty minute journey out in his car we discovered the doors to the dry dock locked, and everybody gone home for the day to let the first coat of paint dry! The following day we made the trip again, with a far more successful conclusion. Seeing my small boat propped up out of the water on three beams of wood was a strange moment. Fascinating on the level of seeing her full body from top to bottom, somehow looking tall and unstable. I had a sense of the fragility of my little floating home. A thin steel shell, rusting away, everything that I owned and based my life around, merely a rusting hull that I hoped would stay afloat. A feeling that I get every now and then, but only here presented to me out of the water in all its nakedness, the feeling of inevitability was overwhelming. The trip home seemed quiet as I wrestled to put my normal face back on, and let distance work its magic of making the feelings fade. It did, but never truly has it vanished.

Once again with Helena onboard as my only crew, we set out from Whixall after the job was done, with a shiny new looking hull. In an unexpectedly long trip we ended up travelling about thirteen miles that day, enjoying the incredible unbroken rural canal for over six hours. As we reached each landmark that would be easy for Helena to be picked up from in a car, we couldn't help but think, just a bit further, just a bit further. So perfect and enjoyable was the trip, Tilly very nearly got her completely home. We decided to stop just before the New Marton locks at St Martins just in case we ended up in a huge queue. The trip had been perfect, no incidents or any kind of drama, just pure boating for boating's sake. About the worst thing that had happened was some confusion over who was going to pass through a bridge first, and my reluctance to try and squeeze through a small gap left by an oncoming holiday boat... Tilly was freshly painted remember!

The following morning we arranged that I would head up to the locks onboard first thing, and Helena would ride her bike down and meet me. Once again the short trip went perfectly, early enough to avoid the traffic, we breezed through the locks and even stopped to fill up with water. Heading temporarily to Weston Rhyn, we had made the thirteen mile trip from Whixall in about the most textbook, perfect, demonstration of boating that I have ever been involved in... Until what was quite literally the last bridge of the trip!

Seeing the final bridge before our mooring spot, I relaxed as we approached its slightly wider and slightly longer than standard arch. It is a highly built road bridge, with two lanes rather than the more frequent, tiny, humpback bridges common on the canal. I was so relaxed that, taking my eye off the ball for one second, to try and stop a rattling sound by the engine control panel, I looked up as we entered the bridge at a slightly off angle, brushing up against the left hand side. Hardly the worst thing in the world, but it was a shame to scuff the still nearly pristine hull. The real problem was just out of the bridge on the other side, a series of gardens run straight down to the canal and over the years there have been various things built into the water that have been long forgotten. This means that just below the water's surface, there are many stone and slab like obstructions that stick out at a right angle. Not good at the best of times, but certainly not what you want to see yourself heading towards right in time to scrape away a fresh coat of paint.

After making it perfectly all the way to barely a hundred foot from mooring, I was thrown into a sudden panic. I handed the tiller to Helena as we veered towards the bank, we had no steering control due to the fact we were in a bridge, so had no space to move either side. I grabbed a huge stick from my pile of uncut kindling wood on the roof, and walked down the side of Tilly to the front, before jabbing away at the bank. Being the start of summer the bank was overgrown with reeds and bushes, so it was a precarious balance of me trying not to fall off the thin step on Tilly, and not let the stick slip from its grassy grip. I heaved with all my might and the bow shifted away to the centre of the canal, this in turn started the stern on a direct collision course with the underwater trouble, so I shuffled down to the back. Stick still in hand, I was wildly shouting out frantic and contradictory tiller commands to a less than amused shipmate. Another huge heave saw us realign out towards the centre of the canal, and by a matter of two to three inches, we avoided a real underwater crunch.

Mooring at Weston Rhyn a minute later, it was a job just about well done. I decided to enjoy a relaxing few days in that spot, before the time came to head up to my first ever marina mooring at Chirk. A much calmer trip over the aqueduct and through Chirk tunnel, saw the remaining few miles of the trip peacefully glide away. So ended my first narrowboat hull blacking experience.

As luck would have it, as I am editing this book for the final time before release, Tilly is back in the dry dock being blacked. Literally as I write these words, she is out of the water with a coat of paint drying. I know this for certain as only an hour ago I was speaking to the person doing the work on the phone, so this is almost a real time account of my second hull blacking experience!

I decided to take Tilly back to Whixall, two years after the initial paint job. This time I made the trip on my own, showing a number of things, mainly that I don't feel the need to have to have somebody else onboard every time that I do anything slightly different, such as going through lift bridges. I arrived at the marina on the evening before I was booked into the dry dock, spending a very quiet night inside the marina, very quiet apart from some rowdy crows at five in the morning, the joy of being so close to nature! I was caught off guard by the arrival of the marina staff in the morning, but had luckily gone through my process of "dock proofing" any fragile items onboard. Seeing Tilly in the dry dock as the water was pumped out at an extremely slow rate, was quite a tense time. I relaxed when I realised how ridiculous I was being as she sat on the railway sleepers, and was out of the water in about as gentle a transition as I could have ever imagined.

This time as well as blacking, a hole in a cooling pipe underneath the boat is also being repaired. Getting up close and personal with the underside of the stern (the "swim" area) has done nothing to soothe my thoughts on how impermanent and fragile a boat is in the scheme of things. Blotches of rust all over the general area below the waterline were quite alarming to see, but important to be completely aware of for future reference and maintenance. The elements taking their toll as time rolls on, as sure as the steady flow of the canal.

Marina Life

As summer took hold of 2013, my first full calendar year afloat, I began my first and so far only "proper" marina stay, a two month period that gave me a lot to think about. The previous year I had only just arrived in the Llangollen area as the summer rush reached its height. Redecorating the interior of a boat over a period of weeks, that saw hundreds of boats going past, was an experience that taught me to appreciate the calm waters of winter when they came. I was keen to be off the main canal and in a marina for the peak holiday months, not only for its lack of waves and rocking, but also because even before the traffic had got anywhere near the level of the summer holidays, I had already been hit by three separate boats. None were serious incidents, but those three were just the ones that I had been onboard to witness, and after getting her hull freshly painted I was hoping to let Tilly remain tidy looking for as long as possible.

The day of moving into the marina was an overcast, damp day with drizzle hanging in the air, a normal British summer day. With the help of Helena (again) we made our way through Chirk, over the aqueduct, through the tunnel and then up the short stretch of canal, edged by a miniature valley of trees before reaching the marina entrance. This was another tense moment, for the first time ever, I was about to enter a full marina to try and negotiate to a mooring spot of my own.

We stopped at the first jetty and a member of staff pointed us in a general direction to travel before walking down to meet us at our mooring. In a true demonstration of the pace of narrowboat life, he reached the mooring long before us. In a true demonstration of my life, even with his instruction I still started to go down the wrong way, out of a choice of two. Trying to reverse slightly with one side being an overgrown reedy and grassy bank, while the other side was made up of other peoples' boats, I took the decision to back into the grassy tangle. Luckily, once again with the help of what can only be described as a big stick from the yet to be cut firewood on the roof, I was able to free us when we became stuck, and point us into the space between the rows of boats, allowing a fairly simple mooring.

Stepping off Tilly to tie the ropes for the first time gave me a momentary wobble, as I stood on the floating jetty and felt it sink slightly below my weight. That first unsteady step was the start of my marina life. It proved to be quite an interesting experience, especially when I ended up spending so much time away from Tilly too.

When I first moored in the marina there were two empty spaces between Tilly and the path leading up a steep bank to the marina car park, on the other side there was another empty space, then an unoccupied boat. I could not have been happier, in a silent marina with no passing traffic apart from a few people passing by on foot heading to their own boats, and the new, interesting scenery of dozens of boats moored up everywhere I looked. The great benefit of living in a marina however, goes beyond peace and quiet.

Having every amenity a boater could want, almost within reach of your window in some cases, was fantastic. I was seconds away from water and electricity if I wanted it. New gas bottles could be bought from the marina shop, and diesel could be topped up on your way in or out of the marina. Of course the all important cassette toilet emptying facility was also about two minutes walk away, that is one facility you don't want quite as close as the others.

After a few days of settling in, and realising that I should really close both of the blinds in the front of Tilly at night, I was over the moon with my new slightly more permanent home. A few weeks of fantastic summer weather followed, which allowed me to walk up the country lanes and really explore the area between Chirk, Llangollen and Glyn Ceriog, that sit just on the outskirts of where I could comfortably, regularly walk to. Add the two wheels of my bike and I suddenly found myself on some fantastic new cycling routes, that allowed hours of almost uninterrupted countryside pedalling. Moving up to four wheels on my mountain board (basically a giant skateboard with brakes), I was in my element as the marina was situated at the bottom of a large hill, that had miles of perfect quiet roads curving around the hill at various inclines. With the weather on my side, a fixed place to call home, and easy access to everything I needed from water to a bus ride, marina life was perfect.

An unexpected pattern emerged though. All this was taking place over the main summer months, which led me to suddenly having many opportunities to look after empty houses as relatives went on their holidays. I found that repeatedly my mother's house, father's house and grandparents' house, were all in turn in need of a caretaker for a couple of nights here and there. Cats needed feeding, plants watering and parcels collecting. For the first time I had Tilly in what was a safe place, away from anyone other than marina residents, I could feel secure leaving her there, without the worry of the wrong person taking a chance on an empty boat. I took the opportunity to jump between multiple deserted houses and Tilly.

For several weeks of summer I could be found with even less of a fixed address than usual. Between four properties and Tilly, I would be surprised if I spent more than a third of my time at any one place. The sheer amount of biking and walking that I was able to fill my days with, also added to the sense of not really existing anywhere. The freedom from the inherent slight concern over Tilly's welfare that the marina gave me, allowed me to live like this happily, and was one of the unexpected side effects of choosing to tie up ropes that I would not untie for six weeks.

It would be wrong for me to paint a picture of a flawless experience with nothing but sunshine and summer fun. As mentioned previously, when I first entered the marina Tilly was the only boat in four moorings, this did not remain the case. It would be outrageous to enter a marina full of boats and not expect close neighbours at some point, first I gained a neighbour to the right. Not directly next door as there was a free space between us, but to the left, the side on which Tilly was tied to the thin floating jetty, I also gained a neighbour. Our boats were about three feet apart with the wooden gangway our only separation. Suddenly one side of Tilly only had windows looking directly into another person's boat, while the other side looked out on the full length of the other boat slightly further away.

Mooring up side by side is standard practice in marinas, and exactly what I had been expecting, but the way the experience changed once this had happened was as unexpected as the spell of good weather had been. Suddenly I went back to having one set of curtains closed all the time, as if I was on the towpath. The extremely close proximity was something that I could not get to grips with.

When you place two boats next to each other, there is an instant change in how private you can be. With windows facing each other it is easy enough to close the curtains and take yourself back out of sight, but not so easy to deal with the noise issue. No matter how quiet you are it is impossible not to be overheard at some point, and also impossible not to over hear things too. In the dead of night a television becomes the loudest sound in the world, as does a barking or even just a growling dog. A conversation in a doorway becomes a public meeting, and after my fourth time of waking up to voices at five-thirty in the morning, I started to set my alarm for slightly later than normal to compensate. At the best of times I am a very light sleeper, so I was particularly concerned over these unintentional wake up calls.

This is not a problem that can really be helped, unless you and your neighbours can live in total silence, without making a sound! Neither people, nor marinas could ever be blamed, it is just the way that it is. The floating jetties also added an interesting issue into the experience. When it is just one boat on one side of the jetty, it really doesn't matter that it is not a solid fixed platform. You step onto and off your boat and as your entire weight moves from one to the other, the platform can rise and fall a good few inches, which, in turn can really give your boat a good wobble. When you add a second boat tied to the other side however, things start to get interesting.

If you or your neighbour jump off without thinking, then the residents onboard the other boat will find themselves in an earthquake simulator, going from perfect stillness to suddenly having everything lurch to one side, and then slowly rock back to a neutral position. Experiencing this at random intervals, not least in the small hours of the morning, makes sure that you don't forget you are on a boat. Once I had realised what was going on, I tried to get on and off as gently as I could, something that was particularly difficult to do delicately first thing in the morning, as I tried to also get my bike on and off the stern in silence.

These minor issues aside, the marina life experiment was greatly enjoyable even though it happened in a period, that admittedly saw me spend far less time than I expected living in a marina. The confidence it gave me to leave Tilly unattended for so much time was key to getting out and doing so much in terms of my my walking, biking and house sitting, and enjoying the outdoors in some great places with fantastic weather. The convenience of having every facility I could ask for on the doorstep took away all thoughts of running out of water, or even worse filling up a toilet. A community of experienced boaters surrounding you, with many stories and experiences of their own, a great pool of knowledge to draw from, or even just a group of friendly faces to give a morning wave and "hello". Much of life in a marina is what you want it to be. For me, coming into a fixed position from continuously cruising for almost a year, I found the simple life in many ways became even simpler when the "boating" element of living on a boat was removed.

The travelling part of boat life however is not something I would want to live without for very long. Even just a short boat trip once a week, the experience of moving to different places and waking up to different views, is still too much of a joy to me to want to give it up, even in return for the benefits of a marina. The emptiness of the canals in winter also offers some of the most private and peaceful places I could ever hope to live, while still holding on to some element of everyday society passing by your windows.

Slow Me The Money

The issue of money is a source of endless questioning and some fascination, both to the people I know in my day to day life, and the people who have stumbled upon my videos online. Questions such as, "what do you do for a living? How many hours do you work? How do you afford it?" are all common, and often I feel that people don't believe me when I tell them that I work part time in a supermarket, and find that the wage is more than enough to sustain my lifestyle afloat.

When I first entered the real world of work seven years ago, I worked every hour I could get, I am not really sure why. I would then invariably spend huge amounts of money each month on games, consoles, gadgets and many other things that marked me out as an obsessive nerd. After suddenly finding myself taking frequent walking holidays to Scotland, and dozens of day trips to various Welsh mountains, I had a thought confirmed to me. I had known all along that the endless stream of games and gadgets was little more than a distraction and that there was something more to life, getting out and experiencing this first hand, merely acted as the confirmation to truly make me see what I wanted, there wasn't more to life, there was less.

In late 2009 I took a decision to cut my working hours drastically and went from regularly doing forty hours or more a week, to just sixteen. I have never looked back. Without a car, and at that point not really interested in my bike, I started to spend my five days off a week out walking the local countryside. I put hundreds of miles a month under my feet, discovered a remarkable amount of hidden places of incredible beauty on the doorstep, and frequently got lost with no panic or worry, as I had seemingly all the time in the world to find my way back. Sometimes I would walk two, twenty mile circuits in two days, sometimes I would walk a similar seven mile route five times in a week. I did not realise it at the time but I was setting the tone for the life that I had truly wanted to live all along, a life of simplicity, enjoying the natural world and stopping every so often to write a few words in my little black book.

I have always enjoyed writing, on and off I had never really stopped since they first gave me a pencil and taught me how to write my name at school. My college years saw tens of thousands of words written in a story, that to this day I am glad I wrote, but also glad I never tried to publish. I was told at one point by a college tutor that it was extremely unlikely that I would have any success as an author, and should leave it and focus on finding a real job. A very confidence inspiring sentiment, that I wish I had been able to shake off as a timid seventeen year old. The years of short story writing and poetry that followed, in sporadic moments of inspiration and flurries of activity were thoroughly enjoyable. Certainly not the best things ever written. As I settled into part time life, my love of writing not only grew back to its former strength, but surpassed it and flourished during my new surplus of free time and thousands of yearly miles walked. Writing became what I wanted to do once more.

Although this talk of writing may seem a little off topic, the significance of the period of my life in the two years prior to my decision to buy a boat, is profound. As I got older my thoughts turned to how I would ever be able to live a life on my own and afford somewhere to live. I was distraught at the idea of having to go back to working full time for another forty years, hoping I would live to retirement, only to discover that with my best years of health a thing of distant memory I could not enjoy the long awaited release of a pension. Job hunting revealed very few options, potential low cost housing was still too expensive, and the topic of an independent life was a depressing and hopeless one.

I have told and retold the story of how the narrowboat idea came to me. After having my second hernia and being generally down about life, my friends (once again Helena and Ollie) invited me to go on a canoe with them at a local stretch of canal. I was unable to do any paddling due to the recent operation, but still found the trip fantastic. As we paddled past a narrowboat with a "for sale" sign in the window, Helena said a passing comment in jest: "There you go Dan, you could live on a boat!" Or words to that effect. My curiosity was too much and I started to spend a lot of time looking at boats for sale online. It seemed like the perfect idea, I could live out in the countryside, change my scenery and walking and biking trips whenever I wanted, and most pressing and immediate of all I could actually afford it.

The fact that it was an affordable option in a world of seemingly impossible home ownership grabbed my attention, and as my current situation afloat shows, kept it. As time went on I decided it was too good an opportunity to miss. A completely different lifestyle, yet also one I had been attempting to live already, based in my mother's home. The ample free time to actually enjoy life out in the countryside was vital, or half of the magic of living on a narrowboat would have been lost to me. When I realised that part time hours would be more than enough to sustain me I knew that a narrowboat was going to feature heavily somewhere in my near future.

The biggest cost associated with living on a narrowboat is of course buying the boat itself. I hope that over the next few paragraphs I will be able to illustrate just how low my general living costs are, which itself enabled me to confidently spend the initial lump sum on Tilly. I have often been quizzed about whether I had a helping hand off my parents to buy my boat. When I reply that all I had was £20 off my mum to go to a pub on the return journey, and the same £20 sum and instruction off my dad, I am used to the surprised responses.

After a short period of haggling, I ended up paying £11,000 for Tilly. Was this a good price? How much a boat is worth can be argued without end. There are so many factors to consider from its condition above and below the waterline, the engine condition, and any major work that may need doing in the near future. Internal features too come into play, apart from all the working parts such as plumbing, gas, electricity there is also the decor and state of the living area to think about. If a boat is laid out in a way that one person likes but another hates, and will spend a fortune renovating and moving components around, then that alone can start to make different people's views on a boat's value vary by hundreds maybe thousands. I would argue that a good price for a boat is different to every set of eyes that look upon it. For me buying an old boat and having all the time I could ask for to paint her up and change the carpet and internal fittings on a limited budget, meant that £11,000 was worth dealing at. A year and a half later I could not have had such an incredible experience without the initial payment and if I had known how it would turn out, would have had no problem paying the asking price.

The important thing that I must stress as we head into a look at the living costs onboard Tilly, is that she is a very small boat even by narrowboat standards. At only thirty foot in length she is just over half the length of many narrowboats that you will see, which are often in the fifty to sixty foot range. The significance of size is vital to understanding how hugely varied the costs of life afloat can be from one person/boat to another. Many of the costs involved such as mooring fees, boat licensing and hull blacking are charged based on a per foot system, which inevitably starts to make bigger boats a lot more expensive than smaller vessels.

At this point I would like to note that the following costs and prices are based on my experience during 2013, as with all things, prices will change with time so current costs are definitely worth looking into properly if you are considering a life afloat. Once again I will say that I live on a TINY boat, which helps me to keep the costs very low indeed, obviously on anything charged per foot, but also less obviously, when it comes to things like having less space to keep warm with heating.

The first cost that you must account for is the annual boat license. Some people misunderstand this and think that it is similar to a driving license. It is not a test, it is more like a permission slip to allow you to use the waterways. In order to get one you must have a boat that meets the requirements of the Boat Safety Scheme (BSS). The Canal and River Trust (CRT) who have recently replaced British Waterways as the governing body of most of the inland waterways, describe this as an equivalent of an MOT for a car. A certificate lasts for four years before a boat needs a new survey, and depending on who you have survey your boat, it could cost between £120 and £180 maybe more or less depending on how lucky you are. I have been lucky with Tilly in two ways, firstly she had three years left on her certificate when I bought her, and secondly my friend and colleague from work is a boat surveyor (so I know who will be checking Tilly out when the time comes!)

There is one other very important requirement before you can purchase a boat license, insurance. Insurance for a boat, as with many other forms of insurance is yet another cost that can vary wildly from boat to boat or by company. For Tilly as a small twenty-six year old boat, I paid exactly £100 for my 2013 insurance. A small saving on the 2012 costs which was a fraction over £104. However during 2014 and now for 2015 my insurance has been a steady £105.

Once you have your BSS certificate and insurance, you can then purchase a license, here I will refer to my license which lasts for twelve months but they do not have to go from January to December. They can start at any time and are often based on when the boat was first placed in the water on construction. For 2014 my boat license fee was £561.97. By far the largest single cost of the year. For reference, if I was on a fifty-two foot boat it would have cost £773.08.

Now we have the three necessary costs, insurance (£100-£105), BSS (if we say is an average of £150 every four years) and a boat license (£561.97), our total figure for unavoidable costs is an annual figure in the region of £660-£700. Not a bad starting point for an entire year. There are however, of course many extra costs to consider. The biggest unknown cost is that of maintenance, you can budget a few pounds here and there for semi regular jobs like an oil change or fuel filter replacement, but as with all engines there can be any number of things go wrong. Luckily I have not had any major costs on this front. One of the biggest things that you could ever need doing is the replating of the hull, where you have new sheets of metal cover all, or part of the boat from the waterline and below. This can cost thousands, but should not need doing for at least a decade on a new boat depending on circumstances.

The major maintenance to be done is blacking the hull. This consists of having the boat out of the water, scraping the paint on the hull away, and cleaning it up then repainting. This is to preserve the hull and fight the onset of rust as best as possible. I have been told by dozens of people that this should be done either every year or two years, then dozens more people have said every three years and every four years, a couple have said they only do it every five years. Personally I intend to have it done every two years, the first of these occurred in the summer of 2013, the job cost £530 to complete. The blacking can be completed by yourself, but it could cost a couple of hundred pound to have your boat out of the water to begin with, being charged on a per foot basis. I felt that it was worth it to have experienced narrowboat experts do the entire job and not have to worry about it. However on a large boat the cost can easily be well over £1,000 which may make you think differently about whether or not you want to get your hands dirty!

The remaining costs then start to become more related to everyday life and far less fixed. For example a £30-ish gas bottle every now and then depending on your usage, bags of coal in the winter depending on how much wood you can personally come across. In my case with an ever expanding range of legitimate wood sources from family and friends, I have found my fuel cost go down over time but with the boat being kept warmer than ever. Diesel for the engine costs me around £50 a year, but a frequent, long distance, traveller could see a few hundred pounds go on that without thinking twice. If you want to spend all of your time in a marina it could cost thousands. On Tilly I could stay in one particular marina for a year at just about the £1,000 mark. Over winter however, I have paid for a full five months towpath winter mooring over the past two seasons. At a cost of barely over £40 a month or £200 in total for one season and then around £225 for the following season; I could have avoided this entirely and continued cruising, so completely optional are some costs if you want them to be.

To sum up these as a total for my personal life afloat, is to give an example of extremely cheap narrowboat life. An extremely low and most definitely the exception not the rule level of cost! The total costs I had for 2013 looked like this: License £561.97, Insurance £100, Full term of winter mooring £200, 8 bags of coal for the winter £72 and a rounded up £50 for diesel costs. This is an overall cost of £983.97. You could subtract £200 for winter mooring as an option, but it is something that I hope to regularly enjoy. You could also divide the cost of blacking by the years interval that you intend to carry it out, and add that to the yearly total as well, and about £35 to go towards the Boat Safety Scheme every four years.

Even with my added costs of mooring, the total price being under £1,000 during 2013, explains in an instant how I am able to work part time and continue to enjoy one or two luxuries. 2014 was a similarly low cost year weighing in at just over £1,000.

Now, in 2015 however Tilly is already out of the water again for blacking and a (hopefully) small bit of maintenance, so again I will find a huge bulk of my boat costs for the year happening in one go. Grasp the nettle!

The stress and worry that is lifted when money is not a constant worry, is a part of the lifestyle I have built that is worth far more than any physical element. Giving up the idea of getting a house, cars, and such things, has also meant giving up the idea of having a huge mortgage, loans, monthly bills etc. For that release from worry and perpetual work, I am truly grateful to have had the idea before it was too late and I was stuck in the cycle.

Some people have said that their boats cost them as much as their houses did. As shown briefly above, costs can vary in their thousands, A huge boat on a permanent mooring with an address, a car parked nearby and sometimes even a small patch of land may seem perfect, and in fact be perfect to many. For me though, the joy of mooring up, sometimes miles from the nearest boat and opening the curtains to nature itself in the morning, is the heart of my lifestyle... and it is cheap!

A Love Letter to the Canal

While I was editing the original version of this book and deciding what needed to be added, changed or taken away, I decided that I wanted the final section to be its own thing. Rather than a summary of the book, I wanted to break with any formality and just write about how I am feeling, now that the third anniversary is upon me. What follows turned into a love letter to the canal more than anything else. These boat life books that I write, have been (and still are) one of my favourite things to spend my time doing. It is the written form of what my friends and family have to put up with periodically… me going on and on about boats and things that have happened on the canal! To round off this book, I have let my fingers go wildly at the keyboard for a few thousand words, and do just that… go on and on about boating! So here is everything that I am thinking and feeling, about narrowboat life and my time on the canal, right now.

After three years onboard Tilly, I can honestly look back and say that these have been the happiest years of my life. I am lucky to be able to say that there have been many good times previous to my boat life. Events such as camping at the foot of a mountain, then walking up it first thing the following morning, then proceeding to do the same thing, day after day, in the middle of Scotland. Wandering off the local roads from my mother's house, to vanish into the countryside for hours on end, returning only after walking thirty-two miles on a scorching day, whether out with friends or walking under a star filled sky to set up my telescope, completely alone and in total silence, I have been lucky to have even a tenth of the experiences I have had.

Even earlier memories stay with me as cherished moments, my school years of practical jokes and hi jinx without a care in the world, accidentally setting off a water pressure bottle rocket in an empty classroom, laughing till I cried at the smallest things, or spending my holidays at my nan and grandad's house, causing chaos for six weeks straight!

All these moments and countless others have marked out my life up until the age of twenty-five. Of all the moments in my life that I thought were pivotal, it wasn't until the day that I bought Tilly that I truly had an important milestone to measure my life from. The signing of the documents to say that I now owned a boat, was the moment of truth, to see if my dreams of being able to live affordably, actively and most of all, enjoyably, was a pure fantasy or not.

Three years on and hundreds of miles boated, thousands of miles walked and cycled and a few dozen miles kayaked, I can say that I would be happy to relive those three years for the rest of my life. After the initial steep learning curve of buying a boat with only a days hire boat experience of the canals, things did not only settle down and become easier due to my ongoing experiences and education, by trial and error. They also got easier because I started to grow up.

I would never go so far as to say that I really act my age, but what I have learned from my early times onboard Tilly has been vital to my future happiness and peace of mind. What is really important in my life? All of the worrying that I did about Tilly, the obsessive panic over leaving her for even a few hours when I first bought her, refusing to not sleep on her every night for the first fifty days, even though for years I had spent at least two nights a week at my friends' house!

The original period of worry over everything boat related, was almost the opposite of what I had wanted boat life to be, instead of having a boat to go off exploring in different areas and use as a base to "keep all my stuff in", Tilly was instead becoming a worry that was stopping me going off and doing all those things.

I am not sure if I could pinpoint an actual event or moment that my attitude changed, and I got back on track with living the relatively worry free lifestyle that I had envisioned in the run up to my boat life. It was more of a gradual thing, a steady build up of shaky confidence. Even to this day I still worry about Tilly, a lot more than I should, if I am not onboard. The difference is, now I don't feel the need to get my nearest friend to bike down and have a look while I am at work!

Casting my mind back to those early days seems like a memory from another lifetime long ago, yet at the same time, I feel as if barely a moment has passed since then. Whenever I talk with what I often refer to as "real boaters" who have decades of experience, I can't help but feel that I have merely taken a couple of baby steps into life afloat.

Those few steps that I have taken though, have been life changing, shifting my ideas of what is important, what is possible in the modern age, and what my future may or may not become. Above all else it has been thoroughly enjoyable to experience so much of the countryside before my ever approaching thirtieth birthday. If for any reason I had to stop my boat life and never see the canal again, I would be more than grateful to have already spent so much time with it as my ever changing garden. If I could write down every amazing rural encounter with wildlife, scenery, weather, boats and of course people, then it would make for a very very long read.

With the benefit of hindsight I can now see that the moments captured in this book, particularly the trip down the Montgomery Canal and my stay in Chirk Marina, are from that time of change in my own personal attitude, and the true beginning of my appreciation for what Tilly has allowed me to do. Without my obsessive worry over Tilly herself, and of engine problems and all sorts of fears, I would never have been able to look back and think "What an idiot I was, this is amazing!" and realise what was right in front of me all along.

While Tilly was moored in Chirk Marina, I attended the wedding of a close friend at a venue right next to the canal. I was extensively quizzed about boats and the canal by another long term friend who I had not seen for a while, as we watched the passing holiday boats. We stood at the canal-side on a perfect sunny day, an activity that for almost everybody at the wedding was a rare moment of peace. As we talked, this became apparent and I realised that where the wedding reception was taking place for its beautiful canal based location, was a place that I had already spent weeks moored up at, literally in line of sight. The usual elements of conversation such as "I can see why you have done it" and "it is not really a life for me" came up, the mixture of reactions and questions all being valid and important to consider for future plans in my life. The common theme that everybody could agree on, was definitely, what a lovely place the canal in the area was. Whether you enjoyed it for a day, a few hours or for weeks on end.

Of all the times spent boating, sleeping, writing, walking, biking, kayaking, filming or whatever else I have been up to as a result of Tilly, it is always in conversations with others that my canal love is demonstrated. The amount of times that I have caught odd glances, as I talk more excitedly or louder at each random thing that pops into my mind when speaking about the canal, is evidence enough. But people tend to politely, and often probably in a state of bemusement, put up with me! These conversations are always best with someone who "gets it". Bouncing off each other, various friends and I have been able to talk for hours, starting on a simple outdoors theme and then building into all kinds of diversions. Plans for the future, directions and distances of canal, what to find there, and a lot of talk about how cosy a boat gets with a roaring fire at its heart.

What I was hoping to sum up with this talk about conversations, was the breadth of things that make up my boat life. To talk of a "typical" day would be impossible. Sometimes Tilly might not move for a week, instead I would see my days filled with cycling or walking. Other times I might boat twenty miles in a day and then practically fall into bed asleep. There doesn't have to be a specific plan, even if there was it would be unlikely to unfold as expected, and that is absolutely fine.

The fact that I can wake up in the morning and potentially have a day that involves, boating, biking, walking and kayaking is enough to make every day that I wake up onboard Tilly a blessing! It definitely keeps me entertained. This is all before even considering inviting friends and family onboard!

As time has gone on there have been many different people added into my life, traditionally I have always been very shy and reluctant to let many people into my floating home. Even with all my YouTubing, Facebooking and Tweeting, at my core I am pretty quiet and shy. I have been lucky to have crossed paths with many great people over the years and have started to let more people get closer and come on frequent Tilly trips. Most recently, a very good friend, also by the name of Dan and (my on again off again girlfriend of well over a year) Sarah, have been joining me for their first boating experiences.

Unlike my early trips with my close friends, I am no longer worried about travelling, wanting to grab the tiller off them every two minutes. Instead it is me who is saying, "Don't worry" as we drift around the canal at all kinds of unusual angles! Getting to share an empty winter canal with some of my best friends, sometimes multiple days a week, is more than I could have ever asked for. Making a short trip around a corner of canal to pick somebody up from a car park, before turning around and boating a bit further away, is the ideal way to spend the last light of the day. Mooring up, then watching the sun vanish and the stars come out, has already formed some of the best memories I am ever likely to have.

To find myself surrounded by other boaters in the summer, with decades more experience and a wealth of knowledge and memories that are beyond my understanding, is motivating to keep going, keep floating and keep striving for what the future of the canal may hold. What I have written here and look back on fondly, would not even be a footnote to the life of many people on the canal. If in thirty years time I can look back and have the experience that they have, then I would be a very happy man.

Then again, if I can look back in another three years, and have more memories similar to those already made, I will consider myself extremely lucky.

As the previous paragraphs show, I really can't sum up my boating experience in anything like a short, coherent manner! So instead of trying to wrap things up nice and neatly with a final paragraph, I would like to share with you something that I wrote, seemingly a lifetime ago. It is a diary entry from Tuesday 24th July 2012. The day that I bought Tilly and stayed on her for the first time.

The excitement that I felt on that glorious summer day was overwhelming, and in constant competition to the nerves, and sense of relief that I was sat for the first time ever in a home that was truly mine. The following years have been amazing, greater than any expectation I could have placed on them. The good times hugely outweighing the glitches and moments of panic. The lifestyle I have been able to live as a result is a reward in its own right. I have been lucky enough to enjoy a large amount of free time to truly enjoy the canals and surrounding areas. Experiencing the passing of the seasons and many miles of water passing under the bow, marina life, towpath travelling and even the madness of the summer rush, have all created memories that I will treasure, both in my obsessive diary writing and in my heart. To sum up narrowboat life is not easy, but to live it has been a dream.

I will hand you over to my very first boating diary entry now, with the final thought, that had I known how good the adventure was going to be, I may have dared not take it!

My first day onboard, in the perfect countryside surrounding the village of Great Haywood...

Got Her! 24/07/2012

I had a phone call from the marina at about nine-thirty this morning. I could have Tilly at noon. Thanks to an impromptu lift in the car from my nan and grandad I was able to make it there in time.

As luck had it we arrived moments before the current owner, he immediately took us in his car down to Tilly to show us around and explain a few of the features onboard, boiler, water pump etc. I call him the current owner but I suppose that is now me! He was a kindly type and managed to settle all of my main concerns about Tilly's innards in his Scottish accent.

After a short but information packed time onboard we drove back to the marina office, his wife had been busy signing all the relevant paperwork while we were out, this meant a quick handshake and they were off on their newly boat free life. I sat down and signed two or maybe three lines and that was it. At twelve-forty-four I walked out of the office with the keys in my hand and the title of boat owner.

Most of the afternoon was spent cleaning and tidying with the occasional moment of being absolutely overwhelmed by the day's events. After eating our first meal of crisps and sandwiches onboard my nan and grandad had gone home leaving me to settle in. I feel that without all the work to be done onboard I could have just sat down and cried for hours on end without ever knowing exactly why. Everything except the shower room and toilet is now rigorously cleaned, not necessarily tidy or presentable, but at the very least very clean.

It has been an incredible day for the weather too, blazing sun all day long. All windows and doors were open as far as they could be for the first four hours onboard, I need to get a hook on the stern door rather than using a bucket full of coal as a door stop!

As I write this the evening cool is coming, so only the back door and one stable door is open plus a few windows! A very warm day indeed. Looking around I can see a huge amount of small jobs that need doing. Painting, cleaning, tinkering with fittings and minor woodwork, I can't wait to get a clear run at fixing her up properly when we get home... I suppose I am home really, what a thought.

In mid afternoon I had a stroll down the towpath in both directions, loads of incredible boats around. I couldn't resist a walk around the village either, a lovely little place that I almost don't want to leave. The farm shop that is visible across the canal from the windows of Tilly was also on my agenda and some ginger biscuits were a "must buy". The time spent walking around was almost too perfect a scenario to be real.

While I have been writing this (around six in the evening), a few boats have passed and the odd sensation of having everything around you start rocking slightly was off putting, but something I feel I will soon be used to. There is a railway that runs along a bank past the farm shop and every so often a huge Virgin train will rocket along and reflect the sun straight into Tilly.

Earlier on while I was in the kitchen I could see dozens of fish swimming around outside, then perfectly timed, a dragonfly buzzed past and landed on the tip of the bow. It was the ultimate scene of being close to nature and just one of the moments today that let me know that I have wanted this life more than I ever dared to acknowledge, and that I am finally living the dream!

A Narrowboat and a Notebook

A Narrowboat and a Notebook

By Daniel Mark Brown

www.thenarrowboatlad.com

To all my friends and family who have helped me make my life what it is. To everybody who shouts hello from a boat or the towpath and to the YouTubers who keep me so busy!

Floating on By

My name is Dan Brown and I live on a narrowboat.

I wanted to start this book with a simple statement to sum up everything you are about to read, it doesn't get more blunt than that! After writing and proof reading the rest of this book those were the words that best describe the following pages. After two years afloat, hours of boat chat, thousands of words written on the subject and a consistent flow of videos posted online, I feel and hope that the following book is me "just talking about boat things". Conversational, casual chat moving from one thing to another. Talking about a few of the things I have noticed, learned and a lot of the things I have loved. With a vast resource of handwritten diaries I hope you will enjoy the few entries I have scattered into this short book.

For many years I have really enjoyed writing. Not always writing as we imagine it. Not sitting down at a desk writing page after page for hours on end, mainly the opposite. A quick diary entry scribbled down secretly by torchlight as a young teenager, terrified of my parents seeing my secrets. A rough poem written in scruffy writing in a pocket notebook filled with battered pages from the wear and tear of use out in the countryside.

From my early twenties until the present, my twenty-seventh birthday just passed, I have written more than ever, even more than my school years. Short stories, poems and diary entries, even some utterly random descriptive pieces that have no relevance to anything or context of any kind.

My love of the outdoors has been a strong theme in all I have written. Getting out and walking, biking or getting up to any kind of mischief outside rules the rest of my life. It was an attempt to find a low cost way of living and if possible living out in the "middle of nowhere" that led me to be a twenty-five year old narrowboat dweller. Working part time in a supermarket and having a floating home that I could move around some of the best countryside imaginable has given me not only the time but also the perfect environment to really let my writing grow to become a main pastime in my life.

As I sit onboard at my desk writing this brief introduction I have six pocket notebooks, two large hardbacks and many scraps of paper that document (in my admittedly terrible handwriting) the two years of my narrowboat life to date. Major events and good and bad days are of course listed and explained, but more importantly so are my thoughts. The joy, the struggles and any feelings that popped up while I had a pen in my hand at each particular moment. It is this that I want to share with you in this book. Not a list of events but my actual experience of narrowboat life.

These diaries contain entries that are sometimes hundreds of words and sometimes simple two line summaries. They let me know that on Friday 7th September 2012 I went collecting wood from the wild for the first time ever and felt ecstatic at the thought of being heated by wood I picked up from the ground. Similarly, I can look back and see my excitement at seeing several good shooting stars from the stern on Thursday 7th November 2013. I can also look more recently and be reminded of the nervous excitement and fascination I had when the UK was hit by a severe storm on Wednesday 12th February 2014. The terror of trees being blown down all around the vicinity but also my reluctance to stay inside and not experience the gales and driving rain first hand. Walking my puncture stricken bicycle seven miles into Oswestry to fix it at my mum's house is also listed for the next day!

I have recently noticed that I have picked up an odd habit when I return back to Tilly, my humble thirty foot narrowboat home, after a day at work or even just a day out. I will walk down the towpath and have a small sense of relief when she first comes into sight and everything is how I left it. More recently, when I get back onboard I will sometimes not even unlock the back door for ten minutes. Instead of going straight in I stand around and shift positions on the stern, carefully walk down the gunwales, the narrow ledges on either side of the boat, and just stare at both my surroundings and Tilly herself.

I think that the feeling of being able to rest and feel safe at home could be a part of this but whenever I catch myself in this quiet time I have no particular thoughts or worries. I am literally just enjoying being on a boat. Often the only boat in sight and surrounded by nothing but water, trees, farmland and the vast array of wildlife that is the true owner of the area. When it rains I still find myself in these blissful daydreams, if I am already soaked through from a long bike ride then a bit more rain can't hurt.

I find myself in similar reflective and quiet moments in the evenings after I have finished whatever grand feast was on the menu that day. Sometimes soup and crusty rolls, pasta and salad, pizza and salad or even something as challenging to the chef as a curry or a tex-mex selection. Full of food, dishes washed and sat at either my desk tucked into the top right hand corner or sprawled out on the sofa-bed that makes up either my living room or bedroom depending on the time of day. A moment of total relaxation, usually nothing but trees, fields or other stereotypical countryside scenes through the windows and the sound of birds from all directions. True bliss.

I have been known to listen to history podcasts for hours on end while I occasionally shift position or view. Just enjoying the cosy little environment that I can truly call my own. At only thirty foot in total length with ten foot outside as a large open stern area and another five foot open at the front, Tilly offers just fifteen foot of indoor living space. A tiny home but just about right to act as a base to launch my outdoor adventures from wherever she is moored up. In this small indoor space I can see almost everything I own. The back door to the side of a walled off bathroom with toilet and shower, along from that my sofa-bed, with a small space to walk between that and the cupboards opposite. The fireplace holds my unusual cylindrical woodburner which is designed perfectly for placing a saucepan on top of for cooking. Next to this the gas cooker with hobs and oven, then my food cupboard finally meeting my writing desk. Opposite the cooker and desk is the kitchen sink and more storage cupboards below. That is the complete and not very grand tour of my humble home.

The small size definitely enhances the cosy factor when I am winding down at the end of the day. No matter how much I move around, the podcasts I love will still be audible and if the fire is lit the heat will definitely find you. The perfect way to shelter in the bad weather but also the perfect floating summerhouse in the good. It is this cosy little place to call my own, floating through the sort of rural environments that would fit in well with scenes from The Lord of the Rings, that has over the past two years been slowly calming me down to its pace. Even to the point that I am now happy to just stand around on the stern or sit around inside as described and enjoy the simple inherent experience of narrowboat life. Does it always go to plan? No, rarely in fact. Are there problems, worries and stresses? Of course, but the way I now react and deal with things has become one of acceptance, relative calm and hopefully sense. Three things that going back only a few years I had no experience of.

What is my narrowboat life experience so far? Hopefully I will be able to share with you some of my own personal thoughts and feelings in the pages ahead. I always wished for a simple life long before a narrowboat was even a thought, little did I know that I was so suited to the simplicity or that it could open up so much to me.

I am lucky to have so many of my experiences documented in my handwritten diary entries. Many things I would have otherwise forgotten jump right back to the front of my mind as I read them. With this source of events, thoughts and feelings, I have put together the following book that I hope will give an insight into my life afloat, how I live it and a few words on various aspects of my attempt to *live the dream*. This book is me doing what I love, talking about boat life!

Two Years Afloat and Counting

At the release of this book I will have been living onboard Tilly for almost two years. One year and eleven months to be precise. What a time it has been. People often ask me if I think my time afloat seems to have gone fast. The answer is definitely a "Yes", the time seems to have flown by, but at the same time I feel as if I have always had a boat. The memory of what it was like to not have my own floating bit of freedom and peace is fading fast, both the good and the bad.

Tilly was (and still is) my first ever home away from my parents, this alone gives her a special place in my heart and also the added joy and novelty of being the first time I ever had a place that was truly my own. If you had spoken to me as a teenager, I don't think I would have been able to believe, or even really understand that my first home would be a boat. It is even less likely that the person who told a teenage, video-game obsessed, near recluse version of myself would have ever believed I would be able to spend any prolonged period of time outdoors. Life works out in unexpected ways and throws obstacles and twists and turns at you when you least expect it. When at the age of twenty-five I stood onboard Tilly with the keys in my hand for the first time, it was a moment that I knew was life changing. The talk was over, the dreams were a thing of the past, life was happening.

My mind that had once been solely dedicated to scraping together enough money to keep a constant flow of games and technology into my room at my mother's house was instead filled with thoughts of the endless hours I could spend out boating, biking and walking in the countryside. Thoughts of what shelves or cupboards to buy to keep my old room looking tidy, were replaced by thoughts of how I would redecorate and reorder my entire home for the first time. Tiny though it was, I could not have been happier to have a home.

The initial months of learning how to boat from a point of almost total inexperience were tough. Getting stuck in locks, an overheating engine, and terror at what might happen every time I left her on her own at the side of the canal were a few of the mental and practical challenges. There were low points, moments that I was certain that I had made an awful mistake. These were often followed rapidly by high points, that seemed to bring a world of endless opportunity, the rapid contrasts between the extreme feelings demonstrating just how over emotional and invested in the events I was. A memory that has stuck in my mind for years as a turning point was near the end of my two week long maiden voyage and baptism of fire. Mooring up for the night after a long hard day of locks and overheating engines, I was particularly low.

My friend Helena was onboard for the trip and as we went about our evening meal in down spirits we were firstly boarded by a pirate... A four legged one rather than a one legged one though, a dog from a neighbouring boat deciding to join us. Spirits were lifted further when an occupant of the same boat fetched us two slices of chocolate cake, anything chocolate is bound to make things better in my book! While doing the washing up the final event to rally my spirits was looking across the canal to see a heron slowly creeping on the far bank. It is an example of how the simplest things can make all the difference, and how regardless of how bad I believed things to be, a few tiny moments could change my outlook on everything.

The evening of the dog, the cake and the heron is a story I have talked about ever since and mentioned repeatedly both online, face to face and in writing. The best of boat life, good people and great nature summed up in less than an hour. The following evening, everyone involved, and the animals would all be miles apart to enjoy their own branching and ever changing canal story. That is the basis that my life has followed ever since, enjoying nature of all kinds through all seasons and from a huge range of locations.

The close proximity to nature is something that I am extremely lucky to be able to enjoy on the Llangollen Canal. It is extremely rural and much of the canal's course through Wales and Shropshire runs through areas that I have been lucky enough to grow up visiting for day trips, and then in my early twenties, enjoy long walks and bike rides around. The canal may bring with it plenty of water based wildlife, but the general Shropshire countryside that stretches for miles around it is almost universally perfect. Areas of low hills, far stretching flatland and farms dotted around even more numerously than the many tiny villages.

Twisting country lanes that occasionally pass almost forgotten old industrial points of interest now make up my pleasant cycling commutes into work or trips to see my friends and family. The scene is as close to idyllic as I can imagine. When the weather is good and everything is running smoothly. Biking from an overheated boat to be met with a road that leads up seemingly endless rain soaked hills is definitely a slightly different experience to waking up to a beautiful day. Turning the boat by hand while a heron watches your movements from over a wide stretch of canal. Hopping on your bike to leave a scene like this, and experience amazing views for nearly all of the ride to your nan and grandad's house, is a great commute to have. When you find yourself arriving in time for homemade chips for lunch, it tips the balance from being a great morning into a perfect morning.

My narrowboat life is made up of a good mixture of the perfect and not so perfect. I am extremely lucky to have friends and family all around the canal. Some a ten minute walk away, some a twenty five minute bike ride... Although when I get a long way down the canal, I have been known to make that commute into two hour long epics, boat life can definitely keep you fit. Following a long watery road through the perfect countryside is my ideal life. The ability to jump on a bike and find a friendly bricks and mortar dwelling within minutes, is definitely a bonus. A fixed address for deliveries and somewhere to upload my endless stream of videos to YouTube are but two of the many benefits. The fact that I can cruise for thirty miles and end up only minutes away from another friends house in somewhere like Whitchurch is a blessing I am grateful for. Not only for the ability to occasionally pop onto dry land and watch Family Guy with a takeaway pizza, but also for the chance to get different people onboard and share the experience of boating on a good day. It also definitely helps to have somebody else onboard to share the difficulty of a bad day, luckily these are increasingly rare in my life.

Two years afloat and my life is settling down into a rhythm of boating, biking, walking and writing. Putting my fears and worries about almost everything to the back of my mind and getting out there to enjoy the world while I can. A sense of urgency sometimes takes over me to make the most of what I have now. Driven half by an obsession with how short life might be, how fate seems to find ways to trip us up, and by my own inability to sit still for five minutes, I have been blessed to be in this situation.

There are some periods of utter rootlessness. Not only in terms of moving the boat every day for a week in a fit of thinking "this view isn't quite perfect enough" or more urgently "better top up the water" or *even more* urgently "better empty the toilets!" As the seasons pass, I sometimes vanish even from the canal itself, for days at a time. Going off exploring over the summer, stopping at friends houses to get an early start walking somewhere into Wales or heading off to the coast to the family caravan two minutes from the sea. Being able to escape to multiple properties during the summer, as family and friends, and even friend's parents go on holiday leaving their houses empty, with pets to feed and plants to water has huge advantages too. The houses themselves are not the key, just like Tilly they can act as bases for walking and biking into even more areas than the already huge potential surrounding the canal. When the owners return, the house is left well stocked, and hopefully in as good a condition as they left it. By the time they step back in through their door I will have probably already unmoored Tilly and moved to another countryside spot to enjoy for a few days.

To say that spending a few days in a house located sometimes near to a town centre is the break from my normal life and that returning to the countryside on a boat is not the holiday, is an indication of how different my life has become. I used to love going on holiday to Scotland or Wales, either camping or caravanning, and getting to walk through new areas and up different mountains to see what the view from the top would reveal. Now those experiences are available all year long, minus the summer weather of course. Moving from place to place, meeting new people and walking down unknown roads with unknown destinations, I have no true distinction between holiday and normal life.

The joy of having a tiny narrowboat floating around somewhere on a canal is its own reward. I can tuck her away in a shady spot for a few days or head down twenty miles of canal in a day, both situations are experiences of "boating", yet completely different. That is why it is so difficult to sum up my two years onboard so far. I can draw comparisons to my life before Tilly but those are more a demonstration of how my life has changed rather than anything else.

I have always been into the outdoors, now I see more of it more frequently than I could have ever imagined, keeping physically fit is even more a part of my life than ever. As time has passed it is interesting that my general diet has "grown up". I have already mentioned my love of takeaway pizzas above, this will not be the only mention they get in this book I am sure. As much as I love pizzas, chips and all the classic unhealthy things, I find that these days I have them less and less frequently. The dominance of chocolate bars and junk food in my diet has been replaced by cereal bars bought in huge quantities when I get the chance. Walks down the towpath to local villages have seen me pick up fresh food and salads instead of a portions of chips, and my bag that was once weighed down by bottles of pop is more often filled with plain old water, and maybe some orange juice. My diet is the source of a few running jokes online which I have done very little to stop but as people have started to ask me to do more "proper" cooking videos it is clear that something is changing in my life.

Food, exercise, listening to audiobooks and podcasts, reading, writing, recording, all these things are completely separate from each other and nothing to do with boats. Yet all of these things are a part of my weekly life. Living on a narrowboat can be different to living in a house for many reasons, but I view everything in the same way that I have always done. Everything you do is "living your life", at work at home, or out walking. I may now live on a narrowboat but I am still also just *living*. It just happens that I have been lucky enough to live my dream!

One of the keys to this whole arrangement is how little money I spend on anything. I have recently found myself at the point of not wanting anything else in my life, I have my boat, bike, kayak and telescope. A couple of ageing gadgets, iPad and iPhone. With the low cost way I have set up my life, the vast majority of months now see my biggest spend being on food. In an unexpected twist I am now able to save more money than almost any other time in my life despite working only two days a week in a supermarket. Saving and plentiful free time are not things I have been able to enjoy at the same time in the past, and everybody who quizzes me on the subject tells me to make the most of it, especially those who are a little more mature in years. For the time being while everything is going well, that is exactly what I am doing. Make the most of what you have while you can.

A Tale of Two Winters

The first winter that I saw on a narrowboat began at the end of 2012. We had a little snow and I was able to enjoy the novelty of being on a boat surrounded by amazing snow covered canal scenery. This was a huge bonus to add to what was already a great experience to me, as the boating novice that I was. Having a fire roaring and logs crackling away throwing out a heat well beyond what was necessary, gave a cosy and safe feeling beyond anything I had ever experienced. The bitter cold trapped outside and the overwhelming heat that would hit you on entering from the winter air were two extremes that only served to make each other seem warmer or cooler.

The novelty of snowy scenery soon turned into a genuine difficulty as the consistently low temperatures led to persistent ice and a reluctance for the snow to melt. Waking up before seven in the morning to hop on a bike and ride five miles over icy roads in the dark was not ideal at all. Neither was the cancellation of bus services and blocked stretches of canal barricaded in with fallen trees.

As the winter progressed it threw the most snow I have ever seen in my life at the already scenic and hilly area of Shropshire along the Welsh Border. Tilly being repeatedly covered in six inches of snow and the towpath at some points being covered in knee depth snow and beyond. At the worst point Tilly was stuck miles away from where I wanted to be, the roads were a no go for cycling or even walking and there were no buses running... but I still can't say that I didn't love the experience! Waking up to find it very dark outside, only to open the curtains and discover the windows are actually covered by thick snow keeping the light out. Very cautiously holding onto the hand rail as I walked down the side of the boat, knocking the snow away with a mop, was inherently a wonderful experience despite the chimney throwing smoke into your face and the potential of slipping into a very cold canal.

Fast forward one year and the 2013-2014 winter has passed with only one morning bringing snow on the ground. Ice had also been almost non existent with icy days numbering in the single figures. The winter had a very mild temperature in general which kept things warm enough in the daytime hours for me to not bother lighting the fire until well into the evening for the majority of days.

It had been wet and overcast for a large percentage of the time but compared to my first winter, the second was like a tropical break. Over the start of 2014 huge storms, gales and rainfall brought ruin and devastation beyond anything in living memory to many areas of the UK. Seafronts and railways destroyed, lumps of Tarmac and huge sea defences were being washed aside as if nothing. Flooding for months on end throughout the South. There was carnage and genuine ground shaking destruction being delivered to both the coast and mainland. However apart from one two day long serious gale, the Shropshire and North Wales Border area that I had paid for winter mooring in, was almost utterly spared any trouble.

Seeing images of canals flooded to the extent that their courses were invisible as they merged with flooded fields. Muddy water that stretched as far as the eye could see was a sobering and terrifying glimpse at the potential for disaster if the situation rose northwards up the country. An image that struck me at just how much water there was down South was that of the top rails of a lock being the only visible part of the entire canal. To think of a lock being submerged conjures up a good few feet of flood water. When you consider that one side of the lock was probably around seven foot lower than the other, you start to build an image of potentially ten foot or a good couple of metres more water than there should be.

In an act of total indifference this weather left Tilly almost entirely alone. Having paid for a full five months of winter mooring on the towpath, I was lucky to not have to do any major travelling when the winds did set in. I was very grateful for this when the rain was particularly relentless at times. But having plenty of dry days and even sunny, dare I say warm days thrown in too, I was amazed at how much less fuel I was adding to the fire and how long my wood and coal supplies were lasting compared to the previous winter.

Being able to get out and enjoy myself while knowing I didn't have to worry about moving Tilly was a great bonus that I had from my mooring. I spent most of the time moored around the outskirts of a pub freshly reopened and renamed "The Poachers". Standing at around one and a half miles from the Welsh Border village of Chirk, I regularly walked the towpath and various footpaths around the area while picking up supplies (mainly pizzas, pop and bags of salad). There were plenty of days filled with little walks and bike rides around the local Chirk Castle grounds that also served the purpose of refilling the cupboards with something that was at least halfway to edible.

The village of Chirk was also a useful base to launch walks further afield from too. There is a relatively frequent bus service that runs from Chirk to Llangollen, one of my favourite of all the local Welsh villages. Llangollen is known for being a tourist hotspot and can get extremely busy at certain times of the year, but for me the real draw of the place is its location at the foot of the Berwyn Mountain Range.

The area is filled with undulating, mountainous landscapes quite literally as far as the eye can see even from some of the highest peaks. Miles upon miles of hills ranging from small steep hikes, to almost nine hundred metre high points at the end of morning long treks. Needless to say that with my background of walking for walking's sake I decided to use the uncommonly good winter weather to get a few of these mountains under my belt... or more accurately under my feet.

I made an effort to have at least one trip a week to Llangollen and found myself once again fulfilling some kind of stereotypical ideal lifestyle. I would wake up early to a boat just about kept warm by a dying fire, quickly get dressed and pick up my bag that had been packed the night before. Make sure the boat was tidy and in order to be a pleasant environment to return to, and then head out on the first mile and a half walk of the day to the local shop. Buy a fresh salad bag and cold bottle of pop or two to go with my already packed supply of cereal bars and chocolate, then head around the corner to the bus stop.

It is worth noting at this point that even though the bus ride was only around twenty minutes long, knowing that I had to get off the bus and then walk back another mile and a half to get to Tilly, certainly made the return journey seem longer after some of the particularly long and ill advised routes I had followed. The addition of three miles to each actual hill walk I did, certainly kept me fit.

Arriving in the centre of the village it was simply a case of walking for a couple of minutes before I would be starting an ascent of some kind. There is a picturesque castle in ruins known as Dinas Bran that sits almost in the village. Following some extremely steep roads and paths you can find yourself standing within an abandoned archway or in front of half a wall on top of a hill in no time and yet this still remains a very quiet place outside of the peak holidays. From the castle you can see miles of the mountainous terrain previously described and that is a comparatively low point in the area. Places with names like "The Panorama Walk" and "Worlds End" are wedged right next to, or at least nearby the ruins, which help to conjure up an image of why I love this area as one of my local places to get out with my boots during the winter.

I will very often spend hours out walking in no particular direction with no ultimate destination in mind other than to sooner or later end up where I started from. This is fine when walking country lanes or very small hills, but when it comes to bigger day long excursions things need to be taken a little more seriously and planned a little better. Unfortunately a decent sense of direction and good judgment of distance are two skills I have not picked up even after all these years. Off the top of my head I can't recall a single Llangollen walking trip that actually ended up going to plan. Some had to be cut short as I had bitten off far more than I could chew in terms of a single days hill walking. Others ended up nearly doubling in length due to the same inability to figure out just what the terrain would be like and how steep it would be.

My only defence is that I have to plan these trips using a giant foldout OS map inside a very small boat. In my old room at my mother's house there is a wall still covered by three large maps of the local area. Onboard however I have to fold out the sofa bed just to have a surface large enough to lay a map on flat, which in turn means that the living room becomes the bedroom and almost all other space has vanished! It is a poor excuse though and I often contemplate whether or not I don't quite pay attention deliberately to add a feeling of discovery into these walks.

Vanishing from contact ,and in many cases even just the sight of another human being for six to eight hours, has a great feeling of liberation for me. Getting back to nature and just enjoying the incredible surroundings and feeling of being such a tiny being in the shadow of vast mountains and hills that stretch to the horizon and beyond. It is a peaceful feeling and similar to the one I get from mooring up Tilly out of the line of sight of any other boats or houses. Over the winter when I sometimes don't see another boat for days at a time, the sense of quiet and peace is only rivalled by the prominence of the sounds of nature. From a random bird call or farm animal, to the inanimate, such as the wind in the trees causing the slight whistle effect that permeates and fills the air itself. The creaking of branches stripped of their leaves and the occasional drip or splash as some unknown object finds itself falling into the canal.

To be able to hop on a bus and leave a lukewarm boat, enjoy a full days walking, sometimes with a race against a setting sun to get back to civilisation. Popping into my favourite delicatessen to stock up on Vegetable Rolls and "Blue Cheese Bombs" to eat in the evening and following day. Then getting back onto the bus to drop me off ready for the final half an hour walk back down the towpath to Tilly is about as perfect a way as I can think of spending a sunny winter's day. So that is exactly what I did repeatedly throughout the final months of my winter mooring. The mild weather and lack of snow or ice made this possible, comfortable and enjoyable. Attempting these trips at some points during the previous winter would have seen me struggle to arrive at the bus stop, only to find there were no buses running anyway!

Winter is definitely a time for idyllic scenery with a warm cosy boat planted in its centre. It definitely also brings some pretty chilly nights and commutes if the weather is against you. There are however, few moments that I have enjoyed more than getting back to Tilly to find her bitterly cold, down a dark damp towpath, but with a waiting fireplace and stacks of wood ready to light as soon as possible...

Water's Whispering

Lonely boat, freezing under a star filled night.
Stone cold boat, hidden, no other boat in sight.
This solitary towpath walker is home,
An empty canal, winter makes itself known.

So dark a path, so silent a way to go,
So remote, yet so close, a strange place to know.
At an empty home, a dark stern door to pass,
The torch light shines off the familiar glass.

Through the door the boat remains a freezing shell,
Home late again, the cold cupboard doors do tell.
Cold metal fittings chill the bone like a knife,
Quick light the fire and bring the place to life!

The Community: On The Network and Online

Depending on the time of year and stretch of canal that you are on, the boating community can look extremely varied. There is a good reason for this, it is! To attempt to write a book about what a standard life on a narrowboat is, would be very difficult, if not impossible due to the fact that there are so many ways you could choose to live onboard. During my time both at the canalside and in marinas I have met people who travel huge distances across the country each year and also people who do not so much as leave their spot in their marina. That is the sort of variation in narrowboat lifestyle that can be found, each almost an entirely different way of life, but both just happen to be taking place on a boat.

With this in mind you can start to create a picture of how difficult it would be to define what the boating community is like, what I can do however is talk about my personal experience onboard. Spending most of my time out on the canal, both cruising over the summer months and stopping in one place to batten down the hatches and hope for the best during the winter mooring period from November to March, I meet a lot of people.

During the summer months the Llangollen Canal becomes filled with holiday boaters and the private boating and livaboard community tends to search for calmer waters, even a nature loving character like me has been known to dive into a marina for a few months! Being out on the canal during this period is still a wonderful experience, you may well be rocked around by passing boats, crashed into and scraped, but the amount of people about is great. The place is genuinely alive, if you can get good weather too then it almost takes on the friendly and neighbourly quality of an old street party. Walking down the towpath back to Tilly on a hot summers evening as dozens of holiday makers moor up or sit out on their sterns enjoying the weather, I find myself saying "hello" and greeting people every ten to twenty seconds at some points. Similarly, the amount of people out on holiday who will stop on the towpath and quiz me all about Tilly and living on a boat is incredible.

Being sat on a chair on Tilly's deck talking about various elements of narrowboating to a genuinely interested questioner is a great way to relax and enjoy the summer evenings... even if I can almost visibly see my pizza getting colder with each passing moment of conversation! The distance that some holiday makers travel with no previous experience is often very impressive, even if the speed at which they do it is equally often a controversial matter among regular boaters, seeing their possessions tipped up and rolled off work tops as another boat zooms past their mooring.

Bumps, scratches and speeding aside, the holiday traffic is part of the lifeblood of the canals, it is one of the things that keeps the whole network ticking, not just financially but also in terms of having canals in a fit condition to travel along. Bumpy towpaths are kept from being overgrown jungles. A quiet stretch of canal that acts almost as its own nature reserve such as the nearby Montgomery, demonstrate how reeds can flourish on the banks if left to their own devices with no frequent traffic.

There are many interesting people to be met during the summer time just as there are all year round, it is just over the summer there are far more people to choose from. Bikers, walkers, boaters, fishermen, bird watchers and the occasional artist make up an often bustling canal at peak travel times. It is important to not only see these as a group of individuals doing their own thing, but also as a momentary heroic set of helping hands. The time and effort of getting through a lock single handed is slashed when a boater ahead and boater behind joins in the effort, many hands make light work indeed, especially if I don't even have to leave the boat. Apart from when I repay the favour of course!

Many times now I have been out biking or walking and given a helping hand to people passing through locks or struggling to moor up their boat. Not only is it the right thing to do for somebody like me with all the time in the world for chatting and cranking handles, but I like to think that it leaves people with a really positive view of the canal network and a great experience to look back on.

The summer months are however the exception in terms of canal traffic, as many people want to pass over the incredible Pontcysyllte Aqueduct with its sheer drop to one side with no railings for safety. A great point of interest along an already beautiful canal.

As holiday season passes and the canals quieten down I tend to revert to my tradition of mooring in slightly more out of the way places. I quite like to be in sight of other boats but not right next to them, firstly so that neither boat disturbs one another if travelling early, but also as I very often like to go out on the towpath late at night with a telescope. I can imagine that hearing a disturbance by your boat in the small hours, and then peering through a crack in the curtains to see somebody on their knees nearby with some kind of odd equipment in the dark, may not be the peaceful experience expected. With miles of canal that often has no boats moored on it during the off peak months there is plenty of room to moor out of the way.

I particularly enjoy speaking to continuous cruisers who travel huge distances over the summer then have a relaxed winter somewhere. The insight and experiences they offer on the wider canal network are fascinating and sometimes make me want to drop everything and go off on my long planned "Big Boating Adventure" right then and there. As I save up money for the day that I can finally head off for a few years of serious narrowboat travel, it is a joy to hear of some of the places various characters have been. The perfect scenery or oddities they come across are definitely points that I one day hope to tick off my ever growing checklist. It is also worth noting down any warnings I am given about places to avoid and some of the more urban areas that seem to be from a different world to the rolling fields surrounding the Llangollen.

One of the more recent people I have met on the towpath is definitely somebody that I could be happy emulating in years to come. Travelling the waterways as he does with his trusty chainsaw and general woodcarving skills, while his artist partner works away at photorealistic portraits. Two skills I will almost certainly never have, and another example of how differently people can choose to live their lives if they are willing to go for it and make it happen.

During the winter months when the canal almost empties entirely of boats, I am regularly the only boat around for miles, something that I still struggle to believe is a real situation. To be the only boat around makes Tilly more of a point of interest to passing walkers. Spending my winter mooring around the area I grew up in, leads to plenty of good conversations on the towpath about the local area, canal, hills, hidden routes and all sorts of random chat in general.

Last winter I paid for a full five months of winter mooring for the first time which allowed me to stay in the area much longer than ever before, (although I am sure I still moved more than some non paying winter moorers!) This led to getting to know some regular dog walkers, very muddy commuters and local residents better than I usually do. This proved interesting in some cases because of their incredible local knowledge and ability to point at random mounds on the canal side and declare what each one of them used to be back in the heyday of the waterways. Beyond that, I thought it was quite reassuring to know that there were friendly people around to keep an eye on Tilly while I wasn't around. If I was at work or up a mountain, I felt that a friendly group of frequent towpath walkers offered me a little feeling of safety, similar, but not as strong as that of the feeling of leaving her in a marina.

An odd side effect of spending my winter in one place comes in the form of how the balance of conversation shifts when speaking to many of the people travelling to the area for the first time. As well as hearing the tales of distant canals and places from them, I am also quizzed about the local canal as if I will know all the answers. I manage to fumble through most of it and give rough mileages and distances to points of interest, a water point, marina or aqueduct. This questioning though sums up how I have become so used to travelling with no ultimate destination. I rarely look at a map and no longer keep an eye on the time to even know how long it takes me to travel from place to place. These relaxations have left me knowing for dozens of miles exactly what is on the canal, in which order, and whereabouts, but with no idea of how many miles or how long it would take to travel. For example, I do know that between the super rural Whixall, and the larger town Whitchurch, there is a span of roughly five miles of canal. Not a huge distance and even at my slow pace of travel it should be well under two hours of boating goodness. However, there are four lift bridges along the way which suddenly throw in a total unknown. I couldn't say how long passing through those would add to the journey, and even if I had timed myself it would be a useless measurement as I have never done all four unbroken without mooring up for a while to have something to eat. Laid back boating at its best.

Moving away from the towpath and completely changing the way you can live on a boat we need to spend a little time talking about marinas. This can be an entirely different kind of community, and the constantly changing group of people you might meet out on the canal can be swapped for the steady sightings of fellow marina dwellers. Spending time at Chirk Marina was an interesting experience and change of pace that I am certainly going to return to at some point. The obvious benefits of a safe mooring away from the canal traffic, but also right next to all the onsite services you could want, are well documented in my videos and need not be pointed out. The community aspect is hard to pin down though.

One of the core things that I took away from my marina stay was that there are a lot more people in the local area who live on boats than you would imagine if you merely walked the towpath. The people and characters you can find and befriend will as with everything else wildly vary from marina to marina, but one thing that is certain, is that you are much more likely to find yourself with a far more regular neighbourhood than the passing boats on the canal.

I would never say that I am really interested in having a huge crowd of close friends but I do like to get to know people and have a random chat about anything, especially boats and especially with someone who knows more than me on the subject... so almost anybody! A marina with a good community of livaboard boat owners is definitely a good place to meet such people. For me I am more of a passing "hello" shouter but regularly bumping into the same people and seeing others going about their daily lives, is in itself a pleasant and somehow reassuring routine that makes you feel like you belong to a group of people.

Hearing people shout to one another from jetty to jetty, heads pop up and vanish between row upon row of all kinds of narrowboat, and the occasional appearance of somebody with an arm full of McDonalds food are all just my sort of thing. So much so, that even now, while thinking about my marina experience, and reading my diary entries all kinds of tiny moments come back to me. The boat cats peering out at me in the dark, an injured pigeon that hung around moving from one jetty to the next to wait on boats that it hoped it would be able to get a little food from. Feeling the boat move when neighbours walked up and down the floating platforms we were all moored up to, and then hearing conversations strike up outside the stern resulting in practically being in the middle of the conversation through the miracle of thin steel walls.

A marina can be far more like a regular street of houses. Everybody has their place and is a far more fixed resident than on the canal, there are people who you see and know the names of, people who you talk to, and people that you never see. Ultimately people are always people whether they live in a house, on a boat or on the moon. If they are all together then a small society will form, but if they are all moving then names, faces and memories will be all you have within a short amount of time. All people are individuals and as such lead their own lives, just as narrowboats on the canal are varied, even more so are the people on them. To brand one group of people as "boaters" and expect them to be different to "housers" is to leave reality behind. Living my low stress and low cost lifestyle has definitely changed me as a person in many ways, but my extreme low end of the spectrum of boat costs as usual makes me an exception and a bit of a fringe non representative character... which sounds like a good place to be!

There is another rather unexpected level of community interaction that I have individually come to experience. This is the side effect of my obsessive YouTube-ing. Over the first part of 2014 my videos and only name of "The Narrowboat Lad" became increasingly popular. This has in turn led to many people recognising me and Tilly. Over the past year or so I have become used to the occasional person recognising me, but recently it has been something else. Particularly over school and bank holidays when the canal gets temporarily busier it has become a frequent event that more than one person a day will shout "Hello Dan!" Or "It's Tilly!" as they go past.

This has proved an incredible way to meet people, to have a stranger say "hello" and start talking about my videos or books and know many things about me already, is an odd experience. It is however a pleasant one, although it is difficult to "get my head around the idea" I am glad to be able to enjoy. There are all kinds of people from around the world on holiday and all age groups that shout my name or take photos of Tilly on their way past, and I can't thank every person out there enough for the support.

Turning up to find somebody has left a note or a gift on Tilly for me is an amazing welcome back to have, hearing people talk about my books, assuming that I am not onboard, is an odd one too. Something that really amazes me though is when people recognise me away from Tilly. While I am walking the towpath I can understand that someone may be on the look out if they have just passed the boat, but when I am at my supermarket workplace it is another thing altogether. Having total strangers ask me questions is a standard part of my job, but having those questions be things like "Do you have a narrowboat?" Or "When's the next video/book?" Or, my personal favourite, in a questioning tone of voice "Dan?"

It is truly humbling to have thousands of people tuning in to my videos each day, and even more so to have some of these people see me in person and strike up a conversation. I have said it time and time again but I thank every single one of you from the bottom of my heart. I am a quiet lad who loves the countryside and happens to enjoy it from onboard a boat. I am truly grateful that so many people have tuned in to share it with me, and I hope my nervous, stuttering conversation lives up to expectations in real life!

Another Perfect Day on the Monty

Whenever possible I like to have friends or family join me onboard for the various boat trips that I make from week to week. It is something that I especially like to do if I know the trip is going to involve anything potentially awkward or slightly more labour intensive than just pushing and pulling a tiller as we trundle along. Locks have become something that if on a quiet stretch of canal where I can take my time, I have been finding myself thoroughly enjoying, but that doesn't mean I am not always up for a bit of company.

On Monday 5th May, a Bank Holiday in England, I was keen to move Tilly about six miles upstream from the beautiful, and in all honesty, perfect stretch of canal by Maesbury Marsh on the Montgomery to the junction where it rejoins the Llangollen Canal at Lower Frankton. This was a trip along almost all of the currently restored top section of "The Monty"

The top section is very much a nature ruled canal, so much so that there are a maximum of twelve boats a day allowed to travel down onto the Montgomery, and all passages up and down have to be booked in, with no more than fourteen nights spent on the stretch. As such there are long intervals between mooring points, with sometimes literally miles of incredibly rural canal with shallow sides leading up to uneven banks and overhanging trees, bushes and reeds. It is the perfect picture of the countryside, farmland, nature reserves, and a very calm canal with a few locks dotted around.

Being a Bank Holiday, I was expecting to see a few more people around than normal with a huge number of people nationwide enjoying a long weekend away from work. This assumption was proved to be completely wrong by the end of the day. My nan and grandad had been enjoying the good weather at their caravan on the North Wales Coast for a few days, so I had been making the most of having a nearby empty house. It was not yet summer so I wasn't needed for gardening duties while they were away, but I certainly had a good number of video voice overs and podcasts that I wanted to get recorded. Taking the opportunity I turned their living room into my temporary recording studio and found myself riding between Tilly and Oswestry multiple times a day. The distance between the two being barely three miles and very flat. It seemed especially flat compared to the terrain I had been covering over my winter mooring months and I was glad of the relative "walk in the park" of a commute. I even found myself riding into town on some evenings to then do a few varied circuits of the town centre, before riding back out to Tilly without having so much as put a foot on the ground.

The night previous to the trip I had met some friends in town to watch a very old comedy film, recorded more audio until around one in the morning, then headed upstairs for a luxurious nights sleep in a big double bed. A rare pleasure! I had arranged to meet my good friend Michael Manning at half nine the following morning, so that he could experience his first lock, the extra pair of helping hands was of course nothing to do with my decision to ask him to join me.

Waking up nice and fresh I was relaxed to the point that I forgot to pack my bag with a few things I wanted to take out with me. I saw my friend roll up nice and early and we rode our bikes out to Tilly. Finding ourselves on empty roads almost the entire journey, only eleven cars passed us, and not a single car travelling in the same direction as our destination. We hopped on Tilly and threw the bikes on the stern, and in unusually efficient form had untied the ropes and were on our way before ten in the morning had struck.

From the very first moment we had an empty canal in front of us, the sun in the sky and a backdrop of nothing but farmland. The speed limit for the canal is sign posted at various points at only three miles per hour. I am a slow traveller anyway, but we kept it even calmer than usual, and as a good measure of our speed we saw a towpath walker zip past us and into the distance as if travelling with a great urgency. The first short stint of the trip saw us moving through a narrow canal with lots of reeds shooting up out of the water on either side, definitely not the sort of banks you want to get too close to. Passing freshly ploughed fields and a huge expanse of nearly fluorescent yellow rapeseed crop, the sun on our backs was hot enough to start us de-layering down to T-shirts. I left "Manning" on the tiller and for the first time in quite a while I just enjoyed being a passenger.

Being able to walk around and go inside while moving still has a certain novelty to me, heading inside to make a drink, grab a snack or just sit down, I love to see the world passing by so slowly through the window. The engine pounding away at the back of the bathroom certainly takes away some of the peace of the scene but doesn't detract from the scenery and the poetic thought of travelling so slowly to an ever changing and often undecided destination. Walking up onto the deck and being free to look over the back and see all sorts of reeds and twigs caught up around the rudder area is always something that causes me to instruct a quick burst of reverse to release them and also put my obsessive mind at ease that the propeller isn't about to seize up at any given moment.

We soon reached the first of the three Aston Locks. After descending them on my own with a time of roughly twenty minutes per lock (I don't lift both paddles when on my own to stop the boat moving around so much as the water drains or fills at a slower rate) I was glad of the hand. Having two people, one for each side of the lock and then one to steer the boat in while the other closes the gates can easily halve the time, especially when the water is at your level to begin with.

Seeing Manning struggle with the windlass on stiff mechanisms and trying to push the gates open before the water had levelled out, was an excellent reminder of how baffled I had been by locks, and why I had feared them so much not too long ago. Not even two years ago I had not so much as touched a windlass, or as I called them (and still do most of the time to this day) a "lock handle". Yet on the way down through these locks on my own, I had outright enjoyed the experience. Taking my time, and even doing one in as flawless a way as I could hope for, while a camera recorded the whole thing for a future time lapse video. Seeing nearly twenty minutes sped up into a five second video was a pleasing result, though it didn't quite convey the care and attention that I always give to one of the most dangerous features of the canal.

As we passed through the three locks in no particular rush, I was pleased to see someone else at the tiller in a lock for the first time since I had bought Tilly. We moored up for a few minutes rest and a quick series of cereal bars on the temporary mooring mushrooms by the top lock, the canal had been very quiet. A handful of walkers on the towpath and only us on the water, the epitome of a calm canal. We were about to pass The Queen's Head pub and start on a series of long straights that were definitely unsuitable for mooring. Tilly had not had any engine problems for a long time, but the faint fear and doubt in the back of my mind stirs slightly at moments like that. We ploughed ahead at our steady but also incredibly slow pace.

To say that I did not touch the tiller for the majority of the day would be an understatement. I love boating on my own and find myself extending the experience deliberately, by slowing down to enjoy the simple act of travelling through the middle of nowhere. Often I will drift from left to right at slow speed while I am distracted by one sight or another, but this problem evaporates when somebody else takes the helm. Getting to enjoy to scenery of the Monty as a passenger allowed me to really look at how beautiful the canal and its surroundings really are. I have always been grateful to have done what I have done in my life and often hearing how other people enjoy their boating experiences onboard with me I know I am extremely lucky. But to lean against the back door and just watch the world pass by as a passive passenger for once was a treat I have been deliberately recreating whenever I can.

Our destination was a small basin by Lower Frankton. Given the limited mooring opportunities, I had passed this area by on my way down the canal as there were no vacant spots. To make sure we didn't arrive there to find it full, resulting in us turning around and backtracking a very long way we pulled a trick that I had learned previously. At a very small aqueduct about a mile away from the mooring point we tied up to the temporary mooring mushrooms that are there to hold your boat steady if waiting for an oncoming vessel to pass through the very short but single file aqueduct. Once tied nice and securely, I hopped onto Manning's bike and pedalled down the towpath to find that there were plenty of spaces available to moor up, largely due to the fact that there wasn't a single boat there! Two weeks beforehand it had caused all sorts of logistical problems, as me with my family onboard had travelled down to find "no room at the inn", and then had to go well out of our way to find a place to moor for a while in order to continue my birthday celebrations!

I pedalled back with a big smile on my face at what was now a trip with a solid destination. When Tilly came into line of sight I saw somebody stood next to her and assumed it to be Manning, as I got closer I realised the figure was on a bike. I got closer and recognised it as another friend, Ashley. In what I can only describe as an exceptional feat of bike based man hunting he had put his extra day off work to good use and cycled to the canal, then scoured at least six miles of it to find Tilly. Find her he did!

Surprised but happy to have another friend onboard I told Manning the good news about us being the only boaters we would see all day, (excluding a pair of kayakers!) I told Ashley to throw his bike on the roof and hop on. In the excitement he forgot to use the classic line that he had been waiting to say to me for almost two years. What was the line? "Permission to come aboard Sir?"

With an unexpectedly bolstered crew I took the tiller for about two minutes before I managed to get a shy and weary Ashley to take control. His reaction was the standard mixture of joy at going boating for the first time, and surprise at how easy it was to control. Once again I distanced myself from the tiller as we approached the Graham Palmer Lock. One of the smallest locks I have ever passed through. The difference in depth of water is barely a few centimetres and easy to miss at first glance. That is the sort of lock that I don't mind doing on my own. We were through in minutes, and I decided that I would actually do some steering for the last leg of the journey. It was a shorter leg than I had thought, five minutes may be an overstatement.

The opportunity to moor up at any point in the small basin at what was once a junction with a long disused canal to Shrewsbury, caused me to face a problem I often deal with at the end of a boat trip. I am never quite happy with where I moor the first time. We pulled up to the bank, stopped the engine and started to tie the ropes. Then I had a change of heart as Tilly was facing towards a dead end, and my mistrust of the weather meant I didn't want to have to reverse in high wind if any other boats did moor up nearby. The ropes were untied, I pushed the bow out, hopped onboard and ran to the front in order to jump off and pull her in by the bowline when we reached the opposite side of the basin. A very nice slow relaxed end to the trip and a classic demonstration of my indecisive ways. Luckily although slightly bemused, my friends onboard have steadily got used to it over the years.

We moored up for a second time with only minor movements and a ten foot change in position and then set off back to town on our bikes. Ashley said a line that summed up the day perfectly "It feels like childhood". The three of us out in the middle of nowhere, boating along without a care in the world and no sign that there was so much as another human being in the country. Hopping on our bikes to cycle down the towpath, walk across farmland and fields. Lifting our bikes awkwardly over every style and gate we came to, until the mud and soil finally turned into the cracked tarmac of the narrow and empty country lanes. One of those rare truly carefree days where good company, surroundings and activity all merge perfectly to leave anything not in the present moment well away from the mind. Biking three wide down the roads we talked and laughed as if there was nothing else in the world to think about. It truly was one of my favourite days for a long time and that is saying a lot as I am lucky enough to enjoy very good days very frequently!

A Not So Perfect Day

Not every boat trip goes to plan. In fact beyond not going to plan, there are on rare occasions boat trips that go literally nowhere. In the past I have seen other people on larger boats give up a trip early due to high wind or torrential rain, at one point I have struggled along with a couple to pull their boat across a mere twenty foot wide canal. Rarely have I had a boat trip planned that, once actually started, represented a literal step backwards.

I was moored at a pleasant and very rural stretch of canal at Tetchill, only a mile or so from Ellesmere. Due to wet weather I had been putting off my trip up to Ellesmere and the services available there for a couple of days previously but finally reached that point of thinking *"Ah let's just go and get it over with"*. I awoke to a very windy morning, wind being my least favourite of all weather conditions due to the potential of being blown into another boat.

I had already let my mind decide that I was moving no matter what. With the wind whistling away and pushing against Tilly at almost a right angle from the towpath side, I started to untie the ropes. I have a system for unmooring that normally works well to keep the boat under control should any issue arise. Firstly I untie the bow rope but leave it coiled around the mooring peg on the front of Tilly, so that it can't unravel on its own but is easily removable within seconds by hand. I then start the engine and untie the stern rope completely, head back down to the front, unwrap the rope and throw it onto the roof before giving Tilly a little push outwards into the canal and hopping on... a nice simple routine despite how awkward it looks written down.

However with the wind pushing Tilly away from the bank, as soon as any slack was available in either of the ropes I could feel her being pushed away from me, so left the back tied. I decided to just try and unmoor quickly, so started the engine to make a quick getaway, then ran to the front and untied the bow line completely. By the time I had started to untie at the back, Tilly's nose was way out into the canal. I ran and grabbed one of the side fenders and heaved her back a little then frantically untied the back rope.

By the time the stern was unmoored too she was at a forty-five degree angle across the canal. Not wanting to lose her to the far bank entirely, I grabbed the middle line that I normally keep in a coil on the roof, and heaved with all my strength (admittedly not a huge amount!) All I managed to achieve was a slight straightening up of her in the centre of the canal, as the back end had blown out too, making my middle rope a pivot for her to twist around in the gusts.

Try as I might I could not pull her back to the bank. Even by my standards it would be a foolish thing to attempt to jump an impossible distance onto a boat that was blown out of control before I had so much as touched the tiller! I was holding her in place just about and as there were boats moored ahead started to walk backwards down the towpath with my newly invented water based kite!

After roughly thirty foot, one entire length of Tilly, the hedgerow along the towpath seemed to offer a little bit more shelter and I was able to heave her back to the bank. Quickly getting her moored back up was one of those moments of relief that reveals just how frantic and stressed you had been a moment before but were too busy to realise at the time!

So all in all, I had effectively travelled minus thirty foot, had a ten minute battle against the wind and then sat down inside to write a frustrated diary entry and cook some pasta. I have said many times to many people, boating isn't all sunny countryside and idyllic cruising. That was the perfect day's non-boating to demonstrate what I mean!

Don't Jinx It! Things I Never Talk About

If there is one trait that I have that is detrimental to my general life, (apart from the obvious shyness and awkwardness around other people!) then it could well be my very strong superstitious streak. I have unfortunately stored in my mind an unusual amount of snippets of folklore and things that you shouldn't do or shouldn't say, because they are "bad luck". Needless to say these are the sorts of things which then come back to haunt me at any given moment, often when it's least appropriate.

The usual things about not walking under ladders, spilling salt, black cats, magpies and many more classic "Old Wives Tales" are represented in my array of superstitions. On the first of each month for more than half of my life I have been saying "Rabbits, Rabbits, Rabbits" for good luck, at age thirteen I then heard an alternative version where you simply say "White Rabbits". This meant that I then had to make my first of the month good luck chant into "Rabbits, Rabbits, Rabbits... PAUSE... White Rabbits"! Absolutely crazy maybe, but I have now been doing it for fourteen years so can't stop now!

As well as the more commonly known superstitions, I also have many words that I will never say and topics of conversation that I wish to utterly avoid so that I don't "tempt fate". The idea of *tempting fate* really does have a hold over me, enough of a hold that whenever I do tempt fate, I normally also find myself *touching wood* for luck. I have talked about the less glamorous and less perfect side of narrowboat life on many occasions, things like the bitter cold or soaking wet cycling commutes. Emptying a plastic camping toilet in a tiny cubicle of a room and my personal favourite, waking up and feeling ill, and then being stuck onboard a boat that is itself being rocked constantly by passing boats on a busy summers day.

What I have not spoken about are the topics that tempt fate. Now at long last I am going to break out of my superstitious prison and talk about sinking, vandalism, crashes and break-ins. Just typing that makes me want to never leave Tilly again so that I can keep an eye on her around the clock.

The subject of sinking is one that I have a lot of questions about in real life. "Are you not scared she might sink?" is the sort of question that sends a shiver down my spine. There is only one answer, "yes of course I am worried" and the fact is that one day Tilly will almost certainly sink. It is easy to imagine that the only thing you have to worry about is getting a hole in the hull and then going down, this is unfortunately not at all the truth.

The engine of a boat can have several pipes for cooling that go out of the boat into the canal, and of course there is the propeller shaft that needs to be filled with waterproof grease. Anything like this that operates below the waterline is a potential weak point and a reason that you need to keep on top of maintenance. I may not know much about the technical side of an engine, but I know that a drip from a propeller shaft can soon turn into two or three, and if left would eventually bring about a disaster. Similarly I found dozens of litres of water below Tilly's floorboards inside, I pumped it all out and was alarmed to get bucket after bucket of water overboard. My mind was slightly eased by a friend who told me that if left long enough, then some boats continue to collect water that has formed as condensation on the actual metal surfaces behind the walls inside. The water level rising in the cold winter and then evaporating a little during the summer. I am sure that I don't need to also point out the dangers of a hull rusting away below the waterline, but these are a few of the issues that a boat can have in terms of its structure.

Nature also has a few tricks up its sleeve that should be taken into account, namely rain and snow. The weight of snow building up on a boat is a common cause of sinking over the winter months. My first lesson of this during the heavy snowfall at the start of 2013 was quite an eye opener. Brushing off six inches of snow from one side of the boat and then going inside to warm up before finishing the job, I found the boat to be leaning at a visibly noticeable angle like some kind of funhouse at the fair. The weight of the snow on just half of Tilly was clearly huge and I shudder to think about what might have happened if I had not been able to get to her to clear the snow. Especially when I awoke the next day to find another huge six inch covering of snow had fallen over night. At that point I did not know that within a few miles of Tilly there were multiple boats sinking under the weight, had I known this then I think I would have been too scared to leave her until the middle of summer.

Less obvious is the problem that the rain can cause and without the weight that snow can put on your roof it takes longer to have an effect, but it should not be overlooked. Unlike snow, rain can easily get into all the openings and nooks and crannies that a vessel may have, and once it is there it may be hard to get a clear path to evaporate out, leading to a steady build up of water over time. On Tilly this is a problem that was particularly bad with water dripping down into the engine bay from the massive open cruiser stern above. Having a ten foot deck that is split up into about six wooden sections that are held up on a wonky metal frame is great in the summer, but as soon as the rain starts, the metal drainage channels will be tested.

Tilly has a few holes in her sides around the deck area to let rainwater drain off, they do get some of the water away. Unfortunately as the frame holding it all together is slightly bowed after years of people standing around holding the tiller there is also a huge amount of water that just drips straight down onto the engine and collects below. A bilge pump can soon get this water out but that relies on somebody being around to flip the switch, which for other boats with similar problems is not always possible. This sort of steady build up can claim a boat over a rainy autumn and winter and is something to take particular caution with on large decked boats such as Tilly. I have found that I am able to almost entirely solve this issue by simply covering the stern with a tarpaulin sheet and folding the edges in a certain way to encourage the water to run off to the sides.

There is one massive external cause of sinking that cannot be overlooked. Locks. The amount of disastrous incidents that have happened in the locks of the waterways must be a huge figure over the past few hundred years. Each summer there are multiple boats sunk as the canals get busier. Horror stories from both novice holiday maker to seasoned boating veteran alike being caught out and realising a little too late that they have made a grave error with nothing else to do other than stand and watch their boat fill up with water, and sink.

Sometimes a boat can be filled with water from something as simple as a leaky lock gate pouring a steady waterfall down from the top gate. A boat can go a little too close to the leaking flow, and before you realise it be taking on water quicker than you can react. The classic danger of a lock is getting your boat caught on the cill. A shelf that the top lock gate closes against, when the water is drained to lower the boat, the cill is left exposed sometimes a few feet out of the lower water level. A boat caught on this will have its back end lifted up and dip it's bow into the water, once again leading to a sinking before it can be saved. The rarer but still terrifying issue of a lock being too tight and pinching a boat in place is also a danger. Over time lock walls warp and in some cases have become extremely tight for a narrowboat to enter. Narrowboats can also warp and alter shape gradually.

Looking down the side of Tilly it can be seen how uneven her sides are and how there looks to be in some areas huge sweeping dents or swells in what was once a flat sheet of steel. Demonstrating how tight locks can be I have at moments forgotten to lift the rubber fenders that hang on Tilly's sides, before entering locks and found myself wedged at New Marton, Grindley Brook and Hurleston. A couple of friends were recently planning a trip up the Llangollen canal but found they could not get their boat into the Hurleston locks at all and had to enjoy a completely different trip instead.

If a boat gets stuck as a lock is filling with water then the consequences are obvious. If it gets stuck as a lock is emptying then the boat can be held out of the water and dropped or held at one point as a pivot to let the free end of the boat dip into the water, and again fill, even if only partially. All things to keep a very keen eye out for while travelling the waterways. Stopping at a lock and treating it as a rest from travelling is common, I have even seen somebody enjoying a cup of tea while in a lock. It may be an amusing sight of the laid back way of the canals, but as time goes on and more incidents involving locks are reported, it is a clear reminder that when operating a lock there is no second chance for a sometimes literally fatal error.

What happens if a boat sinks? There are a few possible scenarios depending on the type of boat and it's location. The general process will likely involve giant airbags being used to float the boat and water pumps to empty out the vessel. It should also be remembered that as well as the boat and the internal furnishings there will also be a high chance that a lot of oil and diesel from the engine will also find its way into the water. The environmental issue of a sunken boat leaking out fuel like a tanker can be tackled in a similar way to oil spills at sea in some cases. The use of "booms" floating barriers made of a material intended to absorb oil can help contain the damage. As with all things of an unpredictable nature though, it is impossible to have an infinite supply of recovery and rescue materials lining the canal, and in some cases abandoned boats can be sunken for months.

In a marina the boat will already be in an easily accessible position whereas a sunken boat out in the middle of a rural stretch of canal may need to be towed back to an easier place for restoration to take place.

I have spoken to older sage-like boat owners who have memories of their own boat sinking. One of the things that strikes me about their recollections is that they don't seem too disturbed by the experience. It is truly the mark of a calm person to be able to look back without a flicker of emotion and recall the events. It is even more amazing to speak to someone on the matter and have them nod to the stern and say "These engines are bullet proof, it's been sunk three times" then add "It was sunk when it bought it". A genuinely terrible situation like a sinking seems to be eased by the right attitude but it is still a scenario I hope to avoid.

If we are still afloat and everything onboard is running fine, then there is always the potential for mischief from the outside. The idea of vandalism and theft seems like an almost alien concept while I sit here, miles from anything other than tiny villages in any direction. The trees, fields and country lanes are not known for their wanton destruction of property (except for a few falling trees, I suppose). The rural ideal that I live in is not the universal canal environment, it has to be remembered that the canal network was once an industrial transport system, and as such, runs through many major cities. The view through the window can change dramatically from rolling fields and countryside into a view of old industrial areas on the outskirts of cities. Factories with broken windows and graffiti stretching sometimes beyond view. Further into a city a canal might find itself cutting through brand new flawlessly kept inner city shopping areas, the bumpy muddy towpath becoming a beautifully smooth brickwork plaza, edged by big brand shops recognisable the world over.

It would be outrageous to say that vandalism and trouble only happen in cities and the above description is loosely based on Birmingham as an example of how the environment surrounding the canal can change. But what is fair to say is that the chance of trouble increases when you add more people into the mix. Out on the Llangollen canal I have only heard of one boat being broken into over the last year or so. The only act of vandalism that I have seen is when I walked down the towpath past some footpath signs that were definitely intact, then walked back an hour later to find both signs were snapped off, and on the ground.

There is one exception to my calm, uninterrupted experience on the canal around here and that is the theft of my bike. In the usual way with this sort of thing the one time that I left my bike out on the deck unlocked while I went inside and had something to eat was exactly the moment that the wrong person walked past and decided that they would help themselves. At the time I was moored up at Chirk Bank, a truly lovely area. To prove the point about more people increasing the risk of trouble, I was moored right by a road bridge that is almost exactly halfway between two very nearby small villages. Even with the comparatively tiny population of all three areas together, I made a mistake and an unscrupulous character was on hand to make off with my months old bike. Had I been moored only a corner or two away in either direction, then chances are that I would have got away with the slip in security, as there is a good probability that not a single person would have so much as seen Tilly, never mind the unlocked bike on her stern.

The issues of vandalism and security I treat as the same thing, having things stolen is exactly as costly, upsetting and worrying as having things ruined. I am lucky to live in a good area where I can travel forty miles down the canal and still not really find many parts of the canal that are anything except extremely rural. The people who walk the towpath are mainly local residents and general walkers or cyclists out to enjoy the scenery. I do though hear of a lot of trouble that goes on around some of the less welcoming areas.

I have spoken to a few people who have travelled in areas that locals have warned them not to stop in, even if they are going to stay onboard. The news will every now and then feature a story about a lock being vandalised, and in some cases a repeat offender of boat breaking will have his name known across his area. As I mentioned in the section about the boating community, boaters are all people and so too is the canal just a feature of the land. The canal network is not at all immune to trouble, and it is just a fact of life that trouble finds its way into everything, the one advantage that being on a boat offers you is the option to float away to less turbulent waters. An option that unfortunately does not exist for somebody with a house in the wrong area.

Speaking of floating away... People often ask me if I am afraid of somebody cutting the ropes and letting Tilly drift off. It is a concern, but I think that a lot of the time the questioner has an image of the ropes being loosed, and then a narrowboat being washed away down some white water rapids never to be seen again! The reality would be far less dramatic. Some canals barely have any current at all and even on the four mile an hour flow on the Llangollen if you let a boat build up a bit of momentum with the current, it will still only be travelling very slowly. It is conceivable that it could move straight down the canal for a while, but in all likelihood would soon become beached on a shallow side or caught in trees, maybe even wedged against a bridge. The remedy to this is entirely in the hands of other boaters, hopefully the first person that finds a drifting boat would be kind enough to pull her over and tie her up but if not somebody sooner or later would be the good Samaritan.

I know this personally, as in the past I have tied up a loose mooring rope on a holiday boat but also have returned twice to Tilly to find that one of my ropes has been retied. The first time a very fancy knot had been put into my stern line that was moored using a hook. It is easily possible that a fast passing boat had managed to make the hook come free from the bank, so I am willing to give that the benefit of the doubt. In a far stranger incident though I came home to find that the bow line was tied in a completely different way to how it had been left. I was moored using chains so they could not possibly have come undone, the rope wasn't loose and the canal was wide so she hadn't been swinging out and cutting into the canal at passing boats. I had even coiled the rope, passing it over features on the roof that would have made it impossible to untie without stepping onto Tilly to do so. I have no possible explanation for why it would have been untied and then tied again unless while I was away somebody had for whatever reason decided to do it for fun. Maybe some character had decided they would just untie her and leave Tilly to her fate. A poor bit of mischief as the current of the canal was flowing with the direction of the boat, meaning that the water itself would encourage her to stay at the bank. A very strange event and a bit of a mind boggler.

I have quite a few little tricks to help improve security in the small way that I can. When a boat is at the side of a canal on its own out of sight of anyone or anything, it is hard to say it is not vulnerable. Apart from mooring in places less likely to attract trouble what I like to do is make it difficult to tell if anybody is on the boat or not. Spending a lot of time away from Tilly doing other things, the boat can look very empty during the day. I usually keep my bike locked up on the stern but to make sure that the bike being present or absent is not a clear sign of whether I am onboard or not I sometimes leave my bike inside while I am onboard going about my daily life. This obviously takes up a lot of room but as long as I am not wanting to go in and out of the back door all the time is not a hassle. Similarly, I may leave my bike nearby at my friends house during winter mooring as within minutes I can be riding it away but don't have to be concerned about its security when I am not onboard and also show that my bike may not be on the boat for a week but I am still onboard.

Simple things like that are handy over the winter mooring period when I will be in the same area for a prolonged time. Having friends around the area helps, as if I do go away for a couple of days they can come down and move things around onboard to keep up the image of constant residence.

When it comes to moving down the canal and stopping at different places for a day or two before moving on, there should hopefully not be enough time for security in the area to become an issue. The mere fact that I might travel a few miles a day gives passers-by the message that I am onboard and constantly moving. If I spend a night away then I have taken up a trick taught to me by many others, LED lights. I have many battery operated strips and fake candles. Even these I am obsessed could start a fire though so only ever leave them in the fireplace!

My irregular trips out as mentioned previously I also hope would confuse and deter anyone paying close attention to Tilly. Sometimes vanishing first thing and returning late at night, other times leaving in the evening and returning after midnight. Hopefully a keen observer would see that even if I wasn't onboard, I could arrive back at any moment. I have a couple of other similar measures to these but do not want to show my hand utterly.

One thing that does give me peace of mind while away from Tilly is the fact that there is nothing of real value onboard. The most expensive thing that I own apart from Tilly herself is an iPad. It is that iPad that I record a lot of my videos on, so I almost always take it with me when I am off adventuring down the country lanes or up hills. Knowing that the most costly thing I may need to replace is more likely to be as a result of me dropping it rather than somebody running off with it has a strange calming effect. There is no security quite like not owning much that anyone is likely to want to steal.

What I would never do however is give a clear indication that a boat was empty for long periods. Putting a cover over the chimney or a padlock on the outside doors are both common examples of clear a "nobodies home" message. If a boat is padlocked shut from the outside then let us hope it is not occupied at least! I have heard a few tips on how to achieve a prolonged smokey chimney but am not entirely convinced that leaving a fire burning, deliberately unattended, would be a wise choice.

Originally when I wrote this section it was going to stop somewhere around this point and I was not going to include the issue of having a crash on the canal. Then at the last minute before I finished adding to this book, an opportunity for an anecdote to be thrown in occurred...

Boats collide, crash, scrape and bump all the time. I am happy to say that I have never hit another boat while moving but I have been hit repeatedly from all sorts of angles while moored up. From my very first time onboard when a marine engineer scraped their way down the side of Tilly, to a few weeks ago when a very impressive boat hit us at almost a perfect right angle.

The boat was Buckden, a boat built in 1936 and still on the canals today, even more impressive but also terrifying when they are heading towards you is the boat that it was towing at the time, Saturn, a 1906 built boat. Today they are both very much showpieces for the industrial past, and turn up at all sorts of boat shows and events. While I was recently moored up at Ellesmere basin however, they both turned up for an unintended standoff with Tilly.

Both of these boats are huge old work boats, controlling one historically important narrowboat would be a challenge, but controlling two, especially when the rear boat has no means of propulsion, makes that challenge even more daunting. Definitely not an activity that I would want to do if there were other boats around. Saturn being an unpowered boat would have once upon a time been drawn by horse, in fact Saturn and a horse can still be regularly seen for demonstration purposes. Being horse drawn means that steering has to be done with a very large tiller and rudder to try and shift as much water as possible in the hope of pointing yourself in the desired direction. You can imagine how unwieldy driving a huge boat and towing something like that behind you would be. Now add in the rain and the distance between the person at the tiller of Buckden and the person at the tiller of Saturn, and the almost ninety degree angle that they needed to turn at Ellesmere basin, a wide area of canal that is similar to a T-junction in a road.

Wide though it may be, it was not wide enough. I was already watching through my window as historic boats are always nice to see, but soon I realised I was going to get an extreme close up. Due to the size of the vessels and the difficulty of the task they could not quite start turning in time, so my view was one of a huge high bow slowly drifting straight towards Tilly. I could hear the engine kick in as a last attempt to avoid a collision but slowly Buckden moved closer and closer.

Just like the corner they were trying to round, the collision was a near perfect ninety degree incident. At a speed so slow that it would seem almost to have stopped if watching from a distance, Buckden crept up to the side of Tilly. It was the momentum of tons of boat rather than the speed that caused the ensuing loud bang, as Tilly was hit on the right hand side, level with the steps down into the boat. I was moored against a concrete bank so there was absolutely no cushion and Tilly just had to absorb the impact of the forces involved. I was inside doing the only thing I knew how to... Film the whole thing! There was no way you could go out and try to push the boat away, firstly you would be very lucky to move a boat of that size at such short notice. Secondly the risk of getting hands or other body parts trapped between two boats is too high and the potential for disaster and terrible injury make actions like that foolhardy at best and at worst outright senseless.

The crash was basically a very loud bang with the whole boat making one very short sharp jolt, almost as if somebody had very quickly pulled a rug a tiny way from under your feet. The video footage that I had recorded (and subsequently made into a longer YouTube video), shows my general attitude to these sorts of incidents perfectly. I am upbeat but have a very nervous laugh, because to have something like this squeeze your boat is terrifying, it is impossible to know what damage may be done especially below the water line. At the same time though, I knew it was completely unintentional and an extremely difficult job they were doing, trying to keep the two boats under control. Going out shouting and kicking off would have been firstly irrelevant and useless, but also unfair to the crew of three people spread across two boats. Already shouting their apologies I waved and gave the passing boats the thumbs up, while enjoying the spectacle of boats from a bygone era passing by. As it turned out they moored up right in front of Tilly, so I even had a quick chat with them later in the evening.

I thought that while I had the opportunity to squeeze the above story into this book I would take it. I am happy to report that the only visible damage so far, is the disappearance of about an inch of paint that was seemingly vaporised at the impact point on Tilly's side. If somebody had told me a few years ago that one day I would be sat on my own narrowboat it would have been hard to believe. If somebody told me that as well as that I would also be watching narrowboats from a century ago come up and give Tilly a very rough kiss on the cheek, and I wouldn't mind too much, that would have surely been something I thought a fantasy!

My Life Afloat As Seen In Handwriting

As I mentioned at the start of this book, writing has been a big part of my life almost continually since the first time that I was given a pencil and managed to write my own name in a sprawling spidery font. From the early days of actually learning how to write and spell. Writing terrible sci-fi short stories as a teen while also keeping diaries of massive childhood events such as when I first played Pokemon. I loved writing anything. At college I started writing more poems, and also got sixty-five thousand words into a fantasy novel that nobody but me has ever seen. For a few years during my early twenties I wrote nothing but very short stories, before my first ever piece of non-fiction writing longer than a diary entry in the form of "The Narrowboat Lad".

When I released The Narrowboat Lad I was terrified by the idea of people reading something so personal to me. The reception it had was a tremendous relief at first. It then became a truly humbling experience as I started to receive messages from readers around the world, and see my book appear on all kinds of websites with favourable words. It was the first time that I have ever felt close to being comfortable about having written something that other people were reading. Writing descriptive pieces, poems, diary entries and short stories for myself, writing for other people and writing books for the Kindle. All of these have become activities that I do at least one kind of, in any two day period, whether in my leather pocket notebook and wallet, on an iPad or a great big notebook. I love it and can't thank everybody enough for their support, both online and my friends and family in "real life"... If that is still a thing!

In this section of the book I hope that I can give you a look into my life, as recorded in my own words long before I ever dreamed of writing a book that would contain any of them. Through these diary entries and a couple of poems I hope that I can offer you an insight into how I try and live my life in a way that involves as many of my best friends and family as often as possible. How I try and have as little impact on the people and things around me as possible and simply live a quiet life in the countryside.

Poetry is something that I have found the rural canal lifestyle lends itself particularly well to. I would never claim to be a poet of any competence. I have a few poems that I am willing to share with the world, and a couple of those are contained in this very book. (For over a year I have had an anthology almost ready to publish, but never quite plucked up the courage). I find the mere act of attempting to catch moments, ideas and feelings in verse, is as rewarding as actually finishing a poem. One of the most agonising poems to write, yet also most enjoyable and lengthy in process was "A Boy on a Boat", in which I attempt to sum up my love of narrowboat life. No small subject matter to deal with.

A Boy On A Boat

Miles away down a towpath and road
There sits an old house that once he called home.
Built of bricks, mortar and slate for a roof
Standing rock solid no grasp of the move.

Miles away down a road and towpath
Now sits a young lad feeling home at last.
A steel tube barely thirty-feet long
Just right for his life not much to go wrong.

The cold winter nights stoking the fire
The bright spring mornings that new life inspires.
Summer days on the deck under the sun
Golden leaves on the bow, Autumn has come.

The cycle of life from morning to night
On the canal brings his daily delight.
Birds above, fish below and boy adrift
Why live like this? The closed minds remain miffed.

A smile on his face he floats downstream
In the cold or the warm, snow or sunbeam.
Forever afloat, voice cheerful in note,
He stands on the stern, a boy on a boat.

Writing with a pen on paper seems to be one of those simple activities that is disappearing so fast it doesn't seem possible to those of us who grew up before the rise of computers. Hearing people say "let me write that down", and then pulling out their smartphone is an interesting demonstration of just how much technology is steadily altering the areas of our lives we don't even think about. From my experience online, especially with posting videos about notebooks and pens on YouTube, the simple act of writing is becoming an increasingly popular hobby. Something that most of us over a certain age spent our entire childhoods doing is becoming an art and activity for its own sake.

I am no master calligrapher at all, in fact I am not even an adequate calligrapher. I have a huge range of notebooks and do often write in them using a dip pen, but the patience, skill and again patience to create beautiful calligraphy escapes me. I do however enjoy just the simple act of writing with a dip pen, a perfect calm way to end a day. Particularly good for those long dark winter nights.

These handwritten records are great to look back on, and my love of recording random events for posterity may explain why I love services like Twitter and Facebook today. Having an easily searchable and public record of all kinds of moments and events from life has proven a fantastically useful tool for me when looking back to find out when certain events happened. It has helped tremendously in writing up my narrowboat life so far.

My true diary keeping though still remains as ink on paper. My expanding collection of notebooks filled with memories and important events serve not only as a reference for what has happened, but also (I like to think) a measure of how far I have come. Starting as the terrified early boating novice, to the slightly less terrified boat dweller who can claim to have "years of experience", despite still being clueless about anything technical to do with engines, electronics or gas and water systems!

There is one feature of these diaries that pops up far too often which you will see below, that is the exclamation mark. I have often edited them out when writing up entries for publication, as well as altered certain terms to make the entries make more sense to read out of context, but will leave the following entry untouched. It was written while leaning on the side of one of the many small stone humpback bridges, over the canal and recalls the previous few day's events. I remember writing this well as I was out on a short walk on a warm evening as Spring was finally moving to become the dominant season. I feel it wraps in many areas of my current life, my calmer attitude to dealing with unexpected events while boating, love of the outdoors and peace, and also the significance of both friends and family.

Thursday 10th April 2014 6:50pm

"Had another good weekend in work and trying to have a nice calm week onboard!

On Monday I managed to finish at eight thirty which meant I could go back to my mum's house and record an episode of the new history podcast so I was pleased with that!

Tuesday was an odd day as me and grandad had planned to do a couple of supply runs to get the last bag of coal onboard but halfway through we had the chance to break with tradition and have nan's home made chips on a Tuesday which meant being in town and able to hopefully do more recording... In an unexpected twist mum was having the boiler replaced which took forever and ended any recording plans.

When grandad and I headed back to Tilly I couldn't resist moving just down from Mad Jack's (*pub*) to just past the old railway bridge to a completely out of the way point. A perfect place to do nothing. Sheep and lambs everywhere on the the far bank. Lovely.

On Wednesday I did nothing at all but film a beginners guide to boating video and a little writing. Helena asked if I wanted to go and watch a film at their house so I decided to make the most it and turned it into a good bike ride by taking a detour into Oswestry. I said hello to the family, uploaded the day's video, ran up into town and bought some food then got back on my bike and rode out to the Jasper's (*five miles away at Weston Rhyn, right by the winter mooring I had recently moved away from*). A fantastic night as usual.

Another calm day today, soon after ten I moved up past The Narrowboat Inn. Had a little drama while I was passing the long line of boats moored up along the canal at Maestermyn Marina.

Right at one of those awkward corner points an oncoming holiday boat appeared. I made the decision to pull over rather than try and squeeze through between the moored boats and their moving one. All was well and as I got to the bank I jumped off to pull Tilly up properly only to find she was solidly beached about two foot away from the side. Not ideal to then have to reverse off the bottom of the canal across towards the moored boats!

The canal has been very busy recently and it has made me even more unsure about what my plans for the summer will be concerning any potential marina stops.

As I write this and think about ending this entry it is a perfect evening with golden sunlight tinting everything slightly yellow. It is still warm and birds are making a din in all directions! There is even a distant woodpecker. Classic canal!

I am about as stereotypical as can be right now, sat writing in my diary on a humpback bridge at sunset. Right then, back to Tilly for a lazy night!"

As perfect a way to end a day as I can think. Lazy nights and early bedtimes have steadily been becoming more frequent over the last two years. I hate to say it but with less than three years until my thirtieth birthday I may well be getting old... I will just have to try and soldier on through my late twenties as best as I can!

Thursday 3rd October 2013 10:15pm

"Once again I am sprawled out onboard as I write this in bed. It is now about 10:15pm and I am currently moored at Ellesmere in my favourite spot just around the corner from the basin and before the services. It is extremely hot onboard as I have already started to overfill the fire!

Last night having Helena and Ollie onboard for a few hours was really nice, just talking on a candle lit boat! It absolutely poured down over night but had cleared up by the morning in time for me to bike out to their house for the day at Weston Rhyn from yesterday's mooring at Frankton. The rain didn't stay away for long though and it poured down from 11 until 4.

When I got back onboard I immediately lit the fire and didn't trust the weather so didn't expect to move Tilly. As it stayed dry I couldn't resist it and ended up moving to my current place at Ellesmere. The chimney was really smokey from the half smothered fire, not ideal to stand in for over an hour while I moved down the canal.

It was another great trip, nice quiet canals, so quiet that I only met another two boats in the entire journey. It even started to brighten up weather wise. That is not too important now though as I have three big bags of wood from Ollie's mum and dad's house stored under the front cover, helping to keep the bow weight up as I use up the water supply making it lighter.

Just before I noticed a small bag by the back door. I have been looking at it the last few days and assumed it had a small amount of ash inside that I had forgotten to dispose of so I had just ignored it. Amazingly I had a closer look and discovered that it actually had a small gnome and a note left inside from an American couple who along with their friend knew Tilly from YouTube. I knew that they had been around the area and that they had stopped to have their photo taken onboard, I can't believe I missed this for so long! I know they passed Ellesmere today so went out to look for them but there was no sign, I will check again tomorrow morning, but now it is bedtime!"

At the time I had no idea that my YouTube videos would double in viewing figures within just a few months. This has led to the previously mentioned very strange situation where people on a regular basis, will recognise me or Tilly. Shout out various things and greetings, sometimes stop for a chat and a photo and generally say hello. As mentioned even when I am away from Tilly people somehow pick me out of a crowd and shake my hand. It is a very strange thing to have somebody ask for a photo with you, a request that I am never sure whether I am meant to laugh off as a joke or if it is intended seriously!

Things like that though are just the icing on the cake, narrowboat life even on a rainy day as mentioned above can be cosy, enjoyable and rewarding just to go about your daily tasks.

Saturday 25th January 2014
(no time but a rushed entry while moored up by the New Marton Locks)

"Cancelled a good walking trip planned for today due to a terrible weather forecast. Awoke to find it a perfect morning, very disappointed but decided to make the most of it by kayaking down past the locks and to the old railway bridge past Mad Jack's...

Unfortunately the weather then turned, wind, rain and hale. A nightmare kayaking upstream and into the wind and weather. Had to shelter by a small brick building at the bottom lock, weather didn't improve so just went for it. Got back onboard soaking wet but thankfully just before it started thundering."

Once again a demonstration of how things don't always work out to plan. Not only was my walk cancelled but then the replacement kayak trip was a scramble back in the rain as well. I remember that day clearly as it was a such a sharp and extreme turn in weather conditions that I could literally see the rain and clouds approaching over the large flat area of farmland leading to distant hills. At some points I thought I could beat it back to Tilly but as history records it soundly defeated me.

Searching through all my old diary entries it is amazing to see that even now I record some of the most random and odd things that looking back seem to make no sense in me wanting to remember for the future. What better opportunity will there ever be than now to share a couple of these odd lines.

On Saturday 4th of December 2013 Helena and I met at Tilly then walked down to the nearby garden centre... *"...for cake and to see some Christmas Donkeys. As far as we can tell the donkeys had run off so we gave up and went home."* Monday the 30th of the same month is marked as important because it was the first time that I had filled in a diary entry using a dip pen. I have got to admit that the writing actually looks more readable than my usual squiggles.

On Thursday 7th of November 2013 I am not sure why but I felt it necessary to add the words *"Still single"* to the end of a pretty standard entry. On Sunday 13th of September 2013 I had the opportunity of an empty house so slept in town instead of biking out to Tilly after work then back into town the following morning. This night did not go well as I noted that while biking around town in the dark I lost my inhaler. I knew I had a spare one at my nan and grandad's nearby house and thought I could last the night. Unfortunately though I woke up at four thirty in the morning and could think of nothing else in my half dazed state and phoned them up to say I was coming over to get it. Luckily they took the event in the usual light hearted way of my family and I felt a right fool waking up the next day knowing I had woken them up at a quarter to five in the morning.

Going back almost exactly one year previously to Monday 17th September 2012 I know that I was joined onboard the previous night by Helena in a break from my usual shipmate Jono at the time. This time in September it seems has not been good for my sleeping as I awoke in the early hours and started being sick, which was not very pleasant for poor old Helena to be trapped with me in the fifteen foot indoor space available.

I note several times during the end of 2012 that I could smell a burning chemical smell while travelling and refer to it as *"The smell of disaster"*. Despite this I still didn't get anybody to give the engine a proper look or service until I convince myself everything is fine. I consider it problem solved when I no longer have to travel after paying for winter mooring. A brilliant opening line to one entry for Saturday 1st March opens with *"I am writing this as I record a piece for my short film"* I remember having a camera right on me while I wrote the entry. A tiny clip of which was intended for my short YouTube film "The Narrowboat Lad" I got carried away and forgot to turn off the camera resulting in about seven minutes of footage of me sitting still. That would make for great viewing I am sure. Although that entry does in an odd way tie together so many of my hobbies and loves. I was writing in my diary while being filmed for YouTube as part of my short film about living on a narrowboat, and now I am writing about it here in one of my books. Everything has come full circle!

What is the plan?

The future has never been a place I have given much thought. The fact that I managed to come up with a long term plan to buy a narrowboat and then actually stick to it, was a small miracle in itself. Things did not entirely stick to the initial plan though. I ended up with a much cheaper and smaller boat at thirty foot, rather than my initial interest in a forty to forty-five foot vessel. I was also intending to give up everything or at least leave work for a very long time to immediately go on a huge nationwide adventure with my freshly bought narrowboat.

Luckily I realised that the immediate adventure idea was probably not a good one. Looking back at how much I struggled on my maiden voyage of just under one-hundred miles, a big trip would have likely been a disaster. The struggle I had during this maiden voyage would have been a swift end to my boating days, had it not been for the constant help from friends, family and other boaters. I also can't believe that I was planning to make the biggest purchase in my life, then give up any income to go off to unknown places on a form of transport I had read about extensively, but had almost no practical experience of. Sometimes it seems that plans, if stuck to may lead to disaster, although the second that you deviate from a plan everything turns into guess work on hypothetical scenarios.

Since moving onto and settling down with Tilly, I have had an ever changing series of plans and ideas of what I will do and when. The content, timeframe and entire construction of these plans varies wildly from the simple "I am going to save up and buy a bigger boat" to "I will save up, go exploring for a year or two, and then move into a marina". Sometimes I have brief moments of thinking "maybe next year I will just go into a marina full time" before I then talk myself out of that, and into cruising further afield than ever. Ultimately though, I know that sooner or later I will have to have a new boat. Tilly is a great little narrowboat, she has been around as long as me, has already had most of the hull replated and has a relatively new engine which had less than two-hundred hours on the clock when I bought her. She has everything I need inside and everything is in working order, even if some fittings such as the cooker are a little dated. Remember she is an eighties child like myself!

There is plenty of life left in Tilly and the ever increasing number of chips in her paintwork outside give a sure sign of the life that she is currently living with me, I have no personal plans to move on from her, but the inevitability of such an event has to be realistically thought about. One day I may need more space, not only for potential shipmates but for things I can't imagine, for example I have seen boats with motorcycles on them ready to drive off. I don't think I would get on well with a full on polished up motorbike, but I can see a future where I would not be up for cycling everywhere so somewhere to keep a moped or small scooter would be a very welcome addition for an ageing less fit future version of myself.

A proper separated office area, bedroom, more modern shower room and larger living area, would also be something that the Dan in his later years would find very useful. Adding a partner into the mix would make it an almost urgent issue depending on their enthusiasm for my current waterways lifestyle. The addition of a "better half" could cause all sorts of changes, but I really struggle to envision a scenario where I am torn away from the canal network and remain happy for long.

To further underline the unpredictable nature of my ever changing future, it has always been an option in my mind to keep Tilly and add another small boat to the equation, that I would then tow around. Adding more space at a lower cost and without all of the hassle of selling and moving home entirely this is an idea I have been so actively following at some points, that I have literally been onboard small fibreglass cruisers that are up for sale. It would certainly be more awkward than one bigger boat, but it is exactly the sort of idea that appeals to me immensely. Having two entirely separate modules could be great, one being the day time boat and the other a big cosy bedroom and bathroom. Maybe one as the office and kitchen and the other everything else... Dare I say it, His and Her narrowboats? Being able to hand over a set of keys to an entirely separate boat to a girlfriend who thought Tilly too small for both of us would definitely be a bonus too. I have seen a large boat that tows a much smaller boat, the smaller one has the words

"The Dog House" painted below the name. There is just enough room below the lettering of "Tilly" for something similar!

To bring us back to the serious topic of what my future may be, I really couldn't put my hand on my heart and say that I know what I am going to do. Firstly I am not in any rush to come up with a grand plan as the fact that I have never really had a plan or ultimate goal for the future, even as a child, doesn't seem to have worked out too badly so far. Secondly there is nothing in my life right now that I want to change or more importantly needs to change. I am less than three years away from thirty as I write this, and have a very strong desire to enjoy my quickly vanishing youth. The amount of people much older than me who have told me to enjoy things while I am young, and how they wish they had done things sooner. Whether they are talking about a narrowboat or land based adventure it is advice that I am keenly aware of and a conclusion that I had come to many years ago. The entire narrowboat idea was based around creating a very low cost way of life that would allow me to enjoy as much free time as I could, while also getting me out into the countryside that I adore. For the first two years this lifestyle has been beyond anything I could have expected and I find myself also able to save more money than at almost any other time in my life. Not knowing what the future is and not being prepared for it are two completely different things.

If I had to say that I had a plan then it would barely be a sentence. Keep saving, keep enjoying the opportunity to do this and see what my situation is when I turn thirty. The first boat themed book I wrote was titled *The Narrowboat Lad* when I am thirty I may have to give up the title "lad". Using my birthday as a completely arbitrary point I will see how my life is going, what condition Tilly is in, and how my bank account looks, and then come up with a new plan that I almost certainly won't stick with!

For the moment though, while I am sat here on a boat being rocked by a strong wind despite a near unbroken blue sky visible through the window, I am content to be typing away at this sentence. To say I am happy to be living this life right now still doesn't explain how I feel, it may be a better description to say that I feel honoured to be living this life.

The opportunity to see the countryside from a different perspective, to open my windows to a new view whenever I want, or to almost completely escape from society for a while in the winter months. The ability to have a debt free life even while only working part time hours is a situation that many people struggle to believe and again something I am extremely lucky to have stumbled upon. The stress of money and full time employment replaced by literally nothing. Just peace, quiet and the occasional rush of holiday makers!

I would like to end this book with another diary entry from the early days of my life afloat, the final paragraph sums up a particularly good night onboard. I have read and re-read it a few times before choosing this as the ending to this book. Without realising it, when I wrote the diary entry for Thursday 13th September 2012, I was demonstrating one of the most important things I have learned since moving on to Tilly.

The scenery, peace and solace that can be found on the canal are truly amazing. The long maiden voyage home and many adventures I have had both on the canal and lost up mountains miles away, are things that I look back on fondly. The real things that make life what it is though are the passing experiences from moment to moment. The little things that you don't ever think "Wow! This is a huge memory being made!"

I get an overwhelming sense of teary eyed nostalgia when I look back to the first time that me and my friend Jono tried to make Jacket Potatoes (Baked Potatoes for those overseas!) in the woodburner. We wrapped them up in foil and dropped them in the fire. We fished them out every now and then with the fire tongs. The result was a mixture of perfectly cooked and charred to ash potatoes. I can remember in full detail events not mentioned in the below diary piece, such as how we saw a huge piece of wood drifting down the canal and thought it would be ideal for the fire. It was too far out to reach, so in a cartoon style incident, I grabbed hold of Jono and he slowly moved towards the bank so that I steadily leaned out further and further, until I could hook it up with a stick. It only got more ridiculous as we then had to try and ride our bikes down the towpath while clutching at unbalancing lengths of wood, like medieval jousters.

It is these random events, the tiny things, the everyday moments that are the true essence of life, alone, with friends, with family. Everything that happens is a part of life, and I am extremely lucky that I have been able to live a life on the canal filled with so many special moments.

Thursday 13th September 2012

"Jono came onboard with his new bike in the afternoon and we set off from The Poachers on what was a really good fun two mile trip down to the New Marton Locks. I have been eyeing up this stretch of canal since I first saw it after Jono's first ever night onboard a few months ago. It turned out to be perfect! Middle of nowhere, awesome wildlife and the widest area of dark sky visible for astronomy that I have ever seen. Also not too far to bike to St Martins.

We had another epic time onboard featuring a duck on my foot, crazy wind overnight, some quick astronomy, wood collecting fun, Jono falling between the boat and the bank... And jacket potatoes cooked in the fire!

Why did I not buy a boat sooner?"

The Narrowboat Diaries

The Narrowboat Diaries

By Daniel Mark Brown

www.thenarrowboatlad.com

To SJO

The Years Fly by at Three Miles Per Hour

To say that I have enjoyed my time afloat over the last three and a half years would be an understatement. However, to say that it has been perfect would be an overstatement! Cruising around the Llangollen and Montgomery canals in a tiny thirty foot long boat called Tilly has proven to be a great way to see the countryside and enjoy a relatively peaceful and active life.

As my third full calendar year afloat draws to a close, I am glad to be able to look back on 2015 with a smile, and maybe even with very slightly more wisdom than when the year began. But that is debatable.

2015 is a year that contains some of my fondest memories of my time afloat so far. A year that saw me settle in, even further, to a life with no particular fixed location to call home. More than ever before, my bike became the key to boat life, putting huge commutes in, or very often huge rides just for fun.

It has also been a year of making new friends, having people experience boating for the first time onboard Tilly, and finding myself venture onto other people's boats more often than in my previous years combined!

In many respects though, 2015 feels like it may have been the last year of my "boating childhood". Finding myself dealing with the few, very small problems I came across, without a trace of my old habit of immediately panicking! Being familiar enough with the surroundings of the canal to create two hour long commutes just for fun... and only sometimes getting lost!

As the year passed I found myself with a feeling of vanishing innocence as a small number of less joyful events afloat unfolded. Rumours of violent crime and burglaries floating upstream caused me to change my cruising plans at one point. Finding a broken lift bridge, discovering the Montgomery leaking halfway down, and no longer being able to settle into my regular spot for winter mooring as the bad weather set in. Situations like these have served to underline how much of my life afloat can be out of my direct control, and often entirely in the hands of others.

Luckily, the low moments have hardly been a blip on the radar of another fantastic twelve months of boating fun! To continue this quick introduction to another year of boating beauty, canal cruising, towpath trudging and very frequent soaking wet cycling, I will give a very brief introduction to the star of the show, narrowboat Tilly.

Many people will already be familiar with her by now, but as these books are not written to be read in any particular sequence, I better take a deep breath and run through the general layout for anybody who has stumbled onto this book at random!

Built in 1987 Tilly is as old (or young) as myself. Her thirty foot length is split into a ten foot open cruiser stern, perfect for sitting out and eating during the long summer evenings. Fifteen foot of indoor space, filled with a shower, toilet, sofa bed, storage cupboards, log burning fire, cooker, kitchen sink, and a desk, that I am sitting at as I write these words on a stormy night of wind and rain.

A further five foot can be found making up Tilly's bow, accessed through a set of miniature stable doors next to my writing desk. This area is also covered by a removable material cover, which means I can lean through and grab more fuel for the fire from the bags of coal and wood that I store there, all without getting myself wet, or having to go outside in my pyjamas! Speaking of outside, I should also mention that Tilly's exterior is mainly painted green with her name in large cream letters.

Tilly has been on the Llangollen and Montgomery canals for the last few years, a truly beautiful part of Britain. The canal that the following book takes place upon runs on a winding path in the Welsh border area, crossing between England and Wales multiple times. The rural nature of this stretch of canal cannot be overstated, the surroundings of fields, trees and general countryside are rarely broken by a main road or at most a small town.

Before this introduction comes to an end, I would like to talk a little about the writing of this book. I have enjoyed keeping diaries for many years, which has helped tremendously when piecing together the events in the words below. An extra level of accuracy with dates and time of day for some of the events, is provided by my huge collection of photos taken during the year.

I have decided to keep the names of some of the people mentioned in this book anonymous, this allows them to keep their privacy but is not at all intended to diminish their importance in my life. I especially do not want to draw attention to some people, as the appeal of time on the canal to many is the solitude and silence... not unexpected book cameo appearances!

A Chilly Start

January continued the weather that December had already ushered in. Plenty of very cold days with a bright sun beaming low in a clear blue sky. Occasional dustings of snow, creating a very scenic world to look out on from a toasty warm boat, heated by a crackling fire. There were also a surprising amount of windy days, with breezes and gusts strong enough to liven up the usually calm canal water into waves, that just about reached a height to mimic a very calm sea.

Of course it wouldn't be real British weather without a generous amount of rain dropped in at unpredictable moments, but the thing that I noticed most of all was the cool temperature. It was in this chilly environment that the year got off to an odd start. With Tilly moored in her usual winter spot by the canal side pub "The Poachers" I was frantically working away on a book that I had, once upon a time, intended to have published on New Years Day!

My winter mooring spot at The Poachers, is one of those popular spots that the canal is known for locally. The pub has always been well known and busy, located as it is, right by a main road and also by the canal. This is not just any stretch of canal though, this is the stretch that sits only about a mile away from the Welsh border, where a small valley opens up. The famous Chirk aqueduct stretches across the open fields below, and next to it, the slightly higher but similar looking stone archways of the viaduct run parallel. Following the canal over the aqueduct to the other side of the valley, you are almost immediately met with Chirk tunnel. The aqueduct and tunnel make for two great features of any boat trip in the area. The village of Chirk is only a short distance from the canal, as is the village of Weston Rhyn, which is where my friends have lived since I met them, several years ago. This section of canal also gives me a five mile or so cycling commute to get to work, so not too bad at all!

The first few weeks of the year also saw me working more overtime at my "proper job" in a supermarket, than I had done since buying Tilly. Between filling shelves, writing and then editing, (with the help of my Nan's proof reading), then also spending time up the road at my friends' house, I felt like I was never at Tilly in these first weeks. Yet when I look back at my journals and photographs, I can see that somehow I was still onboard enough to experience some of the perfect moments that have kept me in love with the canals for over three years. My usual late night returns to the canal and early morning disappearances to work on a bicycle, were a regular and very cold experience over the first few weeks of the year. With the dark nights coming in so early, and the mornings often not getting light until well after my commuting time, the sun itself seemed to elude me at some points. Often though, it is the mere act of including a boat into daily life that gives things an enjoyable twist.

Getting back onboard late at night after work, or a day out with friends, can be a cold and barren experience. The relief and joy at getting a fire lit and feeling the heat start to radiate outwards brings with it a feeling of quiet calm, safety and rest that is difficult to describe. Stacking up the fuel on top of a roaring fire, and feeling the boat get extremely warm can even become uncomfortably hot! This discomfort is balanced by being able to drop off to sleep, knowing that when you awake with an early alarm, the fire will still be warm, and you will have a moment of cosy warmth before heading out into the darkness on your bike. Or at the very least that is how I try and justify some of the extremely hot sweaty moments to myself!

The first day of the year that I didn't spend a good chunk of either at work, or sat desperately trying to rewrite thousands of words in a panic, was Saturday 3rd of January: ok, so that is only two days of the year that I had missed, so not too bad at all! (Friday 2nd would have taken the spot as my first "calm day" had I not inexplicably left my Kindle at my Mum's house in Oswestry, leading to not one, but two cycle rides to the town and back, putting about twenty-five miles beneath my wheels.) Tilly sat nestled in a procession of about seven boats which gave me a morning view of incredible serenity. Moored on a straight next to the pub, Tilly overlooked five boats, most of which had smoking chimneys. This gave the canal the look, sounds and smell of a time long forgotten.

Seeing the smoke blown around outside and feeling the heat from Tilly's own wood burner, it was a cosy scene to say the least! The grey sky and damp surroundings only heightened the sense of warmth and primal contentment of being safe inside my tiny home. The only thing missing was the light covering of snow that had remained in the area for a few days over the Christmas to New Year period.

As the day wore on, the weather brightened to the point that the early winter sunset was one of amazing beauty. Before even reaching four o'clock in the afternoon, the sun was setting to Tilly's stern, sending out an incredible orange light to fall on the boats, trees and humpback canal bridge ahead. By five o'clock the world was in darkness, and the eerie spectacle of the thick mist that often rises off the canal at night was now taking over the scene. Shining a torch even a couple of feet over the canal would reveal the rolling, murky clouds emerging from the darkness.

At this point one final item was added to the scene to make sure that it was as perfect an end to the day as possible. In the distance I could see the headlight of an approaching boat. As it emerged through the bridge a few hundred feet away, the headlight was like a blinding beacon in the night, beaming down the canal and illuminating the misty scene. It was a little spooky looking, but at the same time, beautiful.

Travelling extremely slowly and carefully past the moored boats in the darkness, it approached Tilly. As it did so, I could barely tear myself away from the sight, not of the boat itself, but of the now fully illuminated murky clouds over the surface of the canal. Even at night, it was one of the most scenic things I have ever seen. The water, boats and banks all shrouded in varying degrees of fog that made the environment resemble something from another world. A world sat on top of clouds that you could seemingly step onto... although I didn't try it, and don't recommend it!

So ended the first of many perfect days that were to come. The following morning I was back in work and had my regular early morning bike ride to Oswestry, about twenty-five to thirty minutes away. It was an extremely cold ride. Frost and ice covered not only the fields to either side of the road, but also some of the road itself. Definitely a time to be extremely careful as the sun was still not up. As I pedalled through the empty Sunday morning countryside, the sun did finally start to show its face. Just before it rose, and while I was merely a mile and a half away from town, I stopped for a quick hand warming break by a gateway into a field. The view that this break in the hedgerow offered was absolutely stunning.

A hilly field of grass, covered in a thick grey layer of frost made up the foreground. Beyond this in the darkness, a series of distant trees and hedgerows of all shapes and sizes stuck out as black silhouettes against one of the most amazing skies I have ever seen. The sun was getting ready to appear over the horizon, but before it arrived, the sky above me remained a deep purple that faded through multiple colours on its way down to meet the field. From the purple above, the sky changed to a blueish tint before the incredibly vivid orange and yellow took the sky down to the horizon. With the shapes of the trees in front of it the sky looked like it was man made, a piece of stained glass for a candle to burn behind, or a painted sheet of paper with black cardboard trees stuck directly onto it.

What I can never explain about moments like this, is the silent, still environment that I was privileged to be able to experience this within. Between the hours of six and eight in the morning on a Sunday, when many of my cycling commutes take place, it can be imagined that in rural Shropshire there are not many people about. Add in the fact that this was still part of the holidays for many people, and you find even less sign of society out on the twisting roads and country lanes of a frozen region of farmland. It was quite possibly the most serene moment of my life… until I had to get back on my bike and pedal up the last hill before town!

Moments like this enrich my life beyond words. Sometimes they are rare, other times they come day after day. In this case of the rising sun, there were no narrowboats for miles around, yet the simple necessity of the commute is still an integral part of my life afloat. A couple of days later I would have another picturesque moment on leaving Tilly for work in the morning. On January 5th after cycling for less than two minutes down the towpath, then up a narrow lane, I looked across a low point in the hedgerow to catch a glimpse of Tilly across a field.

There were five boats moored around her, a couple with wisps of smoke rising from their chimneys again. It was mid morning, around ten o'clock, so this time I was actually able to see the boats in daylight! Tilly looked smaller than ever, the angle of about forty-five degrees that I was looking from seemed to shrink her next to the other larger boats. What made this moment stand out in my mind though was the scenery between me and the canal. The boats made a perfect backdrop. Things were taken to a new level of rural stereotype when, in the sloping field that separated me and my home, there stood three horses, all wearing coats to keep the winter chill away. I couldn't quite put my finger on why this moment captivated me so much, but it really did make me stop and try to appreciate the moment to its fullest. The fact that this moment of peace and rural beauty was the first sight of my day set things off on a positive note.

During early January I met a fascinating character, who was on a boat moored just around the corner from Tilly. On a whim one day, we ended up on a random stroll up around Weston Rhyn and the local roads. All the while exchanging stories of all kinds. In what would become an alarmingly regular occurrence, I didn't really have to introduce myself, as my YouTube videos had already filled him in on just about everything anybody needed (or didn't need) to know about me! This was another example of the bizarre effect of the internet. My usual shyness and general awkwardness being massively outweighed by the fact that there are some people who come up to me and start conversations about things they already know about me! The difficult introductions to strangers don't happen when the other person already knows you to some extent.

With decades of boating experience, my new friend had stories from the canals and rivers that showed me for the total novice that I really am! It was fascinating to hear tales from the towpath from far and wide. These stories are more than worthy of a book in their own right, so I won't steal anybody else's thunder by sneaking them into this book. It was a great pleasure to be invited for jacket potatoes onboard his boat the following week, where we then proceeded to talk for hours on end.

Tales of how to get engines out of boats without the use of a crane, rescuing a propeller that had dropped off the back of a boat, and plenty more, gave me a great deal of entertainment and also food for thought. How calm and quiet my own boating experience had been so far was highlighted with all these stories. It was something that I remember being grateful for, but also left contemplating the possibilities of what excitement might be had on a great big boating adventure. Long ago, before I had even viewed a narrowboat to buy, I had planned my own ill thought out huge adventures. Any possible long term huge cruising plans must unfortunately be put off in favour of the practical realities of earning money to do so, for the time being, but our multiple conversations over the coming weeks would be an inspiration for my boat based day dreams for months to come.

The cold weather of January allowed us to have an unusually regular sprinkling of snow, no major snowfalls, but enough to make things just about white over. Still, more than an average winter. Sometimes the snow would start at midday before melting away by the evening, other times it would stick around for a day or two. On one evening I was pleased with the prospect of waking up to a good snowfall, as large flakes started to land on the ground while I was on one of my frequent late night walks to "stretch my back", and generally stop myself from seizing up at my desk! I was disappointed to find that even before I had gone to sleep it had all melted away, leaving the towpath a muddier place than ever.

The cold weather brought with it some of the classic bright, crisp and clear winter days. Clear skies and a shining sun may have been hanging overhead, but just how bitterly cold it was on some of my bike rides ensured that the almost summery looking weather was not to be taken at face value. Still, I was more than happy to wake up to find the sun streaming in, rather than on the few extremely windy days, and of course, the less said about the interspersed damp, drizzly days the better.

The cold was even more evident on a day that I decided to turn Tilly around. I could have simply boated up to Chirk, crossed the aqueduct, then turned around before the long tunnel, going back over the aqueduct and down the canal to where I had started.

Instead of taking that short two mile trip, I decided on an even shorter, but stranger option for any onlookers who might have seen it being carried out. As there were no boats moored behind Tilly, I decided to simply untie her and walk her backwards to the turning point only a few hundred feet away. I left the mooring chains still in position on the canal, and made my slow way back, holding onto the ropes as my boots squelched in the ever muddier towpath. I had a camera set up on the roof and I can see how cold the day must been from the footage recorded. Firstly, smoke from the chimney can be seen blowing around the surroundings. More importantly though, despite only being outside of the boat for a matter of minutes, and never further than a couple of feet away, the footage shows me wearing some kind of tubular scarf, with a thick woollen part around my neck and the thinner part wrapped up over my head like a balaclava. On top of this, sits my usual camo cap, I am wearing my "big gloves" rather than my usual cycling gloves, then to top it off, I am wearing a thin waterproof coat over the top of my thick jumper. A sure sign that I wanted to keep the chill out, my waterproof is worn as a windbreaker as often as an actual waterproof layer!

While this spectacle of me taking a boat for a walk was going on, I was spotted by my boating friend, who had the good grace to watch without comment as the slow process and spectacle of my manual boat turn unfolded! Once I was almost back and moored up, he walked over with a gift of an LED light, the first of many that would change the way I lived! Maybe that is a bit over dramatic, but previously my means of light had been the "proper" lights that are powered by Tilly's leisure batteries, which themselves are charged by the engine. Supplementing these were a few cold, bright white, LED work lights.

With this simple gift, I now had a light that I could attach to a small portable power pack that gave out an incredibly bright, but also warm, yellow tinted light. This could be placed and angled almost anywhere, which has proven to be extremely useful ever since, not only for lighting my endless videos, but also for simple things such as looking at the engine at night or peering outside at rustling in the hedgerows! It also encouraged my attempted art by giving me an extremely well lit workspace when I went through my "trying to draw" phases! The addition of this light has made my previous work lights look as primitive as they actually were! An LED may seem like a small thing, maybe even strange to mention at all, but it is the unexpected tiny things that often prove important, and so beneficial.

January ultimately became a month of great memories from the canal. The changing weather was better than a consistent rain or a consistent frost, but I did get a bit restless with not moving Tilly properly, especially as January marked the third full month of the Winter Mooring period. My time was filled with my usual mix of biking and walking, with the writing easing off when I had finally finished and published "Dan's Narrowboat Life".

There were thankfully only a couple of "down" moments in the first month of the year. It was on a short walk up to the village of Chirk for supplies, that I discovered a truly sad sight. A tiny fibreglass cruiser style boat, sat on the bottom of the canal by Chirk Aqueduct. When it had sunk I had no idea, local rumour said it had been abandoned, or at least nobody had seen anyone onboard for a while. I remember that each time I walked past it subsequently, I would feel a slight fear over Tilly's safety. An uneasy feeling of dread seemed to linger with the sunken boat, in the way that somebody with too much time to think about that sort of thing would dwell on!

The sunken boat definitely added another, sad, feature to the canal, albeit less grand and epic than Chirk Aqueduct and Viaduct, as many people who I knew who visited the stone structures, also went on to mention the boat.

It was around this time that I had my first mis-step of the year. One morning I was hoping to make an early trip into Oswestry to get a few supplies and a couple of things sorted online. In the typical way that things like this work, I found myself with a puncture while riding down the towpath, only seconds away from Tilly. I hopped onboard and quickly set about fixing the situation.

Covered in mud from the towpath, the puncture was still easy to fix. A lot dirtier than I had been when I initially set out, I closed the door behind me, jumped on my bike and started out for town again… Until about thirty seconds into the ride when I realised that I didn't have my backpack. I got off my bike and ran back to Tilly to discover that I had not only locked my bag in the boat but also locked myself out! Something that happens surprisingly rarely, considering the amount of "spur of the moment" mini adventures I go on!

Luckily, still being at my usual winter spot, I was only a few minutes bike ride away from my friends up at Weston Rhyn. A place that I have always kept a spare key for exactly these types of situations. Even more luckily they were actually home when this happened, so I could cycle up and collect it immediately. A minor set back, but one that shows the luck and benefit of having friends and family placed all over the canal's winding path.

On January 30th I finally wanted a change of scenery. It was not a huge trip, just over two miles down to St Martins. An area where the canal runs through some very flat open land, which whenever mentioned, I always point out, gives excellent conditions for astronomy. The low horizon showing you a lot of sky in an area of little light pollution.

If ever there has been a day of changeable weather, this was it. Rain, wind, incredible sunshine, then frost by eight o'clock at night. This day sticks out in my mind as in a demonstration of "not learning my lesson", I once again locked my keys inside Tilly!

I didn't realise this until I was well into my short supply trip, up over the fields to a local supermarket. The return journey saw me coming back down over the fields with a backpack full of supplies and no plan on what I was going to do next. About a mile away there was a bus stop, so I could conceivably get to Oswestry and grab my second spare key from my mum's house. I could also walk about an eight mile round trip up to my friends at Weston Rhyn, but that wasn't particularly appealing. Normally I would be able to cycle the trip, but the keys to the bike locks were also attached to the main cork keyring trapped inside.

As I paced around Tilly's exterior contemplating my next move, I saw my keys themselves, on my small desk at the very front of the boat. I instantly had an idea, it was a long shot but worth a try. The desk and keys sat next to a kitchen worktop, the window I could see them through was directly over the worktop. Tilly has large rectangular windows, the top section of which is hinged to open inwards. I was able to just about open the top section from the outside and then pull it upwards to create a gap (that is not intended to be there), by wedging the pane of glass against the indoor blind.

Then in a very "James Bond" moment, or so I liked to think, I took one of the elasticated strings that held down the kayak on top of Tilly, each end of the cord having a wide metal hook, and proceeded to try and "fish out" my keys. This would have been almost impossible were it not for the huge cork float that acts as a keyring. Many boat keys are attached to these corks to ensure that if accidentally dropped into the water, you have a sporting chance of being able to fish them out from a floating keyring.

As I wiggled the hook around as best as I could, I was overjoyed when I felt a new weight on the line. In one of the most glorious moments of the year to that point, I pulled the cord and saw my keys rise to the gap in the window. Success! More importantly a lot of time and hassle was saved by me no longer having to run to the bus stop.

I would happily say that the above description of a few of the events of January sets the scene for what started with a lot of writing, working and very cold cycling, but soon enough turned into an excellent start to the year.

As February rolled around, the cold weather continued to bring some very clear skies and amazing sunsets and rises, especially with Tilly moored in the low flat fields of St Martins. Waking up on an extremely cold Tuesday morning, February 3rd, I was filled with the sense of calm that I feel at certain moments of boat life. Stepping up on the stern I was treated to another amazing sunrise. Bright blue sky above, that faded seamlessly into a peach tone at the horizon. The thing that really made this a moment to savour was the perfectly smooth, mirror image on the glass-like canal surface. Every detail of the sky, colour and wispy white clouds, was there on the water's surface. The trees and canal bank seemed to merge into one image with their reflection, the real tree stretching upwards, while its watery twin stretched downwards.

As the morning passed, the ice on Tilly's roof and stern did melt away, but it can hardly be described as a warm day regardless of the sun in the sky. By late morning, I decided to head the few hundred feet down-stream to fill up with water from the canal side tap. I passed one of the friendly "local boats" on my way down, and had a chat at the water point itself, but the thing that really sticks out as an amazing feature of that morning was the ice formation around the bottom of the tap.

It may sound an unusual thing to focus on, but it was truly a miniature work of art. Very often the water taps will have a continuous drip, no matter how hard you try to stop them. In the freezing conditions, the splashes of water from the dripping tap had sprayed onto the blades of grass at the tap's base. Gradually these had frozen until each blade was a perfectly smooth, blunt, upward pointing icicle! They all came together to form something that looked like it could have been a small bush from another planet... or at least a prop from an old Doctor Who series!

If that wasn't enough to qualify as an exciting day on the canal (which it wasn't), then there was one final detail from the day. I turned Tilly by hand, pushing her bow out into the canal and using ropes to swing her around on a stretch of canal barely more than thirty foot wide. Then I set off up-stream towards my original mooring place of the year, with the intention of mooring up about a mile or so before my usual winter site, in a secluded spot, just down from another canal side pub (purely coincidental) and surrounded by fields of crops.

About two minutes before I reached the spot, I saw a person walking two big dogs down the towpath, we smiled and said "hello" as we passed (the lady and myself, not the dogs!), then after a few moments I heard a huge splash behind Tilly. I turned to see a dog swimming in the canal, soon followed by the second. A heartwarming sight to say the least. What made things even better was the fact that it just so happened that I had a camera pointed back at me from the roof, which also caught the diving dogs too. Something that made for a nice little video clip, and the perfect end to a slow boat trip. Seeing dogs in the canal is not particularly unusual, although I hadn't seen any while I was actually travelling before, but it just added that extra final twist to an otherwise standard bit of boating.

As the day turned to night, the sun started to vanish and gave the naked winter trees a bath of orange light as it went down. I remember looking at Tilly and thinking that she almost looked like a toy boat in the lighting conditions. As the sun finally disappeared, another great day was brought to a close. There had been a perfect sunrise, some general pottering around onboard, a quick trip for water, then to a new mooring spot. The addition of the dogs and ice as minor novelties, then a calm afternoon on an almost deserted canal. The sunset being the final moment to make it a perfect day afloat.

February had some of the coldest days of the year, or maybe I was just moored in the wrong place! What I can say for certain, is that waking up to find the seat of my bike, that was normally black, almost uniformly white with a thick coating of frost, was not something that made me particularly overjoyed to have to scrape it off, then ride the thing for half an hour to work!

The second month of the year also brought a new friend to Tilly. One of my best friends of recent times, also by the name of Dan, finally came out for a boat trip... then we couldn't seem to stop meeting up for mini boat trips for months to come! The first trip was the perfect template for how our days would usually unfold.

On the morning of February 13th, Dan started to walk out of Oswestry, down the winding lane past the Iron Age Hill Fort. This is a route that has been a huge part of my life, and that I must have walked and cycled, at the very least hundreds of times over the last decade. Getting to hear Dan's thoughts on it, and places of note, was interesting to compare with my own experiences. Back on the canal, I found myself walking down the towpath to join the road that would ultimately lead us to meet after a matter of miles. Ideally we would meet up halfway, which would be about three and a half miles each.

It was a dull, slightly damp day. The sort of day that doesn't really have a cloudy sky, instead a seemingly giant unbroken white sheet sat above the area. After only moments on the towpath, walking away from Tilly, I was convinced I could hear a woodpecker. I passed under the first bridge and could tell the sound was coming from the tops of some tall and still naked trees on the other side of the canal. My progress to meet Dan was immediately halted as I tried to pinpoint the exact source of the sound. It took a moment or two but then all of a sudden the woodpecker itself was clearly in sight. I took a few seconds to enjoy the spectacle and contemplate the incredibly violent nature of its head banging, loud enough to hear goodness knows how many feet away on all sides!

Regaining my concentration I set back on my way. Meanwhile, "Other Dan" was making incredible progress. Managing to almost beat me to Weston Rhyn itself, covering over five miles while I had barely managed two, due to my dilly dallying onboard Tilly, then my very distracted amble up to meet him! With a quick stop for supplies at the village shop, we made our way down to Tilly. A new era in canal based "meet ups" had begun.

I gave Dan the grand tour of Tilly, which basically consisted of a lot of tongue in cheek remarks about the bedroom/kitchen/office/studio/dining room that is all really one tiny bit of space! After the important task of also educating him on how to work the portable toilet, proving just how glamorous boat life can be, we set off! After only a couple of minutes travel we found ourselves slightly grounded while we allowed a boat to head down-stream through a bridge. But after that it was plain sailing.

We travelled at my usual slow pace. Making sure to enjoy the experience to the fullest. I convinced Dan to take the tiller and thoroughly enjoyed seeing him go through the initial phase that I had once been through myself, holding on so tightly and stiffly that it makes your arm ache! As we reached the turning point by The Poachers, I decided we would turn around and moor up slightly back down-stream, away from the pub itself.

I let Dan keep the tiller for the manoeuvre but promised I would be on hand to work the throttle, but despite my best efforts and advice, I managed to get us stuck in the mud! In a huge pond like turning point, there is more than enough room to turn a small boat like Tilly. But under the circumstances I managed to completely derail what should have been Dan's first perfect one-hundred-and-eighty degree turn… as luck (or bad luck) would have it, my friend from the other boat had also moored up in the area again and was there filming the whole thing!

We moored up, got inside and stacked up the fire. What followed was a fantastic day of half finished conversations, flying of a miniature drone inside Tilly and general wandering about. I received a message while we were onboard, from the other boater - he had been down and left even more LED light fittings on Tilly's stern. Again the generosity, thoughtfulness and general willingness to help of so many people I have met afloat, shines like a beacon of hope in a seemingly ever more selfish world.

I have often thought back to that original "two Dan" trip. One of the stand out memories to me is of us being sat inside, a bit of drizzle on the windows, while the fire burned away. I was wearing my usual slippers, while Dan wore my back up pair, "The Jono Slippers" as they are often called in honour of another friend. In hindsight, it was another key moment of the year. For the next few months these trips, along with other friends, would become so regular that the period of February to March is almost measured more by these days, than the calendar.

It took less than a week before us two Dans were reunited on Tilly, boating down to the Lion Quays, (the pub that I had been moored by on our original trip), and back up to The Poachers, for no other reason than to enjoy a boat trip. The actual boating itself was a minor part of the day, we would spend most of the time, literally hours on end very often, either cycling or walking around the local area.

The small villages, Chirk Castle, paths and routes we could barely plot on a map, all of these were just a part of our simple days of exploration. Sometimes the weather would be on our side, others not so much, it didn't really matter. Taking Tilly to fill up with water, moving her for the sake of a change of scenery or simply ending up back where we started. It was great to have found another like minded soul to get out there with, as many of my friends had moved to working night shifts over the previous years, making our meet ups less frequent than they once were. Quite what Amy, Dan's girlfriend, must have thought about him returning home with tales of us "going out to play" I dare not think!

Writing this section of the book has brought to my attention just how varied my boating experience was during the first three months of the year. Considering this time was all spent on roughly only two miles of canal that made up my winter mooring area, I feel as if I have a huge amount of experiences to share. In reality many of these may just be different variants of the same sort of event, such as having friends onboard, getting the kayak out, and finding all kinds of wildlife at unexpected moments. Don't worry, I am not about to break into a repetitive daily breakdown of these events, but I do want to spend a bit of time hopefully adding a bit of colour to the time of year when spring finally started to truly replace winter.

One of the features of February that was a favourite sight of mine, was the appearance of large amounts of snowdrops. Tiny white flowers popping up amidst the still brown and barren woods, hedgerows and canal bank. In a small patch of land just next to the towpath, only a few dozen feet away from Tilly, there was one of the most concentrated collections of them that I have ever seen, literally hundreds of them clumped together like sheep's wool. After the era of the snowdrop, the daffodils took over. Popping up all over the place in similar fashion, the bright yellow flowers made a beautiful lining between the canal and towpath, by the turning point by the pub. They also made the perfect decoration to the grass verges on either side of the canal as you left the Welsh side of Chirk aqueduct. A good welcome to Wales indeed!

Overseeing this changing landscape was the ever more changeable weather, plenty of wind, some sun, a lot of heavy downpours, frequently all in one day, and it made for some very unfortunate commutes. I would find myself on more than one occasion soaked through with rain despite setting out with the sun shining, conversely I would sometimes find myself sweating under far too many layers of clothes when the sun popped out on what I had expected to be a chilly morning. Simple things that I am more than used to after three years onboard, but still not ideal, especially when arriving back onboard soaking wet after work in the last minutes before midnight. Steamed up windows aplenty helped to mark these occasions for any towpath walkers!

It was during these months that I really got back into cycling in a bigger way than I had for a long time. Even though my bike is a huge part of my boat life, enabling me to actually get to and from Tilly whenever needed, I found myself cycling more and more on long commute routes or just going out for fun. The simple acts of commuting to work and visiting friends and family ensures that I ride thousands of miles a year as a built-in statistic, but when my new phase of really going out of my way on the bike started, I found myself worn out to the point of falling asleep in a chair on more than one occasion. Perhaps I am just getting old though!

I am not really sure what it was that started me off, but I found myself with a strong urge to revisit a lot of the places that I had frequently walked and cycled in the years before I had a boat. Being on my winter mooring not far from these areas gave me the perfect opportunity to set out from Tilly at any time of day and cycle through the almost forgotten sweeping curves and bumpy roads of the English and Welsh countryside.

The sense of nostalgia that I had when doing some of these rides was overpowering, even the frequently unpleasant weather couldn't take away some of the memories that came back to my mind from times almost a decade earlier. Remembering walks with friends, quick breaks for something to eat and random strangers I had bumped into, it was a period that gave me a lot of time to think about things, how life had turned out and how I could never have imagined what I would have ended up doing all these years later.

If I could have bumped into my past self on one of those lonely, empty roads, I think I would have been forced to tell him not to worry, and that things would be fine. It would have eased the thread of concern about what I was going to do with my life, that I know used to weave through a lot of my thoughts.

Without getting too deep or spiritual, it is fair to say that I really enjoyed getting back into cycling in an even bigger way than I had been for a while. It was lucky too, as I would continue this theme for most of the months to come, leading April to be one of the most active and productive months of my life.

It is strange to try and write about what happens in my life, as there is so much that needs to be left out to stop this book turning into an in depth look at each of my days. For example, the hours of supermarket work that I put in are completely overlooked, as they are an accepted background theme that makes all the rest possible. It is unrelated to my boat life but it also seems too harsh to not even mention the incredible changes and growing up of my friends' (up the road from Tilly) baby, born in the previous November. Being able to see him grow, change and learn, as the year progressed was amazing. Quite a remarkable thing to witness during all the hours that I spend visiting them or when we go off out on mini adventures together... admittedly the adventures are a little rarer now there is a one year old to consider!

Cycling to my Nan and Grandad's house to sit around a big table and eat with the family, walking miles to a bus stop and then going off to visit my Dad and little Sister, there are so many elements that make up life that I cannot possibly list or detail here, but that I want to mention and draw attention to. I feel it is important to flesh out my character a little more for a change, in order to not appear like a boating, cycling, writing, YouTubing robot in the description of the months ahead!

One of the yearly traditions that I also got around to during March was my trip (by bus) to Llangollen, to walk up and around the hills on the outskirts of the town. I am not sure why I love the whole day so much, but it has become an activity that I try and set aside a day for, with no time limit or expectations set.

Sometimes I have found myself making repeated trips out from the canal to walk around different areas of the Berwyn Mountains where Llangollen lies, this year however, it was just the one trip.

These trips really do seem to sum up the idealised view of a day of boat life. Beginning with waking up onboard with the stereotypical last bit of heat coming from the dying fire. Then walking over the mighty stone Chirk aqueduct right next to the even bigger stone viaduct, offering a morning view down the valley and onto the small Welsh hills in the distance.

Waiting at the bus stop in the village of Chirk itself, the bus that arrives to head to Llangollen is a tiny minibus, seeming to sum up the old fashioned image of tiny village communities dotted around the Welsh border.

Arriving in Llangollen, I have only one real place that I have to visit, the bakery, then stocking up on "blue cheese bombs" and vegetable rolls, which is a vital part of the day. This particular walk is around my favourite route, crossing over the roaring river Dee in the town, it can be only a matter of minutes until I find myself going up the steep roads that lead to the even steeper fields that end up at the castle ruins of Dinas Bran.

Overlooking the town and a huge area of hilly countryside, the old castle ruins do not take long to get to, the sheer angle that the hillside becomes, really did make it an excellent place to defend if needed! The view is well worth the breathlessness! Especially with the added columns of old stonework and arches just about still intact. The hilltop is extremely windy and renowned among local walkers for the almost constant gales.

From that hilltop I decided to continue around the "Panorama Walk" on the neighbouring hill. A hill with a series of huge steps carved into it by time, leaving it as a series of rocky cliffs and half valleys. Spending hours out on these hills, before finding my way down to the narrow lanes that would lead me back to Llangollen is as peaceful and remote, (and sometimes scary when peering over ledges), as I could ask for.

The inevitable late afternoon bus ride to Chirk and early evening arrival back on Tilly brought the day to a perfect close. I have written and talked at length about these adventures in previous books and videos, but I could never tire of them. If in decades to come I still find myself walking these routes, I will have little to complain about!

Finally, A Bit of Warmth!

When the winter mooring period finally drew to a close, I couldn't have imagined how many great times the rest of the year would bring with it. Even moving away from the Poachers and my winter mooring area was a sign of good things to come. On March 31st "Other Dan" and me untied Tilly's ropes and set off over Chirk aqueduct, through the tunnel, before passing the local marina and another smaller tunnel a short distance away from there.

When we started, it was a windy, drizzly day. So windy that when we found ourselves exposed in the open, passing over the aqueduct, the inflatable kayak on top of Tilly's roof found itself turning into a kite and very nearly leaving us for a better life either in a tree or elsewhere being dragged along the towpath! This short trip of about four miles, took us almost two hours, being especially slow due to the tunnels. As with all the best times travelling onboard, the destination was almost irrelevant, the arrival time was never discussed, and a fun time was had by simply moving at less than three miles an hour.

Passing through the final short tunnel, we moored in a place known as the "far side" of Chirk, although it all depends on which side of the village you live! Even though the canal is surrounded, at face value by the usual beautiful mixture of trees and fields, there is also the unfortunate noise of a nearby road and train track. But even with that addition it is still a place I love. The road allows easy cycling access and even easier bus access for any bigger shopping trips.

What was more important on that day in particular ,was the fact that less than two miles away stood the impressive Pontcysyllte aqueduct, with its extremely narrow path and lack of railings on the water side. Without a second thought we tied the ropes, had a quick moment of panic when I dropped my phone within a few inches of landing in the canal, and then set off walking down the towpath.

Even as we walked away from Tilly the weather was improving. Stepping foot onto the aqueduct and doing all the appropriate "oohing and ahhhing" at a genuinely impressive spectacle of engineering, we crossed over with the sun peering out at us, lighting up the valley and the river Dee below perfectly. The naked trees still not showing too much promise of the spring that was meant to be bringing them all back to life.

We had a walk around the Trevor basin and then up into the village to buy a few supplies from the tiny shop that seems almost hidden from the public, giving a feeling that it is "for local use only!" By the time we were off down the towpath again, it was a beautiful sunny day.

Warm, bright and with a blue sky above us we stretched a last bit of exploration out of the day by investigating the culverts that run under the canal, allowing tiny streams to pass through some of the surrounding fields. Then before we ended up getting too carried away and having wet feet, (we didn't actually enter any of these tiny tunnels I should point out!) our paths for the day parted. Dan went cycling down the towpath and vanished into the tunnel at Tilly's stern, I got back inside Tilly to continue editing a book in preparation of recording the audio version. A task that saw me turning my Nan and Grandads empty house into a recording studio.

As luck had it, right when I needed to find somewhere quiet to record the audiobook of my original narrowboat book "The Narrowboat Lad", my Nan and Grandad went away to open up their caravan for the holiday season… meanwhile back at their house, I created the worlds' least professional recording studio! Setting up a laptop and microphone on a stool, and with a cushion to kneel on, I was surrounded by all of their living room furniture making a small echo proof booth. To complete this soundproofing I did the only thing that I could think of, threw a blanket over the top of the entire area to create something resembling the type of "den" that I used to make as a child.

Even though the final audiobook was less than three hours in length, the recording time was unbelievably long, repeating lines over and over and over again… throw in the bike rides to and from Tilly at any given moment and it made for a very tiring period… not to mention actually doing my real job too.

In return for this invasion of their empty home, I like to think that I paid them back a few days later with a boat trip that included passing over Pontcysyllte Aqueduct not once, but twice. This is the most famous landmark in the area. A huge stone and steel aqueduct cutting across fields and a river. Even when Other Dan had joined me for a walk, he was surprised at how narrow the path was, but even more so that in the modern age it was possible to have an aqueduct that had a sheer drop on the waterside. It is probably the most "in your face" dangerous feature on the local canal, the edge of the aqueduct is lower than the step onto Tilly's stern. One wrong step and you could literally fall straight over to a very unpleasant fate. This is one of the reasons that the aqueduct pops up on television so frequently, history, danger and boats, all in one handy location!

It was another pleasant morning when I quickly went around Tilly, dusting every surface yet another time before they arrived. The weather was a perfect mixture of a bit of sun, a slight chill and a hint of pastel like, off white, cloud covering the blue sky that was still partially visible through it all.

When my grandparents came walking down the towpath, carrying with them a classic day trip dinner of rolls, crisps and a Mars bar for "afters", I was all ready to go. That was until we tried to remove the mooring chain that had been holding the stern in place. With all of the Bank Holiday traffic and speeding boats of Easter week, it had become wedged between two bits of the metal canal side. It must have taken a solid five minutes of wiggling, wobbling and heaving before I finally used a claw hammer to apply the tiniest amount of pressure to the situation, only to have the chain slide right out without any trouble or effort! Now we were boating!

The plan wasn't entirely set in stone, apart from the vague idea that we were going to cross over Pontcysyllte at least once. After the first ten minutes, we realised that it may have been a mistake to let one last boat go ahead of us before we set out, as that said boat was travelling so slowly that, even keeping Tilly in a mixture of "tick over" and neutral, we still caught up with it. I am notorious for travelling slow and always make sure that I immediately let any boats pass if they appear behind me, so when I say another boat is slow, I mean slooooooow. This was not a problem at all though, as in the usual way when facing anything resembling even a slight problem while boating, I simply moored up. After barely fifteen minutes of travel, we all sat around tucking into our dinner. Perfect!

A few more boats passed by before we headed back on our journey, so we got in line and headed up towards the aqueduct. It was great to have my Nan and Grandad onboard to experience their first lift bridge… and also help out with it. At this point we also bumped into somebody who knew me from the internet, which is always fun. Then as we approached the narrow aqueduct itself, we saw that we were in for a busy crossing.

Not only were there plenty of walkers, but ahead of us on the canal was a line of boats that had all caught up to the slow boat from earlier. Even though we had stopped and eaten dinner in no rush, we had still managed to catch up with them within a mile of canal. This made for an excellent, very slow crossing of the aqueduct. So slow that at multiple times the entire procession of boats came to an absolute standstill. What a place it is to stop too!

I was happy to have my Nan and Grandad's first experience of the aqueduct on a boat be a slow one, to savour every moment. The view and feeling that you really should back away from the side of the boat when looking down into the valley is slightly more adrenaline inducing than the usual canal moments. There is something very satisfying about being on a boat, suspended over one-hundred feet above a river and a football pitch, (and a sewerage plant), and coming to a complete standstill. With nothing but the hills and countryside to see.

When we did make it to the other side, I had to make up my mind exactly what it was we were going to do next. Carry on further? Moor up further along the canal towards Llangollen? Turn around? What greeted me at Trevor basin immediately made the decision for me. There was total chaos, or at least as much chaos as a canal can get into. Boats of every size were jostling for position. Some missing the turning to continue to Llangollen, others waiting to go one way or another, not sure who was heading where or when. People shouting advice on how to reverse a boat as a huge holiday boat travelled backwards towards them! Without a second thought, I steered Tilly to one side of the canal as it widened out from the aqueduct entry, then when I knew we had just enough room, I pushed the tiller right across and pulled off probably the most perfect one-hundred-and-eighty degree turn I have ever done. The joy of a small boat!

The fact that for once I had managed to do some moderately competent boating while having other people onboard was a bonus, doing it at a crowded Trevor basin and avoiding the chaos that had been ahead was the icing on the cake. Within a matter of less than five minutes of leaving a crowded aqueduct, we were back on it, and the only boat on it too! Just the force of the water being funnelled into the narrow channel was enough to push us at a greater speed than we had achieved on the previous crossing. With that, we enjoyed a slow trip down-stream, meeting only a couple of boats, it was as leisurely as could be. I tried not to touch the tiller at all for this period, and just enjoyed being a passenger on a quiet canal under the sun, whilst my Grandad steered us along.

To add one final touch to the trip before my grandparents left, we decided to go through the small tunnel and moor close to Chirk Marina. With that all said and done, I watched them walk away and out of sight down the towpath. Another great day drawing to a close. April was already becoming a sign of a great cruising season to come.

April also saw the rise and rise of the "Dan and Sarah Adventures" phase of the year. Sarah, my long suffering, "not quite girlfriend but maybe?" is somebody who I have had so many great times with over the past couple of years that they could easily fill their own book. For the summer months about to unfold in this book, Sarah also makes up a good part of boat life.

The excellent turn in the weather during April, led to not only many great days on the canal, but also even more fun and adventures with friends. We certainly had a few good downpours of rain mixed in, but when you have so much sunlight to make up for it, it is difficult to complain. The stage was already set for a great summer afloat.

When I decided it was time to move away from Wales and revisit some of the spots on the canal that I had not seen for six months, I chose what I had hoped to be a calm Sunday evening after work to move down-stream from the marina. When I finally arrived back at Tilly, it was a little drizzly and overcast, but undeterred I immediately locked my bike to the stern and set off intending to put in a good few miles before sunset.

As I travelled down through the tunnel, back across the aqueduct and through the tight bends of Chirk Bank, I was pleased to see plenty of boats moored up. The canal was once again a more lively place, but not quite as lively as the recent Bank Holiday had been. As I made my way back down past The Poachers then waved goodbye to my winter mooring, (not knowing at this point I would not have the option to return for the following winter), I was extremely happy to see the sun come out and the rain stop. Moving further down-stream, past the Lion Quays and through the open fields above the New Marton Locks at St Martins, the sun really came out, just in time for a beautiful sunset.

I came to the first of the two locks, and started to go through the usual very slow and precise routine of raising and lowering paddles. I had a bit of luck that a holiday boat turned up, offering some gratefully received help. We chatted away, and I tried to give rough directions and distances of where places that I often take for granted are, in relation to the canal. It was a really pleasant few minutes. I enjoy hearing other peoples' thoughts and views on the local canal, that I have known for so long that it is almost beyond my mind to notice new things or details that I have assumed are not there, based only on an assumed total familiarity.

After our calm evening chat, I moved down to the next lock. Everything went to plan, and another set of holiday makers helped me get through the lock quicker too. As they opened up the lock gates for Tilly to emerge, I pushed the throttle forwards and with a bit of a splutter… the engine died! Telling myself that I must have accidentally pushed the 'stop' button, I turned the key and restarted the engine… pushing the throttle forwards, I was faced with the reality that there really was a problem, when the engine died again! I looked up at the holiday helpers and uttered a line to the effect of "I'm terribly sorry about this but I seem to have broken down, it might take me a moment to drag her out of the lock by hand".

With that I grabbed a rope and climbed up onto the side of the lock and walked Tilly out and down to moor on the last of the temporary mooring mushrooms. There were two of the regular local boats moored right behind them. It was at this point that I realised, once again, that I knew nothing about boats! But in a promising sign of how far I had come from the trembling nervous wreck I'd been on first buying Tilly and living in fear of everything on the canal, I simply decided to deal with it.

When I tried to move the tiller, I found that it would freely turn at all points apart from when the rudder was passing directly by the propeller. This indicated that there was something wrapped around it. I lifted up the deck boards and could see no obvious problem with the engine, confirming my suspicion that the problem was on the outside. Luckily there is a weed hatch that you can unscrew and get right to the propeller from inside the engine bay. As the light was steadily failing I decided to set straight to work. The seized up bolts that hold the top of the weed hatch in place were not for moving at all, so with the help of a windlass (lock handle), I started to "coerce" (read as: batter) them, to loosen them up. The volume of this metal on metal banging was so loud that I felt I had to go and apologise in advance to the nearby boat for the din. I was pleased to get a good response and even an offer of help, which I declined out of fear for what I would find, and how much it might highlight my lack of knowledge.

So as the last of the sunset turned to genuine darkness, I battered the weed hatch open put my hand in a thick glove and started to feel around the propeller... two things hit me instantly, the freezing cold water, and the fact that instead of a propeller, I was simply grabbing a huge clump of long bramble like vines of greenery. I started to pull at the tangle and with a small effort, huge amounts of strips of stringlike shrub started to come off. The canal had been full of the discarded cuttings from some maintenance work either earlier in the day or on a previous day... the results had been less growth on the towpath, but far more growth than ever before on Tilly's propeller! I would later find out that other boats had succumbed to this issue too. There in the darkness, and with one freezing cold forearm, I was just happy to have found and solved the problem. Making another huge noise, I got the weed hatch back on tightly, gave the engine a quick test and then went inside to warm up and get into bed, ready for work the following day.

My trip had been cut slightly short of where I expected to make it to at the very least, but the open fields as scenery, and easy road access to town were benefits that I was happy to enjoy. When

I awoke the following morning, I had one of my shortest boat trips ever, literally just around the two boats ahead in order to get off the temporary moorings for the lock. Then, satisfied that everything was in ship shape, I set off for work on my bike. Good times indeed!

At this point I would like to insert a random story that doesn't really fit anywhere else. As I left Tilly at "Mad Jack's", (a canal side pub), on my bike, on yet another sunny morning, I heard somebody shout my name on an approaching boat. To my surprise, it was somebody who had been following me online for a while. A friendly chap who was taking an extended break from his usual work as a Reverend, while work took place on the ancient building he was based at. We exchanged a few polite words and I promised to make sure we met up while he was still in the area.

As the days went by and I found myself at work and generally distracted by the good weather, our paths didn't cross. He ended up heading down onto the perfectly rural Montgomery Canal, not too far away from Tilly, but even closer to my home town of Oswestry. This gave me a brainwave, and after work one day, instead of heading out to Tilly, I left town in an entirely different direction, and in roughly twenty minutes I was onboard his fantastic little boat.

I was happy to discover that of all the places he could have moored, the boat was pretty much exactly in the same few feet of canal that I like to moor Tilly, on my way down this overgrown, peaceful stretch of canal. This was a good sign that we were on the same wavelength. A few hours of the evening passed with us walking a few miles around the local canal, while I talked, talked and talked some more, about everything in the area. It was probably a perfect example of how boring I can be about the places I have grown up and seen over the last twenty years!

As the sun started to dip, we returned to his boat and I had to try and look relatively normal for a selfie! The first of many that I would be in during the year. I wanted to mention this moment in particular as it was not only a perfect enjoyable evening, but also an indication of how the summer would be. I had been amazed repeatedly during the previous year when dozens of people had known who I was after seeing me waving my arms and talking excitedly about the canal on YouTube. I try not to dwell on these things when writing as it can easily sound big headed, when in actual fact I find it extremely humbling that anybody would listen or watch anything I had to say. I thought this would be about as suitable a place as I could get, to mention just one of the many great people I met in this way during 2015. Similar to my friend from the start of the year, it was incredible to be able to make a friend based on somebody already knowing all about me! It seems a little more unbelievable the more times that it happens, and I am just as grateful and amazed as it shows little sign of stopping.

One of the benefits of being in the general vicinity of "Mad Jack's" was that it meant I was right on Sarah's route to and from work leading us to meet up and go off adventuring more than ever. I have no idea how many times I would go on to meet her at the canal. We would drive around to different local places of interest, only to finally look back for home when the sun set with amazing pastel colours in a near cloudless sky. The weather that gave us plenty of these moments helped make some experiences like something out of a story book. Local beauty spots, around the hills of Llangollen, Oswestry Racecourse, and Mount Woods (another frequently walked area from my winter mooring time). We saw the sun set on Shropshire and Wales more times than I think I saw the sun at all during winter!

Even on Tilly, we were lucky enough to put in some extremely short trips before the sun vanished. Sometimes we would only move just around a corner or two, simply for the experience of getting another newcomer to take the tiller for the first time! April was truly a great month all round.

On one of the only genuinely dark overcast days, me and another friend made the short trip from Mad Jack's, passed all the moored boats at Maestermyn Marina and moored by the Frankton Locks, that would soon drop Tilly down onto the Montgomery Canal. I remember that day well, it was the usual Dan "plus one" experience. We boated only three miles, yet made it into over an hour of travelling, neither of us being in any rush, things were slowed down even more by me setting up a camera extremely high on a tripod on Tilly's roof. This needed taking down at every bridge we came to, leading to some near miss moments!

After mooring, we went on a ramble through the surrounding fields and back up to Tilly on the towpath. After hanging around onboard for a while we decided to set out on an entirely unplanned bike ride. Again, in usual fashion we spent less than one minute on a "main road", sticking entirely to the bumpy country lanes and occasionally landing back on the towpath for a moment or two. The perfect way to spend literally hours without looking at the time or worrying about doing anything productive!

There was another day while Tilly was moored by Frankton that summed up this active first month of travel. Dan had arranged to meet me on the towpath a short distance away, both of us on bikes. I set out at noon to meet him, not expecting that on the beautiful sunny day that it was, we would end up spending five hours together talking and wandering, never more than a mile away from Tilly. Despite being so close, we were so caught up in talk of Vikings, Rome and mythology, (no honestly!) that Dan never actually set foot inside Tilly during all of that time. Instead when we were with Tilly, we stayed on the stern enjoying the peace and scenery of the canal under a blue sky. It was another rural spot, surrounded by nothing but fields with only a farmhouse to remind us of society.

April was such an active month, that I have decided to gloss over the fact that my birthday occurs during it, as even though I spent the day visiting friends and cycling in the sun, it was not a noteworthy exception for the time period! Neither was an adventure in the Cheshire countryside with my Dad, which could generate a huge amount of writing under any other circumstances. Again both days summarise the month as they were, perfect hot sunny days, with as much countryside as you can reasonably expect to see in the daylight hours.

Yet despite this active outdoors burst of energy, I also managed to somehow record and edit more videos for my obsessive YouTube hobby, than ever before. Dozens upon dozens of videos of walks, boat trips, bike rides, and simple stories to camera were recorded, edited and uploaded during that great time. Setting off yet another trend of the year, having multiple videos ready to post as and when needed, to the extent that by the end of 2015, I had managed to schedule at least one video a week to post online right into March 2016. Along with preparing an entirely new video series and more documentary episodes than I thought possible... It is no surprise that April also saw me sleeping better than ever!

Merry on the Monty

When 2014 drew to a close, I remember looking back and saying that I would be happy to live another year just like it. It seemed at some points, that 2015 was going to follow a very similar path. As on my birthday in 2014, my family had joined me to pass down through the Frankton locks, whereas during 2015 I found myself making the same trip only a few days after my birthday. This time however, with Dan and Amy, his fiancée.

The day prior to the trip through the locks and down onto the Montgomery Canal was yet another perfect illustration of the great summer months I was lucky enough to enjoy. Spending a sunny morning onboard, recording and editing videos, then sitting down in the afternoon to write some letters sealed with an old fashioned wax seal, as cows drank from the canal only a few feet away, opposite Tilly.

A little later, Sarah met me by Tilly and we headed off in the car further up-stream to the beautiful Colemere, a small lake that sits only a couple of minutes walk from the canal. Walking around the perimeter under the trees, a breeze rolling through to add a bit of life to the place, we heard another sound join the trees' hissing in the wind. It was a small stunt plane, something I have seen in the area many times from onboard Tilly. At Colemere it was directly above us, as the pilot executed perfect manoeuvres in an almost unbroken sequence of tricks.

As we stood watching the plane dance around at all angles and speeds, I remember the passing clouds behind it adding an odd sense that we were also moving, which left me feeling a little disorientated... but not so much that it put me off stopping at Ellesmere for a portion of chips to eat on the edge of the lake that the town is named after. While fighting off the seagulls, ducks and geese, we managed to gobble down our food before setting out for a short walk around our second mere of the day.

The early evening saw the temperature drop and by the time we had arrived back at Tilly, the sky was increasingly empty of clouds. In preparation for the following day's passage through the locks, we took Tilly for another of our "epic boat trips" and moved all the way around the corner to moor right by the locks themselves. After Sarah had left, I set about getting Tilly all in order for any potential needs that my guests/helpers may need on the following day. By nine in the evening, almost every cloud had vanished and the stars started to sparkle in the still pale blue and purple sky. Standing on Tilly's stern, I could see for miles over the flat expanses of Shropshire fields, and I could see stars millions of miles away overhead. Only a matter of feet away, I could also see long into the past, the locks and tiny hut next to them, painted in the black and white colour scheme the canals are famous for. The only thing missing from the scene was a puff of smoke billowing from the small chimney that peeked out of the hut's roof.

Waking the following morning, I was pleased to find another day of sun and blue sky for the day's boating. Things went in the usual way at the locks. As the midday opening time got closer, the amount of boats joining the queue grew. As I awaited Tilly's turn to go down, and also the arrival of Amy and Dan, I chipped in and helped wind a few paddles for the boats making their slow trip up or down through the locks. Then as if by magic, moments before it was time for me to hop on Tilly and start her up, my two friends walked down the towpath. So it was that another great day really got underway.

Amy joined me onboard as I gave Dan a windlass (the handle to crank the lock paddles with in order to let water in or out) and sent him off to do the physical work! Luckily the experienced Canal and River Trust (CRT) chap was there to guide him through the process. As a side note here, I will add that the waterways worker is somebody who I consider a friend, and have seen many times at different points of my canal boating career. On Dan's arrival and my quick and excited movements to get things going, the CRT helper summed up my actions (and what others have accused me of on previous occasions) perfectly, with the simple line "You've got too much energy for me!"

As we moved through the locks, helping out and being helped by the other boaters enjoying their own trips, it was great to see Dan figure out the whole process and learn that it was not something that could or should be rushed. Once we had finally dropped through the last of the four Frankton Locks, the three of us were all onboard to immediately witness an amazingly close heron sighting. With the huge bird taking off just ahead of Tilly, sweeping in a huge semi-circle right around us, before returning to the canal bank to our rear. In a nutshell, Dan and Amy had seen exactly the sort of moment that makes the canal so appealing to me.

We soon reached the "Graham Palmer Lock" a tiny lock that only drops/raises your boat a matter of a few inches. A perfect opportunity for us to properly talk and look at the lock mechanism before continuing on our way. As we moved into the more rural and empty section of the canal, I was aware that with every passing minute I was adding to my passengers' walk back up to their car. After an hour and a half of boating, we pulled over onto the temporary mooring mushrooms at a tiny aqueduct, somewhere that I have been lucky enough to spend a couple of peaceful nights in in years gone by. Looking back at my photos from this day I was amazed to see that it had taken so long to get there, one and a half miles in one and a half hours, roughly speaking. The locks, speed limit and jovial nature of the trip, all helped slow down my already slow two to three mile an hour average when travelling. We said our "farewells", and as I do so often, I saw my friends vanish down the towpath leaving me and Tilly in a silent and beautiful patch of countryside.

After a short debate with myself, I decided to press on with the trip. Determined to enjoy every moment, I found myself completing the day's total of over six miles boating in a mere five and a half hours! Travelling that slow for so long was a great way to pass the day and simply enjoy the sun, scenery and serenity of a canal that I met no other moving boat on, after the initial trip down through the locks. With the canal passing through some of the most rural, quiet places for miles around, I think I could have been the only person within earshot for hours of the day. Perfect!

Mooring at Maesbury, the closest point that the canal runs to my hometown of Oswestry, and of course my friends, family and workplace contained within, I was happy to know that my cycling commutes would be less than three miles, and the return journeys to Tilly could take little more than ten minutes... if I had a lot of energy left for pedalling after work! Once again, by the evening time, the sky cleared, the temperature dropped, and I enjoyed a plate of pasta before a late evening stroll down the pitch black towpath. So it was that April finally came to an end, ensuring that it would hold some of my fondest memories of the year.

Spending the next two weeks moored at Maesbury passed in the usual relaxed way. Knowing that there was no huge cycling commute to do to get to work, family and friends, allowed for less worry over the weather as some dark wet days started to filter into the start of summer. It was equally handy for my friends and family to come out to Tilly and actually be able to find her!

On one of the many sunny but windy days that made up a lot of the weather of early May, Dan came back out to Tilly for a short trip. One that I had been hoping he would be present for, due to the fact that we would be passing through a lift bridge twice. Not only is having a second pair of hands at these places always useful, but it would also be his first experience of cranking up the huge bridge, and with it part of an old country lane, at a slow but steady pace. The lift bridge at Maesbury is perfectly placed only a few minutes travel away from a turning point, the turning point itself marks the end of the navigable stretch of canal. The Montgomery soon runs dry after this point before opening up again out into Wales, but unfortunately out of reach for boats travelling from the Llangollen.

The location of the bridge so close to the turning point means that you end up passing under it twice in relatively rapid succession, but not quite quickly enough that you don't have to lower it between passes. The canal is wide enough that I can turn Tilly just before she reaches the bridge... but where is the fun in that?

We moored up at the same place we had set off from, although now facing in the opposite direction, then had our usual series of walks and talks. This time exploring the nearby service station, with water point, toilet emptying facilities, and even a shower, before heading off up the canal to look at an old working boat.

After a few hours of boating, biking and talking, not to mention a very quick kingfisher sighting, Dan headed off home and I had a few hours of tinkering time onboard before meeting Sarah for another adventure in the evening. Taking full advantage of the ever lighter evenings, we enjoyed a drive around all kinds of lanes we had never travelled before in the nearby Welsh hills. Eventually we found ourselves at the foot of Dinas Bran Castle. We parked up, and made our slow ascent up the very steep hillside and for the second time of the year I got to see the fantastic view and feel the extreme wind conditions.

Walking around the ruins as nine-o-clock at night rolled around while the sun sank in the sky was beautiful. The hint of darkness adding to the wind-whipped barren feeling of the place, which in turn made it seem all the more cosy to be up there with a loved one. Simply enjoying the moment after a fantastic day on the canal. Soon though we had to get back, and on returning to the canal on my own I had a warm feeling of peace and calm. The silent canal surroundings being a stark contrast to the wind of the hilltop that roars so loud it is almost difficult to hear your own voice… something that is very rare for me to experience! I settled into bed on Tilly and slept very well after the hours of an active day.

In the usual way that my time at Maesbury seems to pass in the blink of an eye, I found myself heading back up the canal towards the junction back onto the Llangollen in mid May. The days seeming to have zipped by in a haze of cycling, walking with friends, sun, wind and rain. As I made my slow way up the canal on the twelfth of the month, it was again a day of great sun, blue sky but also a slightly higher wind than I would have liked.

Leaving Maesbury, I passed through the overgrown rural canal, finally reaching the Aston Locks, three locks by the small village of Queens Head, known mainly for its pub! As you have come to expect from the "Summer of Dan and Sarah", on reaching the first lock it didn't take long until Sarah had walked down from the car at Queens Head and joined me onboard for yet another short boating experience. We passed through the middle lock and decided that given the windy conditions we would moor up before reaching the third. Nestling Tilly into the side, at the widest or least overgrown part of the canal we could find, we sat onboard and debated what our next move would be for the day.

Keeping it canal themed as we often did, we ended up walking back to the car before driving to Llangollen. Once there we explored more of the rarely travelled roads before a flash of inspiration came over me, "Lets go to the Horseshoe Falls!" Just about the most important place to the local canal that there is.

Hidden away on the outskirts of Llangollen itself, is a huge weir that runs in a semi-circle across the River Dee. The Dee, being the same river that runs below the Pontcysyllte Aqueduct further down-stream, as well as through Llangollen. In the town it runs through a very rocky patch of riverbed leading to some excellent roaring rapids that attract a lot of people to stand and watch, mesmerised from the bridge in the centre of the town.

The Horseshoe Falls also has its own series of small rocky sections of white water, creating a scenic and sometimes dramatic backdrop for a very important place - the small stone building that houses the point at which water is taken from the river and into the Llangollen Canal! On the canal side of the building you get the odd spectacle of literally seeing the canal stop dead at a wall!

Depending on how you want to view it, this is either the start or end of the canal. It acts as a literal source of water, but also happens to be a newer section of canal altogether, originally the "Llangollen" didn't go any further than Ellesmere, almost twenty miles further down-stream. The section that leads from the Horseshoe Falls is almost not a canal at all, being very narrow, shallow, with rocky uneven sides. Add in the overhanging trees and this last tiny section of water seems like it would fit well in an Indiana Jones film in the right conditions.

For me, the place brought back incredible memories and a nostalgic feeling. Having been there as part of a school trip around the age of five, the memories of me and my friends rolling down the hillside flooded back to me. Even stronger were the memories of travelling this empty canal on a horse drawn boat along with my classmates. The canal is so shallow and offers no turning point past the Llangollen basin resulting in it being unnavigable to "normal boats", the horse drawn boat being the only way to go up-stream the last mile or so. What a peaceful memory from a time twenty years before I ended up with my own tiny boat on the canal. What would the five year old Dan thought of that future?

Further beyond this point there is a small, old Chapel sitting by the riverside. We walked up to it and went inside, the sound of the wind and water outside was an extreme contrast to the silence inside the building. The stained glass windows and dark interior created a sense of peace and feeling that you should speak in a whisper, in the way that old churches often do. Walking around the overgrown graves, that dated back hundreds of years in the church yard, it only added to the sense of reverence and almost time travel to a different life. The secluded location, old stonework and huge curving river helped to create yet another scene that could be picked up and placed at any point in the last few hundred years of history. Perfect!

We returned to Tilly for the evening, plotting the next day's adventure before Sarah left. I would wake up and set off again on Tilly at eight the following day, then travel up-stream a further four miles to reach the Frankton Basin just down from the locks. Sarah would then come out and meet me before we set out to walk up the nearest big hill, known locally by the name of the huge stone monument that tops it "Rodney's Pillar".

So it was that the following day the plan went flawlessly. I was slightly late starting off as the lone towpath walker I met as I untied the ropes, turned out to be a friend's mother. After a chat and the usual questions about what I think about boat life and the canal, I finally set off under a cloudy sky that still found room for plenty of blue to show through. The trip was perfect. No boats but Tilly on the move, nothing but nature and peace to be found (apart from Tilly's engine!) Even with the perfect conditions, the four mile trip still took almost three hours, but I arrived well within time for the meet up.

The almost poetic element to this day in particular was that I could see Rodney's Pillar from a lot of different points on the canal as I travelled up towards Frankton. It added a sense of purpose to my day that I find I am often lacking, while I sit onboard and write, film or edit whatever I happen to be working on at that point. Seeing the hill and knowing that I had to get to a certain point onboard before we could drive to its foot and then walk up it, gave a sequence and structure to the day that I really enjoyed having for a change.

Getting into the car and driving out was fantastic as it became apparent the clouds were thinning and a bright sun and blue sky would dominate our walk. The walk itself was as perfect as I could have hoped it would be for one of Sarah's first bigger walks. A few hours were spent in peaceful natural surroundings. Hard work and steep at some points, but rewarding to cut a path over grass, track and through trees. The view from the top over miles of flat Shropshire in every direction was expertly lit by the sun. The passing clouds left shadows on the farmland that could be tracked as they moved across the landscape for miles untold.

Our shortcut back down from the top was not quite as short or quick as the man we had seen take off from the peak with a paraglider! Once we found a small stream, we decided to follow its muddy course down the hillside, leaving us with some less advisable, unstable sections of walking. When we finally reached the car at the foot of the hill we were both pleased for the opportunity of a sit down on an actual seat.

The day didn't stop there, as we then headed out for a drive around some of the countryside we had just been viewing from the hilltop. We spotted the various fields and bright yellow rapeseed crops that made the countryside into a multicoloured patchwork for the time being. Ultimately we ended up getting a little bit lost until we found our way to the local "big" town of Shrewsbury. From here we got back on track with my unusually good memory of the bus route from the town to Ellesmere, a bus trip I have taken many times depending on where Tilly is moored. We grabbed various salad, pasta and soups from a shop on our way back to Tilly.

Once we were back onboard at the Frankton basin, the evening had turned into a very still, warm and bright last gasp of the day. We got our various ingredients in the oven and on the hobs, set up a chair or two on the stern, opened the stable doors on Tilly's bow and the stern door too, before proceeding to enjoy the calmest most relaxing moment of the day.

Sat on the stern, we watched the few people who had arrived during the day and moored up in the basin go about their business. Cleaning, chatting, polishing, filling up with water… the usual boating bits and bobs. In that moment, for the second time in two days, it seemed we could have been witnessing a scene from almost any point of the last couple of hundred years. No phones, computers or anything on show that interrupted the ideal "narrowboat simple life" stereotype. But soon enough we finished eating and we took the decision to move Tilly around to the bottom of the Frankton Locks, ready for their opening the following day.

Once again Sarah was onboard for a trip that lasted only a few minutes. I knew that we would not be the only people who would head there for the night, and not long after, the second place of the queue was taken too. By the time the locks opened the following day, Tilly was at the head of four boats. The practice of mooring on the mushrooms on lock landings is almost universally to be avoided where possible, and leads to a few heated words at certain points. However, it is one of the unspoken (and I assume completely unendorsed) rules at the top of the Montgomery, that because nobody can actually use the locks unless they have been quite literally unlocked by a lock keeper, that it is fine to get your place in the line, over half a day ahead of time. I have cycled past the area previously to find that people have moored there before four in the evening, giving themselves a twenty hour head start!

With Tilly settled for the night it was time to wave "goodbye" to Sarah and then get my head down for an early night. It had been a great day of boating, walking, driving and eating!

Waking up the following morning, a day where I would have to spend a couple of hours standing on the stern and working the locks, it was of course raining!

Loving Living the Llangollen Dream

The day that I passed up through the locks, May 14th, marked the beginning of the next section of the year. The six weeks or so from that point onwards through June and into early July, would bring with it some of the hottest weather of the year. Being Britain, it also continued to pour down at random intervals and throw in completely awful wet days, just to keep us on our toes.

Even on May14th itself, after passing through the locks without incident and then mooring up a couple of miles away at Tetchill, the rain and drizzle gave way to blue sky and sunshine. The bright summer days were even more colourful and impressive around the small village of Tetchill due to the vast fields of bright yellow rapeseed crop. The area is well known locally for this beautiful spectacle. Tetchill, only a mile away from the larger (but still small) town of Ellesmere, sits at the base of the only noticeable hill in the area, known as "The Brow". Even The Brow isn't a very big hill, but it is noticeable because of how flat the area is in general. Due to this open flat environment, the fields of crops seem huge in comparison to the raised, uneven farmland, frequently occupied by sheep only a few miles away around the Welsh Border where I grew up.

Being able to see the landscape uninterrupted, along with the almost over-the-top bright yellow colour of the crops, makes for a fantastic view. The colour adds something different to the usual greens and browns for the weeks when the flowering is at its peak. When mooring at Tetchill one such yellow field, literally borders the canal. Again, the vibrant colour, under a blazing sun, makes for a very pleasant view when opening the curtains in the morning and finding yourself stood looking at it from only about forty foot away.

One of the reasons I have become so obsessed with this crop comes from the fact that I often find myself mooring by it as described, but more importantly I have been able to get out amongst it following footpaths and tracks that sometimes literally lead me to be wading through it, or having the flowers on stalks so high that they mock me from above my head! For a brief week I wandered among the crop at its height. Every time I opened the curtains, looked out of the windows, walked to a shop, or cycled to my friends, family or work, all I saw was a sea of yellow!

At one point I even climbed a tree using some rotting old wood held to the trunk with rusty nails, (not something I advise), to get a better perspective of the fields that ran in every single direction from me. It was great. When I went into the tree there was blue sky, by the time I had got down and walked a couple of hundred feet, it was pouring down… which wasn't so great!

I spent a week moored at Tetchill, a week that I thoroughly enjoyed based on the surroundings, weather and of course time spent outdoors with friends or just with my thoughts. It was also a time when I really started to get a few new writing ideas sorted in my head. Although ultimately hours of writing that I did during this summer period ended up being discarded, I can't say that I enjoyed the days of writing and wandering any less. Especially the moments of peace while sat onboard with the windows and doors wide open, wondering if the weather could possibly get any better.

The following week, I enjoyed one of the random days that I often have as a result of trying to meet up with friends or family onboard. Depending on where Tilly is, it can be a real challenge, especially if those people are unfamiliar with some of the almost non existent villages and landmarks that seem so obvious when setting out from the canal itself.

In order to make things simpler to meet my Dad and little sister, I enjoyed a pleasant early trip from Tetchill to Ellesmere. That was boat trip number one, which ended with Tilly moored on the outskirts of the basin and services that the town is handily home to. After walking to a nearby shop and getting a few supplies, I spent the day onboard Tilly until Sarah turned up for a while. We then embarked on the second, even shorter trip of the day.

We steered Tilly all the way around an entire corner! We stopped briefly to top up some water bottles at the service point before turning around and mooring up back where we had set off from, but facing the opposite way. This was so that once my Dad and sister arrived in the evening, we could just set out on a short trip, without having to worry about heading past the boats that would have moored up on the busy stretch of canal around the basin as the day wore on. This was of great importance, as my sister being only two years old had an attention span that wouldn't tolerate too much dilly dallying!

As the day continued to be very warm, just as the morning had began. I was eager for the final trip of the day. When the good weather starts it is vital to enjoy it while it lasts, so in the evening once I had my two additional shipmates, we set off. The sun, scenery and sheep all providing some welcome distractions and entertainment for my sister. There was one worrying moment, when a sheep managed to get a feed bucket stuck on its head, then walk off the edge of the steep field and fall into the canal! As we approached this scene, I was more than glad to see that just in the nick of time, the sheep freed its head and ran up the bank… a distressed little sister was avoided. What followed was a beautiful evening trip. When the previously mentioned attention span started to fade, I used my usual trick of finding a wide patch of canal and turned tiny Tilly around two miles away from the next turning point. Back up the canal we went, to finally, for the third time of the day, moor Tilly at Ellesmere!

As if to demonstrate just how sweet a two year old can be, after mooring, my sister picked some small flowers from the towpath and placed them on the side of the boat, looking at me and saying "They are for your best friend Tilly". A lovely moment bringing another great day afloat to an end.

The remainder of May soon vanished, and it was very convenient having Ellesmere as a base to get supplies from, meet up with people and even do that rarest of things, catch the bus rather than cycle somewhere! The sun stayed out for the majority of the time, which only added fuel to my mind that was already determined to walk, bike and kayak my body into a deep sleep each night. The canal was already getting busier due to the weather and time of year in general, and being moored at one of the most popular places for miles around only added to the sense of awakening and community. It was a surreal experience to once again find that with the ever rising view count on my videos, more people than ever were shouting "hello", taking pictures, and generally pointing at Tilly after seeing her online. When I was handed a phone to speak to somebody's daughter, I knew that life afloat was not quite as simple and anonymous as I had imagined it would be!

As I often do when moored at Ellesmere, I found myself making the most of the good weather with frequent walks around the main lake. All over the town and outskirts, there is a wide variety of sculptures which range significantly in size and style. I made it a non-urgent goal to finally see them all, including two of my favourites.

One, comprised of a few very small metal figures strewn around a rock that sits by the water's edge. These are barely the size of a coin and include a stone well, figure lying in a boat, a sheep, and on another stone there are a few more, including a sword. All of these are somehow attached solidly to the stone, without any visible sign as to how they don't just fall off at the slightest touch.

If you walk around the lake a little further, you come to my second favourite sculpture. Which is a huge carved tree stump about twenty five feet high. It's not carved into any figure or amazingly ornately decorative piece, but it is much more interesting than that. From the roots is carved a small staircase, these lead up to the main bulk of the tree which has a rectangular hole cut entirely through it: on the other side another tiny staircase leads you back down to the ground. This is one of the more popular pieces and as can be imagined has lead to many photos being taken, not only by me but by the vast amount of like minded people who cannot resist taking a walk up the steps!

This is how I passed a lot of time during these days, the sculpture trail leading me all over the place. There were even a few pieces that were literally in line of sight from where Tilly was moored, others I also knew from their canal side locations. The trail is just another reason that Ellesmere holds a key place in my heart and boating year. It is such a beautiful place to be, as well as an important supply depot and rendezvous point! It also marks one of the final places that I can cycle to and from Oswestry with relative ease, not always the most pleasant ride depending on which route I travel, but still a "realistic" before and after work commute.

Amidst all of this fun and enjoyment, I did also call into the marina right next to the basin and inquire about getting Tilly in the dry dock to have her hull blacked. If I remember rightly, I think that I was given an estimate of the dry dock being free sometime during August and September, which was a little later than I had hoped for, by about three months! This was however what I had expected, the marina is known for its solid workload and frequently full to capacity moorings.

I decided I would leave the blacking for the next few weeks and enquire again at Maestermyn Marina, who had blacked Tilly two years previously. For the time being I decided to make the most of the predicted continuing good weather, although, when the freak showers did hit, I doubted that they would ever stop at some points. One particular incident had me hiding beneath the black and white foot bridge right on the basin itself, only a minute away from Tilly, but surrounded by pounding rain so heavy that I didn't think it was worth leaving cover even for the short sprint to safety!

As time wore on and I had to start leaving the Ellesmere area to keep within the 14 day cruising rule, I decided to spend the last couple of days making a few shorter trips, just to enjoy the area as much as I could before it was time to "clear off" properly. I moved Tilly through the basin, (and was sure to use every facility I possibly could) and spent a couple of nights not far from Ellesmere Tunnel.

The canal leading up to the tunnel is a long very straight line, with fields to one side and a hedgerow to the other, mingled with a few trees for good measure. There is nothing particularly unusual about this place, it is beautiful and rural as most of the canal in the area is... even I had forgotten the one feature that makes this mooring a little noteworthy. After mooring and spending a relaxed moment onboard, I heard an unusual church bell ring out, sounding very close. I sprang up and looked into the hedgerow and trees lining the towpath to catch a glimpse of the monastery on the other side, with the bell tower also just about visible! You know that you have moored your boat in a calm and peaceful place when your neighbours with a monastery!

A few days later, I found that there was such a strong wind hitting Tilly sideways on, that I could barely concentrate on my writing. It is rare to have these moments of such rough weather that the boat rocks enough to put me off, while looking at a screen full of words. The position of Tilly in the open and the direction of the wind, made for (almost literally), the perfect storm of uneasy queasy typing. I decided to make the most of the opportunity and moved Tilly just a short distance through the tunnel, to moor right next to the perfect tree lined scenic lake of Blakemere. Quite literally a matter of a few steps away from the boat, you were practically in the lake if you weren't careful!

Not only did this short move take me entirely out of the wind, but also gave me the great view of nothing but water and trees. I wouldn't usually have travelled in the high wind conditions, but in a common theme with a lot of my short boat trips, I had previously walked down the canal and scouted out the area for any risks. Satisfied that it would be a straightforward trip and be over in a matter of minutes, I went for it. I was also happy to be able to sit in peace and continue obsessively reading my "finished" book that would be released the following month.

I had intended to rewrite my second book "The Narrowboat Lad: Living The Dream" (no longer available), as a listing error had hidden it from a lot of people on Amazon. After writing thousands of words and coming up with all kinds of new additions to the book, I found that I just didn't think I had improved on what I had previously written. This led to a lot of cuts, a huge amount of grammar and punctuation edits in the original sections of the book, until something came out the other side of the process under the name of "Three Years Afloat"! It may not have been the book I had expected, and I was surprised to find that because so much of it had already been written, it was somehow harder to write, but I was happy to have finally taken my first two boat books and got them edited and updated by my nan's expert eye. Improving them hugely and creating something better than I could have ever produced without her. Thanks Nan!

As I have previously mentioned, at the end of 2014 I would have been happy to enjoy an almost identical 2015, and in many ways I did. Another great example of the uncanniness of the similarities between the years at some points came on the 5th June. On this date Sarah and me went off to spend a day and night at my nan and grandad's caravan on the Welsh coast. As things worked out this was exactly the same weekend that my friends and I had done the same thing during 2014. To add an even stranger level of coincidence into things, I was contacted by an online friend, who said he would be in the area and like to meet up… I explained that I was going to be away at the coast, just like we had missed each other on exactly the same weekend the previous year, he was in our local area and I was kayaking on the sea!

Coincidences aside though, it was a fantastic short trip away. In a perfect illustration of the course of the day, I have photos that tell the story with their timestamps. At around ten in the morning, I was onboard Tilly, with the sun beaming on her as she then lay moored by Colemere, a little further up the canal than Blakemere. This gave me the opportunity to rush down the towpath to catch the bus, with the incredible scenery of Blakemere under a powder blue sky, the trees beaming out in bright green on the far banks. A slight clearing revealed dry dusty ground, maybe a muddy beach, with a huge cluster of purply pink blossoms on the distant foliage, possibly "butterly trees".

By the early afternoon, Sarah had finished work and we on our way to the coast. The trip was not long, but longer than usual at around two hours. We passed through a huge bank of cloud and even a drop of rain as we entered the larger Welsh hills, but luckily the sun burst out again as we started to get closer to the coast. My nan and grandad's caravan is out in a secluded spot by the village of Llwyngwril, sitting on the coast in the region of popular holiday locations in Snowdonia such as Barmouth, Twyn and Aberdovey. I am happy to report that after arriving, one of the first jobs was to inflate the kayak. Less than seven hours after leaving the canal, I was back in the water, but this time in a kayak on a sea so rough, and a wind so strong that I could barely paddle myself away from the shore!

We were lucky to spend two days out there in the sun, but the wind did not stop blowing at speeds high enough to make any outdoor activity a little bit more of an intense exercise than it should be! The kayaking was a perfect example, bobbing around on the water it was a genuine struggle to stay away from the beach, or had the wind been blowing off shore then I simply wouldn't have taken the risk of getting in the kayak and being blown away out to sea.

I won't dwell on this trip away from Tilly or the canal too long, but I would like to use it to illustrate a point I like to highlight every now and then. Boat life doesn't mean never leaving the canal! I have said it on many occasions, but there still seems to be a certain amount of disbelief in some people when I say that people from boats really do go on holidays too! An example I have used previously is when I was onboard Tilly at Chirk Bank and was on the stern when a boat moored up behind. I got talking to the chap onboard and he asked me about the area before explaining that he was off to Spain for two weeks. The more I have thought about that the more I realise what an incredible display of trust it was, that he turned up in an unknown area on a boat, and then revealed that nobody would be onboard for two weeks. The idea of tying up a boat with a bit of rope and then leaving the country may seem unusual when taken out of context, but it is only a grander scale version of what many boat dwellers do each week, when travelling, mooring, leaving for work, supplies, day trips or any other reason. I am extremely lucky to have so many friends and family around the canal to go off adventuring and exploring with.

Being at the coast in such windy conditions made me very thankful that the canals are very calm bodies of water. I didn't dare to imagine how long Tilly would last on the open waves, being battered, rocked and almost swallowed up in the foam. As with any of the Dan and Sarah adventures, we barely sat still, visiting the local towns and spending a serene few moments inside a tiny, ancient chapel that sits right by the sea. The sound of the wind howling outside, coupled with the orange light from the ever lowering sun, gave the place a genuine sense of sanctuary and safety. After alarming some of the local cows as we walked around the small graveyard, we returned to the beach by the caravan and watched the sun vanish below the horizon.

I was pleased to find the scorching weather continuing when I was back on the canal a few days later, when on a Sunday evening, after a very warm bike ride, I decided to move Tilly about three miles down-stream to a place that continued the peaceful rural scenery that mooring by the meres had began. Bettisfield is a small village a few miles away by road or canal, from Ellesmere. Ellesmere itself is a small town and pretty calm and rural,

Bettisfield however, is even smaller and makes Ellesmere seem like central London in comparison. It was only during this year's time spent around the village that I realised how few cars I had ever seen travelling there, again the lack of road traffic adds to its peaceful demeanour. Based on this brief description it is probably easy to see why it was on my radar as a mooring spot, especially as the place that I had in mind was slightly out of the village. A short straight of canal is raised on a grassy embankment, higher than the fields to the towpath side, and with the flatness of the terrain in the area, it allows views from your boat over miles of countryside, to some of the smaller more famous local hills.

When I set off on the trip from Colemere to Bettisfield, a chap joined the towpath on a bike, from the first bridge I passed. This led to a very slow race, as he was "in his later years" he would cycle ahead for a bit, then as he rested up for a moment Tilly would retake the lead... all this happened at probably less than two miles per hour! After a few minutes of this I decided to invite him onboard for the trip, what a great decision it was too!

We travelled and talked for the best part of an hour, he had lived in the area all his life and had the stories, anecdotes and knowledge of the canal to prove it. It was one of the most educational moments of my life afloat to hear him talk of canal breaches, maintenance and how the canal had looked decades ago. He offered a very interesting insight into some of the regular boats I have seen many times, and even pointed out a sculpture of a giant chicken that I had never seen before! Yes, that trip really did have everything!

When the trip came to an end, we shook hands and parted as new friends. I was left to witness an incredible sunset over the flat fields in solitude. As I saw the cloudless sky change through the usual series of sunset colours, I had a lot to think about. I pondered whether I might one day find myself as an old man, relating some gems about my time and experience on the canal. I remember being quite sad at the idea of all my current experiences and fun times afloat one day becoming a distant memory with so many forgotten details. It was another reason to be grateful that I had so much of it on film as a detailed long term memory bank. The addition of being able to share it all with millions of viewers on

YouTube is certainly another thing that I am grateful to have been able to do.

When it comes to educational times on the canal, I cannot possibly gloss over one of the best days of the year, (June 10th) the day that I joined my new friends, Hannah and Jon, onboard their boat. This may seem like an average day, canal people on boats, but this was Mountbatten, also known as "The Llangollen Fuel Boat".

The weather that welcomed me when I awoke on "workboat day" was the absolute picture of a traditional summer day. Blue sky, barely a breeze in the air, and a few clouds hanging around just to make sure you didn't get too confident in wearing just shorts and a T-shirt!

I met Hannah and Jon (and of course narrowboat Mountbatten) on the upper side of the New Marton locks. Little did I know what an amazing day lay ahead of me. The first sign that it was going to be good, was that the immediate task at hand was travelling down through the locks with a boat more than twice the length of Tilly!

Taking a huge old workboat from 1959 through the locks with three people was definitely a welcome change to taking tiny Tilly through single handed, with all the constant walking between locks gates, then back to Tilly to hold the ropes so she doesn't go floating around too much and get stuck on the cill... let's just say that to have two people working the lock and one person controlling the boat makes it much less of a "work out". Even with less movement, having a boat so much bigger than Tilly makes it much more hair-raising than I am used to. As the water in the lock drains out, you don't have quite as much room between you and the dreaded lock cill, which can easily help sink a boat. So it is definitely not a task to be taken lightly. On top of this there is an extra step required to help Mountbatten slip out of the lock. As Mountbatten sits quite low in the water, once the lock is drained and the gates are open, it is required that the top paddles are raised again to allow a little more water to rush in and lift up the boat, almost letting the boat surf out of the lock!

One of my immediate realisations on stepping onboard Mountbatten, was just how much Tilly moves about in the water.

Being such a small boat makes her very lightweight in comparison to many other boats, and having a "V" shaped hull also gives her a bit more of a wobble in the water. Setting foot on a seventy foot boat used to carry coal and gas bottles, I couldn't believe how much more stable the boat was. It required a concerted effort to actually get Mountbatten to rock around as much as Tilly moves when I am merely making something to eat in the kitchen!

So it was that a great day of nine hours boating took place on the surprisingly stable, mobile fuel depot! Hearing the old Armstrong Sidderly engine chugging along was a treat, (I know almost nothing about engines, but can at least appreciate an "old" or traditional sound!) More than that, getting to actually see it, situated just ahead of the tiny living area was even better. If you need anything else to make this scene of a brightly painted red workboat travelling through rural Shropshire on a sunny day, any more iconic of an olde worlde canal scene, then add in the bell that is rung by hand to let moored boats know that the fuel boat is approaching and to prepare for any orders or top ups required!

I don't think I have ever been in a situation that could more easily fool me into believing I had gone back in time. As we made our slow trip down the canal, I was amazed at how graceful and deliberate even a huge boat could be. The tighter curves and bends in the canal seemed to serve not only to point out how long seventy foot actually is, but also how in a pair of capable hands, the turns and twists of the canal were almost no effort at all.

The highlights of the trip were definitely the moments of delivery, especially when being waved over by an approaching boat. It might seem like it would be a bit of hassle to deliver bags of coal or diesel between two boats that are travelling. Both boats have to moor up and then make the transaction... contrary to my expectations, that is not what happens at all! Instead, if a boat was approaching and needed some supplies, we would get a big hand-wave and both boats would start to slow down. Then, as the bows drew level, a nifty bit of tiller-work would bring both boats to a complete standstill, along side each other in the canal. A well thrown rope would then tie the boats together to make a floating platform on which to do business. Handing coal over, filling up with diesel, generally having a chat, were all great to experience from this unique perspective!

I was surprised at the level of trade that went on, considering we were travelling during the height of summer when coal is less essential for heating. It is an ideal lifestyle in many ways, a way to earn a living while boating through some of the best places I know, but it is definitely not for everyone. It may be a little too active for some, and for anybody who doesn't "get" the appeal of the canal, I can imagine that they would not enjoy the trip half as much as I did. Personally I can't imagine much better than being asked what you do for a living and being able to respond "I sell fuel while travelling around on an historic boat!"

As the day wore on, we picked up a few supplies ourselves at Ellesmere before heading out into the really rural countryside between Ellesmere itself, and Whitchurch. When we approached Tilly (still moored at the rural Bettisfield), I said a big "thank you" and "farewell", then hopped onboard, leading to much amusement as I rocked the boat deliberately to show how unstable she was compared to Mountbatten!

I stood on the stern for a few minutes, watching Hannah and Jon slowly vanish around the corner. It was a peaceful moment to reflect on what a great day it had been, and what a privilege it really was for all of us to be able to enjoy the canals and countryside as much as we do. Soon though I stepped down into Tilly and made myself at home... for a few minutes. In my usual way, I couldn't resist a little walk to end the day.

Making the most of the still sunny day, I walked the short distance down to where I knew there was an old rope swing. I am not exactly sure why I wanted to go there in particular, but the mood took me and my body followed.

I am not sure how I first discovered it, but the huge amount of time I spend walking or cycling on the towpaths has certainly helped. Next to the towpath there is a short stretch of low stone wall for a few metres. If you step over this, you find yourself on a steep bank that leads down a short way to a stream. More importantly, halfway down the small slope hangs an old tyre on a rope. A seemingly forgotten addition to the secret place that has hung in place for years... waiting for a random twenty-something boater to find?

In a scene that has been repeated many times when I have walked past this place, I of course couldn't help but have a few swings, getting higher each time as I had more confidence the rope and tree would still take my weight! After this interlude of amusement, I headed back to finally settle down for the evening. Another peaceful sunset and good night's sleep brought things to a perfect close.

The summer fun and adventures continued, the 16th stands out in my memory as one of the hottest days of the year. I took Tilly on a short cruise to fill up with water before continuing on down towards the junction to Whixall, only a few miles, but a trip that I stretched out at my usual snail's pace. Mooring up, I found myself opening the windows and doors to get a bit of a breeze rolling through the roasting interior. I had planned on doing a spot of filming but discovered that within moments of talking and waving my arms around in front of the camera, I was sweating like a pig! After a while I decided to head out in the kayak and make the most of the weather.

When I moved the kayak from the roof into the canal I couldn't believe how hot it was to the touch. Luckily I keep it upside-down to stop rain and bugs collecting inside, but had the seating area been baking in the sun like the bottom had been, then it is likely I would have given it a miss rather than get into. I took my usual careful step off Tilly's stern down into the kayak and paddled off. I knew within a few minutes that I would not be out for long, as the sweat was mixing in with the sun cream I had plastered over myself.

Anyway, I took a very slow trip down the Whixall branch, pulling the kayak out and dragging it around the lift bridges, as it would have been a bit excessive and annoying for any locals to turn up to cross the canal and find me winding the bridge up to let an inflatable kayak pass under!

Whixall is a place that has a few houses scattered around, a lot of flat land and marshes and very little else. This is not meant as an insult, as it is all of those reasons that make it a place I love, even if it is a bit far away for commuting and arranging to meet people. In that kayak, on that summer day, I felt like I could have been anywhere in the world. The boats passing by on the main line were a picture of the British countryside that seemed so idyllic and traditional it would be hard to paint the scene without being accused of exaggerating.

Later on, I had arranged to meet Sarah, but due to the difficulty of directions to Whixall and the distance involved, I decided to walk a few miles back up the canal, to Bettisfield, Welshampton and then away from the canal down a country lane. Passing through the empty and almost silent countryside, I saw a sure sign of just how rural it was in the area, as a lot of fields didn't even have gates on them, just huge gaping openings with an occasional "public footpath" sign. It is common for footpaths, even in relatively open field areas, to be visible from the varying degrees of wear on the ground from countless walkers' boots. Out here though I noticed an old footpath sign in an open field entrance, which pointed toward completely pristine grass. It may seem like a tiny detail to notice but after the thousands of miles I have walked on these paths, sometimes these things seem to jump out at you. It would appear that the attraction of the nearby canal and surrounding area are more popular than some less established walking routes, and I realised that it was quite possible that no-one had walked some of these paths for weeks or even months. But I had no time to explore, I was racing a car to a destination!

There were a few blips in the weather but nothing too bad as June passed by. I will remember it mostly for the amazing summer adventures, my many meetings with friends and pretty long bike rides when there was definitely a tint of sunburn creeping in. Sometimes on our bike rides we were brought to a halt to let cattle pass over the road, other times we took last minute detours to prolong the ride a little longer. Driving around the countryside with Sarah we discovered a few new secret places with amazing views, and a fantastic field full of tiny horses!

Mixed in with all of the fun and games were two notable events. Firstly I arranged for Tilly to come out of the water for hull blacking and repair work to her cooling system, at the marina in Whixall. Secondly it was my Dad's birthday, which led me to make some terrible choices of where I was going to be and when.

Tilly was scheduled to leave the water on Wednesday 8th of July, which meant that I was at Whixall way too early to hang around due to the continuous cruising rule of only being able to stay in one area for two weeks. Equally, I couldn't really turn around and head back up the way I had travelled from, so soon after leaving. Add in the distance that Whixall is to travel from any of my friends houses or work, and it all got a bit confusing, especially as my Dad lives in the opposite direction from the canal than Oswestry!

As his birthday approached I decided on a master plan, brace yourselves for the most steps ever taken in going to the zoo... I decided that it would be best to stop in town after I worked a late night at the supermarket. This meant I could wake up in the morning and catch a bus out to the town of Wrexham, along the way a friend would also join me on the bus, and we would go out for dinner.

From Wrexham, I would then catch another bus to my Dad's house to drop off some presents to save me having to carry them about six miles down the towpath to Tilly. If I had planned it better, I could have stayed at his house for the night and this would be the end of the story. However, as I wanted to get back to Tilly and move her a bit further towards Whitchurch things were not so simple. I then got on another bus back to Wrexham, got a few supplies and caught yet another bus out to Whitchurch, by this point I had spent the best part of three hours on buses! From Whitchurch I walked to the canal and followed the towpath the six miles all the way back down to Tilly. In the heat and from being "on the go" all day, I actually felt really tired and the walk took me almost two hours, way more than it would have normally.

Arriving on Tilly, I was a lot later than I had hoped but as it was a beautiful summer day there was still plenty of light. I then untied the ropes and boated a mile or so in the direction I had just walked from. This was a great relaxing end to the day, and with the sun at my back too, everything perfectly lit, and a tiny hint of sunset gold creeping in to the fully grown bushy trees in their summer prime. Along the way there were plenty of boaters out enjoying the peace and scenery of their rural homes for the night. I decided to cut the trip short and moored by Platt Lane, another equally rural place just like Whixall junction I had just moved from. On the walk down it had given me a sight of something from a time forgotten, when I saw a farmer guiding his cattle down a canal side lane then up and over a small brick bridge, bridge number forty-three to be exact. That was not the reason I stopped though, my reason was far more pragmatic - I didn't want to start working the lift bridge so late on in the day or I would have likely ended up travelling in the dark.

The sheer amount of time it had taken me to get back to Tilly had in turn cut my cruise towards Whitchurch short. As I got in bed that night I knew I still had a long way to walk back to eventually get two final buses from Whitchurch to my Dad's house once again. I couldn't boat any further in the morning as it would take too long and I would end up arriving at my Dad's house in late afternoon or early evening, and that was before considering the fact there lay at least three lift bridges ahead.

So the following morning, I woke up, was pleased to see the sun shining in the sky, and I started walking back, only a mile less distance than I had had to walk the previous day. Finally though I found myself at my Dad's, ready to stay for the night and head out to the zoo with him and my sister the next day. All it had taken to get there were six bus journeys, about twelve miles walked and barely a mile on a boat... that is just one example of how having Tilly miles away from anywhere, coupled with my ridiculous lack of planning, can cause me a lot of trouble and difficulty. Luckily though it was fantastic weather and we had an awesome time at the zoo. It was all more than worth it.

The end of June came with more unexpected adventures. Exploring abandoned old buildings, driving around abandoned sections of canal at night, and of course finding more horses to look at and be slightly scared of... these were big horses!

On the final day of the month I thoroughly enjoyed an impromptu picnic at the side of the canal as some friends I had made pulled up on their boat and came and spent an hour chatting in the shade of the trees. What a life! Once again this was a friendship based on them already knowing me from YouTube.

As the evening arrived, I decided that I would head up towards the next lift bridge, with a plan on an early morning trip to Whitchurch the following day. This would more than satisfy my continuous cruising status in the run up to Tilly heading back to Whixall for blacking.

It was a perfect clear sky, I travelled slowly as usual and moored exactly as planned, a few hundred feet around a corner from the lift bridge. I then went for one of my usual evening strolls around and noticed something odd about the bridge. It seemed to be a bit wonky looking! As I got closer I could see that one of the chains that links the main bridge (that sits flat over the canal) to the top counterbalanced frame way over head height, was loose. Looking at the bridge head on, it was clear that the top and bottom were completely out of line and that one of the hinges was completely snapped in half. The final evidence that it was not right at all was the broken hydraulic pump and fluid all over the base of the bridge.

I did't know what to do! It was obviously never going to be possible for me to lift or fix the bridge and in an area of notoriously poor mobile phone reception I was struggling for signal. I walked further down the canal and found a boat that had just moored up after attempting to pass through, comparing notes and thoughts, we confirmed our suspicions that the bridge was indeed definitely broken!

I then walked up one of the winding country lanes to a hilltop and field that I had previously been able to get phone reception from... again my almost comically specific knowledge of some areas came in handy. Oddly, I could get internet sites such as Facebook and Twitter to load, but when making a test call to my Mum we could barely communicate. In light of this, I did my duty and Tweeted and Facebooked the news to any potential boaters heading this way. I also alerted the CRT via Twitter, which somehow never seems legitimate for this sort of thing.

When I walked back down to the canal I bumped into a pair of dog walkers who said that they would phone up and make sure it was reported officially. The final two things that I did that night were, walk back down the canal to where I had just moved from as I knew there was a holiday boat expecting to travel this way the following morning. I found the occupants enjoying the evening out on the towpath and let them know the issue so that they could plan what they were going to do. Then I returned to Tilly took her right up to the bridge where there was a turning point, spun her one-hundred-and-eighty degrees and moored back up just around the corner.

With the approaching date of Tilly's blacking and the unknown situation with the bridge, I had discussed my best course of action with the other trapped boater on the other side of the bridge. I decided it was better to turn around and head back to Bettisfield rather than stay with the bridge hoping it would open, but risk getting caught at the head of a huge traffic jam, or if the bridge was raised, head through and potentially be stuck on the wrong side and unable to get back to the marina, if any ongoing work closed the canal again.

Strangely it turned out that this bridge was one of the few not owned by the CRT but instead by the local council, who arrived to close off the road and assess the situation first thing the following morning. I know how early they were, as I went to have one last look at the bridge before travelling off early on and instead of finding a quiet canal, discovered it a was hive of activity. The reason I note this here is because I had walked up the towpath in my slippers, looking half asleep.

It was on that note that July began! With me and Tilly heading miles back in the way that I had come from. So much for my rigid adherence to the cruising rules, but these were exceptional circumstances. Given that my entire plan had fallen apart I did the only thing that I knew how to, enjoyed a few hours calm, slow boating under a cloudy sky! Now feeling like I was at a bit of a loose end, I moored and arranged to see Sarah and my other friends, we would meet at one of our local easy meeting places and I would bundle my bike in her car. That plan soon fell apart, when for the first time ever, one of my bike tyres popped! With an actual pop sound too! I wasn't travelling fast as the towpath was so bumpy it was impossible, especially with tiny road bike tyres, it was enough to make me jump and doubt what I had actually heard. The end result was proof enough though, and with a flat front tyre, I slowly started to push my bike down the towpath.

Of course the first thing we did on meeting up was head straight down to even more canal at Maesbury for a walk. Then in a shocking twist, the clouds began to pour with rain on us! This was the first sign that the best of summer had been and gone. This is not to say that it was going to be an awful summer, there were still plenty of great days to come, but things just never hit the heights of the previous weeks weather-wise!

A Bit More Summer, A Few Problems and a Good Time

Having taken Tilly back up to Bettisfield, I felt like I was at a bit of a loss, my intention had been to have a relaxed week or so, writing and filming out at Whitchurch. As it was miles from where most of my friends and family were, it would be ideal to be a rural distraction free environment. Bettisfield is just within my range of "oh go on then" cycling and meet ups with most people and so I couldn't resist a few more fun times with friends.

Sarah came out for her first proper boat trip on July 3rd and we turned Tilly, took her back down to the Whixall Junction, then boated back up to the same spot in Bettisfield (again!) To be honest it was a great day, really slow boating as usual, and also with me not touching the tiller for huge portions of the trip. We were lucky to have a blue sky with passing clouds as we made our way, both down and up-stream. In the evening we drove to my friends at Weston Rhyn and enjoyed a few hours there until it got dark. With no desire to end the fun there, we then set out on a couple of hours driving around the small Welsh hills. As we drove we saw a flash of lightening in the distance - this was our cue to go storm chasing!

I can honestly say that even with the amount of miles I had put in over the years, walking and cycling around some of the areas we were driving through, I had no idea where we were at some points. There was at least one point where we were genuinely lost, attempting to drive in the direction of the lightening, down winding narrow lanes with quite literally no street lights for well over ninety percent of the time. Needless to mention the fact that we both thought it was awesome, the random flashes of light and rumbles of thunder creating the ultimate horror film setting for our trip!

This continued until after midnight, we had found a few good hilltops to sit and watch the flashes ebb and flow and move across the distant black hills, which were only visible when the lightening struck. As we had been out for such an unexpectedly full day of fun, I decided that it was unreasonable to expect to be dropped off back at Tilly and add another twenty plus mile round trip to Sarah's evening. Luckily, as this during was the summer, my Nan and Grandad were on holiday at their caravan, luckily I had been keeping my spare key to their house with me for just this sort of occasion, it paid off. I let myself in, hoping not to alert the neighbours with unexpected rustlings at such a late hour, and soon fell asleep with more great memories.

On July 7th I once again found myself boating down to the Whixall Junction, this time though to actually go to Whixall in preparation of the following day's trip into the dry dock. Lucky enough to be doing this under a blue sky, it was the perfect way to spend an afternoon. Passing onto the Prees Branch of canal that would lead me a mile down to Whixall Marina, I was as relaxed and contented as I have ever been. Working the procession of lift bridges on the extremely quiet piece of canal, I was amazed just how calm it was.

The creaking of an old wooden bridge as you wind the handle to see it rise up into the sky above you, is a good sound to hear as it's the loudest most unnatural thing around. Walking Tilly below the bridge by her ropes then lowering it again to the same sounds of the straining wood, is yet another example of the sort of moments that could be plucked from a lot of the canal's history… until I started the engine up and the peace was shattered!

I arrived at the marina and moored Tilly next to the dry dock area, close to the other marina services and facilities. Through the windows to the waterside though, the marina opened up, making a nice change to the usual rural views I could now actually see other boats! Admittedly the marina was surprisingly empty, but it was nice for one night of the year to be able to see something different. I don't think that I will ever be able to settle into a marina long term, sat side by side with other boats is not the sort of thing I signed up to boat life for! The issue of mooring next to other boats lengthways is slightly worse with Tilly as her short length almost guarantees that not only will the windows open up to look directly onto/into another boat, but also that the others boats will be longer and stretch out further behind Tilly too.

I settled down for an early night and was able to grab a few pleasant hours sleep… however the night did not pass undisturbed. Of all the unbelievable things to happen, I awoke in the early hours of the morning to the sound of someone banging on a metal drum. I had no clue what was going on and peered through the windows, still unable to figure it out. Finally I got up and went onto the stern for a proper look in the very early dawn light. I couldn't believe my eyes, the noise was not being made by a human, but a crow, the huge bird was banging on the side of a nearby diesel pump!

I shooed it away and was surprised to find there were actually two crows there. For the few hours before I got up properly, I would be locked in a battle of broken sleep, shooing the returning birds and then shooing them again as they came even closer to Tilly and start squawking from on top of the dry dock! The joys of boat life!

I really don't have much to say about the morning, as once had I started to pack away any fragile items onboard Tilly, two chaps from Maestermyn Marina turned up, said hello and then started walking Tilly backwards into the dry dock! It was the first time ever that I had travelled backwards on Tilly in a competent and controlled way… and the engine wasn't even switched on!

A very kind and friendly fellow, who I won't embarrass by naming here, chatted away to me as I watched the dock slowly empty and Tilly gently sit down on the chocks. It was as slow and gentle a process as I could have envisioned, the speed was reduced even further by not having all of their pumps running, but the gentler that the descent was, the happier and more relaxed about it I became.

Seeing her out of the water for the second time since I had bought her brought back the same thoughts that I had had on the previous occasion. Everything that I had in the world was pretty much contained in a rusting metal shell that was getting on for thirty years old. Out of the water you can (obviously) clearly see the hull that is usually hidden in the brown murk of the canal. This makes the boat look a lot taller and top heavy, giving the slight impression that it could topple over at any moment, particularly with Tilly, being an old Springer narrowboat with a slightly V-shaped hull.

The periodically leaking cooling system that sits below Tilly's stern was also visible, resembling a series of very rusty uneven pipes. We were all pleased to see that the issue causing her to leak water from the cooling system, sometimes at an alarming rate, was as simple as had been previously predicted. There was a hole in the pipe right over the propeller. When Tilly would leave the dry dock this would have a temporary patch up job, with the thought of a full pipe system replacement further down the line. This discovery and confirmation that it wasn't a more serious problem was a huge weight off my shoulders and help cancel out the general feeling of unease I had from seeing her out of the water in her fragile glory!

In a perfect bit of timing, again due to the usual summer holidays of my various family members, while Tilly was out of the water for a few days been scraped down and painted, there was an empty house back in Oswestry with a cat waiting to be fed also in the vicinity! My Grandad came to see Tilly out of the water later in the morning, and I had a lift back into town with him and set about wandering some of the local fields, based from my Mum's house for a few days. This was a time of many meetings with friends and a lot of retracing old steps.

As if by magic by the morning of the 11th Tilly was back on the canal, my Nan and Grandad joined me for a short trip out of the marina and around a corner or two to moor on the Prees Branch, just out of the way of the main Llangollen traffic. A job well done, a patched up cooling system and a few months of summer still to go. Not bad all in all!

When I moved back onto the main Llangollen Canal a few days later, I wasn't sure where I was heading. I knew I wanted to go back towards Frankton but with rain falling from the moment I started the engine, I wasn't sure exactly how far I would get. Equally important was the fact that the Montgomery Canal had sprung a leak in the section of canal between the locks that I liked to moor at, and where I had previously met my friend from the Internet. I was hoping that at some point it would soon be fixed and opened up for a nice summer cruise again.

Soon enough, and a little damp, I found myself back in the region of Ellesmere, just before the small tunnel on the outskirts of the town. I couldn't resist stopping for a night or two by Blakemere. Finding it almost deserted, I had the choice of exactly where along the canal side lake I wanted to open the curtains up to in the morning. Even with a grey sky, the view from the canal onto a lake with three swans bobbing about on it, was beautiful.

The Montgomery Canal got a good series of explorations by me during July. With trips to sections inaccessible from the Llangollen and still in a state of disrepair, as well as a journey out with Sarah to look at the situation regarding the leak.

Seeing the leaking section all but empty was quite sad to say the least, although the low water level did give an excellent view of some of the lock workings and system, even so I would have much preferred to have never seen it and instead had a canal free for boats to pass down! I was asked a few times about how much I would have enjoyed being stuck down on the bottom section, with no choice but to stay at Maesbury and very close to Oswestry. It was logical to assume that I would have enjoyed the chance to stay there far longer than the two week maximum, but in my heart I know I would have likely found it incredibly tedious after a while. The same bland commute down a wide main road and tiny stretch of open canal would both have been the complete opposite of the ever changing and varied places I would have been missing out on. Even on my winter mooring I would move around four general positions, and that was when I had paid money to be able to stay still!

With Tilly moving back into cycling range for my friends we restarted the boating "meet ups" and after a few very sunny trips Tilly ended up back by the Lion Quays at the end of July. The final trip of barely two miles from Mad Jacks up through the two New Marton Locks took us almost two hours, due to the summer traffic backing up as we passed through the locks. Again, patience and willingness to help others always makes for a better boating experience. Once moored and after seeing a few more familiar faces on canal boats… or at least people who recognised my face, we set off cycling up the towpath. Determined to enjoy every bit of sun, we went to Chirk Aqueduct, took a load of photos and then joined the road over the tunnel. Zipping down a steep bank on our bikes we then veered off back into the country lanes that were just about in Shropshire. Hours of boating followed by hours of cycling was a good enough day to hold a few memories, such as my friend taking his first trip through a lock onboard, rather than working the paddles. I was happy, and also a little put out, that he controlled the boat perfectly.

The months of July, August and September were the last truly ideal times afloat of the year. July and August saw the end of my family and friends needing a house sitter while they were on holiday. With Tilly brought back into closer proximity it made for some ideal days of cycling, meeting friends, feeding a cat, watering gardens and then either cycling or walking an untold amount of miles with a friend or two. We would be in and out of town at all hours of the day and night. Sometimes meeting somewhere on an anonymous Shropshire country lane halfway between town and Tilly, then spending a few hours on the canal before both of us headed into town for the night, then meeting the following day to continue the adventure!

As July and August merged into one, sometimes overcast, sometimes sunny, I found that for some reason I especially enjoyed the boating aspect of life. Not just the time spent onboard in the varied weather conditions, but actually travelling on the much busier summer canal. The reason I mention this as a thing of note is that traditionally I have always much preferred the winter time, with little or no traffic while travelling and no endless procession of boats going past while you are moored up.

Perhaps it was just the amount of time that I got to spend doing the things I loved with people I loved, but on days such as August 4th when me and a friend travelled from the Lion Quays up to Chirk Marina, I could have not been happier. We set off with some very windy conditions making things a little tense. Had I have been on my own it was the sort of weather that would have made me stay where I was, however with a competent second pair of hands onboard I knew that we would be able to moor up at any given moment, if things got too rough.

As we moved up the overgrown canal, complete with a big bushy weeping willow tree hanging down like a curtain, we were happy with how things were going, a bit chilly and a bit wet for the middle of summer, but happy! When we reached the Chirk Bank area and got into the shelter of the hillside that leads you to the aqueduct, we were completely fooled into thinking the weather and the elements had finally relented. Once the aqueduct came into sight we realised how wrong we had been. In a repeat of the conditions that me and Dan had passed this way in, many months earlier, we saw wind-driving rain sideways through the valley. As I was attempting to record a video of the trip, I crouched down at the side of Tilly as a bit of shelter, while my friend had to brave the elements on the tiller. Never have I seen somebody look so much as if they had just been taken from a warm bath and thrown into an icy river! When we arrived at the tunnel entrance we were both genuinely glad to get underground for a few minutes of warmth!

In the end we moored opposite Chirk Marina and that is where Tilly stayed for a full two weeks. Over this time I met a lot of new friends onboard the many holiday boats passing by. As usual when asked questions, I attempted to sound like I knew what I was talking about, but found myself instinctively trying to give directions as if people had any idea where my own obscure landmarks were. Gifts were left on Tilly, photos were taken, and at one point a bike ride even had to catch up with a boater, who had tweeted at me while I was just a few minutes away from the canal! Life was all good.

I don't wish to repeat myself with all of the repeat cruising I did during this time, but for context in the seven weeks or so after leaving Whixall Marina to the start of September, me and Tilly racked up almost forty miles of cruising, ultimately ending up moored back down at Maesbury for the first week of September.

Although the cruising in all weather conditions had been great, the time spent with loved ones was a blessing to become memories, and with the general habit of writing and filming still going strong, there were a few points of concern.

As mentioned, the Montgomery Canal itself had been closed due to a breach, which was sorted in time for me to head down at the end of August, but that coupled with the discovery of the broken lift bridge gave me a lot to reflect on. How fragile the canal and my life was, was perfectly illustrated by two issues happening at the same time, that temporarily had simply shut off sections of canal with no chance of passing.

Adding to this sense of how out of my control things were, the new CRT winter mooring rules were announced, which saw the end of the general towpath permit, meaning that I couldn't moor anywhere near to the places around Chirk where I had spent every winter since buying Tilly. Mooring was an option at Ellesmere or Llangollen but they were both too far to make long term bases, especially during the winter weather. On top of that it would cost hundreds of pounds more than my previous moorings to do so. This was a real worry as it meant that Tilly would spend more time at places that I couldn't reasonably commute from and therefore I would be able spend less time onboard in my favourite calm winter months.

In a less obvious but also still very important way, the sale of my friends' house at Weston Rhyn, next to my old winter mooring place, also spelled the end of an era. As much as I was glad to see them moving on with their life to a bigger family home in Oswestry, we all felt a little sad that their life in the village was coming to an end. As they weren't moving until early 2016, it gave us the chance to make some final memories, and gave me a few last ridiculous "after work night rides" to their house before moving on further to Tilly, the following morning!

It may be a strange thing to dwell on, but my friends' house had been one of my many "second homes" since long before the narrowboat idea was even thought of. I have often mentioned the amount of times I had walked or cycled to their house, at one point one of the people from the village let slip that everybody assumed I lived there, so often could I be seen in the area. Although a lot of this was also caused by the fact that once I had the boat, a lot of my commutes from the canal to town would naturally see me ride through Weston Rhyn.

As the time of their moving draws closer, I realise that it will probably make my life slightly easier in some ways. Every time I visit them I will now have access to a full town of shops and supplies, whereas previously I would be cycling miles and miles out of my way to spend time with them, before back-tracking to town to stock up. In other ways it will make things a lot less convenient. Commutes to Tilly when she is up on the Welsh side of the border towards Llangollen will have to be completed in one go rather than having a break halfway, or having somewhere slightly closer to leave any heavy items I might be carrying.

One final situation arose during this time that shocked a lot of people that I knew on the canal. One night Facebook started to come alive with rumours of assault and robbery on the canal, people were posting stories of being advised to leave the canal for a while by Police, and how there was a pub full of boaters down by

Whitchurch. The community of boaters really shone during this time, with people helping to keep others updated and advised on what was happening and where.

It did however create an odd atmosphere with people not wanting to leave their boats unattended in certain areas for a while. I don't wish to dwell on this topic too long, especially as the victim was on a boat I see very often throughout the year, but I have no hesitation in telling you that it scared me. It scared me enough that I altered my route and ended up boating down The Montgomery, rather than head towards Whitchurch as I had planned.

As the weeks passed, boats kept moving and as the legal process was underway things did return to normal, but it was just another thing to add to the recent events that showed how fragile this idyllic life on the canal can be, and the many ways in which the good times can be interrupted without a moment's notice.

Getting back to a happier theme, while I was moored down at Maesbury I decided to attempt to revisit some of the roads that were on my longer walks from when I used to live in town before Tilly. I looked at the old routes and figured out a twenty-three mile walk that would take me past many of the places I had visited dozens of times during the previous decade.

The day before the walk, I cycled the short distance to town to make sure that I had enough supplies and provisions for the trip. I packed a bag with everything I would need and left it at my Mum's house before cycling back to Tilly for the night. What a night it was too, a perfect sunset with just about the brightest pink, purple and orange colours I have ever seen in the sky. The weather was so calm that the canal was acting as an almost perfectly flat mirror. The overall effect of this was that of somebody pasting thick blobs of paint of vibrant colours on a piece of paper, folding it in half and reopening it to see an almost perfect recreation of the first painting... throw in the silhouettes of a few trees, add in a narrowboat and you have just created the perfect sunset!

I won't bore you with the details of the walk, but in brief I woke up on Tilly early, immediately cycled to Oswestry, then as quickly as possible grabbed my bag from my Mum's house and then started walking. I walked, walked a bit further, and a little bit more. I was hit with many feelings of nostalgia and a bit of surprise when I found new buildings or slight alterations along the way. I was slightly sad to see it had taken me so long to walk areas that I had breezed through in my early twenties, but also grateful to be seeing them again at all.

My destination was Weston Rhyn, where I planned to stop the night, usually only a five mile trip from Oswestry. The route of almost two dozen miles to get there was as out of the way and rural as I could have realistically made it, something that I started to regret during the last few miles. To say that my foot became sore is an understatement, but even though I was tempted, after walking twenty miles I couldn't bear to phone for help. Instead I started to try and cut a direct route over fields to get to my destination. Even though I managed to cut a few corners, the uneven ground and crops caused even more pain, and barely over a mile away from my friends house I was even more tempted to call them to come and pick me up… I resisted, and in one of the slowest miles of my life, I eventually found my way to their door.

I tore off my shoes as if they were on fire, pulled down my socks and discovered a huge bruise all over my right foot. Immediately I regretted being such a stubborn fool, and the following morning when my foot was not only bruised but also swollen, I regretted it even more. This put me out of action for any serious walking for over a month, cycling was ok but on some of my longer trips in the coming months I would still find my foot playing up. The case was finally closed, I really am not as fit as I used to be!

When my time at Maesbury was up, I decided to head back to Ellesmere for a week, taking time to stock up and get back to the general area of anybody who might have important news about recent events on the canal. After being reassured that the canal was definitely open and that the broken lift bridge had been wedged upright, allowing boats to pass (but not cars!) and that there was no sign of trouble in the region either, I decided to head straight to Whitchurch on one slow day of boating.

The almost full day of boating that I managed to make the twelve mile trip become was great. Taking the other three non broken lift bridges slowly, I spoke to many other people and heard of various holiday makers' thorough enjoyment of their time on the canal. I also heard an almighty crash as a boat loaded with people hit the concrete base of a lift bridge, the loudest crash I have ever heard. Everybody was ok fortunately, and a pair of towpath walkers informed me that they had already seen them crashing on a straight section of canal a few minutes before... the joys of boating!

I don't wish to appear to brush September aside too much - my usual boating, cycling,writing and working had taken place as I moved from Maesbury to Ellesmere. However, when I took Tilly out to Whitchurch, well over twenty miles of cycling away from work, I decided to stay onboard for most of the time during the week before cycling the huge commute to stay at my friends' house at Weston Rhyn during my working weekends. This gave me the experience of cycling a twenty mile ride to their house, and then still find my work day commutes to be a ten mile round trip!

It was a really nice experience though, to just be forced to get on with stuff! (My usual writing and filming mainly) I did also enjoy the epic bike rides that I had on a few occasions, especially one particular day that I tried to not only reach Weston Rhyn, but also do it via trying to track down the fuel boat to pay for coal that they would leave onboard the next time they went past Tilly. Cycling almost non stop for two hours was something I hadn't done for a while, and certainly not with a backpack full of things I didn't want to leave on Tilly over a working weekend! These were exactly the sort of bike rides that would make my foot play up and lead me to curse my ridiculous walk a few weeks earlier!

Two weeks flew by in this manner, I did have a couple of visits from people I knew, and even a trip out to explore the ruins of an abandoned water mill and castle, but all in all I just stayed around Tilly. I would walk up into Whitchurch for supplies or wander off into the local crop fields and woods, quite often several times a day! The weather grew cooler and damper in general, so many of the evenings were spent onboard writing with the background noise of a rumbling fire heating the place just enough to take the chill off.

After my two weeks were up, I had a beautiful bright sunlit early morning trip back up the canal to Platt Lane, the extremely rural place towards Whixall where I had moored before discovering the broken lift bridge. As Tilly was one of the only boats moving, it made for a very relaxed time as I passed back through the working lift bridges, and I felt a slight regret as I passed some of my more secret mooring places knowing I wouldn't return for quite some time - in one such area I had found a bounty of damson fruit the previous year! It would be beyond ungrateful for me to complain about being able to spend weeks at a time in the secluded spots that I had done though, so the regrets were soon forgotten as the sun shone in the blue sky, and seemed to bring the morning world to life.

What is the Sun?

As Tilly sat on the canal at Platt Lane, September gave way to October and the end of the year really seemed to hurry by. I didn't realise it at the time, but the few moments of blue sky and dry weather that October would offer, needed to be used to their full, as sunshine would soon be at a premium. Luckily, with the help of a boat, kayak, bike and some friends, very few of these sunny moments went to waste!

One of the first signs that things were changing came in the form of thick damp mist that started to hang around a lot longer than some of September's beautiful misty mornings, lit by a rising sun that would soon burn away the vapour. After the first two beautiful days of the month, October 3rd was one of the mistiest, greyest days since the bizarre morning of early September that saw Tilly pass back up through the Frankton Locks.

During the first week of October my Mum was unexpectedly away on holiday, so I had temporary cat responsibilities. It was a shame that I had moored Tilly in one of the most awkward places to get to during this time, but I thoroughly enjoyed the time anyway. As luck would have it I had slept out at my friends' at Weston Rhyn the previous evening, so the morning bike ride to feed the cat was not the greatest distance ever cycled. When I arrived in town, my clothes were covered in the tiny droplets of water that the mist magically forms on the outside of my clothes, whilst inside I sweated away in the cat food rush! Nothing unusual to report there.

However, a few days later on October 6th, I found myself boating a few miles down from Platt Lane to the Whixall Junction in the evening with a slight mist descending. As the two miles or so passed slowly under the bow, I gained a couple of odd looks from passers by, with a friendly wave and a cheery "Hello". I like to think that I confused some people even more as I boated down the canal dressed from head to toe in a Halloween costume! This was for a Halloween special video that I would post online later in the month, all good fun and quite nice to do some anonymous boating too! Although soon after I took the costume off, I arrived at the last lift bridge between Tilly and Ellesmere to find a boat just passing through, one of the friendly crew immediately recognised me and we generally shared a great moment as they waved me though the bridge, kind enough to do all the hard work themselves!

At this point I decided to moor up just before the junction leading down to Whixall Marina. This turned out to be one of my best decisions of the month. As the last light of the day started to fade, an faint mist started to gather. Within a matter of minutes I could see thicker clouds of mist silently moving across the canal and through the surrounding fields.

Whixall is located in an extremely flat part of the local area, and this helped me see the incredible scenes of mist covering everything at an alarming rate. The even better feature for viewing the incoming mist was the small black and white painted metal footbridge that rises up over the canal at the junction. As soon as I realised that I was about to witness an almost tidal onset of mist, I headed up onto the bridge, even with that small extra elevation, the flat land around seemed surprisingly more visible. I stood, turning to look in all directions as during the last moments of light, it appeared as if the world was being slowly erased back to a white sheet of paper.

Tilly was the only boat around, there are a couple of houses at the junction but these too were silent. The only sounds came in the form of random drops and splashes in the canal along with the occasional chaotic interruptions from the nearby flocks of Canada Geese. The entire situation seemed surreal, I literally stood and watched the mist roll over the countryside until it was hidden by darkness. A truly beautiful moment, just the sort of moment that I needed somebody there with me to confirm that it was all real and that I wasn't actually sat onboard hallucinating after being exposed to too many diesel fumes! That was another night that saw me sleep well.

In several short trips I moved back up the canal to Colemere, and while there I experienced some moments of complete silence. The towpath is so thick with trees and the rural location literally meant I could hear no sound at all on times, for several minutes. It was an eerie experience to be honest! Before I reached Colemere though, I spent a few nights at Bettisfield, where the weather became beautiful and sunny, the chill in the air and shorter days made for some classic autumnal experiences as the trees turned to gold and brown rather than green.

While moored not far from Bettisfield, I enjoyed some great kayaking under the autumn trees, with the sun beaming and the almost cloudless sky. It was a relaxing way to spend a part of my afternoon after the excitement and terror of catching somebody quite literally walking off with my tripod and camera that I had left filming a time lapse earlier in the day.

Although I got it back and nothing really happened as I was too confused as to what on earth was going on, and relieved to have grabbed my items back from a dog walker chap in his fifties. It was another unbelievable example of how somewhere as rural and quiet as Welshampton... a tiny village that is not even as close to the canal as Bettisfield itself, there could be somebody waiting to ruin your day! I dread to think what would have happened if I had run up the towpath and onto the road bridge to discover a more aggressive thief, but luckily all was well that ended well. Another lesson learned and another bit of canal innocence unfortunately lost!

It was that incident that encouraged me to move up towards Colemere rather than stay at the scene of the crime, and it made me wander how I would have felt if I couldn't have moved my entire home out of harms way. There's an old joke about being able to move your boat if you don't like your neighbours which had a very real and serious use in that particular moment.

My time at Colemere was probably one of the most perfect stints of mooring of the year. Even though I was only there for a week, the peace that I have just described was a real treat. Being able to step off Tilly and walk to the mere itself in two minutes gave me plenty of outdoor time, and being in that particular spot as autumn ruled the landscape was a spectacle well worth seeing.

My trip from Colemere to Ellesmere basin, to use the services and get supplies before moving further down to Tetchill, was as autumnal as it gets. Having to put the engine into reverse every few minutes to clear the leaves from the propeller was a sign of just how clogged the canal was. At some points the surface of the water was almost entirely covered with brown leaves. Looking behind Tilly it was possible to see the channel she carved in the leafy water close up, as the water settled. The leaves that had collected on the roof and stern were blown around and overboard by the small gusts of wind that we would pass through, at breaks in the tree lined canal.

When I reached Blakemere before Ellesmere Tunnel, I had another moment of thinking "Wow, I can't believe this is what I am doing". Boating very slowly down the canal as it skirted around the lake, there were a few boats to pass, adding their own cosy feeling to the autumn scene of a leaf covered towpath, which acted as a small stretch of land between the canal and lake. The trees on the far side of Blakemere didn't seem quite as brown and subdued as those on the canal, but that only served to add a little bit of green life to the scene.

Getting through the tunnel and stopping in Ellesmere for an hour while doing the usual stocking up and emptying out was a reminder that there was still a real world going on away from the canal… but I soon put that out of my mind as I headed off down towards Tetchill, the final perfect touch of the day and its boating was the slowly setting sun that started to turn the world yellow and orange ahead of me!

I nestled in behind a few other boats at my usual Tetchill mooring spot and was happy to be closer to town. As the days passed I was even happier to be there as the weather went through a series a rapid changes, there were perfect days, awful days, and a lot more rain that I was hoping for. My waterproofs became a must-have fashion accessory once again.

The mist and general dampness that defined late October was a warning of things to come. As November took hold of the calendar the rain really took total control of the weather. It would not be an exaggeration for me to say that as far as I can remember, there were only three days during the entire month that it did not rain at some point.

In addition to all the rain, the wind increased significantly, resulting in a rather unpleasant month outdoors. There were some days when beautiful sunshine would change and become cloudy, and within minutes the rain would be torrential. Equally on some occasions the heavy rain would stop abruptly, only for the sun to appear! During these brighter intervals I got "caught out" a few times, when I made a mad dash either to town or to my friends, only for the heavens to open once again. Even when it wasn't actually raining, the roads and lanes were so wet, muddy and often flooded, that waterproofs were a constant requirement.

At the start of the month it was amazing how quickly some of the roads became flooded. I remember commenting at the time that cycling through the miniature floods, often measuring over one-hundred feet in length was a slightly annoying novelty. By the time the month had ended and the UK had started to see unprecedented flooding and rainfall there were very few people who saw this as anything other than a real problem. I am extremely grateful that the Shropshire to Welsh Border area doesn't tend to see too much serious flooding, otherwise it could have been a genuine disaster for the area.

I don't mean for this to be a downbeat or sad, depressing part of the book, but it is important to put into context just how wet this month was, especially as December did very little to change things. I have never known weather to be so consistently bad in all my time onboard Tilly. One of the side effects of this was that I ended up spending more time onboard than ever before as it was literally a futile hassle to leave on many occasions. All of my usual wandering around the areas local to the canal were pretty much brought to an end for the year, as the fields and paths had turned into some of the muddiest I have ever seen. When I did venture out, it meant that when I returned to Tilly with soaking wet muddy clothes, it would steam the place up and, so I had no motivation to get out on my bike or in my boots… but this did mean that I enjoyed some of the cosiest relaxed times I have ever had onboard. In terms of my usual online antics, I simply couldn't do the vast majority of filming that I normally would have done, but I found myself writing more than ever, working on the multiple projects I had ideas for. There was nothing else I could do, stay inside, listen to podcasts and write!

I feel that looking back at this month there are very few moments that stand out or make for an interesting story! The first and second days of the month were so misty and foggy that the moisture in the air was constantly condensing on the trees over Tilly, creating an endless drip, drip, drip in a steady rhythm. My cycle rides were an eye opener as to how accidents can so easily happen. Even with all my lights shining bright with new batteries, I realised as soon as I got to the main roads that I must be almost invisible, cars in the oncoming lane with their headlights shining were visible only from a distance that could probably be best measured to the nearest ten feet.

The above paragraphs may help to paint the general picture of how the year came to an end, but that doesn't mean there weren't some great moments during November. As Tilly was now closer to Oswestry and within sensible cycling distance for my friends again, we once again started to enjoy our more regular meetings. Particularly on a Tuesday, when even on the third day of the month two of us boated our way a few miles down-stream, managing to only be sprinkled by a small amount of drizzle on the way.

As usual I let my friend take the tiller for the majority of the trip, and he thoroughly enjoyed the experience of the canals outside of peak times. No matter how much I explain how quiet the canal gets during the winter, it still surprises many. After we had travelled miles without meeting another cruising boat and passing through many popular places which get very busy during the summer, such as the Frankton Locks, he couldn't believe that when I say there are no boats around, I literally mean that sometimes there are no boats on miles of canal, apart from Tilly!

This particular trip down from Tetchill to just past Frankton, was particularly good as it was the last time I travelled below the golden trees of lingering autumn. Many of them were already bare, and the canal was nowhere near as coated in leaves as it had been, but there was still enough colour in the world to make it irresistible to my camera... just one of the benefits of having a friend onboard!

We moored about five minutes from an access to a main road, under an almost naked tree by the towpath and with open fields to the other side. A few days later it was the perfect place to enjoy the sunniest day that the area would see for weeks on end, although also one of the windiest there had been for a while too. Let's not get too carried away and think it was an all round good day outside!

This sunny day, November 7th, was probably the last "classic" boat life day of the year. I found myself writing and tinkering onboard, then heading out to take some bags of rubbish down the canal to the Frankton service point, before heading back and generally meandering around the local area as I went along. I really am struggling to think of another day during November that I actually strayed from the towpath or even went outside for a prolonged period of time for fun!

When the sun set, I was pleased to be able to enjoy the sky going through its phases of pastel colours rather than simply changing from grey to black. At this point I realised it was going to be a very cold night, for the time being though, I was off down the towpath to find my way over the canal to the nearby pub, where I would meet Sarah for a few hours random driving and milling around town… and to spend some quality time with Gary, her pet hamster!

As a side note, before going to wait in the driveway leading to the Narrowboat Inn, I had a quick look around the huge array of hire boats at the neighbouring Maestermyn Marina. Over the summer, these boats would very often all be out cruising, but by November they were all sat at the side of the canal, as the following week some of them would literally be sat on the carpark at the canal side itself, having been lifted out for maintenance. When I did finally go and wait for Sarah in the dark driveway, I somehow managed to mistake a small work van for her car. This resulted in me smiling into the invisible driver seat, slowly walking towards them while fumbling around in my backpack, I can only imagine that seeing this stranger in a dark place would have been a little bit creepy. Needless to say they didn't slow down!

Later in the evening as we said our "goodbyes" by the canal, we were treated to a very clear sky. Reminding myself once again that there were actually stars above the usual layer of cloud, I set out down the towpath for a good night's sleep and an early start to cycle to my friends' house the following morning. I was wide awake at about half six the next day, with plenty of time to see the reverse of the previous night's sunset. The sun was rising and peaking through fish scale clouds to Tilly's stern, and adding the perfect finishing touch to this picture was a jet black silhouette of a thick trunked old tree not far away from Tilly… within an hour it began pouring down. So the month continued.

The weeks passed quickly and all blurred into one indistinguishable period of writing, cycling in the rain and occasionally boating a bit further down the canal towards the New Marton locks. The weather was so bad that at some points not only were there no boats travelling for days on end, but I was the only person on the towpath around Tilly for periods of forty-eight hours and probably more!

My friends joined me for another short boat trip and I made a couple on my own. "Meet ups" were cancelled and were rearranged when possible, and boating was entirely dependent on the wind conditions. As if to prove once and for all that things in the sky were not too good, the UK was hit by Storm Barney around the middle of the month. Damage and flooding was caused on a national scale, with gusts of wind up to eighty-five miles per hour. On the night of the 20th as the wind howled and battered around Tilly, I was amazed to see flakes of snow start to fall, or rather be blown around, during the general storm. I thought it might be refreshing to take a walk down the towpath in the conditions but was soon feeling rather foolish as I ran back down the pitch-black towpath to some warmth and safety.

Storm Barney would be one of many storms to hit the Country before the end of the year. Fortunately Shropshire was well out of the path of destruction compared to some parts of the country, where hundreds of millions of pounds worth of damage would take place. Out on the canal, I had some of the roughest nights I have experienced onboard as the canal was repeatedly being whipped up into a series of miniature waves instead of its usual calm flat surface, this created no fun at all when trying to sleep. If the wind was coming from directly ahead or behind, the boat would be almost unmoved by it, but when it caught Tilly from either side it was time to hold on tight - well that might be a slight exaggeration, but it was not as relaxing as being rocked to sleep might sound!

To be completely honest apart from the deteriorating weather, the only real unusual point of interest of November was the scheduled maintenance due to take place on Bridge 15W near

The Lion Quays restaurant and hotel, which is only a short distance from my previous winter mooring area. The CRT listed this stoppage as being from November 2nd to December 18th, which had led me to slow down my progress a little, rather than continue until I got stuck! I was especially keen not to get stuck at the closed bridge as I knew it would leave me with about a quarter of a mile of muddy towpath to pass through every time I wanted to leave the boat.

As November passed and I continued to cycle on the towpath in the area to visit friends, I was a bit confused to see no sign of any action going on at the bridge, until I was told it had been delayed by a couple of weeks. Then one day at the end of the month, while walking down to meet Hannah and Jon on the coal boat, I discovered the canal was closed and with scaffolding around the base of the bridge. I felt relieved to know the work was underway and that it would likely be done in time for me to take Tilly up to moor by The Poachers for Christmas. What I didn't expect was to cycle past a few days later and find that the work was completed, the canal open, and there were no signs of anybody returning.

Something that I had been planning my cruising around for over a month, had turned out to be a non issue. I would go as far as to say that, had I never seen the stoppage notice, there is a chance I would have never even known anything had gone on! A little confused, but mainly pleased that I was free to pass through and make it to the Poachers for Christmas, I cycled merrily on down the towpath.

As the days continued to pass in a way that could be described as "only a bit lighter than the night" I continued to write, write a bit more and then rewrite all of that. By the time December arrived I was happy to have got most of this book almost complete. I was also very happy to wake up on December 1st and see a blue sky and a hint of the sunrise colours in the broken clouds.

I unmoored and headed on back up through the New Marton Locks for the final time of the year. Despite the promising sky, I was a little tense about how windy it was (again!) and had I have known just how strong the wind would be as I moved up the canal I may well have decided to give it a miss and travel on another day. Despite this, the locks and trip wasn't problematic apart from trying to keep her at the side of the canal below the locks. Once I was above them, the towpath was on the side of the canal that the wind was blowing towards, from the far side of the water.

The strong wind and open fields in the St Martins area led to the unusual situation of being able to bring Tilly over to the side of the canal, bring her to a halt, then see the wind pin her in place. As I pulled over at the water point I decided to take a moment to watch and see if she would start moving backwards with the flow of the water. There was no movement at all!

Just as I had pulled up to the side of the canal where I intended to moor for a few days, my friend from the Canal and River Trust pulled up in his van, on the way to check the water at the locks. He stopped next to me as I stood on Tilly's stern and we had a good old chat, with many mentions of the weather and the unusual spectacle of the sun showing its face. After he left ten minutes or so later, I realised that once again I had not actually moored up and the wind had been keeping Tilly in place all along. That was probably the high point of the month outside of Christmas!

December is a month best summed up in a few simple sentences. Lots of cycling to and from Tilly in the dark morning and night time, lots of writing and a lot more overtime at my job in the build up to Christmas.

After going to my friends' house to get my haircut one evening, we then discovered while I was sitting half stripped down in the kitchen in readiness, that there were no actual hair clippers in the house, and I ended up staying the night rather than get another soaking. The following morning I cycled back down the towpath to Tilly to find the kayak on the roof not quite how I had left it. Then a moment later, I found a note on the stern steps, from Lewis of the CRT who had been kind enough to put the kayak back onboard and tie it down. It was lucky that I had a bike lock to keep the kayak tethered to Tilly at least partially, or I fear it would have turned into a kite and never been seen again. For my part, I wrote a huge note saying "Thank You Lewis" and stuck it in the window!

Again, it seems an anticlimax to this book that the last two months of the year were "write offs" in the grand scheme of things.

During the week that I spent moored in the open area above the locks, I only left Tilly once for anything like a mini adventure, as the only trips I really made were to go to work and to visit friends. Very few of these trips left me in the most presentable of appearances when I arrived. As far as I can remember it was the first time in years that I had moored for a week at St Martins and not ventured up over the fields to the village. Knowing the general conditions of the fields and paths in the winter, and especially this one, I had no desire to discovered just what they had turned into during the previous weeks.

Soon enough, I moved a little further up the canal to be closer to a main road and avoid the bumpy track filled with mud and puddles where I had been moored by. Even though it was a short trip, it was one I enjoyed, and with December 8th seeming like it might be a dry day, it had enticed me to make the early morning trip and organise a "meet up" with my Grandad at the road bridge I was moored by. This was one of our utility trips, exchanging a bag or two of firewood from his car with two toilet tanks from Tilly to be emptied. Driving around with that as cargo is something I won't go into too much detail about, but be advised that, in the most literal sense possible, it doesn't sound good. As an almost needless side note at this point I will say that after mooring up, it absolutely poured down.

Me and my friend took a couple of train trips out to Chester to do some Christmas shopping during December, which was a welcome, if minor, change from the cycle of working, writing and raining. The Chester trips helped demonstrate my life once again, as even though it might seem a simple thing to hop on a train, there was actually more to it. I would set a nice early alarm, wake up onboard, cycle to their house, then we would drive to the train station at Chirk and catch the train for the last leg of the journey, and then follow these steps in reverse on the way back. Again it was a demonstration of how the location of Tilly can make certain things either easier or more difficult, especially when we realised that at the start of 2016 I would have Tilly moored about a mere one minute walk away from the train station. This in turn means that all of the previous cycling and early alarms can be forgotten, as any trips to Chester can simply be made by waking up and having a quick stroll down to the train station! More than that, if needs be I could literally moor Tilly barely a few hundred feet away from the station itself!

As the month wore on and Christmas drew ever nearer, I moved Tilly up to my old winter mooring spot next to The Poachers, and I decided that I would stop here for the full two weeks allowed as a continuous cruiser, the first time for quite a while that I had broken my weekly moving habits. It was an ideal location, not only with road access for meeting friends and family and getting supplies onboard, but also because it was where I had woken up on Christmas Day for the previous two years, the year prior to that it had been just up the road at Chirk Bank. I am a sucker for tradition!

One of the things that made me feel a little sad was how quiet the canal was. Don't get me wrong, I love a quiet winter canal, but there were barely a handful of boats around. Previously during winter, when the old mooring rules were in force, I would have already been in the area for two months, as would a couple of other winter moorers. This time though as I moved around the long curved bends of the canal, I realised that Tilly was going to be the only moored boat in over two miles of canal, apart from one boat moored long term on a private mooring.

The following day another boat came to join Tilly, it was one that I had passed and been passed by a couple of times during the last few weeks. I had a chat with the owner who was in the same position as I was, having to keep moving as his usual winter spot nearby was no longer available under the new rules. I had a walk down to Chirk to pick up a few bits and bobs on one afternoon and found that my suspicions had been correct, there were no other boats apart from the private mooring boat, Tilly, and her new mooring mate. This was a place that my jacket potato cooking friend from the start of the year had described as quite a popular place. Twelve months later and he could have moored up and been just one quarter of the traffic on miles of canal! Another boat did moor by Tilly for two days, but soon they had vanished too… amidst the rain and wind storms that were making my commutes pretty damp, I was in no mood to charge off down the canal looking for more boats! Again, at this time of year I would normally have made at least one trip right down to Llangollen by boot or by bike, but time and the weather were not on my side.

As if these wet months were not a big enough anti climax to the year and this book, when Christmas week arrived and my overtime really kicked in, I was ill. Not just a bit sick, probably as sick as I had ever been since childhood. It is rare that I ever take days off work, in fact apart from when I had to have hernia operations, I think that I have only missed about three days in almost nine years… during Christmas week I added two more to that total. Not only was this disappointing in terms of letting work down at a vital time, and when I had managed to go so long with so few days off, but also because I was so dizzy and out of it that I literally couldn't leave my mum's house!

It was lucky that my bug had hit me while there, as I daren't think of how much worse it would have been on a boat in the gales! One slightly positive thing did happen while I was groaning and staggering around my old bedroom, I was randomly mentioned for writing books and doing videos about boating on BBC Radio Two. Of all the places I have been mentioned or popped up unexpectedly over the years, I think that on a programme titled "Sounds of the 70's" must be at the top, with my appearance years ago in Lauren Laverne's column in Grazia magazine! What was even crazier to me, was the amount of people who had heard it and already knew who I was and started to send me messages about the shoutout! What a strange world!

Soon though I was back at work and then finished for the Christmas break. On Christmas Eve I met my Dad and little sister, we had a great fun time as usual before returning to spend some time on Tilly and show my sister the lights… I was however told by her that I had to take my Santa hat off because it wasn't snowing, but apart from that I think she enjoyed the day!

I woke up just after eight on Christmas Day, the familiar sound of wind and rain rushing around Tilly greeted me. Still, I got up opened my presents, and then when the rain had miraculously stopped, I set out down a very muddy towpath to visit my friends up the road at Weston Rhyn, just as I had done for the previous three years. I got wet before I arrived, but was still hopeful of making my usual bike ride into town for the day's festivities. Needless to say that not long after I had arrived at my friend's, the Heavens opened and for the first time at Christmas since buying Tilly, I had a lift into town with them rather than cycle.

No big deal though, a fantastic day with my family followed. I received the usual presents of food and drink rather than many actual "things". I have never been one for wanting loads of gifts, even as a child, but now with such limited space on Tilly I am more than happy with what amounts to a few bags of "normal shopping" things that take little room and will soon be consumed!

The day never really brightened up and in the end another two traditions came to an end. Firstly my usual trip up the local hill known as The Racecourse that I had been doing for years before even having Tilly, the second and only real disappointment of the day being that due to the fact that by about seven in the evening I had already fallen asleep twice, and the with deteriorating weather outside, I decided to stay in town as I was working at nine the following day. This proved to be a fairly good decision as the weather wasn't so much deteriorating as it was becoming yet another huge storm.

The following day, December 26th, while I was working, then back at the dinner table with my family in the afternoon, flooding caused even more chaos and destruction to add to the disasters of the previous weeks. Once again my local area was spared the worst of it, but the reports, videos and pictures that things like Facebook were filled with from around the country was beyond anything I have ever seen. Buildings collapsing, bridges washed away and thousands of people watching their homes be destroyed. The news was once again filled with images of raging waters running through streets and homes, or mockingly, still waters, seemingly calm and stationary as it submerged homes and shops almost to the top of their front doors in many cases. Rescue boats in the High Street were a bad enough sign, but seeing rescuers struggle to wade through water that was literally up to their armpits, showed just how much water there was in some of these areas.

It was a scary and sobering sight to see the night pass to day with little sign that the rain wouldn't continue for the foreseeable future. It was a reminder of how lucky those of us unaffected were, yet also a demonstration of how fragile we could be if nature decided to raise its hand against us. It was in this way that Christmas week drew to a close and the year neared its end.

On Tuesday 29th I took Tilly on my last boat trip of the year. As usual, first thing in the morning, as the sun rose, finally revealing a blue sky and a dry day, I headed off over the aqueduct and through the tunnel, mooring just through the other side. I couldn't believe my eyes when the morning continued to pass with the sun continuing to shine in the sky! It was actually looking like a good day.

I moored at the spot near the tunnel as this was also a place right next to the road that led a short distance up to the village of Chirk and the shops within. I had been wanting to get a few new bottles of water onboard so took this as my chance to do it with the least trouble possible. By the time I had made the short shopping trip I found myself sweating from the mild weather, sunlight and backpack full of litres of water.

I knew that this weather wouldn't last, as the media was full of warnings about the next approaching storm. Little did I realise that this was not only bringing a lot more rain with it but also some extremely windy conditions yet again, and if I had have known this I would not have remained moored where I was. The tunnel behind Tilly was about the only secure thing in sight. Both of the banks to the sides rose up steeply, covered in huge trees that already swayed around in even a gentle breeze. It was in this area that I had found eleven trees fallen during the snowfall on my first winter afloat... needless to say that as the storm grew, there was a very wet, windy and nervous night.

The following days brought calmer conditions but with very little break in the rain, even as the New Year began. That is unfortunately the damp whimper of a finale to this short book about another great year on the canal!

A Few Final Thoughts

To spend one year on a narrowboat was a blessing and an experience that changed my life totally. To have then continued my adventure, for almost four years (so far!) is something that I will treasure for a lifetime. The fact that these years of boating have continued to improve, as my own experience increases and obsessive worries have been subdued, has led 2015 to be another year I would love to live through again.

There have been so many high points, both on and off the canal, that I can't easily pick the best moments without fear of missing out some of the less obvious ones. The day spent onboard fuel boat Mountbatten was incredible, yet so too was the split second moment that I saw a stoat swim across the canal and run up the towpath. It would probably be impossible for me to make a summary of all those tiny moments of surprise without walking away and realising that I had missed another ten moments… then another ten… and so on!

What I hope this book has done is given you a taste of the kind of active life I have tried to create. I hope this book also gives enough emphasis to some of my friends who have joined me onboard. I have been lucky to find people willing to be equipped with a bike and told they are about to join me on a trip to places they have never been before! It is definitely a test of friendship, but almost always results in great times including a short trip onboard.

2015 has perfectly embodied my mantra of "I didn't buy a boat to sit inside and never leave it, I bought one so I could be in the outdoors all the time!" At some points, such as having two hour bike rides to get from Tilly to where I needed to be and then return to her, I have pushed this overly active lifestyle idea beyond even my own limit of comfort. Yet I still look back at these moments fondly. Past experiences of boating down the canal in pouring rain and freezing wind have also not been the best of moments, but how much sweeter that made the sunshine or the warm interior of Tilly and the crackling fire, even things out. Life is all about making the most out of the situations that come our way. If having to cycle from work, through miles of amazing countryside to end up on a tranquil canal is the hardship I have to face, then I will face it willingly!

In all seriousness though, my life may not be glamorous, luxurious or particularly easy, but that doesn't mean it can't be fun and that I can't love it, even the late nights after work and the early mornings before work! All these silent hours of cycling, when the world seems to be asleep have given me sights of sunrises, sunsets and nocturnal wildlife that few are lucky enough to see, especially with such frequency. The late night sweaty bike rides up the Brow Hill when Tilly is moored around Ellesmere seems a hard way to end a workday, yet it is cycling through the pitch black countryside on that mile or so of road that has led me to see more shooting stars than almost any other place in the past year.

The few negative moments of this year, such as first hearing the confused rumours of assault and robbery, make up such a small part of life that it may seem insignificant. However, in some ways they are almost more significant than other positive moments as it is the bad things that prove how lucky I have been for so long. There are questions that hang in the air unanswered about what my boat life will look like in the future, due to things like the winter mooring rule changes, or even my friends moving away from the canal after all this time. If my time afloat so far has taught me anything, it is that even if I don't know it yet, things will work out… especially with the help and advice of a community of amazing people that can be found on many parts of the canal.

I would love to live the last few years again, but even more than that, I cannot wait to live the years ahead. There are so many places to see on the canal outside of my small watery world, there are so many people to meet and boating experiences to have, that it is impossible for me to begin to imagine them all. It is just a question of getting out there and finding them all!

Even onboard Tilly there is still a lot to be done. Things that will stretch my very little skill as a handyman, modernising her interior, installing solar panels, even just a (long overdue), coat of paint on the exterior. When this will all be done is another question, what the end result will be is both a motivation and a mystery!

While writing and editing this book, my friends have been judging my ideas for the future of "Dan and Tilly" and it has put me in mind of the year before buying her. A time when my friends would join me in planning huge routes with canal maps, all over the floor of my Mum's house. We would also plot and plan the ultimate basic boat layout, coming up with all kinds of schemes to use camping equipment to make a low cost and almost entirely removable interior. In hindsight many of our ideas were admittedly terrible and probably dangerous, but it was great fun to contemplate! Some of our recent conversations seem to be bringing back that feeling of excitement, but built upon years of experience rather than total conjecture as to what having a boat might be like.

To bring this book to an end, I would like to focus on that excitement. Even as my fourth anniversary with Tilly approaches I still love what the canal has to offer. There were some people who thought I might get bored after a while, and to be honest I had doubts myself, but even now I still find a huge amount of enjoyment in the simple things that life on the canal offers. Whether it is the ever satisfying hum of a roaring fire on a cold night, the chance encounters with nature, or walking around inside Tilly watching the world pass by, as a friend or family member takes the tiller for miles on end.

My life has taken turnings and gone down avenues that I never could have predicted, the amazing people I have met along the way are too numerous to list, but all are important. My friends and family have seen me change from a video game obsessed young man in his early twenties, into some kind of boat based, cycling obsessed attempted writer! The people I have met out on the canal, from boaters, towpath walkers, CRT and marina staff, have all played their part in helping me on my journey and making life afloat such an enjoyable experience. The people online, who tune into my videos and read these books are hugely important, offering insights and advice into parts of my everyday life that I may have otherwise overlooked.

Despite all the adventures, experiences and people that make up my days, I have often summed up my life jokingly as "literally going nowhere slowly". As I prepare to find somewhere, calm, quiet and dry to paint Tilly's exterior, "going nowhere slowly" is as true now as it has ever been… and that sounds perfect to me!

So That Was Boat Life

So That Was Boat Life

By Daniel Mark Brown

www.thenarrowboatlad.com

To HMJ

A Boat Load of Fun

For almost four years I was lucky enough to experience my dream of living on a narrowboat. It would be an understatement to say that I merely enjoyed my time onboard Narrowboat Tilly. Drifting off to sleep with the sound of wood crackling on the fire, waking up to the sights and sounds of nature through every window. I was able to move my home around some of the most scenic places that I could have ever imagined, enjoying boat trips at a moment's notice, sometimes just for the sheer pleasure of boating down the canal under a blazing sun.

So why on earth did I give it all up? This book is going to bring you along for a look at my final months onboard and offer some insight into the various reasons that led me to sell up and move back onto land.

This book isn't a series of pages of me moaning about boats, or a collection of reasons that boat life is awful, I loved boat life right until the final moments. Neither will this book be a lamentation of how much I miss the amazing times I had with my floating home. Instead I hope that this book will be a personal examination of the practical realities of the life I built on the canal, the good, the bad and importantly, why I felt that it was not my future.

After writing many short books about my life afloat, I can honestly say that this one has been the most difficult. The editing seemed endless, sometimes it seemed too negative, other times, my attempts at humour seemed too sarcastic and came across as if I was disregarding my near four years of boat life as nothing more than a big holiday! I would also like to say that I am not intending to put anybody off boat life with my writing, I have genuinely enjoyed my time on the canal!

To set the scene of what my life afloat was all about, I will briefly introduce myself and Narrowboat Tilly. I moved onto the water not long after my twenty-fifth birthday. I grew up in Oswestry, a small town in Shropshire, just on the English side of the Welsh border. Oswestry is surrounded by all kinds of countryside, plenty of farmland, woodland and small hills that lead to some bigger Welsh mountains. It is also only a matter of a few miles away from a large section of the Llangollen Canal and even closer to the Montgomery Canal.

Living my entire life in a rural area like this had given me an ever greater appreciation of the outdoors. By my early twenties I was walking and cycling thousands of miles a year in the surrounding areas, it was truly a perfect place to be an "outdoorsy type"!

Ultimately I found myself drawn to the simplicity and extremely rural lifestyle that I could build on the canal. As I researched boats, I found that I would be able to afford a boat and to live on it while also to keeping commitments to work at a minimum. The idea of living in the calm rural locations the canal ran through and being able to enjoy as much time in the great outdoors as I could possibly get, was ultimately too much to resist!

Boat life called and I went running (and cycling!) towards it!

The boat that I ended up buying was a small thirty foot boat called Tilly. She had a huge outdoor back area which cut away a lot of space that could have otherwise been an indoor living space. The fifteen foot indoor area was still enough for me at the time. I had a shower, toilet, sofa-bed, kitchen with sink, oven, grill and two hobs, even a small storage area that I later turned into a writing desk sat at the front of the cabin. The heart of the boat was always the fireplace. One of Tilly's previous owners had installed an unusual custom made cylinder wood burner, I was warned not to put too much fuel in it when I bought her... I will still never be able to quite explain just how hot it got!

The fireplace not only acted as an incredible and vital source of heat in the winter months, but also as an occasional hob for warming soup or even for toasting bread and rolls! Tilly was never more homely than during some of the cold dark winter nights, when the only sounds to be heard were the occasional splash from an unknown source outside, the rustling of trees in the wind, and the roar and crackle of the fire.

The tiny space that I lived in was absolutely fine for me when I first bought Tilly. There were a few moments where I wished I had more room, which we will look at later in this book. The entire basis of my decision to get a boat was not specifically about living on a boat, but rather for living in the rural areas that the boat could travel to! Tilly was my base for further fun in the outdoors rather than the tiny self imposed prison she could have been!

My four years onboard were every bit as good as I could have wished for. I was lucky to spend a huge amount of time travelling around Shropshire, discovering all kinds of random places and almost forgotten paths and routes as I went. I had the perfect environment to sit down and write my short boat life books, along with my diaries and journals. Being surrounded by so much natural beauty also led me to make more and more videos for YouTube.

My YouTube hobby turned out to be quite a life changing influence. I had been posting videos to the internet for years, many about my love of the outdoors, however I was totally unprepared for people to suddenly take so much more of an interest once I had the boat! My channel, that had previously been lucky to get a few thousand views in a year, soon found itself counting views to the nearest million, currently sitting at over well over five-million views.

Narrowboat Tilly suddenly became a very recognisable boat to a lot of people… although I personally refuse to use the word "famous"! Sometimes while I was onboard, multiple people in a day would sail past and shout out about Tilly from the internet. Others would stop for a chat and a photograph, in some instances I was recognised while many miles away from the canals! It was all an amazing experience, completely opposite to the anonymous quiet lifestyle I had intended to live in the countryside, but at the same time, great fun.

The green paint and cream lines that made up Tilly's exterior came to be recognised all over the world. It was truly humbling to meet people from all over Europe, the US, Australia and more! It was even better to meet these people while they were first experiencing the canal on holiday, sharing in my love of the peace and the beauty of the seemingly endless fields and rolling small hills. It is fair to say that the longer I was with Tilly, the more "she" became her own entity as far a other people saw her.

So it was that I spent so many great times onboard. There were of course some low moments, like when I had engine troubles during my early months afloat and I was not as relaxed as I had hoped I would be. I would go as far as to say that my first ever trip of almost one-hundred miles onboard was almost enough of a shock to me that I was tempted to give it all up right away! Once I had got over my initial learning curve, and the realisation that I knew absolutely nothing about boats, it was plain sailing... excuse the pun!

The winters offered some of my favourite moments, the canal would be practically deserted, often I would go for days, maybe even a week without seeing another boat. The freezing weather could transform the surroundings into a rural landscape coated in ice as if it was a film set, waiting for the actors to show up. Heavy snowfall could cause serious problems getting to and from Tilly and could bring down trees all across the canal, but in contrast I have never seen a more perfect, magical place than the canal after a foot of snowfall!

So was boat life always perfect? Of course not, but it was pretty close! Now that the introduction is out of the way, lets take a look at my final months afloat and why I decided to leave.

The Beginning of the End!

2016 began in the same wet, damp and drizzly way that 2015 had drawn to a close. When I say wet, I mean very wet! The winter of 2015-16 was a record breaking winter, with flooding all over the country bringing destruction that had not been seen in a generation. Luckily the Llangollen Canal (my home territory) isn't prone to flooding. Those of us moored up around the Welsh Border were very lucky to avoid some of the devastating damage which occurred on other canals and boats.

The rain would continue to be an issue for months to come, but at the start of the new year I was full of hope and excitement at the prospect of getting to Spring and Summer. I would continue to deal with the watery cycling commutes and the days stuck inside, but I would do it knowing that we were heading out of winter and that better weather would be on its way. With this in mind I was determined to continue to make the most of whatever weather the sky threw at me.

The wet days onboard had been an excellent time to sit down at my desk and get some serious writing and editing done. I was in the frantic final stages of preparing "The Narrowboat Diaries" for publishing, so I had plenty to keep me busy. Sitting at my desk, rewriting the same sentences over and over again, the rain on the roof, coupled with the comforting sound of firewood crackling away in the background, made for a pretty perfect distraction free environment.

As of the beginning of 2016 I had also started work on an in depth diary that I was writing with the intention of publishing after a full year of boat life recordings… needless to say that when I sold my boat, this idea completely fell apart, so I will use a few entries here to give you a glimpse into just how much I was still loving life afloat, lest it sound like I am too negative in this chapter!

For example here is my recording for January 1st:

"A fantastic start to the year! Today I worked a short shift of 9-1, once finished I left the shop while saying the appropriate number of "Happy New Years"! I had a quick trip into town to get a few supplies before I met Grandad to then go to Tilly for a short boat trip.

We had already arranged this mini boat adventure, it was only a journey of a mile in order to move Tilly from under the trees by Chirk Tunnel and out into the open by Chirk Marina. The heavy rain and wind storms made the trees a constant risk, as many had fallen in years gone by.

The trip went well and without any major incidents to report, unfortunately though, the weather has decided to continue to be as wet and grey as it had been during the final few months of 2015. I will say we were extremely lucky that during our twenty-five minute or so boat ride, we may have had as many as five entirely dry minutes!

I am still picking up a bit of overtime at work, so it is now good to have a little more peace of mind that Tilly is no longer surrounded by huge trees, whilst I am miles away from her filling shelves in a supermarket with gales blowing outside!"

All in all this would set the tone for the next few months, especially as me and my grandad would find ourselves making far more trips out to Tilly than we had during previous years. This was largely due to changes in the Canal and River Trust's Winter Mooring Scheme, as in previous years I had paid a fee to be able to moor Tilly for five months in the same place, rather than have to move every fourteen days as the standard mooring rules dictate.

For the 2015-16 winter period, the Winter Mooring Scheme saw that "General Towpath Permit" removed as an option, meaning that I would have had to moor Tilly miles away from my usual convenient winter place. Worse still was the new pricing that would have seen the cost of mooring Tilly for the winter shoot upwards... but we will get to these changes properly later on in this book!

Having taken Tilly over the border into Wales just before the new year had begun, I had brought Tilly to one of the most famous stretches of canal on the UK network. The few miles of canal that lay ahead of Tilly contained the Poncysyllte Aqueduct and scenic narrow canal up to the Welsh town of Llangollen. Behind Tilly the canal stretched back into England and featured Chirk Tunnel leading right onto Chirk Aqueduct. An absolutely beautiful place to travel, whether by boat, bike or boots!

Mooring in these areas, with the small village of Chirk a short walk away, brought a lot of fascinating features into everyday life. A commute to work could feature a tunnel, aqueduct and even a bit of ice to keep you on your toes, a trip to friends could see "unofficial shortcuts" taken over bridges and across fields until I found a road I recognised!

Travelling down miles of famous canal in the summer is not necessarily as peaceful as you may imagine, as thousands of tourists flock to these areas, the towpaths can get surprisingly busy. Add to that the huge number of boats that head up the Llangollen during summer, and the water turns from its crystal clear winter composition, into a light brown muddy complexion. Being in these same places in the middle of winter can be the complete opposite experience. The towpath and canal can seem almost abandoned! It is possible to stay onboard for days on end without seeing a single boat go by, and moor up with no boats for a mile ahead or behind you, truly a peaceful time of year to take in the incredible sights and surroundings of the canal as it cuts through the hilly terrain of Wales.

Over the course of the first two weeks of January I slowly took Tilly closer to Pontcysyllte Aqueduct, famous not only for being an incredible piece of engineering that cuts across a beautiful Welsh valley, but also for the lack of safety railings on the waterside. If you were to get too carried away in admiring the scenery, you could literally step off your boat right over the edge of the aqueduct! It was unusual for me to spend so much time in that particular area, but thoroughly enjoyable to be able to make that incredible canal feature into a regular part of my daily life. Quick walks, trips to the shops, meeting relatives, and other simple activities found themselves having a vertigo inducing walk down the narrow aqueduct towpath, high over the River Dee, thrown into them!

I don't wish to dwell too much on the rain, but it was truly a blessing to have even a few brief dry spells thrown into these early weeks of the year. Spending time in such a great area was refreshing in its own right, but having a literal ray of sunshine was welcome beyond belief. A brief note in my diary entry for Tuesday 12th January says that while cycling to my friend's house in the evening, not only was it hammering rain down on me but I also pedalled through flood water that rose well over my feet. That in itself is bad enough, but it was later discovered that the fire service was called out to rescue a stranded car from those same flooded roads. Even more alarming is that the car became stuck less than an hour after I had passed through.

I was more than used to cycling down pitch black country lanes and flooding by that point, but the fact it had got so bad and so quickly really gave me quite a shock, more than that, it was one of the first times that I really thought about my general safety when out riding in these conditions and places on my own.

Given all this talk of rain, it is important to highlight just how much this made me get out there and enjoy any scrap of sunshine that I could! Friday 15th January proved that point as wholeheartedly as possible...

"What a perfect day! I awoke to a nice early alarm and immediately set out on a huge boat trip... around a corner or two! I wanted to get Tilly a little closer to the easiest road access for the next week or so in order to meet up with my Grandad at some point in the days ahead.

As the morning wore on, the weather got better and better. The sun dominating a blue sky, with only minor interruptions from the passing clouds. A very welcome change from the months of rain. With this weather came one of the rare opportunities to get back outside and do the things I love while remaining relatively dry!

My first instinct was to get the kayak fully inflated, grab a camera or two and then to paddle up to Pontcysyllte Aqueduct. What an incredible trip it was. The aqueduct is a popular feature on the Llangollen Canal, the towpath is a very thin strip of tarmac to one side, wedged between the canal and the much needed railings.

The water side of the aqueduct lacking any railings whatsoever, was quite daunting to peer over to the ground and river over one-hundred feet below!

Crossing this feature is great onboard a boat, especially Tilly, as the railings around her stern give you an extra feeling of security. Making this crossing in an inflatable kayak was a slightly different experience. I paddled over the aqueduct with the sun beating down from overhead, however the air was freezing, and the towpath was covered in ice at many points. Every so often I felt the irresistible urge to peer over the edge and look down.

Even though I was sat in the kayak at water level, with the aqueduct side rising up a few inches to just about the kayak's height, I could not help but feel that I was about to spontaneously tumble out and tip over the edge. I took a few photos and some video clips as I went, each time I held the camera over the aqueduct, I found myself leaning back away from the side as much as possible, again feeling that for no apparent reason I might be pulled up and over into oblivion!

Once I was across I took a few minutes to paddle around in the Trevor Basin, it was full of the holiday boats that will be scattered all over the canal once the summer comes, but are left dormant during the cold winter months. Paddling back to Tilly, I found the wind to be especially biting and cold. Getting onboard and opening the door to be greeted by the usual wall of heat from the fire was a moment of such relief that I feel I could have curled up on the sofa and gone back to sleep!

After a short while of warming, I couldn't let the sun go to waste any longer. I decided to get on my bike and head down the road to Llangollen. The "main road" way to Llangollen is luckily almost entirely downhill for the last few miles, so it took only a matter of minutes to zip down the surprisingly good road surface to the scenic town. My progress was held up as I had to stop a couple of times to take in the views of the surrounding hills and mountains that had managed to keep their coverings of snow. The most iconic of which, was the hilltop holding the ruins of Dinas Bran Castle. The old archways and walls mixed poetically with snow on the ground on the distant hilltop.

I once again took a moment to enjoy being near to the river, the sun lit the old railway and steam train across the water, and at the moments when there were no cars crossing the old stone bridge, it felt like you could have been looking at a scene from a century ago!

My return journey from Llangollen was equally as sunny but amazingly even more scenic! I joined the canal and followed the almost deserted towpath about five miles back to the Trevor Basin. The canal goes extremely narrow at this top section, leading to a lot of fun and games for boats during the busy holiday season. Today however there wasn't a single boat moving, partly due to the fact the very end of the canal was closed as work was being carried out on a bridge, but also largely due to the time of year. On such a beautiful day I was surprised at how few walkers there were on the towpath.

Even cycling down the flat towpath surface, I barely broke seven miles an hour, with frequent stops to take photos of some of the unbelievable rural, sun soaked sights, while also slowed my progress to a crawl. Once I reached Trevor, I decided not to cross the thin path on the aqueduct and instead followed a road that not only took me a slightly longer way round towards Tilly, but also gave me an incredible view up to the Pontcysyllte Aqueduct itself. Again with the sun gleaming down into the structure, a blue sky behind, it seemed like the perfect day.

I arrived back onboard Tilly and settled down to enjoy a quick rest. Soon, I decided that I would make a short trip into Trevor, to visit the small shop and stock up with a few supplies. The weather however took a turn for the worse. Typically, after having such a beautiful day with the prospect of the ground drying out a little, once the evening had rolled in it was absolutely pouring down. I decided that the rain couldn't last too long and as the downpours eased a little, I took the risk and started walking very quickly down the canal and over the aqueduct.

I will not dwell on this final section of the day, but by the time I had returned to Tilly, I was absolutely soaked through! I had been hammered by the wind and rain, especially when exposed while crossing the aqueduct. Once back it was a case of a total change of clothes. The sun was nice while it lasted, but the rest of the evening was passed beneath a constant sprinkling of water!"

Yes that really was a diary entry that I wrote all that time ago! If I had stayed onboard Tilly and kept up my diary for publication, I can't help but feel it would have been the longest book I had ever written. Perhaps the fact I had spent so much time indoors shines through in the length of these early diary entries, as mentioned earlier, with nothing but the sound of rain drops on the roof and wood in the fire, it was as stereotypically calm and peaceful as any postcard could depict.

One of my favourite memories from my final few months of my time with Tilly has to be Tuesday 19th January, a day that really sums up the chaotic way that I had lived my boat life. Half of it being loosely planned, the other half being those plans going out of the window and me just trying to figure it out as I went. Brace yourself for another classic Dan and Tilly diary entry:

"After spending one of my "working weekends" in town, I arranged to meet a friend and catch the bus from Oswestry back out to the canal. Our plan was to move Tilly, exactly where to was not quite certain. We got off the bus at a small village by the name of Cefn Mawr, not far from Pontcysyllte. It was just over a mile to walk to Tilly from the village, including crossing the epic aqueduct itself.

The overcast day was cold enough to make it a hats and gloves situation when we arrived at Tilly and prepared to set off. Before we untied the ropes, I took a few minutes to create a relatively secure tripod setup that would allow us to film a good angle of Tilly crossing the aqueduct. After some debate on whether we should simply cross this, then moor up in the Trevor Basin or head up to Llangollen, we set off, deciding to pass by the basin.

The trip went perfectly… at first! Having an extra pair of hands to get through the lift bridge made things a lot quicker and easier, then crossing the aqueduct, I learned that my friend really did not like heights. The effect of passing with no railings on the water side caused him a lot of queasiness after his earlier mention of feeling "a bit funny" when we had crossed on foot!

We continued past Trevor and up the increasingly narrow stretch of canal towards Llangollen, not meeting a single boat on the move! It was great… until we started to smell burning plastic! In a very rural area where it is common to have fires in fields where farmers and others are burning rubbish, it was difficult to figure out if the smell was in the air in general, or coming from Tilly.

Once again in a sign of how much times had changed, whereas this would have once sent me into a panic, this time we simply pulled Tilly over to the towpath and lifted the deck boards to see the engine... laughing and joking as we did so! There was no smell or sign of burning plastic below the deck but in the circumstances it was hard to tell if the smell was still in the air. As two walkers passed by, I stood up in the engine bay and asked the odd question about whether the air smelled of plastic or not! The answer didn't really clarify anything so my friend and I came up with a very manual solution to the potential problem!

Due to the concrete and solid sides of the canal in the area, it wasn't really possible or necessarily wise to try and drive mooring pins into the ground, especially when considering how narrow the canal is at parts. We decided to take Tilly up to the next turning point, spin her around and then drag her half a mile backwards by hand, finally reaching the next officially marked mooring point, with mooring rings for security. This may sound like a lot of work... and it was!

It took the best part of an hour to complete our task, the boat drifting in and out, sometimes running aground and needing the engine switched on to get us free again, but we did eventually find our way to the moorings. Finding a narrowboat moored just ahead of any free spaces made for some pretty intense reversing as we tried to delicately pass and not crush the small lightweight boat it was also towing!

Needless to say that once the ropes were tied, we both got ourselves inside to warm up and have a rest, while I started to sample different kinds of non dairy milk! Our day finally came to an end when we both found ourselves walking about three miles down to where we had left the bus, for my friend to return home, and myself to meet my Dad to go and watch Star Wars Episode VII, which I thoroughly enjoyed! It was during this walk back down the towpath that my friend and I where amused to discover the same burning smell in the air that we had previously thought was coming from Tilly! We chuckled about how a random person buying rubbish, had led us to have some serious exercise in dragging a boat backwards down the canal!

After enjoying the film and as the night wore on I was finally dropped off back onboard to enjoy a calm and cosy end to the day as I drifted off to sleep!"

In hindsight, it seems that some of my favourite memories of boat life were the days that didn't go to plan. Days such as the one just described, but also days in the past where a friend might see me walking down the towpath and persuade me to hop onboard for a very slow lift as they travelled down the canal. Other times, the surprises would come from nature, an unexpected fox vanishing into the distance, herons watching patiently barely a few feet away from the stern. On one occasion I heard a loud splash, only to look through the kitchen window and find a cormorant rising up from the water before flapping its huge wings and flying off down the canal! With the benefit of the passing years, I even look back at some of the times that Tilly was hit by other boats with a slight smile. I was so worried about things like that when I first moved onboard, for some reason thinking that a great big steel boat was the most delicate thing in the world. But lets get back to January.

As the first month of the year continued, I enjoyed a few towpath walks down into Llangollen, the epitome of a scenic Welsh town, a steam railway, the river cutting the town in two, and of course the canal. As I have done on so many occasions, I would walk down from the canal, cross the bridge over the River Dee and then pop into my favourite bakery, filling my backpack with all kinds of vegetarian goodies, some "olde worlde" style drinks, and of course something sweet for dessert.

At Llangollen itself, the canal was closed for maintenance. Beneath a road bridge the canal was blocked off and emptied, seeming to make the total depth look shallower than ever, a pipe and pump allowed a stream of water to keep flowing from one side to the other. It would have been nice to have been able to take Tilly right up to Llangollen Basin on her final journey in that direction, but at the time I didn't realise that I wouldn't be taking her that way again.

Cycling between my workplace/friends/family and my mooring spot by Llangollen was both a blessing and a curse. If the weather was good then it could be a beautiful twelve mile bike ride, almost exactly half of it on the towpath and half on quiet country lanes. The perfect activity for anybody wanting to enjoy a bit of nature to start or end the day. However, in the dark winter evenings the route was almost entirely unlit. This made for some particularly hair raising moments when doing six miles along the towpath. With a lot of this section of the ride taking place in areas where the canal cut through woodland or under huge trees, I would occasionally find myself hitting sticks, rocks and random objects seemingly emerging out of the darkness from nowhere! It is easy to see how people end up falling in the canal, although I am pleased to say that never happened to me... or at least hasn't happened yet!

Because of the nature of the commute, I found myself relying on the bus service more than I had done previously. It was a three mile walk to get to the bus stop, and sometimes I would find myself talking to people on the towpath for so long that I would have to wait for the next bus after the one I had originally set out to catch, but this seemed to help to add to the unexpectedly pleasant experience of being moored in an awkward place to get to.

January gave us a few true winter days, where ice formed over parts of the canal, not enough to stop boats, but still nice to see. Some incredible golden sunsets seemed to light the hills on fire as I travelled up and down the towpath. If I was lucky enough to be around at the right time, I would find the sun setting at my back, lighting up the naked trees and canal bridges with a yellow hint as I passed below them.

As you may have come to expect from this book though, when I actually wanted some good weather, such as days when I moved Tilly, the sky was not so blue. As my diary tells, this led to one particularly unfortunate incident on Wednesday 27th January...

"The last weekend of being moored up here by Llangollen has passed in a blur. The sheer amount of miles I have put in on my bike heading both to work and to my friends, along with walking to and from the bus stop has seen a lot of time eaten up. Add in my attempt to plan and start filming a series of daily "Ultimate Boat Basics" videos to go online during February, and my days seem to have slipped away faster than ever.

The real thing to talk about today though, is my trip down from my previous Welsh mooring spot to arrive at Chirk Bank. What a fantastic, but also disastrous boat trip it has been! To start with it was (as usual) a grey, overcast day, quite windy when I set off and with passing rain showers throughout the day. Together the wind and the rain seemed to help make it feel even colder than it actually was.

In total the whole trip was just under seven miles of travelling, it was a very slow seven miles too. With the wind instantly pushing Tilly around, we passed through the narrow stretches of canal, over Pontcysyllte Aqueduct, filling up with water, going through the lift bridge, heading through the small Whitehouse Tunnel, then through Chirk Tunnel before crossing the final aqueduct and mooring up.

At some points it seemed like I had made a terrible mistake in moving at all, huge gusts of wind would come from nowhere and push Tilly towards some of the very shallow parts of the canal. Crossing over Pontcysyllte Aqueduct was quite an experience, being exposed in the middle of the valley over one-hundred foot up with high winds blowing from almost a perfect right angle! Tilly was rocking around like never before, being forced to rub and scrape along the edge of the towpath by the wind! In all honesty, despite not being in any real danger, it was actually quite scary.

After this battering from the wind I moored up by the nearby water points to fill up a few bottles for drinking water… and to take a moment to warm my hands up. Moving on a little further again, I was happy to get into a little bit of cover from the wind as I took Tilly through the lift bridge and down the tree lined canal towards Chirk. The only thing of real note that happened during this stage of the trip was that I passed a huge walking group who were heading up toward Llangollen… like I say there isn't much to report from this point in the journey!

The final and disastrous part of this trip came as I passed through Chirk tunnel and then headed out over the aqueduct. The weather had started to pick up and the sun was shining through a break in the clouds as Tilly moved into the open valley on the old stone aqueduct. I had my iPod filming as usual, it was sat on a tripod on Tilly's roof. To get one good panoramic shot of the rare appearance of the sun I took my iPhone out and started to point it at the perfect scene. Then a big gust of wind started to push the tripod over, I threw my hand forwards to save it, but unfortunately in doing so I also threw my phone out of my hand!

The tripod was saved but the phone fell over the side of Tilly, hit the concrete towpath and then landed on the wooden fenders that run along the side of the water's edge. For a split second it looked as if it might be saved, but it slid along the wooden surface before finding a gap to fall down into the water. I was gutted!

I moored Tilly at the nearest possible point just around the next corner at Chirk Bank. I had barely tied the ropes before getting back up to the aqueduct to search for any signs of my phone. Unfortunately in the heat of the moment, not only could I not see any sign of the phone, but I also wasn't sure exactly where it had fallen into the canal. The aqueduct being one of the few places where the water flow keeps the canal relatively deep didn't help, and after a few minutes I gave up. The loss of a phone and the cost of £540 to replace it was bad enough, but what I was really disappointed about was the fact that I had lots of great footage from the days boating on there, as well as all sorts of clips from the previous days of cycling and walking all over the place. I took a few minutes to think about things logically and tried to tell myself that it was "just money"... something that did little to console me when I reserved a new phone online a few hours later.

All in all, a fantastic day has been marred by a very expensive mistake!"

As January drew to a close, it was fair to say that it had been a month filled with the best and worst of boat life. I had thoroughly enjoyed spending time on a very quiet canal surrounded by beautiful Welsh hills, but I had also been hit hard by the weather. Spending a lot of time sheltering onboard writing and recording videos was fantastic in terms of productivity, but maybe a little tiresome after a while. Somehow at the same time, due to the distance I had to travel to my workplace and friends and family,

January was also an incredibly active month with a good few hundred miles put in on my bike alone.

Through all this, in the back of my mind the "Tilly Question" had been niggling away! What was I going to do for the long term? In hindsight I don't think I really know exactly when I decided that my boat life was reaching its final chapter. A mixture of fear, doubt and simple "kidding myself" all helped to keep my future plans anything but clear, even to myself. Perhaps it was just a bit of sulking about the weather and losing my phone, but I remember being moored at Chirk Bank at the end of January and feeling like my heart wasn't in it for the long term anymore.

A late night walk across Chirk Aqueduct into the village for supplies had been an unexpectedly thoughtful trip. As I had done on many occasions, I stood on the aqueduct for a few moments, in the past I had done this to look at the stars, but this was yet another cloudy night. Instead I just leaned against the railing and listened to the River Ceiriog flowing beneath the stone arches of the aqueduct and watched the lights of cars dancing between the trees in the distance.

I didn't feel sad, I didn't feel like this was the last time I would ever moor a boat at Chirk Bank, but I didn't feel any great motivation to run out and buy another boat or to get to work solving the many small issues that Tilly had. In hindsight, the reason that this totally random moment has stayed in my mind, may well be because it was the first time I felt at ease. Perhaps a secret sigh of relief that I was going to be able to hand my boating concerns over to somebody else.

As you would expect a wet January soon became a wet February, on the fourth I decided to move Tilly a little bit further downstream to moor by The Lion Quays, a restaurant, pub, spa and hotel right next to the canal... if I was looking for the opposite experience of my basic boat life, then perhaps I should have booked a few nights in there!

Thursday 4th February:
"In a less than shocking turn of events, this morning I opened the curtains on Tilly to discover a grey, overcast day! Ignoring the potential for rain, I decided to press on with my planned morning

boat trip. Soon after nine in the morning Tilly was untied and we were off downstream, leaving Chirk Bank, passing The Poachers, then further on around a few long bends, and under a main road bridge, before finally mooring just past The Lion Quays.

To be completely honest, the trip was quite uneventful, the few boats we met were all moored up, there were no moments of excitement, and only one person was seen walking... it may not have been notable, but that doesn't mean it wasn't a perfect peaceful trip! Passing under the main road by The Lion Quays, the traffic roared overhead as it always does, at around sixty miles per hour. On almost every occasion that I pass beneath a busy road like that, I can't help thinking about the contrast between me travelling around three miles an hour, as they zip off above me at literally twenty times Tilly's speed! I often contemplate what life would have been like if I had taken other choices and it was me in one of those cars... but we are getting too off topic and deep here!

The one unusual thing that happened on this trip occurred just as I was mooring up, when from around the long corner that stretched ahead of Tilly appeared two sheep! They ran down the towpath towards me, not really a sight I had been expecting. As they approached down the towpath I had an alarming thought like "oh no, I am going to have to try and get them back in a field" and started to imagine "what if one of them fell into the canal?" Luckily not far behind a human figure also emerged, who I assumed to be the farmer. He was not looking flustered at all so I allowed the sheep to barge past me. It was only when the figure reached me and we exchanged a few surprised words about seeing sheep on the towpath that I realised he was not a farmer or connected to the sheep at all. Where on earth those sheep must have wandered to in the end I have no idea!

As the day wore on, it became extremely windy, but also quite sunny. For the first time in quite a while, Tilly was moored in a place where the sun falls on the side of the boat unhindered by trees for hours on end. Today I have been reminded just how much the sun can warm up the interior of the boat, even when outside it is a cold windy day. Again this added heat together with the fire inside created an unbearably warm boat! Get those windows open!"

On the subject of animals on the towpath, I will also throw in a bonus moment here. The night before I made this trip downstream, I had been sat onboard editing videos when all of a sudden I heard a small animal land on the boat and start running around all over the roof! After a brief moment of shock from the sudden interruption to my peaceful evening, I grabbed my camera and ran out onto the stern. As I did so, I saw one of the local cats jump off Tilly and vanish into the darkness! Not the most exhilarating of incidents, but just about as exciting as I ever wanted boat life to get!

I ended up spending a full two weeks moored by the Lion Quays, while I was there it just so happened that I had a holiday booked from work. Luckily the weather started to perk up a bit so I was able to get out and about a bit more, which was great for filming and general fun! However, all of this free time definitely saw me thinking about life a lot more. I remember distinctly getting back onboard one night and attempting to record a video discussing whether or not I should buy a new boat or just do up Tilly. I still wasn't talking about selling up completely, but the fact I was actually putting those thoughts into a video shows how serious it was all becoming!

During this period another huge change happened. It may seem trivial, or even an odd thing to bring up, but some of my best friends moved from by the canal to my home town of Oswestry. They had previously lived a few minutes away from the canal at Weston Rhyn and had been absolutely instrumental in the early days of my boat life. It was actually one of them who had first suggested that I buy a boat to live on as a joke, many years ago. We all went viewing boats together while I was still looking, and they helped me move Tilly for a large part of the one-hundred mile maiden voyage I had onboard.

My winter mooring spot of previous years had been only a few minutes away from their house and as such we had spent many great times together. It was also always handy to be able to get a sneaky lift into town when they went shopping too! In all seriousness, I have said many times about what good friends they have been over the years, so to have been "almost neighbours" for five months of the year had been a true pleasure. Life moved on, and pretty soon I would find myself sleeping on their living room floor, before wake up and heading into work in the morning rather than commute from Tilly on the canal! Something that I had done many times before from their previous home, despite the fact that Weston Rhyn still left me with a five mile bike ride to work!

I don't want to dwell on this slight change too much, at the risk of it sounding like it was a big part of my decision to leave boat life. It is however something that really gave me a lot to think about as their lives moved into a new era and their family grew. My mind was already open to the idea of moving on in my own life, perhaps their example gave me a bit more courage to make a big change and follow in their footsteps... all the way to Oswestry!

The days wore on and I found myself really enjoying getting out on my bike. Being in an area that I was far more familiar with, I would go off exploring on short trips, sometimes several times a day. I would find myself taking detours to add a few more miles into my genuine commutes to see friends and really just wanted to get out and exercise, after being stuck inside so frequently over the previous few months. There was one small issue, the towpath! Opposite the Lion Quays is a small stretch of towpath that gets extremely muddy, when I say muddy, I mean it must literally be the muddiest stretch of towpath in about twenty miles! As if I haven't mentioned it before, we had had a lot of rain during the winter, so it was the worst I have ever seen it, bumpy and muddy... a potentially disastrous combination, when only two feet away from a very cold canal! This stretch of path was so slippy that my road bike tyres could gain no grip at all so I would have no option but to get off and walk!

Apart from that minor inconvenience, it was a really pleasant time. On the 9th my friends Hannah and Jon came by on their old working boat "Mountbatton" which they used as a canal delivery service, supplying coal, diesel, gas bottles and more boating essentials. Hearing Hannah ring the bell, I quickly ran up onto the stern and waved them down. It was extremely cold and seeing them wrapped up nice and warm and wearing bright yellow jackets really made me think of the hardship and "toughness" of boaters in years gone by. They moored up alongside Tilly and started to hand supplies over. It was the last supply drop that I ever took onboard.

After two weeks at the Lion Quays, it was finally time to move on... of course the weather had something special lined up, as my diary entry records:

Thursday 18th February

"Wow! What an extremely chilly morning! Today, I woke up just before eight in the morning, ready for an early boat trip down to one of my favourite spots at St. Martins. I knew that it would be a cold day but I wasn't prepared for it to be the one, real, wintry day of the season. The sky was completely clear of clouds, just a huge blue sheet above the canal. The naked trees stood tall over the canal as they were lit by the rising sun in the warm yellow/orange tint of morning sunlight.

The most important thing to note is the frost and ice. As usual for a cold winter morning, the grass was grey with frost, Tilly was also covered in a grey, shimmering film, making the stern and gunwales treacherous to walk on. The most notable thing, and something that hadn't happened for a while, was that the mooring ropes were frozen solid. The coils that I make with the end of the ropes were frozen into a solid pizza shape that could be lifted up as one flat object rather than simply uncoiling to a length of rope! This made for a very cold, tricky unmooring. My gloves were immediately saturated and freezing cold around my finger tips, as I tried to force the rigid ropes to become more... like actual ropes!

It was a beautiful trip down the short distance from The Lion Quays to St. Martins, the sun and chilly winter scenery were such a welcome change to the previous boating experiences of the year so far. Mooring up in the sun and heading inside, it was amazing to feel just how warm it was onboard, with the last tiny bit of heat still coming from the fire, and the sun streaming in through the windows, the heat radiated through the walls as the day wore on.

The day passed by with a bit of tinkering onboard and a perfect sunny walk over the fields up to the village of St. Martins itself, to get a few supplies. The fields were predictably muddy, but luckily with many of the temporary electric fences taken down, as the cattle were in different fields, there was plenty of space to avoid the worst patches.

During the entire day, I saw only a handful of boats, I am not sure if the number passed five in total, including a few familiar faces from this part of the canal.

As I have been sat writing this quick entry, it is pitch black outside apart from the silver light of the moon. The sky is filled with stars and this spot continues to be an excellent area for astronomy. Earlier in the evening, a short walk outside was enough to convince me that my adventures were done for the day, ice, frost and very cold fingers being the main reasons for that conclusion!"

I only stayed at the peaceful spot at St Martins for two nights, but they were two of my favourite nights of the year. A beautiful and really quiet place to be, surrounded by flat fields and very little else, I have spent many perfect nights moored in the area just above the two New Marton Locks. As my diary remembers, the area is so perfect for astronomy, because the low horizons offer a view of a vast expanse of sky compared to other locations with more trees and hills that rise up and block out the sky!

I was lucky to be able to spend those two nights peering through the boat windows up at the stars, in the past I had spent some nights in the quieter months with the curtains open on the waterside of the boat. This allowed me to nod off and get as close to "sleeping under the stars" as I ever wanted to! On this particular occasion I decided not to risk the open curtain plan, for one thing a holiday boat had come down stream and moored up on the far side of the canal for some reason. Their unusual decision to place their boat slightly down from Tilly and on the "wrong" side of the canal made a chicane type layout for boats to pass through... not that it would be any trouble for a vehicle travelling around two miles an hour.

When I woke up on February 20th, I was disappointed to find it raining, as I had planned on an early start to boat down through the two nearby locks before hopping on my bike to head into Oswestry. I didn't fancy having another soaking wet boat trip so I decided to get on with some odd jobs and video editing to see how the weather turned out. By about ten o'clock it looked a lot lighter and as if there may even be the potential of some sun, so I quickly unmoored and set off on the short trip to the first lock… however by the time I got there I was being rained on!

Passing down through the locks went nice and smoothly, I am glad to say that Tilly didn't break down as she had previously once done in the bottom lock. I was soon moored up by Mad Jack's (yes, I know.. yet another canal based pub!) My hands were absolutely freezing from working the locks in the rain which led me to almost drop my bike lock into the canal as I prepared for the short ride into town.

Mad Jack's offered one of the shortest and flattest commutes from the canal back to Oswestry, based on this, I decided to spend almost a full two weeks moored just down from the pub. It was an absolutely perfect time to be there. Some beautiful sunny days rolled in over the end of February and I managed to spend a lot of time out in my kayak, as well as cycling around the extremely quiet country lanes of the area. With it being such a short and easy ride to town (around twenty minutes), the good weather meant that one of my best friends managed to get out to Tilly a lot more than the previous months to join in the fun. It was truly a wonderful time to have a boat!

One of the things that I loved about mooring by Mad Jack's during the winter months was that the sun rose at an almost perfect angle to hit the boat from ahead (or behind, depending on which way you were travelling!) This final stay outside the pub was no exception. On many occasions I awoke to a boat filled with such dazzling sunlight, and the interior being so bright, that it was almost as though the curtains were not there at all.

Taking a moment to walk up onto the stern on these sunny winter mornings, I was met with the sight of the sun rising over the canal ahead. So low and so unobstructed it seemed to change the scene from a colourful rural sight into a black and white silhouette of a classic humpback canal bridge, together with my friends' boat that had been moored just down from Tilly.

Turning my back to the sun where my eyes could focus, it was like seeing a photograph that had been edited to be oversaturated with vivid colours! The golden hint of the morning sun making the bare trees seem even more vivid against the bright blue background of the sky. These sorts of tiny momentary things really stand out in my memory as I started to think to myself "this might be the last time I see this!"

On February 26th my little sister and dad visited me onboard. As they were bringing chips for tea, I made sure to have the plates, drinks and cutlery ready to go... along with my abnormally large selection of ketchup! My sister was only three years old at the time, so keeping her occupied was always a priority. After eating we had a short stroll down the towpath towards the locks.

This is a moment that stands out to me as it was on that walk that I told my dad I was thinking about selling up and that I wasn't sure of whether or not I would get another boat. I was still not completely clear on what my plan would be, but at that point I know that I had really started to look at the practical realities of moving back to dry land. Again I think that simple moments from those last few months afloat, such as that evening family visit, stick in my mind more as I thought to myself "enjoy it while it lasts".

As February drew to a close I was looking forward to a nice calm week in town. My mum was off on holiday, so I took on my usual role as "cat-sitter in chief" and generally enjoyed living in a house for a week. With Tilly being so close to town I ended up cycling out to her repeatedly, both alone or with a friend. I also took an unnaturally great deal of pleasure in laying a new carpet in the bathroom at my mum's house. It was one of those strange things that once I had got the hang of, I felt compelled to spend hours obsessively cutting it to absolute perfection.

If anybody had seen the state of Tilly's paintwork and some of my handiwork onboard then they may well have assumed the carpet would be a disaster. It was always my only real regret that I had not kept on top of Tilly's paintwork and odd jobs, better than I did. I was always finding things to tinker and mess about with onboard, but if I could have shown Tilly the level of obsessive care that I showed that bathroom carpet, then the idea of leaving her may not have been in my mind so soon. Saying that, if I had have been as obsessed with Tilly's appearance as I could have been, then it is unlikely that I would have loved boat life as much as I did. Rough and ready as it was, I learned a lot from living as simply as I did and trying to figure things out as I went along!

On March 4th I moved Tilly a very short distance down the canal... again to another pub! This time I moored opposite the appropriately named "The Narrow Boat Inn". I was also directly opposite the huge selection of boats that sit alongside the canal at Maestermyn Marina. They own the non towpath side of the canal bank and have a great deal of private boats moored there. Always a lovely place to pass through onboard, even if it does get a bit tense sometimes if you meet a boat coming towards you, and you then have to try and slot into a thin slither of canal between two boats.

When passing this area in the months out of the peak holiday season, you can see the full fleet of hire boats that operate from the marina, all moored up and looking quite sad on a drizzly day! It is an eye opening sight though and makes you realise just how many hire boats make up the traffic over the summer months. When kayaking and boating through the Trevor Basin by the Pontycyllte Aqueduct in January it was a similar story, a vast amount of boats waiting for the summer to arrive. When viewed in the context of all the other marinas in just a small stretch of canal it really is amazing just how many boats are out travelling the canals during the summer. Other marinas in the area with their own hire fleets include Chirk, Blackwater, Whixall and Whitchurch and along with Maestermyn that makes five marinas within around twenty-five miles of canal. A recipe for some beautiful summer boat chaos!

Once I was back spending my time onboard I decided to once again move on a short distance as I wanted to spend some time in a completely rural spot away from anyone. The Frankton Junction was practically made for the job! There are a couple of houses in the area, but in my usual way I moored up just out of sight, only a couple of minutes walk away from the locks that allow you to drop down onto the Montgomery Canal.

With total peace and quiet, rural scenery and the occasional herd of cows drinking from the canal opposite your boat, it was a place where I had loved to spend time ever since I had bought Tilly. It took me about forty minutes to cycle from Oswestry to this particular point... if I wanted to get there fast! There was also a completely impractical and ridiculous route that I also liked to take back to town from the area.

I would cycle along the towpath, down past the four locks at the junction, stopping just before the fifth lock to hop over a fence and drag my bike into a field. A public right of way crossed the field to bring any walker out onto a very rural, barely used country road. There was no actual path over the field and it was simply impossible to ride my bike so I would often find myself picking the bike up, hooking the frame over my shoulder and then walking as fast as I could. Sometimes I would have to wade through waist high crops, other times over extremely loose, freshly ploughed soil and mud. Once over this field, it was roughly six miles of almost entirely quiet country lane to ride until I would end up at Oswestry. Just about the perfect start to any day!

A small but significant thing happened while I was moored at Frankton. Previously, I had looked online at different options for selling Tilly, not as a guarantee of intent, more as a cursory check of what my options were apart from selling privately. While at Frankton, I noticed one evening that I had a voicemail message waiting. I listened to it and found that it was a marina getting back to me after I had filled in an online inquiry form, they were interested in buying Tilly.

This was a moment in which everything I had been thinking about, suddenly became real! To be honest it completely knocked me for six, I just didn't know what I wanted at all for the moment. In a bit of a panic I phoned them right away, even though it was obvious there would be no answer at that time of night. I left a message thanking them for their interest and saying that I had decided to keep my boat for the time being. Even as I said the words, I knew I didn't really believe them.

So it was on a cold night in March, completely alone on a boat in a rural spot, I went to bed even more confused than ever about what my plans would be. It did however seem that whatever happened, Tilly would no longer be with me by the end of the year.

As if by magic my two weeks moored in this quiet calm place vanished! I decided to move down onto the Montgomery Canal for a couple of weeks, knowing it would likely be the last time that I did so with Tilly. Ensuring that we made the most of it, my grandad joined me for the passage down through the locks. In order to regulate the flow of boating traffic on the nature reserve-like Montgomery Canal, you have to phone ahead to book a passage through the Frankton Locks. A member of the Canal and River Trust staff will then turn up and literally take the locks off the locks!

On this particular day, Tilly was the only boat heading down onto the Monty, so my grandad, the CRT chap and myself enjoyed a nice calm hour where we all stayed together and descended all of the locks flawlessly. A really enjoyable trip, with no other boats around and the added help of the staff member, it was about as relaxed as dropping a few tons of steel boat down watery chambers can be! I stayed onboard and worked the tiller (the easy job!) while my grandad and his new friend chatted away lifting and lowering the paddles.

Once through the locks, my grandad jumped onboard and took the tiller, steering us the short distance to the deserted basin that marks the top of the Montgomery Canal. As we had done on so many occasions, we walked back up to the car park and travelled into town where my nan had been cutting and cooking some home made chips for dinner... perfect!

On previous trips down the Monty, I had tried to get right down to the bottom of the seven mile stretch in a single day. Mooring at the end of this restored section at a place called Maesbury, was the closest that the canal passed to Oswestry. A short commute with barely any incline was the best thing I could hope for while travelling on my bike, this final trip to Maesbury however, took me a week to complete! I wanted to enjoy every moment that I could on the very quiet stretch of canal, especially quiet as I was travelling it during March, well out of the peak season.

From March 23rd to the 30th, I travelled seven miles in total, and it was great! I stopped at some really obscure random places that could barely hold a boat, sometimes it seemed that I was living in a hedgerow as the towpath side windows were covered by all kinds of greenery from the verges. On the 24th, I moved down from the Frankton Basin to the "Queens Head"... yet another canalside pub! It was a simple and pleasant trip, but I was not prepared for how extremely windy it would be when I arrived at the only lock of the trip. "The Graham Palmer Lock" should have been a simple one to pass, the water level only drops a few inches and is barely noticeable. This time however, the wind was blowing across the canal, which as I slowed to a stop and lost the forward momentum, meant that Tilly was blown all over the place.

After playing canal bank pinball I managed to drag her into the lock, drop the small distance and then started taking her back out the other side. Immediately on leaving the lock her bow was blown right into the tree on the off-side. I ended up leaving her pinned while I closed the lock gate and then managed to straighten her up and vanish downstream, pretending it had never happened.

The following day, I would make a tiny trip of barely a few hundred metres down through one single lock with my grandad. We hadn't planned on a trip that day, but the weather was so warm, sunny and generally perfect, that it seemed only appropriate to go boating! As you can see, I really did make the most of the trip to ensure I moored at my favourite spots and got the most of the environment.

On Easter Sunday (27th), my dad and sister came out for a visit. Although it was a windy day with a mixture of sun and drizzle, this didn't have any impact on us as we had an absolute riot trying to entertain my sister onboard while she demanded I open my Easter egg! The real moment of note of the day came after they had left. The weather seemed to perk up and I decided to take the blue sky as an opportunity to get into town to see my family.

I hopped on my bike and just before I left the canal took a picture of some swans at 1:23pm, the blue sky can clearly be seen in the background… as I cycled towards Oswestry I saw a huge dark storm heading my way. I pedalled as fast as I could, but it was no use, by 1:30pm I was attempting to shelter by a tree, away from the driving rain and hailstones. It was a shock to the system as it had been a while since I had been that cold and wet while riding, yet alone the sheer force of the hail hitting me in the gusts of wind. It may sound silly now, but I was genuinely worried they were going to split my lips, so I ended up cycling while trying to keep my waterproof coat pulled up over my face!

When I finally arrived back at Maesbury, the cycling to and from town seemed like nothing. As such I was sometimes making the trip a couple of times a day to see different people, maybe just for fun on occasions. I managed to sneak in a nice calm kayak trip or two at the sleepy "dead end" of the canal. With so few boats around it really was like I was the last boater in the land… or should I say on the canal!

I wouldn't like to say when exactly, but I feel that it was likely at some point on the Monty trip that my mind finally moved over fully into the "sell up" column of pros and cons. Part of the reason that I was enjoying the trip so much was because I had started it expecting it to be my last with Tilly. As time had gone on and I had not found a boat to my liking online in terms of something I wanted to live on for the long term, my boat life doubts had only grown in strength. There was no single moment where I threw my hands in the air and shouted "I'm done!" It was just a gradual realisation that I was going to sell Tilly but had not come up with another boat to replace her with. It would be less than two weeks between my time at Maesbury and my "official announcement" that Tilly would soon be up for sale, and that I didn't have another boat ready to move onto.

The day that I left Maesbury, I was joined by a good friend. We both had our bikes onboard and were determined to spend as much time "doing something but nothing in particular" as we could. It was a beautiful day, we hadn't done anything active together for a while and we were both off work, so we decided to get onboard and go for it!

The seven mile trip we found ourselves taking back up towards the Llangollen Canal took us well over two hours. Under the gorgeous sunny sky, it was beautiful. We were so relaxed and slow in our progress that at one point we even had to pull over, and let the only other boat we had seen all day, pass us by in order to get to the top locks before they were closed up for the day! I made sure that my friend spent a huge amount of time on the tiller, again in the theme of "enjoy it while it lasts!"

When we finally arrived at the Frankton Basin it was almost a shock to the system to see that we were joined there by another boat! Reflecting on the trip now, it speaks volumes that we were surprised to see two occupied boats in seven miles of canal. It probably speaks even louder about the peaceful nature of the trip that the biggest moment of excitement was when a swan came into a lock with us! We had to raise Tilly through very carefully to keep the swan safe as I feel it would have been too stubborn to move out of the way of Tilly... or that it may have gone on the attack and chased us away from the canal!

Once Tilly was safely moored up, my friend and I jumped on our bikes and started riding aimlessly down the country lanes. It wasn't until we reached the top of the only hill in the area that we made a decision on where to go... not wanting to go down the hill only to have to climb it again later! So we slowly made our way towards St Martins and after two hours of very slow riding we found ourselves topping up with supplies at the village before zooming downhill to join the canal again.

After being out on our bikes and a boat for around six hours, we sat on a fence by a canal bridge as the sun shone, admittedly lower in the sky, not only over us, but also a few horses in a field on the far side of the canal. Eating our vegetable samosas and other impulse purchases from the shop, we talked, said "hello" to a few walkers and even saw another boat moving downstream. After a while, we decided to both head into Oswestry together, he to return back home while I was going to call at another friend's house.

We took the longest route we could think of (without heading in the completely wrong direction!) and finally arrived at our destination after a full day of boating, cycling and fun in the middle of nowhere.

Days like those I have always considered as the days that you really make friends... or perhaps it is just a different level of friendship when you trust someone to work a lock single handed while your boat is in it!

The Last of Boat Life

April was to be my final full month with Narrowboat Tilly, and it was a month well lived! You may well have noticed how there are no more huge diary entries at this point in the year. Seeing my boat life coming to an end so too my book concept drew to a close. My diary entries from the final few moments are far more factual than anything else, informing me of the weather and events in a spartan fashion.

The truth is that even when looking at my photographs from the month, I see it is almost a perfect mixture of canal memories and "general outdoors around Oswestry" memories. In many respects this made it a perfect month!

Things had started off well with the boating and biking day I had spent with my friend. The high continued on the 6th as my grandad joined me, for what we then knew would be our last time, rising up through the Frankton Locks onto the Llangollen canal. A windy but sunny day for it too, we slowly rose up lock by lock. The hood on my grandad's coat was repeatedly being filled by the gusts of wind, making it rise from his head and at a distance giving him the look of Napoleon, complete with golden topped bicorne hat! We travelled a short distance up the Llangollen towards Ellesmere before deciding that we didn't want to give ourselves too far to walk back to the car down the towpath.

Later in the evening, I cycled back out to Tilly. It was the first time that I had moored in that particular spot, and I was amazed that away from anything that really passed as "society", I had yet again found one of the many locations on the canal where it is possible to sit back and listen to nothing but the sounds of nature. I was less inclined to view the scene in a romantic light when I awoke the following morning, ready to take another short trip to the tiny mark on a map known as Tetchill… as soon as my eyes opened in the morning I could hear the rain beating down. I decided to press ahead with the short trip regardless and proceeded to get soaked through, the last time that it would happen!

I stayed at Tetchill, a short distance away from an absolutely gorgeous black and white canalside house, for almost two weeks. The location was slightly awkward to get to as the commute pushed towards ten miles, with the mile closest to the canal being one of the narrowest, bumpiest and muddiest lanes around! It was hardly the worst thing in the world but it did serve to give me some quiet time to gather my thoughts and plan for the future. Not only did the slightly longer commute stop me from having so many spur of the moment trips to my friends, but I was also in an area with very poor phone signal. My time at Tetchill was truly some of my last real peaceful secluded canal experience. I decided during this time that I would put the boating book that I had been working on (along with my diaries) on hold. To this day I have never got back to the near twenty thousand words that were already written! Instead, I just decided to enjoy boat life for what it was, and beyond that just enjoy life itself without worrying about videos or writing etc.

Mingled in with the canal pictures, I have mentioned the general outdoors pictures as well. The sheer amount of walking that I did with a friend during April was really quite something. We came up with a simple idea, to look on a map of the areas surrounding Oswestry, find a point of interest, and then try and get there on foot. Roads were walked, footpaths followed, fences scrambled over and streams jumped. Some of our days spent criss-crossing farmland and woodland could be written about as if happening one-hundred-and-fifty years ago. Descriptions of coppices interrupting the patchwork of fields and hedgerows, stumbling across the eggs of an unknown waterbird sat in a nest by a lake we should not have been at, it was as if we were kids again… and it was great!

On April 19th, I enjoyed what was my last truly awe inspiring boat trip, there would be more boating to follow but this one was extra special. It had been a day of sunlight and blue skies which in turn became an evening of increasingly yellow sunlight as the sunset crept closer. Not wanting to miss my chance I found it impossible to resist untying the ropes and taking Tilly up to Ellesmere, another short half an hour trip or so.

Setting out soon after seven, Tilly was moored up in my usual place just around the corner from the Ellesmere boat service point by seven-forty-five. I had travelled with the setting sun at my back almost the entire way. The world ahead of me was lit with an increasingly golden light, the sun being so low in the sky made every shadow stretch out far longer than the object that cast it. Travelling at my usual slow pace, it was almost hypnotic to see the shadows slowly passing over Tilly's roof, stretching as they passed over the air vents before vanishing forever.

Passing by a string of boats moored up alongside the canal as the residents washed up after tea, sat back watching the television and otherwise just going about their lives, was enough to make me think about what I would be leaving behind when Tilly was sold. Yet another bittersweet moment of beautiful canal scenery mixed with all kinds of emotions. Mooring up that night, I must say that I felt quite happy to be quite close to other boats and a small town.

My time at Ellesmere passed very quickly, as I started to make preparations for Tilly to go up for sale. The weather was mostly beautiful and judging by the amount of photos I took, it seems that I spent almost as much time walking around the town and lakes of the area as I did onboard Tilly!

Having decent bus access between Tilly and Oswestry also lead me to start leaving my bike in my friend's coal shed in town, while I took the easy option out to the boat! This in turn only encouraged me to spend more time out walking when I was on Tilly. Again, it was truly a time of simply enjoying every moment as best as I could. Occasionally that was by bike, but for the majority it was by boot!

I was pleased to spend one last birthday onboard, and I was even happier to find that April 23rd (my 29th) was yet another day of blue sky, sun and then takeaway pizza at my mum's house! I really do think that it was the first day that I had a genuine sadness at the idea of leaving the lifestyle behind. At five-past-nine in the morning, I was on a small bridge over the canal at Ellesmere Junction. A bright blue sky seemed to tower over the long row of boats that were moored up along a short canal arm that lead to the town. It was an exceptionally thoughtful moment. The days were suddenly counting down to my thirtieth birthday, the lifestyle I had built over four years and planned for years before that was coming to an end, yet somehow life seemed perfect!

As a beautiful April became a slightly warmer May, I took Tilly through the short tunnel on the outskirts of Ellesmere. Once through I moored Tilly at one of my all time favourite canal places.

The stretch of towpath that overlooked the great big lake of Blakemere. This was where I chose to officially end my time of living aboard.

The Last Day and Night

On Friday 6th May I spent my last full day, and more importantly night, onboard Tilly. What an absolutely perfect end to boat life it was. At this point she was still yet to be put up for sale. I wanted to move my things off her first and then spend a little bit of time "doing her up" to at least make her more presentable on the inside, even if the outside paintwork was rapidly turning to rust!

Friday was a beautiful day, some cloud cover but with plenty of sun finding patches of blue sky to shine through. I had a lot that I wanted to do on this final moment of "living the dream". Firstly, as Tilly was moored up right next to the absolutely stunning Blakemere, a huge expanse of water that sits just outside of the town of Ellesmere, and has its banks right at the edge of the towpath. With that incredible view through the window I wanted to make sure I took one final towpath walk to thoroughly enjoy it!

Secondly, I was determined that in the evening I would walk into Ellesmere itself, head to a chippy, buy some chips and then eat them sat on a bench overlooking the lake of Ellesmere too. Thirdly, as had been a tradition from the times when I had first brought Tilly to the Ellesmere area, I wanted to take a night time stroll down to get a few supplies from the canalside supermarket... of course as I wasn't going to be stopping onboard after that particular night, my scope for supplies was limited merely to a bottle of pop and some chocolate!

Mingled in with all of these active and distracting goals, I was also keen to have Tilly ready to go up for sale. This saw me packing up all of the random items I had accumulated onboard, a surprising amount hidden beneath the sofa-bed, including a tent, camping mats and outdoors equipment which were soon added to the bagged up items by my desk onboard. The inflatable kayak that had lived on Tilly's roof for the last few years was all packed up, the toiletries from the bathroom sat in bags and the various notebooks and diaries I had kept onboard were skimmed through then slipped into my backpack.

It was the small things that really caught me off guard in terms of making me face the reality that my boat life was all over.

For example, when I started to remove the keys to my bike locks from my main floating keyring, it struck me that I was preparing the keys for somebody else, somebody I had yet to meet, who would in time have their own tales of Tilly to recollect.

Being blessed with a dry day, I made sure that I got all of the walking and outdoors time that I had wanted to, and then some! As I walked along the towpath it was a strange thing to see other boats moored up and say hello to the occasional walker, all while knowing that these were likely the last characteristically casual and friendly canal interactions that I would have.

Passing through the rural setting and seeing the dusty dirt paths that make their way off the towpath into fields and remembering how me and various friends had ended up getting completely lost in these places years before, gave me a sense of just how big a change in my life this was going to be. Sad but also necessary, the end of boat life did not mean the end of adventure, yet in moments like that, it almost seemed like an overly dramatic "end of the world" type of moment!

The absolute killer moment in terms of cranking up the emotions of that final few hours onboard, was lighting the fire. Something that I had done probably two-thousand times over the past few years, yet this time, all of a sudden, it was the saddest thing in the world. I always considered the fire to be the heart of the boat, the crackling of wood, roaring of flames when it really got going, and the slight smell of smoke in the air. All of these things that had come to define a cosy, warm, dry and safe home for myself over four years, had in one instant become something to remind me of all the good times and the amazing life that Tilly had allowed me to lead.

The fact that I was lighting it at night, all the summery distraction of the world outside now in darkness, probably made things much more intense. As darkness had come, it had left me with only my thoughts and a silent world to be with them in. Sat in front of the fire, I knew I was making the right decision, but I must have argued against myself with all of my might.

I tried to record a few final videos, but I had gone to pieces. I was literally crying proper sobs at some points! If a passer by had seen me through a crack in the curtains then they may well have thought that I hated boat life! After months of decision making and being as cold and detached about leaving the canal as I could be, I found myself an emotional wreck. All the bottled up feelings pouring out of me with no control, the last night in my tiny floating home was truly a bittersweet moment.

As I made up my sofa-bed for the final time, I felt a great deal of something that I can only describe inaccurately as "pressure". Knowing that I was about to settle in, with a crackling fire at my side and nothing but the endless swirls of thoughts to keep me company was the strangest mixture of emotions I have ever felt. However once my head hit the pillow, the night passed in a blur and without any ceremony I was asleep!

I awoke the following morning, to an absolutely stunning scene under the sun at Blakemere. The light poured in through the windows, a peek through the curtains revealed the beauty outside, while the birdsong told the tale of another great rural morning.

Stepping out onto the stern, the moment had come, my time of living onboard Tilly was finally over.

If You Love Boat Life So Much, Then Why Give It Up?

The question of why I gave up my life onboard Tilly, is very difficult to give a satisfactory answer to. There is no single issue that ended my boat life, no massive controversial shock that sunk my floating dreams. It was simply a number of minor issues and inconveniences that led me to think seriously about what my plans were going to be for the future.

Let us start at the absolute beginning… of the end! 2016 was always going to be a big year for me as it was my final full year before my 30th birthday, a milestone that I had long said would see me decide what I wanted to do with my life with regards to staying on a boat or not.

In all honesty I went into 2016 expecting to finish the year sat onboard a completely refurbished Narrowboat Tilly. I was willing to spend a small fortune doing her up completely. Stripping the interior down to the steel and starting all over again. I spent a lot of time scribbling down new layout ideas and taking measurements for various new kitchen and bathroom fittings for Tilly's imaginary refit.

The exterior would also undergo big changes, including new windows, replating the hull with new steel, a completely overhauled paint job… all in all I was expecting to spend a lot of money and have a lot of work on my hands, much of which I would hand out to different people with infinitely more skill than myself.

As the incredibly wet winter of 2015-16 continued to dampen me in a literal sense, it also started to tame my enthusiasm for the Tilly project. Continually getting soaking wet and covered in mud, while commuting to and from work, then dragging wet muddy clothes into the small interior of Tilly, gave me a lot to think about on those long dark nights of steamed up windows and clothes drying by the fire.

I realised that I could spend all the money in the world, have the most spectacular refit that any boat had ever experienced… yet I would still only have a tiny thirty foot boat. Having to look at the situation with cold, hard facts as my basis, I realised that for any long term plans to stay afloat to be viable, I would need a bigger boat.

I could not guarantee that I would always travel so light with so few possessions and no requirement for a larger working area or workshop. I had already seen the difficulty of having more than one person onboard when friends would stay over, or romances would burn brightly from time to time. These were all reasons that were far more complex than the simple concept of needing more space for more comfortable day to day living.

I have always been obsessively tidy, which was one of the reasons that Tilly never seemed too cramped to me on my own. Pretty much every surface possible was always free of any clutter. Even that did not make it any more fun to arrive at Tilly, soaking wet in the middle of the night, for the tenth week in a row (yes it really was a record breaking wet winter!) before dragging what seemed like half of the canal inside the boat, ready to steam the place up yet again! I concluded that I would need more space. I secretly started looking for a new boat, the level to which I was actually seriously intending to buy is something that I am not sure even I will ever be certain of!

My privately decided budget for the new boat was to be £25,000 to £35,000. I didn't have any set criteria and was more interested in the layout and "comfort" of a boat rather than simply getting an outright huge boat! I knew the advantages of having a small boat as well as the drawbacks, so looking to upgrade from a thirty foot boat with fifteen foot of indoor room to a moderately sized forty-five foot boat with thirty five foot of indoor space, sounded like a great upgrade.

It was while browsing the internet endlessly for a new boat, just as I had done years earlier when looking to buy my first floating home, that the enormity of the situation started to settle in. I was looking to buy a new home, a place to live for the long term future, a place that would define my life in many respects. As I looked at the huge array of boats for sale, the idea of that kind of investment started to play on my mind. When I had bought Tilly, I had all the excitement and nerves of doing it all for the first time to help me "just go for it" and take a chance to live my dream. Four years onboard had passed, and I suddenly found myself with some excitement, but also a lot of actual practical experience and plain old factual reality joining it in my mind.

I had seen the potential issues and worries, I had seen the good and the bad of boat life. While I had my tiny boat already bought and paid for, the good seemed to outweigh the bad many times over, but as the years had passed I had to admit a growing concern over my future life on the canal had settled. Now faced with the ultimate moment of truth, to really commit to boat life by spending tens of thousands and effectively declaring that the canal was my long term home, every niggle and concern rose up in my mind like a chorus of doubt!

To really understand my reasons for leaving boat life, it is important to understand that I had based my entire life around a simple, minimal and very active way of living. The reason I loved the canal lifestyle was that it allowed me to spend huge amounts of my time in beautiful rural places. Many of the "issues" that I am about to talk about may seem like they have a simple solution, to just move into a marina and live on a permanent mooring.

Although it would be possible for me to go out, get a boat and then settle down with a marina spot, a car parked a few feet away and a relatively easy and low cost life still ahead of me, that is fundamentally not what I wanted from my own personal boat life experience. Over the years I have talked at great length online about the various ways that living on a boat can differ from person to person, boat to boat and place to place. I would again like to say at this point that I love the canals and still visit regularly, so if the following appears as overly negative then that is simply a result of talking about this topic, rather than my actual feelings and thousands of happy memories and moments spent on the canals. Right, now that we have got that little disclaimer out of the way... lets get stuck in!

Selling Tilly was a deeply personal decision and as such the reasons behind it are also relatively personal to me. Firstly, the mere fact of getting older was enough to throw up a lot of doubts in my mind. Every year on Tilly I cycled and walked thousands of miles as part of my "normal" life, commuting to and from work, visiting friends and family and simply getting supplies onboard.

Living such an active life was fantastic, especially as I bought Tilly at age twenty-five, my prime, after I had spent years building stamina on my bike and doing long distances walks for dozens of miles at a time. However, as I had been a keen journal writer in my younger years, I was able to look back from age twenty-eight (after a few years on Tilly!) to my very early twenties, and see that the walks I had done for almost a decade were now taking me a noticeably longer time.

Despite all of the activity that my everyday life included onboard Tilly, I was demonstrably not as fast or fit as I had been in years gone by... dare I say that I was just not as *young* as I had been! It wasn't as if I was struggling, but I knew that I was ageing slowly but surely. I could still go out on near thirty mile walks, but they were no longer the simple "do it and forget about it" events that they had been in the past. I remember having a conversation with a friend during the wet December of 2015 where we both declared that we felt tired a lot of the time... both of us in our late twenties, we even joked about how we were talking like old men!

This realisation that even as a fit young lad, I could feel myself getting older and slower, gave me a lot to think about for the long term. As the years would pass, when approaching forty, how much would I be enjoying having to get on my bike and pedal to the nearest shops or head into work. Then repeat the process to get back home before lighting the fire and settling down for the night. All great fun while just about fit enough to do it, but as the wet winter had served to highlight, not without its draining drawbacks even during my boat life up to that point!

The fact of me getting older was far more relevant than simply saying "I am not gonna be cycling this far forever" though. As time passes, life can change in many unexpected ways and with my twenties rapidly drawing to a close, there was a lot on my mind relating to what I wanted from my life. It had been great to spend four years on a boat, working part time hours in a supermarket, writing books, making videos and generally having a lot of fun doing random things that popped into my head, but I knew this couldn't last forever.

There would come a point in my life that would need me to be a "real grown up", whether that was through choice or circumstances would be impossible to predict, but I felt that investing so much in a new boat could easily come back and haunt me in the near future. The potential influence and opportunities of jobs, relationships and generally unexpected circumstances were things that I was keenly aware of.

As various relationships had been and gone during my time with Tilly, I knew the advantages and disadvantages of living on a boat while having a non boating girlfriend. The novelty of going boating and spending time onboard had been a great activity to share with somebody, but the impermanence and difficulty in getting to each other sometimes led to a figurative and literal *drifting apart!*

As for work, living very cheaply as I did, it had never really been a problem to turn up to a supermarket a couple of times a week and then vanish back off to the canal. However there had been many occasions where I had turned down overtime and taken strategically timed holidays to avoid some of the more punishing cycling commutes. The terrible winter once again played a huge role in highlighting just how awkward things could get, even with shorter commutes, when something as simple as the weather was not in your favour. The idea of changing jobs, or taking on full time work to build towards a more secure future, almost guaranteed that I would need a car to commute from the canal to work. This in turn would almost certainly see me moving into a marina and therefore lose the rural, peaceful, scenic, travelling principle that drew me to boat life to begin with. Not to mention the additional costs that these changes would bring with them.

Finally, I would like to talk about the changing nature of the canals and the role that played in my decision. Once again, I am in no way sat here typing out these words in a spirit of "woe is me, things should stay how I want them!" As a lover of history, I accept fundamentally that times change and things move on.

The Llangollen Canal served as my home for the majority of the time. It is an extremely busy canal during the summer months and can be an extremely quiet canal in the middle of winter. In recent times there have been a number of new marinas proposed along the length of this canal, which brought along with them various reactions from the many different people and groups involved.

One proposal that was of particular interest to me and many of the people I knew on the canal, was that of a development at the canalside town of Ellesmere. A very popular mooring place as it offers some of the easiest access to shops and supplies for miles around. It is known as a place to see boats moored up in their dozens for long stretches of the canal. A service point and marina also make it a popular and useful place for boaters to be. For the last few years there have been proposals, objections and new proposals drawn for a new marina, hundreds of homes and a hotel to be built at one of the most popular and busiest parts of the canal, a very short walk away from the current marina.

Due to the busy nature of Ellesmere, I always chose to moor up on the outskirts, slightly further away than may have been considered "easy access" to the shops, just enough to be on the fringe of all the activity rather than in the middle of it. The idea of making this place any busier or crowded didn't really appeal to me, but I was not terribly disturbed by the various things I heard from local "people in the know" predicting various outcomes and results of what the future held for the town. I knew that if it got too hectic then I would simply keep away and moor in different areas, so the idea of the change and building work wasn't the concerning part for me. What it really highlighted in my mind was just how little control I had over the environment in which I lived, and how things could change for the better or for the worse, regardless of their impact on an irrelevant lad floating around on a little boat.

The biggest reality check relating to how dramatically things could change due to factors outside my control came in the form of the 2015-2016 Winter Mooring Rules. When I had first seen a winter on Narrowboat Tilly, the Winter Mooring Scheme had allowed me to pay a small fee in order to stay long term (up to five months) in the same area during the winter, rather than having to follow the standard rule of moving to a new place every 14 days.

In that first winter, the list of available mooring places was huge, and I had chosen to spend a lot of time at Chirk Bank, a convenient place to spend the cold, wet months. It offered easy bus access and a relatively painless cycling commute to Oswestry.

The following two winters had seen a much shorter list of specific winter mooring sites, this was balanced out by the introduction of a new "General Towpath Permit" which came with some restrictions, but really allowed me to spend two full five month long winters moored just around the corner from Chirk Bank, by a canalside pub of all places!

The summer of 2015 brought bad news out of the blue. For the winter of 2015-16 there would be no General Towpath Permit, just the short list of fixed locations. On top of this the price would be roughly three times what I had previous paid, and finally the winter mooring period was reduced from five months to four. That was a major blow to my yearly routine and the way that I set up my cruising plans. Little did I know at the time, but it would be the worst, wettest winter on record, just to make sure that I really felt every extra mile I had to cycle!

The nearest places to my previous winter spot listed, were Ellesmere and Llangollen, which although I have commuted from both, were simply too far away to be long term bases, especially during the winter months.

At face value, it might seem like I am mentioning this as a direct reason for my vacating of the canal, although this news didn't fill me with joy, I knew that it would be a situation I could work around even if it did make life more difficult. Personally I saw this as a deeper issue that highlighted once again just how little control or influence I had over decisions that could completely alter my life! Moving around on a boat had admittedly never given me much of a sense of permanence, but as time went on and I saw different people have issues and disputes with different Authorities, I realised how lucky I was to have never had any such problems.

As far as I could tell I had always stuck to the rules, I was quiet, clean and tidy and liked to keep myself out of the way when it came to mooring up around other boats. As such I had never had any trouble with the CRT or anybody else. I did however have my own eyes, ears and mind to understand that there were certain issues that arose for various reasons amongst boaters and officials. The idea that the rules could be changed and I might find myself unable to live the way I had, in my calm rural locations, was a worry that was made more real with the Winter Mooring example. Again, the idea of finding myself forced to live in a fixed place in a marina didn't fill me with positivity for the future of boat life.

As a side note, during 2015 there seemed to be a mini crimewave targeting boats in the area, rumours and reports made their way up and down the Llangollen and Shropshire Union canals of break ins, vandalism and mischief. This was at one point enough to make me change my cruising plans and stay in somewhere that I viewed as being "safe" rather than head further afield. I wouldn't say that it had any big impact on my decision making, regarding the future of my life, but in the context of worries over things being taken out of my control, it certainly gave me something to think about on the nights that I spent away from Tilly, sleeping on a friend's living room floor!

When all is said and done, I can honestly say that there is no major single reason that pointed my life away from the canals. Instead there were just a series of small doubts and concerns, some personal, others relating to the canals themselves and other reasons simply based on cold hard truths.

There will be some people who look at this chapter and still don't see why I would give up such a calm and peaceful life over seemingly small matters, some people might be disappointed that there is no major reason to point to and say "this killed his boat life", and some people may even ask why on earth I bought a boat in the first place! All that I can say is that after nearly four years I felt that it was simply time to try something else.

I have often said that almost anybody can live on a boat, but not everybody will like it! I never really thought that I would be one of the people who would choose to go back to dry land, but time passes, people change and life goes on. I am just incredibly grateful to have enjoyed such an amazing experience while young enough to really get out there and enjoy it!

The Two Happiest Days of Your Life

Many years ago, when I had first brought Narrowboat Tilly back to my local area, a boater passed by, saw my family and friends onboard in a celebratory mood, and asked what the occasion was. My family pointed to me and said "he has just bought a boat!" With a smile and almost a wink, the boater replied "The two happiest days of your life are when you buy a boat, and then when you sell the boat!"

Fast forward a few years and you would find Tilly moored up in almost the exact same location, but this time she was up for sale. The joy of moving onboard was replaced by a mixture of sadness, stress and a few strange moments of absolute bliss! With my final night onboard over, and all of my possessions taken back to dry land, it seemed to me that I should be less connected to her than ever before.

However, I found that my trips out to her were more charged with emotion than ever! Which gave me a few quiet moments while waiting to meet people who wished to view her. I won't dwell on this too much or give any personal details away of the people who viewed Tilly, but despite the perfect locations, the actual sales process was a source of huge concern to me.

I listed Tilly for sale online and spread the word via YouTube and Facebook, and knowing the attention this would likely get, I had to use a separate phone number to that of my personal phone.

I posted the video tour and announcement that Tilly was for sale on May 19th, it would be a rapid, but stressful few weeks until she was actually sold on June 5th. One month later I would find myself moving into my own place on dry land, having been stressed, relaxed, overjoyed and a bit sad too!

Within the first few days of her going online, I had had multiple messages and phone calls from "fans" who just wanted to chat, as always it was humbling to have this happen, but also, ironically came at a time that I wanted to talk less about boats than I had ever done in my life!

There were many calls and texts of interest in purchasing that didn't lead anywhere, then there were a few that resulted in viewings and even offers. I agreed to sell Tilly three times, but it wasn't until the third time that I actually got as far as completing the deal and handing over the keys!

The first time the offer simply fell through by the next afternoon, which was stressful. The second time, myself and the potential buyer reached a stalemate over how and when payment would be made and keys handed over. Ultimately ending in me making the statement "Well I have got a boat and you haven't," while on the phone half struggling with anger and half struggling with the despondent feeling of hopelessness that the deal had fallen apart.

For these first two "almost sales" Tilly had been moored at Ellesmere, one of my favourite places on the Llangollen. I had enjoyed my bike rides out to Tilly and back, while showing people around and generally checking up on her. I found that amidst the chaos of emotions, there were some truly perfect moments. Not being based onboard anymore meant that when I hopped on my bike, I wasn't taking a heavy backpack filled with supplies, so the cycling commutes were much easier and surprisingly shorter in terms of travelling time.

Walking around Ellesmere itself, a place with many old picturesque places, country lanes winding up a hill, a large lake with a wooded area, I found some kind of bittersweet calm. As I knew I would likely never take a boat around those places again, I think that I was determined to fully enjoy the surroundings. Cycling out to check up on Tilly became an opportunity to follow some of my less used routes, almost as part of a "Farewell Tour".

When the hopes I had held of selling Tilly while she was at Ellesmere really did fall apart, and I felt so worried by the prospect of having to keep moving her around hoping to sell, I did two things I thought I would never do. Firstly, for a brief period of time I was convinced I would sell her in a marina, but backed out of this due to the fees involved. Secondly I tried to sell her for a bargain price to a local small independent boat hire company. It really was a low time, and when the small company did not want her, there was a period of a few days in which I felt like I was "stuck with her". If somebody had caught me at that point they could have had the bargain of the century!

After sulking for a few days though, I pulled myself together and decided that I would slowly bring Tilly back up the canal towards Llangollen. If I didn't sell her by the time she arrived at Chirk Marina, then I would put her up for sale in there.

From that particular low point, I have to say that I suddenly found myself absolutely loving every moment that I spent with Tilly! The fact that the weather was now absolutely beautiful was a big help, but just getting to take Tilly for a few last summer boat trips reignited my motivation and love of the canals. As Tilly got closer to Oswestry, my friends would join me on bike rides out to check up on her, before we would head off in seemingly random directions with no mission other than to enjoy the sun. It truly was a beautiful way to draw a close to my years with Tilly.

The last few boat trips brought Tilly right up to "Mad Jack's", a canalside pub that was barely twenty minutes bike ride away from Oswestry. It was here that she stayed until I handed the keys to her new owners. For thirteen days I was able to take a quick trip to go and check up on her. This was a time that my friends and family came out to have one last look at the tiny boat that had meant so much to me, many sad moments were mingled in with a huge amount of quiet reflection. I would go out to Tilly for an hour or so, bringing with me some writing to do, or a journal in need of a quick sketch adding to it. This was the true ending of my boat life, me sat onboard in silence, waving at passing holiday boats while I scratched my head and thought "What next?"

When the people who would end up buying Tilly came out to view her, I was over the moon. Not only did they instantly make an offer, (and accept a price that was the highest deal I had made for her) but they also seemed like they would take good care of her. Unlike the previous pair who had made failed deals, these were actual boat owners who knew a lot about boats and the maintenance required. With my neglect of Tilly's general paintwork and cosmetic upkeep, it was good to think of her going to a home which would see her given a new lease of life for years to come.

Later in the evening they made a deposit and, from that moment on, I knew that this time Tilly had really been sold. At that moment I didn't feel sad, I think my sadness had all been dealt with on my final night onboard. Instead, I felt an overwhelming sense of relief. I was happy to have the responsibility taken from my hands. It was a night that saw me sleep very well indeed.

On June 5th, I made my way out to Tilly for the last time. It was a beautiful sunny day, the short bike ride seemed at the time to last forever, yet once I was onboard seemed to have been the briefest moment of my life. I arrived at Tilly over an hour earlier than I was expecting her new owners to turn up. The agreed price had been paid fully, so all that was left to do was hand over the keys. I wanted to be there and enjoy one last hour on the boat that had not only been my home, but had come to define me as "The Narrowboat Lad".

As I waited for the last few minutes before her new owners arrived, it seemed almost like one of those times where you feel you are not really there. Anybody watching me from over the canal would have seen somebody who probably looked a bit frantic, pacing around inside, stepping up onto the stern and peering down the towpath, then heading back inside when there was no sign of anybody else.

When they arrived, the handover was as quick and straightforward as possible. After exchanging pleasantries and good wishes, it wasn't long before I was cycling away down the towpath, no longer a boat owner! I will be completely honest and say that I felt a bit distant and my legs seemed to lack a lot of the strength they had previously had while pedalling out to Tilly! I stopped not far down the road to record a video of my thoughts and feelings at the time, then took the long way home to make the most of the sun, and my sudden lack of any responsibility!

Tilly had been my home for almost four years, was for sale for less than three weeks and seemingly taken off my hands in an instant. It would be exactly one month later on July 5th that I would move into my own place in Oswestry. At the top of a beautiful old building, I am now able to look across the rooftops of town and onto a small section of Shropshire and see the landmarks which indicate where the canal runs and my old mooring spots sit.

All this time later, I will often stand on the balcony and point these out to people, reliving random tales of hijinks and fun on the water.

So That Was Boat Life.

Finalising this last chapter has taken months of writing, rewriting, deleting and starting over. Knowing that there is a good chance that this is the last thing I will ever write about boat life, I want to make sure it is good! Or at least accurately represents how I feel about the life changing experience that I have had over the last few years on the canal.

Firstly, I feel like I have been the luckiest person alive to have enjoyed the second half of my twenties living an extremely active life, travelling around some of the most perfect, peaceful and beautiful rural places I have ever known. To have been able to moor up a boat, on a stretch of canal surrounded by nothing but countryside for miles around and call it home, is something that I not only view as a pleasure, but also as a privilege that few get to experience.

To make this lifestyle possible there were some compromises. I tried to live as low cost as I could, ensuring that I could keep my work hours down to part time and therefore be able to enjoy as much time as I could out in the countryside.

Living in such rural places also made life difficult on a practical level quite often. For the vast majority of the time I had only my boots and bike to travel to and from Tilly. Whether I was heading to work or to get supplies, even just to meet friends, miles of cycling or walking were often involved, sometimes requiring a makeshift bed on my friend's floor to help ease the burden of my sometimes forty-plus mile round trips! Being (just about) fit and healthy enough to put in the thousands of miles of cycling and walking that were required over the last four years, is again a blessing that I can't be thankful enough for.

The calm, simple, maybe even basic, rural lifestyle was well worth the trade-offs of ease, comfort and luxury to me. I got to wake up and open the curtains to see perfect sunrises, cows or herons on the far bank of the canal, or sometimes an early morning mist still settled over the water. I was able to end my days cycling back through deserted country roads on summer evenings, letting the worries and restless thoughts out of my system as I pedalled. Arriving at Tilly under the sun, locking up my bike, having something to eat and then heading out for a quick walk before bed. All these simple things sometimes made me feel like I was the last person on earth, offering peace and tranquility like nothing I could have ever imagined.

Of course, as this book has shown, there were times when all this was done in terrible weather conditions with little fun involved, but those were the down moments that were necessary to also experience and appreciate the incredible high points.

The winter months, I feel in hindsight, could well contain some of my favourite memories along with some of my least favourite. A wet winter day could be boring and sapping to ones motivation, but a cold, frosty day under a dazzling winter sun sat low in the sky, even at noon, could be one of the most beautiful conditions to spend a day or two in.

Waking up before seven in the morning, ready to head into work on my bike, might not sound like the best way to start a freezing cold, pitch black winter day. Wrapping up warm, scraping the ice from my bike seat and then cycling through the deserted, silent, countryside was truly a joy. I have never felt so alive as when pedalling away in the bitter cold as the sky began to move through the colours of sunrise. Seeing the ice glisten on the fields while watching the sun peer over the horizon for the first rays of light to spread over the world ahead, was something that could literally stop me in my tracks to appreciate and enjoy for one moment longer.

So much of what I have talked about in this chapter already has been based not onboard a boat, but in the environments that the boat let me enjoy. I have said many times in the past that I didn't buy a boat to spend all of my time sat indoors, I bought a boat to get out into the countryside. I really did make the most of the opportunity to do that! In hindsight there are many ways that nature intruded into my time onboard that I didn't realise until after it was over. For example, in the spring months as the days grew lighter, there were certain places I would moor where I would constantly be woken up at unearthly hours by the dawn chorus of birds in a nearby hedgerow! An annoyance in some ways, but also a perfect sound to wake up to and hear, while spending a few minutes staring at the water's reflection on the ceiling. An early start on a sunny day would usually result in a lot more productivity too!

I always talk about it as "boat life this" or "boat life that" but really it was "rural life" or maybe even some kind of watered down easy version of "nomad life". That is really what I remember. The places I travelled and moored, the walks, bike rides and miniature gentle adventures that I had. Even in the final months of my life afloat I was still discovering new routes and features of the landscapes in places where I had moored for weeks at a time, three years in a row! My inability to sit still for too long made sure that I was rarely bored while there was a beam of sunlight in the sky, or a path that needed to be followed.

The final thing I want to say about the rural and peaceful element of life afloat has to be dedicated to the night times onboard. Whether it was the tremendous heat coming from the stereotypical crackling fire, the smell of wood burning in the air, or the almost near silence of a rural midnight, the dark hours onboard Narrowboat Tilly were far from unpleasant.

I was rarely ever scared or spooked at being so alone in the dark hours, instead I found that they offered themselves up as a time for reading, writing and reflection with very little disturbance. The ultimate joy that the rural nights could bring for me, came in the form of crystal clear dark skies. A fan of astronomy for many years before boat life, I was amazed at how many thousands of stars could be seen from my many mooring places far away from any light pollution.

I would set up my small telescope on the towpath and be stunned at what I could see in the night sky. Tens of thousands of stars would become visible when peering into the eyepiece. These were the moments of total peace, not only in my surroundings but also in myself. I have always found astronomy to be the most humbling hobby around. Viewing stars, planets and galaxies that are unimaginably distant, and incomprehensibly vast, really helps to put life in perspective. Viewing these things only a few feet away from my tiny home and with no sign of humanity around, was an almost out of body experience. I remember one such occasion while moored by the very rural Whixall, where I had the feeling of "Is this really my life?" not in a good or a bad way, simply in a "Is this actually real?" sort of way. The overwhelming sense of "remoteness" of my location, together with the vastness of the universe, and the fact that I was only a few steps away from my home. All these things coming together to create a feeling of calm and that "everything is all good" that I have never had since.

I couldn't possibly try and sum up my boat life without taking a moment to talk about the incredible people I have met on the canal over the years. My experience with other canal users has been exceptional and apart from one or two small instances it has been an almost unanimously positive thing. This speaks volumes for the general sense of community or camaraderie created by a shared interest in boats, canals or the countryside. Online I have seen many reports of tensions on the water but I have been lucky to avoid almost any issues. Instead I have enjoyed many long chats with other boaters, many random encounters with walkers and CRT employees and even the occasional trip on other peoples' boats.

I do not want to start listing people by name, as there would firstly be too many, and secondly I would feel awful about the names I inevitably forgot to add to the list! I will simply say that during the fours years I spent onboard, I met literally hundreds of people who helped bring more knowledge, colour and sometimes just outright comedy to my life.

The help, advice and support I received whenever I had even a slightest problem tells you everything you need to know about the character of many people dwelling on boats. I heard incredible stories of travelling far and wide, or of an adventurous life before the water, from so many people that it was eye opening, that so many people on the canal had lived lives that were a far cry from the peaceful, rural and comparatively sleepy paths they now followed.

When my youtube channel hit its peak and millions of people were tuning in, I was amazed at the kindness of people from around the world. The amount of people from all over the globe who would come to the Llangollen Canal on holiday, already knowing that they would likely spot Narrowboat Tilly, was humbling. Being woken up by keen "Tilly Spotters" or arriving home after work to find somebody who lived thousands of miles away had been on holiday and left me a gift, was yet another of the experiences that I have been privileged and humbled to have. When I decided to make the move back to dry land, the incredible amount of support and well wishes that I had from both people online and from the canals, proved yet again how lucky I had been to be surrounded by such amazing people for so long.

Having a random passerby retie your mooring ropes if they came undone, rescue a kayak that was blowing away, or even just check everything was ok while I was away from the canal for a few days, again proves the integrity of so many of the people I have been able to call my neighbours.

I truly cannot speak highly enough of so many of the people I have met, and I want to make sure that there is no doubt that many of the characters I found on the canal are some of the best friends anybody could ever have. The fact that I can say this while knowing that I am overly shy and reclusive compared to many, should also reflect well on the people who brought me out of my shell to become friends.

So to reflect on my narrowboat life and wrap it all up for one last time, I will simply say that it was the best time of my life.

Thank you for taking time to read this book.

You can see Dan's latest adventures along with hundreds of his boat life videos on YouTube at:

www.narrowboatvideos.com

Dan also welcomes you to add him on social media at:

www.facebook.com/sortofdan

www.facebook.com/sortofinteresting

www.twitter.com/sort_of_dan

Printed in Great Britain
by Amazon